THE MODERNIZATION
OF JAPAN AND RUSSIA

Written under the auspices of the Center of
International Studies, Princeton University

A list of other Center publications appears
at the back of this book.

Perspectives on Modernizaiton
Cyril E. Black, General Editor

Comparative Modernization: A Reader, Cyril E. Black

The Modernization of Japan and Russia,
Cyril E. Black, Marius B. Jansen, Herbert S. Levine,
Marion J. Levy, Jr., Henry Rosovsky, Gilbert
Rozman, Henry D. Smith, II, S. Frederick Starr

*Modernization and the Transformation of
International Relations,* Edward L. Morse

The Modernization
of Japan and Russia

A Comparative Study

Cyril E. Black
Marius B. Jansen
Herbert S. Levine
Marion J. Levy, Jr.
Henry Rosovsky
Gilbert Rozman
Henry D. Smith, II
S. Frederick Starr

THE FREE PRESS
A Division of Macmillan Publishing Co., Inc.
NEW YORK

Collier Macmillan Publishers
LONDON

The Free Press
A Division of Macmillan Publishing Co., Inc.
866 Third Avenue, New York, N.Y. 10022

Collier Macmillan Canada, Ltd.

Library of Congress Catalog Card Number: 75–8429

Printed in the United States of America

printing number

1 2 3 4 5 6 7 8 9 10

Library of Congress Cataloging in Publication Data
Main entry under title:

The Modernization of Japan and Russia.

(Perspectives on modernization)
Bibliography: p.
Includes index.
1. Japan--Civilization. 2. Russia--Civiliza-
tion. 3. Comparative civilization. I. Black,
Cyril Edwin
DS821.M6395   301.24'3'0947   75-8429
ISBN 0-02-906850-9

CONTENTS

THE AUTHORS

Here is a brief introduction to the authors of this book:

CYRIIL E. BLACK is Shelby Cullom Davis Professor of European History and Director of the Center of International Studies at Princeton University. His teaching and research interests include Russia and Eastern Europe, and comparative history. He lectured at the Slavic Institute, Hokkaido University in the summer of 1965. His publications include, as editor and coauthor, *The Transformation of Russian Society: Aspects of Social Change since 1861* (1960); *The Dynamics of Modernization: A Study in Comparative History* (1966); and, as coeditor and coauthor, *The Future of the International Legal Order* (4 volumes, 1969–1972).

MARIUS B. JANSEN is Professor of History and East Asian Studies at Princeton University. He is a specialist in Japanese history and taught at the University of Washington before coming to Princeton in 1959. He has written *The Japanese and Sun Yet-sen* (1954); *Sakamoto Ryōmo and the Meiji Restoration* (1961); as editor and coauthor, *Changing Japanese Attitudes toward Modernization* (1965); and, as coeditor and coauthor, *Studies in the Institutional History of Early Modern Japan* (1969).

HERBERT S. LEVINE is Professor of Economics at the University of Pennsylvania, and a consultant to the Stanford Research Institute and to the Department of State. He is a former Executive Secretary of the Association for the Study of Soviet-type Economies, and is Chairman of the ACLS-SSRC Joint Committee on Soviet Studies. His publications include, as coauthor, *Comparisons of the United States and Soviet Economies* (1959); as coeditor and coauthor, *Mathematics and Computers in*

Soviet Economic Planning (1967); and, as coauthor, *Comparison of Economic Systems* (1971).

MARION J. LEVY, JR. is Musgrave Professor of Sociology and International Affairs in the Woodrow Wilson School and Chairman of the Department of East Asian Studies at Princeton University. He served with the U.S. Navy in East Asia during World War II, and has visited Japan subsequently for purposes of research. His publications include *Family Revolution in Modern China* (1949); *The Structure of Society* (1962); *Modernization and the Structure of Societies: A Setting for International Affairs* (1966); *Modernization: Latecomers and Survivors* (1972); and *Levy's Ten Laws* (1972).

HENRY ROSOVSKY is Walter S. Barker Professor of Economics and Dean of the Faculty of Arts and Sciences at Harvard University. His research interests include both Russian and Japanese economic history. He has served as visiting Professor at Tokyo University and Hitotsubashi University. His publications include *Capital Formation in Japan, 1898–1940* (1961); as editor, *Industrialization in Two Systems* (1966); and, as coauthor, *Japanese Economic Growth: Trend Acceleration in the Twentieth Century* (1973).

GILBERT ROZMAN is Associate Professor of Sociology at Princeton University. He has conducted research on premodern urbanization in Japan, the Republic of China, and the U.S.S.R., in preparation for writing *Urban Networks in Ch'ing China and Tokugawa Japan* (1973), and *Urban Networks in Russia, 1750–1800, and Premodern Periodization* (1975).

HENRY D. SMITH, II is a Junior Fellow in the Society for the Humanities at Cornell University in 1975–1976, specializing in Japanese history; he was Assistant Professor of History at Princeton University from 1969 to 1975. His research interests include the student movement between the two worlds wars, reflected in his *Japan's First Student Radicals* (1972), and the urban development of Tokyo.

S. FREDERICK STARR is Associate Professor of History at Princeton University and Director of the Institute for Advanced Russian Studies at the Woodrow Wilson International Center for Scholars in Washington, D.C. He specializes in Russian institutional and cultural history in the nineteenth and twentieth centuries. He has written *Decentralization and Self-Government in Russia, 1830–1870* (1972); as editor, *August von Haxthausen, Studies of the Interior of Russia* (1972); and *Konstantin Melnikov: Architect* (forthcoming).

PREFACE

We doubt whether this book could have been written by a single author, although undoubtedly it could have been written by fewer than eight. An understanding of change in the modern world must draw not only on a considerable range of disciplinary specialties, but also on the comparison of societies undergoing change from a base of widely different heritages of premodern cultures. There may occasionally be individual scholars qualified to handle this range of knowledge in regard to two or more countries, but they would be quite exceptional; and we do not know of anyone equipped to undertake a comparison such as this one of two countries as diverse as Japan and Russia.

The advantages of collaborative scholarship are accompanied by problems that we have sought to overcome. Juxtapositions are sometimes confused with genuine comparisons. After separate and more or less parallel descriptive accounts, comparisons are generally limited to concluding remarks that only skim the surface of the many-faceted similarities and differences. Even when they take the form of parallel chapters comparing discrete aspects of the societies, authors rarely give the impression of having discussed each other's work in adequate detail to have achieved a common understanding of their task. We have sought to overcome such difficulties by frequent group discussions and the sharing of drafts and by undertaking virtually paragraph-by-paragraph comparisons so that the similarities and the differences of the two societies would emerge in as full detail as possible.

The discussion and writing took place over a period of five years, in the course of which we had many other concerns. In each case, however, our principal research interests were closely related to the main theme of this book. All of the authors are specialists in either Japanese or Russian studies, and two have worked in both areas. Two are economists and two sociologists, and the four historians also lay claim to an understanding of political science adequate for our purposes here. In the course of our work we held six general two-day meetings at Princeton to discuss drafts of sections and to revise plans in the light of experience. These meetings were attended by all of the authors in the country at the time, and we sought to keep in touch by correspondence with the four engaged in research in Japan and Russia at various times during our collaboration. An uncounted number of consultations were also held by two or more of the six Princeton authors.

A collective study by eight authors who have worked in sufficiently close cooperation to assume joint responsibility for the resulting project is a sufficiently unusual occurrence to deserve a few additional words of explanation. After consideration of numerous outlines and proposals, we agreed on the allocation of first rough drafts of chapters. Black and Jansen prepared the first drafts of the chapters on the international context (2, 8, 14); Smith and Starr, those on both political structure and development (3, 9, 15) and knowledge and education (6, 12, 18); Levine and Rosovsky, those on economic structure and growth (4, 10, 16); Rozman, those on social interdependence (5, 11, 17); and Levy contributed drafts of the interpretative framework presented in the introductions to the three parts and in the concluding chapters (7, 13, 19) of the three parts. The introductory and concluding chapters (1, 20) are to such an extent the result of our joint efforts that it is scarcely possible to disentangle the contributions of individuals.

In the course of our work we have found it convenient to adopt a few usages that should be explained lest they are misunderstood. In the title, and more often than not throughout the text, we refer to Japan before Russia because this is the order in which they occur in the English alphabet. In Russian, but not in Japanese, the order would be reversed.

The term "Japan" is clear enough, because its territory has been relatively stable (its overseas territories were never incorporated into Japan proper, and are discussed separately where appropriate) and its people are exceptionally homogeneous. The term "Russia," by contrast, has no such simple or clear meaning. We use it as a convenient and conventional term to refer to the Union of Soviet Socialist Republics, and to its various antecedents from the Russian Empire back through he Muscovite, Mongol, and Kievan periods. We also refer generally to the peoples of Russia as "Russians," despite the fact that the ethnic Russians, or Great Russians—as distinct from the other major Slavic groups, the Ukrainians and Byelorussians, and the numerous major and minor non-Slavic peoples—have in recent times formed only about half the population of the country (specifically, 43 per cent in 1898, and 53 per cent in 1926 and in 1970). We assume that readers will appreciate the advantages of this simpler (though technically inaccurate) usage, and will note our efforts to take into account the complexities of the territorial and ethnic structure of Russia when these are relevant to the comparison.

We have also used the term "West" to designate the English-speaking and West European countries that began to adapt their societies to the scientific and technological revolution before Japan and Russia did, and were perceived by both as threats, stimuli, and models. Specifically, as of about 1900, the West included the United Kingdom, France, Belgium, Luxembourg, the Netherlands, Switzerland, Germany, Italy, Denmark, Norway, Sweden, and Austria-Hungary, as well as the offshoots of Europe in the New Word—the United States, Canada, Australia, and New Zealand.

It is significant that the Russian term for the West, *Zapad*, has had this same meaning both before and since the revolution, and continues today to have the same general connotations as the English. The Japanese also use the term West, *Seiyō*, or more narrowly Europe, *Yōroppa*, in this same general sense, although they have normally thought of Russia as a part of the West. Only at the height of the so-called cold war, did they make a rather tentative distinction between "Soviet" and "Western" orbits. This important distinction between the Russian and Japanese perceptions of the West is examined in some detail in our study.

In the course of our work we received advice and assistance from quite a variety of colleagues. In October 1970 we held a meeting with guests from other institutions who discussed the feasibility of a study such as this and offered encouragement and warnings. In the later stages of our work several graduate students at Princeton made helpful criticisms of or drafts. Neil B. Weissman (Russian history) and Dante Yip (Japanese history) participated in a number of our discussions, and in the summer of 1973 Barbara Anderson (sociology), Susan Chizeck (sociology), James Conte (history), Adele Lindenmeyr (history), Anne D. Rassweiler (history), D. Eleanor Westney (sociology), and Michio Umegaki (politics) met with the Princeton authors in four sessions to review draft chapters. Professor William L. Blackwell, Department of History, New York University, also reviewed the manuscript at this stage.

We also wish to acknowledge the advice and assistance of Clifford Geertz, James T. C. Liu, Frederick W. Mote, Joseph Strayer, and again to Barbara Anderson, who discussed the manuscript with us in 1974 during the final stages of revision. Particular thanks are also due to Susan Watkins, who in a general editorial capacity eased the difficult task of reconciling the styles and points of view of eight authors. The authors are greatly indebted as well to Elsbeth G. Lewin for the efficiency with which she coordinated and edited their corrections of galleys and page proofs.

We wish to take this opportunity to thank Jane G. McDowall, Administrative Associate of the Center of International Studies, for bearing the main burden of the numerous and complex arrangements that facilitated our collaboration over considerable dimensions of time and space; and Patty Adams, Marianne Caldeira, June Carr, Dorothy Dey, June Traube, and Joanne Weissman for typing innumerable drafts of sections and chapters.

                                                                                    THE AUTHORS

Chapter One

THE PROBLEM

THE DIVERSE PATTERNS associated with modernization have come increasingly to dominate the contemporary world. Their appearance followed long after the beginning of the industrial revolution; they were sped, as Henry Adams was perceptive enough to note, by the intellectual breakthroughs and technology associated with electrical energy as a source of power. Three special characteristics mark the patterns of modernization as we perceive it. They are unrecognizedly recent, unprecedentedly subversive of the past, and unbelievably bizarre.

First, these patterns are, as a set, recent. They have gained such supremacy in the contemporary world that we tend to take them for granted and ignore the fact that none of them existed before 150 years ago at the outside and many are no more than a few decades old.

Second, these patterns have come to constitute a universal social solvent in two senses: They have shown a potency to invade and influence the institutions of all countries, whether they were introduced voluntarily or imposed by force, and they have tended to dissolve many of the major commonalities of the previous heritage of human experience. In both senses modernization constitutes something new under the sun.

Third, these patterns, so much taken for granted by the already modernized and so casually picked up by the nonmodernized, are on point after point at wildest variance with the general lot of humankind. Most people (well upwards of 90 percent of them) prior to these recent developments lived most of their time (well upwards of 90 per cent of it) within eye and earshot of members of their own families. That and a mass of other commonalities that underlie the rich variance of human conduct begin to vanish overnight upon

1

contact with modernization—whatever form that contact takes and whatever the degree of "success" or "nonsuccess" with modernization.

The study of modernization is very recent and has focused in particular on its origins, on the problems of latecomers to the process, and on the future of modernized societies. This study is concerned with the second of these issues: the problems of latecomers. Whatever the origins of modernization, and however compelling the future that awaits modernized societies, there is pressing need to understand the problems of peoples who have had to confront societies already transformed to some degree by the patterns of modernization. A search for comparisons and contrasts among nations participating in that process can reveal factors that must be central to the course of modernization itself. Of the many comparisons possible, two hold a special fascination. One is the contrast between the experiences of China and Japan. No nineteenth-century observer foresaw the speed with which Japan would join the small group of modernized societies, an experience in sharp contrast with the different course and pace of China's special development. There is a literature on this contrast.

Far less attention has been devoted to a second, equally provocative comparison, the one between the experiences of Japan and Russia. That case is the subject of this volume. It is of compelling interest for comparative analysis, but for reasons quite different from those that have invited comparisons of China and Japan in the past. The Chinese and Japanese cases seemed immediately comparable by chronology, cultural tradition, and exposure to the Western challenge. The Russian and Japanese cases, however, have seemed so different in setting and tradition, and the paths that were followed in the creation of the modern states presented such contrasts, that the similarities between their achievements have been all but ignored. Their very juxtaposition of successes with rapid modernization is an historical anomaly. Yet, in most of the ways in which their development can be measured—in education, urbanization, production— the two have achieved comparable levels. A search for antecedent patterns and milestones, as is undertaken here, also shows surprising areas of commonality in those earlier stages of their development that underlie the vast differences between them, differences that have generally commanded attention. That at least is our own general hypothesis.

This similarity of outcome is the more remarkable when one considers the historical contrasts that are so much more obvious. Russia was a huge continental power, in close contact with West European developments and an active participant in European culture in general. Japan was an island country, carefully sequestered from such contact. Japan was highly homogeneous; Russia covered a great variance in ethnic and social characteristics. Their religions were different, their economies were different, their governments were different. Their social patterns presented striking disparities even within the great reservoir of human variance to be found among nonmodernized peoples. The Japanese and Russians differed along almost all the dimensions ordinarily invoked in discussions of comparison, and yet the third quarter of the twentieth century found them the prime examples of "successful" latecomers to the patterns of modernization. In the last quarter of the century they will surely share with the English-speaking and European communities the responsibilities that devolve upon the most modernized regions of the world.

In this study devoted to a comparative analysis of the modernization of Russia and Japan, we are conscious of the inadequacies of empirical research in both areas and of the shortcomings of most analyses of modernization itself. At the same time, we believe that a search for explanations of such startling similarities of outcome from such widely divergent beginnings can shed new light on modernization. Specifically, we hope to locate special characteristics of Japan and Russia that made this process "successful" for them. And we hope that our objective will throw some light on the problems and possibilities faced by others.

Modernization

Several terms used throughout this study have a reasonably precise connotation to the authors but do not yet have a standard meaning in the language of the social sciences. The most important of these is "modernization," a term whose use in much current writing is sometimes confused by false assumptions and extraneous judgments.

By modernization the authors mean the process by which societies have been and are being transformed under the impact of the scientific and technological revolution. In this study we view modernization as a holistic process affecting all aspects of society. In comparing Japan with Russia we have been concerned especially with the international environment, political structures (patterns of coordination and control), economic growth, general social interdependence, and knowledge and education because we think these are the strategic areas for making comparisons and for examining their significance.

We would distinguish between a definition of the process of modernization and its description. We are less concerned with its definition than with its description. We would define "modernization" as an increase in the ratio of inanimate to animate sources of power to and past a point of no return as far as the accompanying social patterns are concerned. In this sense we consider a society or people modernized if a relatively small decrease in inanimate power cannot be "made up" by increases in animate power, or cannot be made up without having inevitable far-reaching social changes. Our concern here, however, is with a description and analysis of the patterns holistically associated with our concept of "modernization."

In its political aspects, modernization is concerned with the growing capacity of the members of a society to mobilize and allocate resources through public and private institutions with a view to implementing the various possibilities implicit in the advancement of knowledge and technology. In all cases this process involves increasing coordination of and control over resources and individuals.

From the economic point of view modernization entails an increase in growth and per capita production made possible by new technology. This growth is fostered by a wide variety of policies, allocation of resources, investment, the creation or borrowing of technology, management, and trade. Without exception modernization always involves a radical and continuing escalation in the ratio of inanimate to animate sources of power, so much so that some—erroneously—regard the animate sources of power as no longer of any importance. The new reliance on inanimate sources of power is in such contrast with all the rest of human history as to constitute a special defining feature in and of itself.

Social interdependence has to do with the patterns of settlement and general social organization that accompany urbanization. It also pertains to the changes in roles and values resulting from the greater specialization of functions and opportunities for education. These changes, ultimately accompanied by longer life-spans, always involve greatly increased densities of settlement and instances of human interaction. This rise in interdependence invariably set aside previously localized and self-sufficient preferences for governance and general social organization.

A widespread belief in rational inquiry is a primary characteristic of modernity, and the advancement of knowledge and its dissemination through education are essential in the process of modernization.

The production of knowledge through basic research, applied research, and the development of technology comes to absorb a growing share of a nation's resources. This knowledge is distributed through a wide variety of means of communication, and particularly through formal education. In modernized societies such education is the principal concern of all youth for a dozen years and for more and more of them between fifteen or twenty. As the amount and diversity of specialized knowledge expand and proliferate unimaginably by previous standards, the amount of basic knowledge common to all must also expand enormously.

Modernization also has a psychological aspect in its impact on the individual personality, which is as yet relatively little studied. We have approached this aspect somewhat indirectly through our treatment of knowledge and education, but we have not sought to describe it in detail. A full discussion of it would include changes in personality resulting from the move from relatively isolated, highly self-sufficient rural communities to interdependent urban societies. Appreciable differences in the tensions between individual security and independence in those societies in the process of change should be discussed as closely relevant if the material for analysis were at hand. The innumerable forms of alienation and anomie that seem to accompany the relative freedom from family and other social restraints in modernized societies are significant, but we know very little about them.

The various aspects of change that we discuss in this study interact, in ways that are by no means fully understood, to transform societies from those where four-fifths or more of the population lived in relatively isolated communities and were principally engaged in fishing, hunting, and agriculture to those in which a similar proportion of a growing total now lives in cities and works in offices and factories. Even those who continue to fish, hunt, and farm do so on a basis quite different from that of their predecessors.

There is no single indicator or formula that provides a comprehensive description of the entire process of change. Many of the characteristic features of change, however, can be measured with reasonable accuracy, and these become essential to comparisons. Political changes can be measured by the changes in the resources allocated by central decision-making bodies and by the concomitant growth in the interaction of bureaucracies, political parties, and interest groups. Economic changes can be measured in aggregate and per capita terms in relation to the volume of production and trade, the productivity of labor and capital, and the more comprehensive estimates of a society's wealth known as gross national product. This transformation to modernity can likewise be measured in terms of the growth of population and its movement from villages to cities, from manual to nonmanual occupations, and from one social class to another. It can also be assessed in terms of the proportion of the population exposed to different levels of education and affected by the shifting patterns of marriage, divorce, illness, crime, or suicide. None of these measurements is entirely accurate or satisfactory. The evaluation of many features of modernization, therefore, must depend for the present on judgment rather than measurement.

Modernization is a continuous process that has no self-defined stages. For purposes of description and analysis, however, one may justifiably define phases so long as the criteria for doing so are made clear. No obvious boundary separates the age-old acceptance of the physical environment from the search for understanding and change that characterizes the modern era. Nevertheless, one may locate the immediate antecedents of the process of modernization in Western Europe in the scientific revolution of the sixteenth and seventeenth centuries, the political revolutions in seventeenth-century England and eighteenth-century France, and the industrial revolution of the late eighteenth and early nineteenth centuries.

Since these beginnings, the impact of change has encompassed the entire world and the rate of change has accelerated. The process will go on so long as knowledge continues to advance, although specific aspects of change may reach their culmination. Urbanization, for instance, must come to an end, or at least change its character, when all members of the society live in cities; industrialization will run its course when all aspects of production are fully mechanized. Reference is sometimes made to a "postindustrial" or even a "postmodern" era in which industrialization and urbanization reach levels that permit societies to devote their attention to distribution, integration, organization, and the cultivation of values other than those of subsistence. Such points of view imply change in emphasis rather than an end to change, however, and we assume that the process of modernization will continue into the indefinite future. The value of speculation about the future is that it permits one to envisage long-term changes in emphasis. Most ideologies of modernization share the belief in a future in which the distribution of goods in the interest of human welfare will replace their production as the principal human concern.

We can conceptualize the process of modernization in terms of three phases: an initial stage in which the premodern foundation for change is laid, while modern ideas and institutions begin to challenge these existing premodern patterns; a transitional stage in which a society is transformed from a predominantly rural and agrarian to a predominantly urban and industrial way of life; and a further stage in which the rural and urban proportions are reversed and a condition of high modernization achieved. One may also speculate about a future phase, probably within relatively few generations, in which sufficient wealth will have been produced to permit an emphasis on quality and distribution to replace the emphasis on quantity and production. At that time the term industrialization might connote more than factories, for services and agriculture will then be as industrialized as manufactures.

There are several terms that we avoid using in this book because they have tended to confuse many discussions of modernization. The first of these is "traditional." In some presentations, "traditional society" describes an undifferentiated monolith that stands in direct opposition to modernity. Actually, the range of variety and complexity within nonmodern societies is very large indeed, and we shall point to ways in which the premodern basis contains critical variables for the process of modernization. Other writings stress "traditional features" as though some people orient themselves more importantly to their traditions than do others, and lag behind in modernization for that reason. But in fact all peoples orient themselves to tradition, some old traditions continue to be important even in highly modernized societies, and the highly modernized create their own, perhaps more evanescent, tradition. In most respects measurable change in the modern era is incremental at per capita rates that do not rise much above 2 to 3 per cent a year over long periods of time, and traditional forms cast a long shadow into the modern era. Nor does the doom of the previous traditions prove the viability of modernized forms to replace them. All relatively modern characteristics of societies represent transformations of previous characteristics. For latecomers especially, these transformations are more likely to be the results of changes in the context in which older patterns persist than the result of direct conversions of the old to the new. When the old exists beside the new it is not the old old at all. Indeed, limits to the capacity of a society to modernize can have only two sources: its premodern patterns and the viability of the modernized patterns. Elements of tradition, like the British Magna Carta or the Japanese throne, may be well adapted to modernization. For this reason we have placed particular emphasis on what we term "the heritage of the past" for both Japan and Russia.

Two other terms we avoid are "Westernization" and "Europeani-zation." These are often used in reference to the fact that for all latecomers to modernization the challenge has been an external one. We have been discussing the process of modernization as though it took place within the confines of individual societies. But in truth, ideas and institutions of modernization were disseminated in Europe by the wars of the French Revolution and Napoleon no less than they were conveyed to Latin America, Asia, and Africa by the ex-plorers, traders, missionaries, emigrants, and military forces of the West. The term "Westernization" implies that Western or European institutions are themselves the essence of modernity and that other societies may forget their historical heritage and adopt modern values and institutions in their Western or European form as they might abandon the ox cart for the automobile or the fez for the hat. The fact is that the members of each society must manage the transforma-tion of their society's own previous institutions. Additional con-tradictions present themselves in the use of "Westernization" and "Europeanization." Twentieth-century Japan, for instance, has func-tioned as a modernizing but not necessarily a Westernizing force at certain times and places. On the other hand, several indubitably European and Western societies are at the present time still in the category of relatively nonmodernized societies. Finally and especially, the modernized Westerners are as different from their forebears as the modernized Japanese are from theirs. All the nonmodernized have more in common with one another than with their modernized descendants. Only a very few greats like Shakespeare speak across all the gaps, and when they do so they speak of the commonalities that underlie all the variance of moderns and nonmoderns alike. The advent of the moderns with their new commonalities made manifest commonalities among the nonmodernized that were previously lost in their variance.

Our emphasis on the foundation provided by the heritage of the past derives from the fact that values and institutions must at each stage of development be comprehensible in terms of the social in-heritance of previous generations. Even when a people adopts a foreign religion or legal system intact, the results of that adoption are substantially colored by the context in which those systems have to function. Consequently, we warn also against a hasty assumption of "convergence" by the rest of the world on the patterns of those societies that are at present the most highly modernized. It is not, after all, foreordained that these societies will remain so. If, as some suggest, Japanese growth and rates of change should continue, whatever convergence takes place might conceivably shift from "Western" models, such as the United States, to other models, such as the Japanese.

We are also sensitive to occasional complaints that discussions of modernization lead to criteria of "success" and "failure" with insufficient allowance for costs and ambiguities. It is necessary to recognize that the process of modernization is arduous and agonizing. Modernization certainly has something in common with the older idea of "progress," but it should not be assumed that every society can survive the transformation intact. Nor is it a requisite for our purposes here that the changes that are achieved be regarded as "progessive." The characteristic development of institutions to a more highly interdependent level is accompanied by the disintegration of older patterns that have been superseded. Not all go at once, and some do not seem to go at all, but even those that survive do so in an altered context. During the process of modernization some always regard themselves as discomfited, regardless of whether or not foreigners are involved, and it always occurs to some of those who are discomfited that salvation lies in returning to the good old days. Fundamentalist reactions always ensue. Powerful interest groups seek to defend existing or previously existing values and institutions, and they come into conflict with those who seek, request, or demand change. Civil wars, revolutions, and international wars are characteristic of the modern era, for the struggle between interest groups favoring the status quo and those favoring change, and particularly the advocates of rival conceptions of modernity, add new issues to the many that have caused bloodshed in the past. The peoples of the world have now developed military technology capable of destroying their enemies and themselves. Exploitation of the natural environment has reached the point at which indirect effects may be more devastating than direct despoliation. The consumption of raw materials and the pollution of the land, water, and atmosphere cannot continue at the present rate for more than a few decades. Will there be sufficient resources available to permit the two-thirds of humankind that is still relatively nonmodernized to attain the present levels of those that are relatively modernized? Can all three thirds survive with these patterns of modernization if they are achieved? Whatever the answers to these questions, all attempts to retreat from this situation by stopping or turning our backs on the patterns of modernization have thus far proved to be self-defeating.

Modernization is certainly not "progress" in any simple sense of the term. Given any standard of values, modernization enhances creative capabilities for both good and evil, and the age-old problems of ends and means are exacerbated by virtue of these increased capabilities. Indeed, failure is as likely as success. It is quite possible that many societies may not have the capacity—in terms of both institutional and natural resources—to attain the levels of achievement of those societies that are today relatively modernized. It is no less possible that the relatively modernized may not be able to survive what they have achieved.

Stages and Periodization

We regard the period in Japan and Russia from the seventeenth century to the 1860's as the base from which modernizing change took place. This first stage is not so much an unmoving line or point as it is a dynamic continuum in which trends are set in motion that greatly affect the modernization drive. Though the members of these two societies in this time span were, of course, the heirs of preceding centuries of development, it was they who confronted the challenge of modernity in the nineteenth century. The impressive era of reforms inaugurated by Peter I is seen in this context as a form of defensive change designed to strengthen the capacity of the civil and military bureaucracies to defend the nation against foreign threats. Similarly, the limited Tokugawa efforts to follow developments in the West through their window at Nagasaki and the hasty attempts by Japanese at defensive changes in the decades after the coming of Admiral Perry did not alter the essential characteristics of the premodern society. Part I of this volume is concerned with the historical bases from which later change took place.

The second stage is that of transformation. Modernizing elites come to power in response to internal and/or external challenge, and they conceive and undertake sweeping plans for institutional reform that are designed to strengthen the state and their power to influence it. It is possible and sometimes desirable to distinguish within this stage shorter periods of transition. One such shorter period encompasses an early stage of experimentation, often accompanied by facile optimism about the models to follow. It is gradually followed by another of consolidation in which the leadership is sobered by the realization of the need to combine control with a slower pace of fundamental innovation. At some point, when educational, industrial, and political institutions begin to assume an inertia and produce a new and participating citizenry, the transformation accelerates. This point was clearly reached in both Japan and Russia early in the twentieth century. Though these and further subdivisions are possible, however, we have chosen to treat the eighty-year period from the 1860's to the 1940's as one of continuous transition from an agrarian and rural to an industrial and urban way of life. We have made this choice because the stage that follows the 1940's and 1950's seems to us different in kind, by all our quantifiable indexes and analytical procedures, from any of the earlier substages that we could have distinguished. The long-term trends in the period of transformation to the 1940's seem to us to outweigh in significance the shorter-term variations within this period. They can even be seen to bridge such cataclysmic political events as the Russian Revolution. Consequently, we have chosen to treat that revolution and the First Five Year Plan within the larger framework of transformation. We fully realize the significance of the changes that resulted from these events, and we are aware of interpretations that regard the October Revolution as a watershed in world history. Those who were involved in those events, however, saw their importance in the context of profound changes that came over the longer period of time. Part II deals with this period of transformation.

The third stage is that of high modernization. Like the first, this is not so much a fixed point in time as it is a developing dynamic. In our view Japan and Russia have been moving into this stage since the 1950's, although by quite different paths and with quite different handicaps and advantages. Per capita production, income, and amenities are at a high level. Upwards of 60 to 70 per cent of the population lives in cities, and a radically increased access to educational opportunity produces a population increasingly prepared and anxious to participate in the bureaucratic arrangements that characterize all areas of society. Quantitative indexes for measurement and comparison now become far more numerous. As in earlier periods, however, such indexes tell little about how political and social constraints influence the life of the individual.

One of the clear indications why it is necessary to distinguish high modernization as a stage is that institutions that are useful and perhaps essential to the earlier transformation can become dysfunctional in later stages of modernization. The extremes of central control—though not of integration in an increasingly interdependent society—become counterproductive in complex societies, and ideological devices, like the Japanese emperor system or the Soviet party ideology, which are useful for marshaling support during transformation, prove too rigid and inflexible for the problems of modernity.

It should hardly be necessary to add that we do not consider the present stage—itself a time of change—as a fixed goal toward which human history has been pressing. Our earlier cautions about terms like "convergence" and "success" remain valid. Yet it is clear that in terms of productive and destructive capability a new plateau has been reached by a small number of advanced societies, and that Japan and Russia are joining their number during the last decades of the twentieth century. Their change has been qualitative, and not merely quantitative. Part III addresses itself to this third stage.

Comparisons

Societies in the process of modernization can be compared in a number of ways. They can be compared on the basis of the relative point in time at which they undertook modernization, for there are vital differences in the problems confronting a society that depend on whether the process occurred early or late in relation to other societies. It is important also to determine whether the initial challenge to premodern values and institutions came from leaders within the society or from outside in the form of war or colonialism. Further, the capacity of the members of a society to manage their own transformation is contingent upon the extent to which that society is characterized by continuity of territory and population during the modernization process, or whether it is wracked by struggles over unification, secession, independence, irredentism, and other problems of nation-building that tend to divert resources from their allocation to the needs of development. Societies may also be compared in terms of levels of achievement in such matters as political stability, economic growth, and social mobilization. Moreover, component institutions of a society can be taken out of context and compared separately with those of other societies.

The comparisons of Japanese and Russian development selected for analysis in the three parts of this study provide the point of departure for an interpretation of their experience and of its implications for an understanding of the process of modernization. We have concerned ourselves within each of the three chronological periods with five broad areas: the international context, political development, economic growth, social interdependence, and knowledge and education. The questions for each period that we regard as of salient importance for this purpose are elaborated in the brief Introduction to each of the three parts, and Chapters 7, 13, and 19 report our findings. Our general conclusions regarding the entire process, and some thoughts regarding the relevance of these conclusions to other latecomers are set forth in Chapter 20.

We have sought to present an interpretation in a systematic form, and at the same time to be as economical as possible in the use of methodological apparatus. The central questions we are asking concern the preconditions relevant to modernization that may be discerned in premodern Japan and Russia, the ways in which these peoples have met the functional requirements of transformation in the period of the 1860's to the 1940's, and also the ways in which they have met the distinctive requirements of high modernization. We are also interested in the relations between the preconditions, and the requirements of transformation and of high modernization.

By preconditions of modernization, we mean the conditions necessary for achieving the capacity to accept science and technology and to undertake the policies leading to radical and comprehensive social change. And by requirements of transformation and of high modernization, we mean the conditions necessary for maintaining this system in these two different sets of circumstances. The preconditions are met by structures of social action, or institutions and values, appropriate to the needs of the situation. The capacity of the members of a society to convert their institutions and values without losing the cohesiveness that comes from stability, and also to adopt institutions and values from abroad when necessary, is a fundamental element of their ability to meet the distinctive requirements of transformation and of high modernization.

Comparisons of Japan and Russia are noteworthy on their own terms, but the significance of their differences and similarities as they relate to modernization can be judged only by comparing them to the experiences of other societies. For this reason we have presented comparisons, offered at the end of each of the fifteen substantive chapters, with other societies in the same three phases of development—the premodern, the period of transformation, and high modernization.

There are three types of premodern societies with which we compare premodern Japan and Russia. First, we make comparisons with some nations that were to become early-modernizing societies, such as England before the eighteenth century. The utility of these comparisons is premised on the assumption that to the extent similarities between Japan and Russia were shared with the early modernizers but not with other societies these factors are likely to represent

preconditions for modernization. Second, we have compared Japan
and Russia to other latecomers to modernization that seem to have
been in an advanced state of premodern development. China is the
most frequently cited case, but certain aspects of Ottoman development are also pertinent. It is our assumption that whereas the preconditions for firstcomers and latecomers to the process vary considerably,
the preconditions for various latecomers are likely to be quite similar.
To the extent that similarities between Japan and Russia were not
shared by other latecomers, we can hypothesize that these were critical
factors underlying the ability of Japan and Russia to transform their
societies. Third, we have made some general comparisons with considerably less developed premodern societies, showing ways in which
premodern Japan and Russia were more advanced societies and
indicating how these factors may have contributed to speedy modernization.

For the transitional period, comparative cases are drawn from
latecomers to modernization. We have sought to compare the rate
of transformation in Japan and Russia with that of other countries
and to explain the relatively greater achievement of these two cases.
Many of the explanations refer back to conditions present during
the premodern period, but we have also not wanted to neglect the
new policies and processes that seem to have accelerated the pace of
change. The international comparisons with Japan and Russia after
the 1940's focus primarily on other relatively modernized societies.

For the purposes of this discussion, limiting our consideration to
countries with populations of a million or more, we consider the
relatively advanced Western societies to include: Australia, Belgium,
Canada, Denmark, Finland, France, the German Democratic Republic, the German Federal Republic, the Netherlands, New Zealand, Norway, Sweden, Switzerland, the United Kingdom, and the
United States. In 1970 these countries had per capita GNP's (calculated at market prices by the World Bank) ranging from $2,250 to
$4,760. Major countries that may be considered to share with Japan
($1,920) and the U.S.S.R. ($1,790) the characteristics of advanced
latecomers include Austria ($2,010), Czechoslovakia ($2,230), and
Italy ($1,760). This leaves as less advanced latecomers some 170
independent countries and dependent territories with per capita
GNP's ranging from $60 to $1,650. Included in this third category,
as countries with higher GNP's per capita but representing exceptional cases, are Israel, Puerto Rico, and the oil-producing states.

These categories are admittedly arbitrary. The estimates of GNP
are tentative and subject to a considerable margin of error, especially

in regard to countries with centrally planned economies. These estimates also fail to take into account the extensive stockpiles of goods and skills produced during past generations by the more advanced societies. In nations like Australia, New Zealand, the United States, and Israel it was possible to import skills, technology, and capital. Despite these problems, and the false impression of precision conveyed by figures for GNP per capita, we believe that these categories correspond rather closely to informed evaluations of the record of the early-modernizing Western societies and certain relatively advanced latecomers in taking advantage of the opportunities offered by the scientific and technological revolution.

In extending this comparison to other societies we are interested in learning which of the distinctive common characteristics of Japan and Russia are common to all societies before 1800, or only to latecomers to modernization, or only to modernizing countries in their early stages, or only to highly modernized societies. We also wish to know whether these distinctive characteristics are relevant to modernization generally or only to particular phases of modernization. Because comparisons involve differences as well as similarities, we also wish to explore the relevance to modernization of the critical differences between Japan and Russia, either in general or at particular stages of development. In studying the implications of the Japanese and Russian experiences for other societies, finally, we wish to explore the extent to which the distinctive common characteristics and critical differences of these two countries that are particularly relevant to modernization are present in developing societies or can be generated by their adoption of other institutions.

Why Japan and Russia?

A short answer to this question has already been suggested: Their relatively similar per capita levels of development over a period of a century, despite markedly different premodern and modern institutional frameworks, suggest some significant conclusions for thinking about the process of modernization. There are no two other countries with such a striking interrelationship of similar results under differing institutions. The long answer to this question is set forth in the rest of this study, and especially in Chapters 7, 13, and 19, in which we draw conclusions with respect to the three chronological periods, and in the more general conclusions provided in Chapter 20.

There is also a need at this point, however, for an intermediate answer to the question, Why Japan and Russia? It is needed both to offer a more detailed formulation of the reasons why this comparison attracted our attention in the first place and to provide some background for readers who are not familiar with these two countries.

The similarities that particularly deserve to be stressed in this context are those circumstances that set these two countries apart from the other latecomers to modernization. These are the common attributes of Japan and Russia that may have been factors in producing a rapid transition to high levels of modernization. The timing of their transformation and the per capita levels of their development since the 1860's provide the basis for the comparison between them. The differences between them are, of course, also striking. These pertain to physical size, resources, and climate; culture; economic and other social developments; political institutions; and international roles. These differences may have been alternative sources of patterns conducive to rapid modernization or simply irrelevant to this process.

A basic similarity is the relation of Japan and Russia to other countries in terms of relative levels of development in the nineteenth century. Though Japan was largely isolated from England and France from the seventeenth to the mid-nineteenth centuries, and though Russia underwent a period of active if limited interaction with these countries in this period, the two latecomers were at an approximately similar distance behind the early modernizing nations in their development in the latter part of the nineteenth century and occupied, even then, a common median position. More specifically, it is estimated that in 1870 their real gross national product per capita was about one-quarter to one-third that of the United Kingdom, with Japan at the lower and Russia at the upper level of this range. As compared with most countries of the world, other than a few of the early modernizing ones, Japan and Russia were relatively advanced.

The importance of these dimensions is that Japan and Russia may have been among the few countries that had both the capacity and the determination to catch up with the early modernizers. They were stimulated by the examples they saw, and they were sufficiently well mobilized to be able to convert their premodern systems to the opportunities offered by the scientific and technological revolution by learning from the achievements and the failures of the more modernized countries.

It is also significant that in the 1970's Japan and Russia are at about the same level of per capita development. Individual indicators naturally vary, due to many factors. On a per capita basis, for example, Japan produces twice as much steel as Russia, but consumes only three-quarters as much energy. In terms of real gross national product per capita the two countries were at about the same level in the 1960's, though since then Japan has forged ahead. Instead of being one-quarter to one-third the level of the United Kingdom in real GNP per capita, as they were in 1870, they are now about equal with it. In the meantime new standards have been set by other countries, however, and the per capita economic level of Japan and Russia is about two-thirds that of the United States and three-quarters that of the most highly developed European countries. In any case, Japan and Russia have not only transformed their countries in about the same degree over a period of a century, but they have also to a considerable extent closed the gap that separated them from the earlier modernizing countries.

The populations in 1970 of 242 million for Russia and 104 million for Japan may seem more of a contrast than a similarity until several other considerations are taken into account. Russia and Japan are both comparatively large as far as population is concerned, ranking third and sixth among the 144 independent nations of the world, and first and third among those that are relatively modernized. Both, among very few countries, have the human resources to develop a fully diversified modern industrial society and to exercise influence as great powers in the international system.

It is also significant that until modern times Japan had a larger population; Russia overtook it only at the end of the eighteenth century. An important factor in this difference in the size of populations in the past century is that Russia is a multinational state whereas Japan is ethnically homogeneous. If one considers only the ethnic Russian population of Russia, as distinct from that of other Slavs (Ukrainians and Byelorussians) and the non-Slavic peoples, the difference is considerably reduced. The Japanese population of 44 million in 1900 and 104 million in 1970 compares with a Russian ethnic population of 59 million in 1900 and 129 million in 1970.

Not only have Japan and Russia been among the most populated countries in the world since premodern times, they have also been among the few with a continuing tradition of effective central government from the seventeenth century to the present. It is also likely that the experience Japan and Russia shared, of existence on the fringe of the larger cultural areas of China and Byzantium, played a crucial part in their ability to employ modernized models as successfully as they have. A good deal is said about this adaptability later, but it is worth noting here that the political systems of Tokugawa Japan and early imperial Russia were probably superior (for purposes of subsequent development) to those of late feudal and early modern Europe insofar as the central governmental officials and local authorities responsible to the center were able to meet internal crises, to initiate change, and to order the relationships among social groups. Their governments were much more effective in these respects than those of most other countries, and perhaps only the Chinese and Ottoman empires, among the other premodern countries of the world, had political systems with comparable capabilities. Indeed, the premodern governments of Japan and Russia were probably more active in resource mobilization and allocation on a regular and long-term basis than other governments in Europe and Asia at that time. One consequence of this capability was that Japan and Russia developed the capacity to resist colonialism by the West, unlike most later modernizing peoples, and to meet the challenges of the modern world essentially by their own efforts.

The development and maintenance of this administrative capacity was accompanied by a value system with a firm historical base in the official ideology of the country, in the operational modes of the bureaucracy, and in the political thinking of active citizens in most walks of life. This value system stressed the predominance of common interests over individual interests, the belief that the central government should play a leading role in development, and the moral virtue of dedication and sacrifice to the national interest as defined by authoritative political figures.

Though these two nations have been approximately similar in per capita levels during the past century, there have also been differences in the rates of change in specific aspects of their societies. From a somewhat lower economic base in the nineteenth century, the long-term annual average growth rate of GNP per capita was about 2.2 per cent for Japan, as compared with 2.0 per cent for Russia. Japan also developed more rapidly as measured by the proportion of the labor force engaged in industry and services, and in the production of consumer goods. Russian heavy industry, however, was generally more advanced. Japanese society was more urbanized than that of Russia in 1870, and it continues to have a larger proportion of its population in cities. Russia has devoted greater resources to research and development and to centrally administered social services. On the other hand, until very recently both countries skimped on consumer demand and social overhead.

These broad similarities in structure and development over a period of two centuries must be evaluated in the light of certain important differences. None of these is more striking than the physical contrasts in size, resources, and climate. The territory of Russia is some sixty times larger than that of Japan—8,263,100 square miles (22,402,200 square kilometers) as compared with 142,766 (369,881). Their size results in a density of population of 25 per square mile (11 per square kilometer) for Russia and 654 (280) for Japan. Russia is generally well supplied with all the natural resources required by an industrial society; Japan is lacking in almost all natural resources except water power.

There are also marked differences in those aspects of the natural environment so vital for national development, although both have a wide variety of climates. Russia is located north of 45° latitude and nearly half of its total land area is permanently frozen; Japan is south of this latitude. Russia has a continental climate, with a long cold winter and relatively little rainfall, whereas Japan has a temperate climate and plentiful rain.

Russia has been landlocked for most of its history. Its warm-water ports, most of which are frozen in winter, were acquired only as a result of territorial expansion in the eighteenth and nineteenth centuries. Even these, apart from Murmansk and Vladivostok, are restricted in their access to the open oceans by the narrow straits of the Baltic and the Bosporus. Japan, by contrast, has easy access to seaborne commerce even though she landlocked herself for more than two centuries. Russia, moreover, has had few natural barriers to protect it from its populous and threatening neighbors, and the plains that link it with Europe have for centuries been a major route of population movements and invasions. With the exception of the unsuccessful Mongol invasions, however, Japan's insular position has provided adequate protection until modern times. To the extent that one can generalize about such matters, it would seem fair to say that climate and geography have represented much greater obstacles to development for Russia than for Japan, whereas Russia's wealth of natural resources has given it decided advantages.

Apart from the similarities already noted in the effectiveness of the political systems of the two countries, their cultural heritages contrast strikingly. From a Western viewpoint, Russia is essentially European, albeit European in a somewhat different historical context from that of its neighbors to the West. Like them its origins are traceable to the ancient world through Greece and Rome, it became Christian, and, after the tenth century, its ruling families intermarried with those of Central and Western Europe. Its Christianity grew apart from that of the West as a result of theological controversies between Constantinople and Rome, but these differences in outlook were relatively minor when compared with those between Christianity and the other major religions of the world. There have also been differences in values and outlook that can be attributed to a variety of factors, not the least of which was the Mongol conquest. Nonetheless, by the end of the eighteenth century Russia was again very much a part of Europe.

Japan, by contrast, has no historic links with Europe, and because of its relative geographical—and later political—isolation, it was less well known to Europeans than China or southern and southeastern Asia. Those Europeans who came to know the Japanese could find little that was familiar to their culture. A Jesuit who visited Japan in the sixteenth century reported that "it may be truly said that Japan is a world the reverse of Europe; everything is so different and opposite that they are like us in practically nothing." Russians considered themselves to be Europeans, especially after 1700. But the Japanese regarded Europe as alien and actively sought to maintain their ethnic distinctiveness. The exclusiveness of the Japanese has continued into modern times, in spite of their successful adaptation to the challenges of the scientific and technological revolution. No foreigners, whether Asian or European, have been accepted into the Japanese civil, military, or economic elites, let alone into the imperial family, and the process of acculturation has been carried out without weakening ethnic barriers.

The greater participation of Russia in Western culture is also reflected in its contributions to modern science. In the nineteenth century not one Japanese scientist made an original contribution to knowledge comparable with those of Mendeleev, Timiriazev, Lobachevsky, and Butlerov, among others (some of foreign origin). In the twentieth century, the 276 (1901–1973) Nobel laureates in physics, chemistry, and medicine have included eight Russians as compared with three Japanese.

The relatively similar levels of development of Japan and Russia in 1870 and 1970 have already been noted, but there has been a notable difference in some of the components of these levels. What is striking about Japanese society in the mid-nineteenth century is that the degree of mobilization was higher than in Russia even though the level of economic production was somewhat lower. This greater mobilization is reflected in better communications, a relatively larger volume of domestic trade, more and better trained bureaucrats at the disposal of the central government, and a generally more tightly knit and integrated society. It was probably because of these characteristics that, once industrialization got under way in the latter part of the nineteenth century, Japan was better equipped to take advantage of its potentialities.

Since 1917 the formal institutional systems of Japan and Russia have been categorized as "capitalist" and "socialist." Although the differences in the two systems have not in practice been as great as implied by these two descriptive terms, there have nevertheless been marked contrasts in the processes by which decisions were made, in the allocation of resources among the main sectors of the society, and in the distribution of income among social groups. In the half century before 1917, however, the two countries tended to resemble each other in the formal structure of their national institutions. Both based their formal political structures to a considerable degree on German and Austrian models.

The contrast in the international roles of the two countries should also be noted. Though Japan defeated Russia in 1905, it remained a relatively secondary power on the international scene until the Second World War. As a defeated state without either nuclear or conventional strategic arms, Japan has been no match for a Russia that after 1945 became one of the two great powers with worldwide interests, authority, and military power. Only in the 1970's, as international relations have moved from confrontation to accommodation, and production and trade have gained in importance as indexes of international influence, has the role of Japan in world politics again become noteworthy. Statesmen have now begun to assume that in the next decade or two Japan will join with the U.S.S.R., the United States, the European Community, and China as one of the principal actors in a future international system.

Finally, it should be noted that we have been forced to leave certain other areas of interest and importance untouched—the political and economic relations between Japan and Russia, their changing perceptions of each other, and their achievements in literature and the fine arts. Russia was one of the first European countries to "discover" Japan in the nineteenth century, although the frequent contacts of these two peoples did not prevent serious mutual misperceptions, a point well worth exploring in the context of their confrontation in 1905. Many of the developments discussed in this volume were sensitively reflected in the literature and art of these two peoples. The temptation to expand our comparative treatment to include these topics, however, had to be resisted because they are not, in the final analysis, central to our main themes.

Political Chronology

JAPAN	RUSSIA

I. Heritage, to 1860's

7th c.–8th c.: Establishment of Centralized State	10th c.–13th c.: Kievan State

13th c. Mongol Invasions

	15th c.–18th c.: Muscovite State
1600–1868: Tokugawa Period	
1639: Seclusion Edict	
	1689–1725: Peter I (the Great)
	18th c.–19th c.: Expansion of the Russian Empire
1853: Perry Expedition	1853–56: Crimean War

II. Transformation, 1860's–1940's

	1861: Emancipation of Serfs
1868: Meiji Restoration	1860's–1870's: Other Major Reforms
1871: Abolition of Feudal Divisions	
1890: Meiji Constitution	

1904–1905 Russo-Japanese War

	1905: Revolution
1914–1918: World War I and Siberian Intervention	1914–18: World War I
	1917: End of Tsarist Rule
	1917: Bolshevik Revolution
	1928– : Five-Year Plans
	1929–30: Collectivization Drive
1931–32: Manchurian Incident and End of Political Party Government	
1937– : China War	

III. Contemporary Era, 1940's–1970's

1941–1945 World War II

1945: Loss of Empire	1945– : Expansion of Communism Abroad
1945–51: American Occupation	1953: Death of Stalin

The Heritage of the Past

Part I is a comparative study of Japan and Russia as premodern societies. It asks two questions: (1) What were the main similarities and differences between these two societies, and (2) Did they have distinctive similarities that were not shared by most other societies and that seem to have given Japan and Russia significant advantages in the subsequent process of modernization?

To answer the first requires both the selection for comparison of a wide range of characteristics and the search for similarities even where differences at first appear most conspicuous. To answer the second we must hypothesize about the preconditions, that is, about the strategic factors in the historical past from which the changes characteristic of modernization took place and which assisted in the process of rapid modernization that started in the 1860's. So little comparative analysis of premodern societies has been carried out that even the question of what factors generally operate as preconditions remains largely unanswered. Given the dearth of previous comparisons of societies prior to the start of modernization, an important task in Part I will be to demonstrate that such comparisons do add immeasurably to our understanding of this process.

By choosing to compare Japan and Russia before the 1860's with other societies not yet transformed by initial modernization, we are consciously seeking to avoid a pitfall commonly associated with comparative statements about premodern societies. Frequently these statements describe Japan and Russia in negative terms; they focus on those elements present in modernizing societies but which were completely lacking in these two countries. Of course, like all premodern societies before the second half of the eighteenth century and all but a few societies before well into the nineteenth century, Japan and Russia were rural and poor by the standards of modernized societies. And yet by the standards of the vast majority of societies still untouched by modernization, they may appear quite different. It is to the universe of premodern societies that we should direct our comparisons to determine why some responded to the scientific and technological revolution as firstcomers to modernization, why some did quite well as latecomers, and why most have done very poorly indeed in the transformation as latecomers.

The notion of premodern societies should not suggest an absence of important elements that contribute to making modernization possible at a later date. There undoubtedly are many ways in which the heritage of the past can either "assist" or "hinder" the leaders and peoples of countries facing the challenge of the modern era. But which are important? Which matter? We are seeking to trace the roots of the later but rapid modernization of Japan and Russia to the premodern period and to take a first step toward a comparison of premodern societies from the point of view of a capacity for modernization.

In two important respects we should expect the heritage of the past to influence the outcome of the subsequent transformation. Many students of the history of societies have noted the contrasting forms of social control in societies of the past and the present. First, since the conversion from family- and community-centered controls to impersonal methods is likely to be a disruptive process, we should expect to find a difference between societies in the degree to which old forms of control are smoothly converted to new forms. In other words, how well was a period of general breakdown avoided? Second, since some characteristics of premodern societies appear to develop in an orderly fashion from century to century, it should not be surprising if the degree of modernization reached has a great deal to do with the type of development previously present. Examination of the dynamic features of societies during the centuries just prior to the beginning of modernization offers the prospect of determining in what respects an exceptional point of development had been reached. In the following chapters we shall look for similarities in these two respects, and in other respects as well, between Japan and Russia. We shall also consider briefly how they compare both with the earlier modernizing countries and with countries that have been slower to modernize.

In each case, countries will be chosen for comparison at a time when they had not yet entered the initial phase of modernization. For Western Europe this generally means prior to some time in the second half of the eighteenth century, while for other parts of the world not settled by recent European arrivals the cutoff usually falls in the middle or late nineteenth century. In order to locate Japan and Russia in comparative perspective among this universe of premodern societies, we can examine wide variations in such variables as government development and urban growth.

By choosing to begin our study of modernization with a comparison of the historical bases for the process, we are expecting to find that how the modernized elements were eventually introduced by outsiders and insiders is far less important than what strategic factors of social experience antedated these contacts. Comparative study of preconditions in the following chapters focuses on the internal social structure of Japan and Russia prior to the 1860's. If we are indeed able to identify preconditions for these two countries, it would point to the desirability of paying a great deal more attention to the premodern period than is customary in studies of modernization.

Chapter Two

INTERNATIONAL CONTEXT

ONE IS INCLINED at first glance to see only contrast in the relations of Japan and Russia with other societies during the millennium before the latter part of the nineteenth century. The Chinese and Byzantine influences to which they were subjected were as different as the original native cultures of the two countries. Japan remained essentially alien to and unfamiliar with the West until the mid-nineteenth century. Russia was in a very real sense a part of Europe, although the Mongol invasions of the thirteenth century led to a break of some two centuries in the previously close relations between the Kievan principalities and the West. After 1700 Peter sought political models in Europe, and thereafter Russia abandoned the Byzantine tradition in favor of the West. Japan's relationship with Europe was far more tenuous. The brief encounter of the Japanese with the European traders and missionaries during the sixteenth and early seventeenth centuries was a contact without consequence so far as institutional borrowing was concerned. It was followed by a period of almost complete isolation for more than two centuries.

Offsetting these striking differences, however, were similarities that may have had considerable bearing on the modern development of Japan and Russia. Both nations drew on a single foreign culture—Chinese in one case and Byzantine in the other—to such an extent that generations of leaders of these two countries became accustomed to accept ideas and institutions from abroad, and to this extent may have prepared their descendants to welcome the scientific and technological revolution of which the "West" became the agent. With the Chinese and Byzantine traditions came values and institutions that were conducive to national unity and effective government, and both Tokugawa and Muscovite rulers drew heavily on these in structuring their societies.

The institutions and values of China and Byzantium that were adopted in Japan and Russia over many centuries were not simply imitated there. They were adapted and employed for the solution of particular problems in such a way as to become expressions of the national identities; when these borrowed institutions lost their earlier effectiveness, Japan and Russia turned away from China and Byzantium.

Initially, Japan and Russia both sought to employ Western technology to defend their institutional heritage against Western influences, which were perceived as subversive. Russia's defensive use of Western technology to bolster traditional institutions began a century and a half before the Tokugawa shogunate tried similarly to shore up its position in the mid-nineteenth century. The Japanese decision had been preceded by a century of growing interest in Western medical and military advances, however, and the crisis of the 1850's had been anticipated by the lively concern individual scholars had shown for Russian expansion in the North Pacific after the late eighteenth century. For example, Fujita Tōko, a prominent but poorly informed nationalist, concluded in 1826 on the basis of similarities in clothing styles that Holland had lost its independence to Russia and that Japan was now threatened by a monolithic Roman Catholic West.

Significance of Chinese and Byzantine Influence

The close relationship of Japan and Russia in their early history with a predominant foreign culture, followed in more recent times by interaction with the West, represents an important parallel in the development of the two countries. The substance both of native traditions and of foreign influences was in many respects markedly different. Yet there are some striking similarities in the forms of the relations of Japan with China and of Russia with Byzantium and in the specific content of certain aspects of the foreign influence. Russia was much less indebted to a single major foreign influence than was Japan, interacting before the mid-nineteenth century with Mongol, Ottoman Turkish, and Western and Central European ideas and institutions. For Japan, on the other hand, China, unlike Byzantium for Russia, remained powerful and continued to be impressive with its institutional and cultural development.

Religion was initially the principal agency of foreign influence. Buddhism, after some five centuries during which it became fully integrated into Chinese and Korean culture, was introduced into Japan in the sixth and seventh centuries and brought with it institutions as well as values. Similarly, the conversion of the rulers of Kievan Russia to the Byzantine version of Christianity in the tenth century had implications that were as much institutional as spiritual. In both cases the initial influence was restricted to small ruling elites who saw China and Byzantium as centers of power and achievement vastly more impressive than their own. The new religions were first taken up by the court and high aristocrats as a vehicle of status and of power; not until much later did Buddhism and Orthodox Christianity come to dominate popular culture in Japan and Russia. Interestingly, countries on the periphery of the larger civilizations were instrumental in the transmission of these values and institutions. The Balkan lands—Bulgaria, Greece, Serbia, Romania, and especially the monasteries of Mount Athos—played an important part in the spread of Byzantine culture to Russia; Japan's first detailed knowledge of Chinese civilization, and of Buddhism, came via Korea.

Because they came as part of a civilization and not just as a set of religious values, Buddhism and Orthodox Christianity brought with them literature, art, architecture, and legal and political values. The temples of Nara and the churches of Kiev, Vladimir, and Novgorod bear witness to Chinese and Byzantine influence, as do the systems of writing, the forms of literature, and the conceptions of man and nature that gradually flowed down from the privileged classes in Japan and Russia to the population at large. Each country thus developed in the backwash of a larger cultural sphere. Korean and Chinese priests carried Chinese influences to Japan, as did the returning clerical and lay students who were sent to China by the early Japanese governments. In Russia the clergy of the Byzantine patriarchate, of which the Russian Church was a metropolitan diocese until the sixteenth century, acted as intermediary and served as influential guide and adviser in many realms of activity. In Japan the Chinese influence was rapidly absorbed and internalized, though Buddhism itself gradually went into decline in China. In Russia, however, many of the metropolitans of Kiev and later Moscow were Greek until the Russian Church finally gained its autonomy in 1589.

Another marked effect of Chinese and Byzantine influence on Japan and Russia was in the realm of politics and administration. The Chinese example represented for Japan a pattern of political integration through the institutions of a centralized state directed by an imperial court bureaucracy. The Chinese model offered great advantages over the less structured and more regional hegemonies of the great families of the Yamato state in the sixth and seventh centuries A.D. The specific institutional emulation was only partial from the start and slowly eroded in the centuries that followed. Thereafter it survived in atrophied form under an overlay of familial, regional, and, finally, feudal decentralization. Nevertheless, the ideal of an integrated, bureaucratic state survived as part of Japanese tradition. In Kievan Russia, Greco-Roman law came to replace pagan custom, and ecclesiastical courts gained jurisdiction over beliefs and morals. Byzantine administrative procedures were likewise introduced, and with them came the theory of the equal roles of church and state in their separate realms. The Russian principalities retained their confederative form, however, and were not at this stage centralized along the lines of the Byzantine autocracy.

Formation of Distinct National Identities

The predominance of foreign influence in Japan and Russia was important in providing sophisticated models for the development of values and institutions, but the content of their respective cultures depended primarily on native inspiration. The early annals of both countries—the Japanese *Kojiki* (712) and *Nihonshoki* (720), which document the divine descent of the imperial family from the Sun Goddess, and the Russian Primary Chronicle (about 1110), which provides an account of the people of Rus from the time of Japheth, son of Noah, to the twelfth century—employ the style of Chinese and Byzantine chronologies to record native traditions. In religion, art, and politics, no less than in literature, the evolution of a native culture and the development of institutions that responded to immediate local needs made for the development of distinctive national identities.

The Mongol invasions of the thirteenth century had a crucial influence on the development of a Russian and a Japanese national consciousness, although their impact on Japan was relatively minor compared with their traumatic effect on Russia. After the Mongol incursions, culminating in 1241, destroyed the confederation of Kievan principalities and much of their culture, it was a century before a new grouping of principalities began to coalesce under the leadership of Moscow, some 750 miles to the northeast of Kiev, and another century and a half before a relatively centralized state

emerged under a Muscovite leadership that was able to deal decisively
with the Mongols. Indeed, the characteristic institutions of the
emerging Russian state were formed between the fourteenth and
seventeen centuries in the process of unifying some twenty-five
principalities and territories, subordinating their princes to Muscovite authority, and at the same time defending them not only
against waning Mongol power but also against threats from the West.

Geography, weather, and military preparations frustrated Mongol
efforts to conquer Japan. The two attempted invasions in 1274 and
1281—the first from Korea and the second and much larger from
Korea and China—were later remembered as the only foreign military threat to Japan before the nineteenth century and proof of
Japan's special protection by the national gods. The Mongol challenge, however, confronted Japan's leaders with unprecedented
problems of mobilizing men and resources, and the strains of prolonged preparedness against invasion had important institutional
results.

In the subsequent development of Japan and Russia, Chinese
and Byzantine precedents were employed primarily to give form and
authority to institutions and policies arising from current concerns.
Indeed, unlike Byzantine authority, which could dogmatically confer
exclusive truth or legitimacy on its Russian heirs, Chinese authority
did not lend itself to claims of direct transmission and legitimation.
In any case China remained a vital center. It may have been easier
for the Japanese to retain an independent self-confidence in their
own standards despite the Chinese influence. The Chinese tradition,
at any rate, was never one to which the Japanese surrendered completely. Furthermore, being universalistic and nonspecific with regard
to time and place rather than parochial or competitive, it did not
need to seem "Chinese." Japan's indigenous cultural tradition, highly
specific and parochial, tended to convert the imported universalism of
Chinese culture into its own particularism. The Shinto mythology of
divine origin and of sacred rulers sprung from the gods was the first
tradition to be recorded in the *Kojiki* in the newly imported writing
system. Japan possessed and retained a tenacious and resilient tradition in folk religion, language, poetry, and aesthetics. For centuries
the "import," though influential among the elite, scarcely affected
the patterns of life by which most Japanese dressed, worked, ate, and
lived; by the twelfth century Japanese religious leaders began to
break away from the Buddhist denominations established during the
early phases of borrowing. The flowering of Buddhism in the Kama-
kura period saw the evolution of distinctive Japanese emphasis in

the Amidist sect, in Zen, and especially in the writings of Nichiren, who proclaimed Japan as the center of a Buddhist universe. These developments made Buddhism more accessible to the common people and represented a distinctive Japanese trend of recasting imports to suit local needs.

It is a reflection of the extent to which the Japanese and Russians had developed a sense of national identity that when they experienced a second wave of Chinese and Byzantine influences in the fifteenth to seventeenth centuries, they were even more positive in adapting them to their needs. Neo-Confucian thought, introduced by Zen Buddhist monks, freed Japan from its earlier dependence on Buddhism, and provided a conception of a political and social order that met the requirements of the Tokugawa rulers. Confucianism came to dominate the thinking of the political elite, while Buddhism and Shinto continued to guide popular religious observance and daily life. The Chinese example was unique, however, in that its exemplar remained dominant in East Asia and provided the unbroken continuity of a single cultural colossus.

After the mid-fifteenth century Byzantium remained only a memory for Russia that survived in the tradition of learning associated with sacred books and legal texts. Even so, Muscovite rulers turned again to Byzantine tradition in formulating political doctrines to justify their unification of the Russian principalities. The fall of Constantinople to the Ottoman Turks in 1453 served to strengthen Byzantine influence by showing that the weakening of autocratic rule would lead to disunity and defeat by foreign enemies. It also permitted Moscow to claim later to be the "Third Rome" that would maintain the traditions of autocratic rule where Rome and Constantinople had failed. The adoption of Byzantine symbols and titles by the rulers of Moscow was an assertion of their divine right to rule, an assertion that was strengthened by the marriage in 1472 of Ivan III to Zoë Paleologus, niece of the last Byzantine emperor.

There are also significant parallels in the manner in which Russia and Japan later turned away from Byzantine and Chinese influence. After the fall of Constantinople the Muscovite rulers saw themselves as successors rather than disciples of Byzantium. Their perception of alternative cultures was also broadened in a series of confrontations with Lithuania, Poland, Sweden, and Turkey. When Peter I turned decisively to Europe at the end of the seventeenth century, he was by the same token rejecting Muscovite culture with its deep roots in Byzantium. It was not long after Peter's reign that Russian intellectuals began to refer to the pre-Petrine era in terms of backwardness obsolescence, and sterility; the continuing elements of the old Russia in religion and popular culture were regarded as survivals of an unhappy era, survivals that would in due course be overcome.

In Japan Tokugawa culture marked a high point in the diffusion of Chinese culture among Japanese intellectuals, but some Confucian writers were already prepared to praise their country's development as superior to that of China. Placing even more emphasis on native traditions in the eighteenth century, a new school of "national" scholars, by glorifying the Shinto tradition, tried to free Japanese culture from the artificial rationality they felt Confucian-Chinese influence had imposed upon it. By the early nineteenth century some writers identified the national characteristics of their culture with the ability to appropriate useful forms of knowledge, whatever their sources. The Shinto scholar Hirata, in his *Summary of the Ancient Way* (1811), argued that the good features of all traditions should be put in the service of Japan, and concluded that "we may properly speak not only of Chinese, but even of Indian and Dutch learning as Japanese learning."

Initial Challenge of the Scientific and Technological Revolution

As noted in the preceding chapter, some profound contrasts existed in the Japanese and Russian heritages. Yet there were also certain common features in the reactions of these two countries to the initial challenge of the scientific and technological revolution. This challenge took the form of a variety of Western influences in the centuries before the critical decision of Japanese and Russian leaders—in the latter part of the nineteenth century—to undertake a thorough transformation along Western lines. These common forms of response began with a tendency in both Japan and Russia to try to isolate themselves from the West and its influence. Finding this unsatisfactory and inadequate, they next sought to employ Western technology not as a means of transforming their societies but as a means of protecting their territories and institutions. Among leaders of both countries there was an insistent emphasis on the maintenance of the "traditional" heritage of values and institutions, a heritage that now included Buddhism, Confucianism, and Orthodox Christianity.

Just as the first major foreign influences on both countries had come through religion, so also they first perceived the West in terms of Catholic Christianity and considered this Western religion a threat. Europeans had first come to Japan in the 1540's, a period of tumultuous change when a succession of military leaders were making important gains toward national reunification. Western ships, with their cargoes of goods and weapons, were of strategic importance in this setting of competition and strife. But Portuguese ships also brought Jesuit missionaries, and later, Spanish ships brought Franciscan and Dominican preachers. The Japanese tolerated the missionaries because of their association with trade and weapons. But as the Jesuits began to meet with success among the feudality and the Franciscans and Dominicans made converts among the commoners, the rulers became fearful of a combination of religious and political subversion. After 1600, while the Tokugawa shoguns were establishing their control, English and Dutch ship captains gladly confirmed fears of Catholic imperialism. Reunification of Japan ended the need for firearms, and when missionaries and their converts flouted restrictions on Christianity, persecutions began. In 1637 a Christian rebellion convinced the shogunate that it should shut Japan off from further European contact.

In Russia the situation was quite different, due both to the relatively close political and economic relations with Catholic and Protestant countries and to the preoccupation of Orthodox Christians with the growing schism between Old Believers and liturgical reformers of the official church. Even so, proselytizing by Catholics and Protestants was strictly prohibited. Foreign Catholics and Protestants were allowed to reside only in specially designated urban areas, while those who entered government service were required to convert to Orthodoxy.

Although the initial reaction of Japan and Russia to the modern West was thus to isolate themselves from its subversive influence as much as possible, there were significant differences in the extent and nature of this isolation. For two centuries after 1640 Japan was shut off from the Western world under the terms of a seclusion system that became part of orthodoxy and tradition. Small-scale trade was kept up with Dutch East India Company representatives at Nagasaki, but Japanese were forbidden to go abroad and to return if they did. Regular checks were carried out among the entire population to guard against the continued propagation of Christianity, and particular care was exercised with the descendants of former or recanted Christians. The result was that persecution and martyrdom extinguished Christianity or drove it underground. Among the elite, Western civilization was usually denigrated in all the terms of reprobation common in China. Westerners were regarded as ignorant of classical values and proprieties, though clever in the fashioning of ingenious objects. To cultural disapproval was added a Shinto concern for the pollution of the sacred tradition and soil of Japan. Individual Westerners who did penetrate these defenses, however, usually reported a lively curiosity about Western civilization and a reception made cautious chiefly by fear of official disapproval.

The first Tokugawa shoguns authorized trade with Southeast Asia, experimented with invitations to Spanish mining engineers, and patronized English and Dutch trading missions that seemed to bypass Catholic influence. Even so, as merchants in a warrior-dominated society the Dutch traders at Nagasaki were given little status and their movement was sharply restricted. Even after they were worked into the system of ceremonial visits to the shogunal capital, they were treated as objects of curiosity, and their gifts aroused little interest until the eighteenth century.

In Russia, as trade and diplomatic contacts increased, the policy of isolation was reflected most rigidly in the intellectual sphere. The restrictions imposed on Catholicism and Protestantism were only a special phase of the general effort to exclude Western thought, considered potentially subversive of tsarist rule. Until the seventeenth century the education of the ruling elite was limited essentially to the Byzantine tradition of learning, and the limited number of Russians who went abroad were concerned primarily with specialized training. In the technical sphere, however, borrowing from the West was initiated in the fifteenth century and grew steadily thereafter. English, Dutch, and Swedish artisans helped to establish shipbuilding and the manufacture of arms, and they often entered Russian government service for long periods of time.

The policies of Peter I in the first quarter of the eighteenth century marked a rapid expansion of this technical borrowing and are customarily described as "Westernizing" or "Europeanizing." Nevertheless, it is important to recognize the limited character of Peter's "reforms": the aim of his extensive borrowing from the West was not to transform Russian society but rather to protect it. Peter visited English shipyards, but was not interested in Parliament. He adopted the administrative structure of the Swedish church for purposes of political centralization, but did not concern himself with Lutheranism. What were transformed, and profoundly, were the military and civilian bureaucracies and the education and way of life of the elite. The traditional culture and rural economic institutions affecting nine-tenths of the population, however, were almost as well preserved in the Europe-oriented Russia of the mid-nineteenth century as in isolated Japan.

Japan's policy of isolation began to change after 1720, as the Dutch mission at Nagasaki gradually came to be used as a source of information on Western advances in medical and military technology. By the end of the century shogunal and regional rulers sponsored "Dutch" studies, and in 1811 a translation bureau was established at the capital. Book requests given the Dutch grew in number and length, and Dutch and Chinese traders prepared regular reports on developments in the outside world. Private and sponsored programs of "Dutch" study produced a corps of specialists who were aware, to some extent, of Western advances in science and in military technology, and their warnings prepared and increased the sense of crisis that came to a head with the defeat of China in 1842 and the advent of Perry in 1853. Japanese writers commented with approval on attempts of Peter I to learn from the West, they described the achievements of Napoleon, and they warned of Japan's weakness. A questionnaire to the Dutch in 1842 asked: "Why have the Tartars lost, since they are said to be brave enough?" The answer was discouraging but direct: "Bravery alone is not sufficient, the art of war demands something more. No outlandish power can compete with a European one, as can be seen by the great realm of China which has been conquered by only four thousand men."

The Dutch contact and transmission were important less for their content and continuity than for the attitudes and awareness they produced. Most of the literature of translation prepared in Tokugawa times disappeared without a trace under the flood of Western learning that entered Japan after the ports were opened again in 1859, and "Dutch" scholars soon found they had learned the wrong language as Yokohama replaced Nagasaki. But shogunal efforts and bureaus prepared the way for the institutes of late Tokugawa years and early Meiji. The Translation Bureau within the Bureau of Astronomy (1811) was a prelude to the Institute for the Study of Barbarian Books (1856), later renamed the Institute for Development (1862) and ultimately absorbed into Tokyo University (1877).

International Comparisons

Comparisons among nations with respect to the relative importance of influences and borrowing— the role of foreign influences, the formation of distinct national identities, and the challenge of the scientific and technological revolution—are of necessity much less precise than those involving economic and social indicators. It is nevertheless important to ask how the interaction of Japan and Russia with their international environments compares with the experience of other countries.

Such comparisons are limited by the fact that Japan and Russia are among the very small number of countries that have experienced continuity as clearly defined national units for several centuries. In Japan geography provided relative freedom from external aggression, and this permitted the development of distinctive institutions by a relatively homogeneous people. The formation of the Russian national identity came somewhat later, and the establishment and enlargement of boundaries and the consolidation of security was accompanied by constant violence. Still, by the tenth century the Kievan state was in being. The opportunity and the time for the development of a rather clearly defined national consciousness were thus present to an unusual degree in both cases.

This lengthy experience of autonomy and separate identity also facilitated selective borrowing from foreign cultures. Their experience permitted greater opportunity to control and to limit foreign influence, less reason to fear submersion by it, and a broader selection of experiments in political and other social engineering. Imported institutions could be blended with indigenous tradition, and the conscious nature of the borrowing often served to define rather than to dilute the native culture. Western Europe's debt to classical culture, and the Ottoman Turks' obligation to Arab and Byzantine culture, offer parallels to the influence of China and Byzantium on Japan and Russia. In Western Europe and in the Ottoman Empire, the religious traditions of Christianity and Islam were frequently vehicles not only for the entry of religious values and institutions but for secular ones as well. But Russia, and certainly Japan, were distinct in that so much of their debt was to a single model state, and the relationship of Japan and China was particularly affected by the stability and continuity of the Chinese Empire.

The countries of Western Europe, especially England and France, resemble Japan and Russia in the way their native institutions interacted with foreign influences to form distinctive national entities. They developed impersonal institutions that came to command the loyalty given earlier to family, community, lord, and church and that retained basic differences derived from heritage and the political environment. They differed, on the other hand, in that their modern intellectual and institutional changes developed slowly and from internal sources. Japan and Russia, after greater isolation than Western Europe had known, responded rapidly and purposefully once they acknowledged the inadequacy of their institutions. To a considerable degree their response could be guided and made systematic by the leadership of modernizing elites.

The Chinese and Ottoman empires lacked adaptability. At key points the Chinese leadership placed a higher value on the legitimation of its role through the values of a past tradition than through the pragmatic adjustment to crisis that characterized the Tokugawa military leaders. The tendency of the Chinese to see their country as "Central" to its world required impressive evidence of failure before any fundamental change could be undertaken. A relative imperviousness to Western influence was reinforced by a political system in which modern and technological knowledge long remained irrelevant to career patterns. China's nineteenth-century contact with the West was further complicated by popular rebellions that strained the resources and capacity of officials and commoners alike. It was only at the century's end, after defeat by a Japan suddenly grown powerful through the application of borrowed technology and institutions, that the special relevance of Western knowledge was finally recognized. In the words of the reformer Liang Ch'i-ch'ao, "Our China was awakened from the dream of four thousand years by the defeat in the war of 1894, the cession of Taiwan, and the indemnity of 200 million *taels*."

The Ottoman Empire, although it did not have an autochthonous culture comparable to that of China, nevertheless possessed an impressive tradition of political and military and cultural accomplishment. Here it would seem that Islam operated as a major obstacle to Western influence. Though the Ottoman leaders were in frequent contact with the armed forces of Europe, in the seventeenth and eighteenth centuries they preferred to insulate themselves from that contact by employing Greek subjects as intermediaries. They maintained almost no personal knowledge of the West. They viewed Europeans as Christian infidels subject to conversion. The Turks did not begin to take the West seriously until the Ottoman confrontations with Europe toward the end of the eighteenth century.

Chapter Three

POLITICAL STRUCTURE

BY THE EARLY nineteenth century the polities of Japan and Russia bore marked similarities to each other. Their people were among the few on earth to be ruled by well-organized and accepted governments functioning at the national level. Both countries were unified politically under institutions of long standing that had become powerful symbols of national unity. Both the tsarist administration in Russia and the central *bakufu* and local *han* administrations in Japan had stable structures extending down to the village level that were staffed by a class whose status derived not merely from birth but also from obligations to specific governmental service. Independent interests were closely regulated by governments in the two countries, each claiming an exceptionally wide range of powers and thus reinforcing the prevailing idea of duty to the state rather than of rights against it. Village political life, dominated by a strong collective spirit, remained largely autonomous in its day-to-day affairs.

The most significant contrast between the two nations lay in Japan's greater degree of decentralization of civil authority into loosely federated domains (han). The Russian autocracy was far more centralized. This difference is partially attributable to the sharply contrasting geopolitical circumstances of the two societies. But in comparison with other premodern societies, both Japan and Russia had developed effective government to a relatively high degree.

Geopolitical Contrasts

The physical contrast between the two is striking. The insular position of Japan secured its inhabitants from foreign military threat

—with the sole exception of the unsuccessful Mongol invasions in the thirteenth century—until the nineteenth century. The task facing Japanese leaders was to integrate power in many local areas, a task essentially completed by the seventeenth century but complicated by the chains of mountains separating the numerous tiny plains on the main islands. The large open plains of Russia, on the other hand, limited the development of local power and also deprived it of clear political boundaries vis-à-vis the outside world; much of Russia's early history was devoted to the definition of national territory, both through defense against foreign invaders and through expansion to new territory.

The first and most obvious implication of this contrast is that during the late premodern period the Japanese were obliged to invest far fewer resources, human and material, in military institutions than were the Russians. As we shall see, warfare had been a major influence on the political development of both countries, but when internal political struggles suddenly ended in Japan, the Japanese needed a smaller military budget than did Russia, whose wars required large defensive works and vast and well-equipped armies to meet the challenge of external foes. The difference between the two nations in military expenditures is conspicuous during Japan's Tokugawa period (1600–1868) when, despite the calculated maintenance of a military ethic, only minimal resources were expended on warfare. During the same period in Russia a series of major international conflicts demanded that enormous resources be extracted from the populace and directed into the complex of institutions that together constituted the army. Had this not been accomplished Russia could never have expanded its territory to the degree that it did, and even its sovereignty might have been lost.

The constant pressure of large-scale warfare in Russia stimulated the development of certain types of national political institutions that were long absent in Japan. The army of Muscovy could not go into the field without weapons and other equipment, which were paid for through taxes levied and collected for Moscow by agents of the tsar. The institutional and personnel arrangements to support the army, more than anything else, gave definition to the early Russian state.

Russia's intimate involvement with, and Japan's isolation from, hostile neighbors meant that the more frequent crises in Russia spurred institutional innovation to a far greater extent than they did in Japan. Formed under the pressure of war and often based on foreign models, Russian institutions were frequently introduced "from above." Once the crisis that had given rise to them passed, they then either evolved to assume new functions, as with the Senate, or died leaving few traces, as in the case of the Assembly of the Land (*zemskii sobor*). As noted in the previous chapter, foreign influence, whether forcefully imposed or voluntarily adopted, figured less prominently among the stimuli to institutional change in Japan —with the major exception of the massive borrowing from T'ang China in the seventh century. Because Japan did not experience grave periodic crises in its international relations, and therefore a compelling motive for abrupt and disruptive innovation, its political institutions developed gradually and with few sharp breaks. To be sure, major innovations were made, but only after being tested for many years at local levels; nor were old institutions often discarded. The perpetuation of Japanese court institutions and ranks long after power had shifted away from them is the most important example of this respect for continuity.

Sovereignty

When in the nineteenth century the leaders of Japan and Russia embarked on what was to become a concentrated modernizing drive, both had in common an important political institution: the imperial office. In both countries the centuries-old emperorship was sufficiently stable to serve as a shield for the modernizers, the more readily because the Russian "tsar" and the Japanese "tennō" were recognized by most of the political elite as the focus of national loyalty.

Moving beyond this broad level of similarity, however, a conspicuous difference becomes apparent: the Russian tsar was both political ruler and divinely ordained symbol of national unity, whereas in Japan the emperor had symbolic force but virtually no political power. The functions of ruling and reigning had for many centuries been almost wholly separated in Japan. A military delegate, or shogun, was charged with the actual work of ruling, but only in the name of the reigning sovereign. The prototype of the Japanese sovereign emerged before the introduction of Buddhism in the sixth and seventh centuries, and he seems from the beginning to have derived legitimacy less from military strength than from the sacerdotal functions of clan chief. Onto this native institution was grafted the rather different Chinese concept of the emperor as a ruler with total political power who derives legitimacy from the mandate of Heaven.

During the seventh and eighth centuries Japan did in fact possess an imperial institution which operated according to the Chinese model, that is, with an emperor (or empress, as was often the case) serving both as political autocrat and divinely sanctioned symbol of national unity over a federation of great families concentrated at the capital. This situation proved to be a passing one, however, as the emperor in the course of the Heian period (794–1185) gradually lost political power to delegates of various sorts, primarily regents of the Fujiwara family. The political dimension of the Chinese imperial institution became muted and a shift also took place from the Chinese concept of the monarch as divinely selected by a cosmic force to the indigenous concept of the ruler as himself divine, the direct descendant of the sun goddess and ultimately of the creators of the Japanese islands themselves. But even if the imperial institution was not believed to have been divinely sanctioned to exercise political power, it served to legitimize the exercise of power by others, and was thus a potentially active force in public life.

The Russian imperial institution was derived from the Byzantine concept of the caesaropapist prince (later caesar or tsar) endowed by God with full authority in secular matters and charged with leadership of the Orthodox flock. Taking inspiration also from the extensive powers of the Tatar office of khan and from the Ottoman sultanate, the leader of Muscovy from an early date came to be the most potent political force in the state, the "ruler by himself" or "autocrat." The Grand Prince of Moscow played a pivotal and personal role in the process of national unification. In Japan, however, the unification of the sixteenth century was accomplished solely through military leaders who sought legitimacy as delegates for the sovereign. In the course of the social and political strife in seventeenth-century Russia, the dominance of the autocracy in *both* secular and churchly affairs was confirmed anew against those who wished *either* oligarchic or theocratic rule. Hence, the figures of Peter I and Tokugawa Ieyasu, who in many respects bear comparison with each other, stand in contrast. Peter exercised power in his own name, whereas Ieyasu carefully maintained the distinctness of the authority delegated to him as shogun.

The implications of this distinction bear emphasis. On the one hand Japan had a more stable focus of national political attention than did Russia—one which was far less subject to the disruptive influence of disputes over succession and attempts at usurpation and regicide, yet one under which virtual revolutions in politics could be accomplished smoothly thanks to the legitimizing force of the sovereign. On the other hand, the correspondence between ruling and reigning gave much more vitality to the office of the tsar, whose occupants in many cases acted with the dynamism and resolution shown only by the early shoguns of the Tokugawa period.

Distribution of State Power

By far the clearest contrast between the Japanese and Russian political systems by the mid-nineteenth century was in the distribution of state power between central and regional or local institutions. Because it long acted primarily to raise funds with which to mount military operations against hostile neighbors, the Russian state was organized nationally and along highly centralized lines. Even when, of necessity, considerable independent authority was exercised locally by representatives of the tsar, there was no question that the power they possessed was due to their link with the central regime. In Japan fear of foreign invasion and of outright secession from the body politic was minimal. Local territorial (han) leaders, therefore, could be left a far greater degree of autonomy. With a proportionately smaller volume of taxes and duties administered from the center, the most intensive institutional development in Japan occurred at the han level. Russia, on the contrary, was more highly developed at the national level.

The peculiar configuration of central and local power in Japan is known technically as the baku-han system, that is, the division of political authority between a central government (the bakufu) and the approximately 250 separate local domains of varying size known as han. The bakufu had a dual character. It was a central government to the extent that it was responsible for all foreign relations, including trade (although trade relations were minimal during the Tokugawa period), for the administration of the three major cities, for all relations between the separate han, for occasional relocation of barons and reallocation of land between han, and even for certain affairs—succession of leadership, for example—within the han. Yet, the bakufu was itself the largest of the han, holding about one quarter of the country as its own realm under its own administration. Each of the han owed various services to the bakufu but at the same time enjoyed a very wide degree of autonomy in the direct governance of its individual territory. All tax collection, for example, was wholly internal to the han; revenues were collected by han officials and used to finance han expenses, in particular the stipends of the han's service class. The bakufu controlled the han barons (*daimyō*) negatively, by exacting loyalty oaths and limiting fortifications, and positively, by requiring them to spend alternate years in attendance and homage at the shogun's capital.

The Japanese baku-han system was feudal in its origins, the relationship between the shogun (the bakufu leader) and each individual domain lord being based on a personal bond of loyalty. In practice, however, the feudal quality of the relationship between the center and the provinces changed through the centuries and the system came to be maintained by each shogun through a cautiously engineered balance of power. Thus one finds such a curious term as "centralized feudalism" used to describe the Tokugawa polity, even though the feudal character of the system had been drastically eroded by the mid-nineteenth century. The absence of a high degree of political centralization reflected not merely the persistence of personal bonds but more importantly the lack of any outside threat to provoke centralization. Here the contrast with Russia, constantly forced to assert its unity against foreign foes, is obvious.

Whereas Japan's political institutions were highly developed at the han level and fairly loosely united at the center, Russian political power was polarized between a highly centralized autocratic state and highly localized (even intravillage) institutions, notably serfdom. The institution of serfdom was by its nature localized. It was, however, intimately related at the same time to the central government because the state itself owned and exercised direct control over nearly half the peasant population and had transferred control of the other half to local gentry, whose indebtedness to and dependence upon state authority was always evident. Functions of local government that in Japan were carried out by officials of the various han were in Russia performed either by local gentry endowed by the central state with police and other powers over their serfs, or directly by officials appointed in the capital. This division of authority was the consequence of the process of unification of Russia, when regional governments and elites were often obliterated and only rarely blended into the centralized Muscovite administration. This jurisdictional division was also given a certain logic by the natural division of Russia into territories so large, so lacking in sharp distinctions, and often so thinly populated as to hinder the development of strong regional institutions and loyalties.

These different distributions of national and local control provided each country with distinct advantages and liabilities. There was more consistency among governmental levels in Japan, as well as greater opportunities for intensive local development and adaptation to local conditions. In Russia, for all the problems of articulation between center and locality, central administrators over many centuries necessarily gained valuable experience with managing extremely large units. For most of their early history the primary experience of Japanese authorities was with relatively small-scale governmental operations.

Governmental Powers and Personnel

Moving from the general distribution of public authority to the specific powers of governmental bodies, one finds in both countries by the mid-nineteenth century an extensive and highly structured system of political controls. The range of functions over which governmental institutions claimed direction and the amount of national production they controlled were unusually comprehensive compared with other premodern societies. In addition to such usual state functions as the minting of currency, the preparation of periodic cadastral surveys, and the mustering and provisioning of an army, government in both Japan and Russia also came to monopolize, or at least closely regulate, such diverse activities as domestic prices, foreign trade, and communications. Systems of education were developed by governmental power in both countries (including han schools in Japan), although much primary education remained in private hands. Both governments were capable of constructing vast public works projects prior to the 1860's, including castle-building, irrigation systems, and land-reclamation projects in Japan and an intricate canal system and extensive urban planning in Russia. Finally, governmental spokesmen in both countries from an early date stressed that their guidance of the populaces in ethical matters was not only proper but essential.

The political role of manufacturers, merchants, guilds and other potential interest groups will be dealt with in a separate section, but mention must be made here of a general contrast between Japan and Russia in respect to governmental control. The distinction would seem to be that in Japan leaders of both the bakufu and the han usually regulated the commercial activities of individuals and groups quite closely. The Russian government on the other hand, though at times pursuing a similar policy, more frequently arrogated the very functions in question and incorporated them into the state structure. The Russian government, for example, traditionally managed its own banking and credit operations, whereas in Tokugawa Japan the private merchants of Osaka were authorized to fulfill comparable functions, albeit under close state regulation. Similarly, the Russian government figured prominently in certain industrial undertakings and directly regulated the nearly one-half of the agricultural populace of the country classified as state peasants. The reason for this contrast probably lies less in the effectiveness of the Russian state in making good its extensive claims than in the faster growth of independent economic interests in Japan during the two centuries prior to the 1860's. At the same time it is probable that large-scale inter-village control was more appropriate to the extensive operations on the recently settled areas of the Russian plain than to densely settled Japan.

The personnel of these two governmental systems were similar at a broad level of generalization, yet they were also quite different at more specific levels of comparison. In overall terms, one may stress the similarity of Japan and Russia in having sufficiently large elite classes of bureaucrats to staff much of the middle and upper levels of their state apparatus. Increasingly, officials owed their jobs to competence in the art of governance and less and less to either independent wealth or to hereditary considerations. Although heredity in Japan constituted the first criterion of selection, the large number of potential public servants gave considerable room for performance criteria to come into play. Yet within the broad pattern of convergence toward modern-style bureaucracy, there exist some marked differences between the Russian and Japanese governing elites, which can best be understood by looking at the origins of this class in each country.

The Japanese *samurai*—military retainers—were in origin a "feudal" class, with a primary stress on personal loyalty to overlord in return for salary or fief. In the process of the unification of Japan in the late sixteenth and early seventeenth centuries, the samurai had been removed from the land and placed in regional castle towns as a measure of political control by the emerging daimyo. From this point on, most samurai were recompensed in rice stipends. Originally this rice came from specific parcels of land, but by the end of the Tokugawa period the stipends were indistinguishable from hereditary salaries paid to the family head. Meanwhile, the specifically military role of the samurai gradually gave way to more broadly gauged forms of public service, since the Tokugawa period was one of both domestic and foreign peace for Japan. The stress on military virtues survived in the training of the samurai class, but the bond between samurai and lord gradually found its usual expression in less personal and more abstract relationships associated with administrative functions. In short, the samurai was moving from warrior to bureaucrat.

The Russian gentry (*dvorianstvo*), by contrast, did not develop like the samurai from a land-based feudal class, but was rather a bureaucratic service class from its beginning. From the mid-sixteenth century most of the older landed hereditary aristocracy was slowly replaced by a service nobility that held land not by birthright but in return for service. Ennoblement through service alone was clearly formulated in law by the time of Peter I in the eighteenth century, so that the Russian gentry was more open than the strictly hereditary samurai. It is true, of course, that the Russian gentry generally held hereditary land and serfs, quite unlike the stipended samurai. Still, the possessors of such land never fully lost sight of their initial indebtedness to the state, and hence the Russian gentry as a whole never developed into an independent estate that could successfully assert its interests against the autocracy, often as it endeavored to do so. Thus, by the mid-nineteenth century the Russian gentry and the Japanese samurai, despite very different origins, had evolved in a very similar direction—toward being service classes wholly dependent on the state for a kind of status that was closely linked to achievement. Because the privileged classes were also dependent officials, government leaders enjoyed relative freedom to act without fear of provoking the samurai or gentry into determined self-assertion as autonomous estates.

Beyond the common role of service in defining rank within, and to some extent membership in, the elite of both nations, two important differences prevailed down to the end of the premodern period in both Japan and Russia. First, the Japanese elite was considerably more numerous than was Russia's (see Chapter 5), which made it possible in Japan for far lower offices to be filled by samurai. Russia's smaller gentry put it at a relative disadvantage in the staffing of its administrative offices, especially in the early nineteenth century when the number of offices multiplied rapidly. Furthermore, the fact that quite modest offices could be filled by members of the Japanese elite was a circumstance that introduced broad differences among the wealth and status of individual samurai. The Neo-Confucian ideology of the Tokugawa era, with its emphasis on the nobility of public service, could only partially remove the effects of these differences.

A second contrast between the elites arises from the fact that even after the ownership of land and serfs in Russia was made contingent upon state service, living on the land remained an ideal and a possibility. In this context, state service appeared to the Russian gentry as a means to an end rather than an end in itself. The autocracy never could effectively combat this lack of enthusiasm, and instead regularly recruited some of its most important officials from lower classes and from abroad. In most of Japan, however, the samurai had been decisively resettled from the land to castle towns. State service was widely accepted by the samurai as an end in itself. Reflecting this contrast between the two elites, leaders in Japan experienced more direct control and could expect more undivided loyalty than their Russian counterparts.

Special Political Interests

It has already been stressed that the state in both Japan and Russia laid claim to an exceptionally broad range of functions. This situation was the result in part of the relative absence of independent forces and interests, such as religious bodies, banks, and merchant organizations, that might challenge state power and in part of the efficiency of the state in asserting its regulatory powers against such groups. The absence of a hereditary aristocracy that could act as an effective independent interest group against the state has already been mentioned as a salient similarity between Japan and Russia.

In medieval times the greatest independent challenge to official political authority in both Japan and Russia was institutional religion, because both the Russian Orthodox Church and the various Buddhist sects were major landholders—and hence wielders of considerable autonomous power. Though religious bodies in neither case posed any major ideological challenge to the legitimacy of the state, they were sometimes a threat to political stability on a short-term basis. This threat was particularly real in Japan, where certain Buddhist sects fielded substantial private armies and set up heavily fortified regional strongholds. By the seventeenth century in both Japan and Russia, however, the political power of the church had been largely broken. In Japan it was broken through outright destruction of Buddhist military strength, confiscation of church lands, and manipulation of the Buddhist temples to serve as an instrument of state political control through the registration of commoners. In Russia, where the church participated actively in the creation and preservation of the state, the only serious threat to the caesaropapist arrangement occurred in the seventeenth century when the Patriarch

Nikon attempted unsuccessfully to assume an active and independent political role. The confiscations of church lands, conversion of the church into a bureau of state, and other measures over the century after Nikon's fall, led to a result similar to the one in Japan. By the eighteenth century institutional religion in both nations wielded little independent political power, and the entire polity was, in most practical respects, secularized.

It was rather the economic growth of the two nations that posed the greatest independent political threat to the state by endowing new groups with considerable resources and, potentially, power. Yet in Japan the exchange houses of Osaka, which achieved such eminence as to be able to serve as bankers for the government, came under needed regulation on account of the great responsibility entrusted to them. Similarly, many han manufacturers and purveyors of services requested permission from government to organize in order to protect themselves from competitors. Merchants may have escaped close regulation because of their low place in the hierarchy of occupations in the Neo-Confucian order, but governments never hesitated to expropriate merchant wealth on the few occasions when it appeared to have become so great as to tempt its owners to assume an independent political posture.

If the Japanese style was generally to regulate the manifestations of commercial power from without, in Russia new commercial interests were usually incorporated into the single structure of tsarist absolutism. This effort broke down partially in the nineteenth century, but over several generations before that time the new commercial classes had been organized into corporations or guilds which the state held accountable for the affairs of their members. Moreover, the very extensive and direct involvement of the autocracy in manufacturing of various types and in agriculture further discouraged the formation of a bourgeoisie with a strong and independent voice in public affairs.

As for the military, which in many traditional polities has established a substantial degree of distinctive political power, it appears to have remained tightly integrated within the power structure in Japan and Russia to the end of the early period. In Japan, as we have seen, the samurai class staffed what began as a military government, but the centuries of peace and scarcity of occasions on which it could exercise its martial training, along with its intimate involvement in the functioning of all agencies of government, transformed it into a more civilian bureaucracy and obviated any likelihood of its acting independently. In Russia, the military had both a large organization of its own and ample opportunity before 1860 to perform its functions. Nevertheless, from the time of Peter I military ranks were equated with, and made largely interchangeable with, ranks in the civil administration, which was in turn "militarized" by placing its members in uniforms. Such measures were among many that enabled the state bureaucracy to control the military closely and to prevent it from developing the personnel or ideology of a distinct caste.

The Village Level

In speaking of premodern Japan and Russia, it is necessary to differentiate between rule in the village and all other levels of governance. Notwithstanding the greater visibility of government at the regional and national levels in both countries, as in other premodern societies, it was in the village that most public functions were executed. It is to the village, and to the specific nature of its contacts with regional and national authorities, that we must look for an understanding of much national political behavior.

Violence and instability were by no means uncommon in the Japanese and Russian countryside. Yet, by the eighteenth century the villages were sufficiently stable to enable higher civil authorities to follow a "hands off" policy toward their internal management with little fear that chaos would ensue. This license was surely due in large measure to peasant practices that reinforced the prevailing spirit of communalism and mutuality. In Japan the investment of huge amounts of human labor in the cooperative preparation and upkeep of rice paddies generated this spirit, and beyond that made it difficult for a member of the community to withdraw and lose access to communally owned resources. In Russia the periodic repartition of the communally held land and collective planting and harvesting fostered the same sort of mutuality, just as serfdom had as its end to bind individual peasants to a given village and its land. Such factors preserved a high level of mutuality in the political life of the village by discouraging any strong manifestations of individualism.

However similar the political life of villages in both countries may have been with respect to the community's stability and autonomy vis-à-vis higher authorities, the exercise of power by peasants on the local scene differed considerably. Though there was considerable variety in village institutions within both countries, and though these institutions were subject to change in both countries in the last centuries before the modern era, power in the Japanese village was based on a hierarchy of families corresponding largely to landed wealth, whereas power in the Russian village was based to an unusual extent on seniority among males.

In Japan a strong and persistent striving for full community consensus lay at the core of village rule, at least until the mid-nineteenth century. This collectivity, however, was early subjected to strains by the rise of tenancy and by the economic and social differentiation that increasingly took place in the village after the seventeenth century. Each village possessed numerous "mutual responsibility units," made up of five families each (*goningumi*), which further strengthened the element of collectivity. Leadership more and more came to be vested on a hereditary basis in individuals from dominant farmer families. A tradition of village assemblies (*mura yoriai*) existed, but in many areas their political position was merely secondary—to conform with the consensus of the community decisions already taken by the political leaders.

The Russian village retained its collective character in even stronger form, notwithstanding the emergence in some areas of wealthy peasant entrepreneurs. Undoubtedly, in the quest for consensus differences in wealth were reflected in differences in influence. Yet leadership was exercised not primarily by leading families but through village assemblies presided over by periodically selected elders representing the entire community. In the exercise of their responsibility, these elders relied strongly on consensus, which was particularly important because only a united village could deal favorably with gentry or state officials.

Most public functions in both nations were relegated to the village as an autonomous unit. Even so, the state (or in Japan the han) had an abiding stake in the village as the source of tax revenue. In this context it is well to consider those means by which village institutions were linked to higher levels of authority. The vast distances within Russia and, to a lesser extent, the mountainous terrain of Japan placed impediments in the way of easy physical communication between village and metropolis, while the imposition of taxes on the village as a unit rather than upon its separate members further curtailed the number of transactions and even points of contact between individual peasants and higher authorities.

Other factors also served to strengthen ties between various levels of governance. Such contacts were doubtless more numerous and conducted with less friction in Japan, where a remarkably effective system of written communication existed between han and village, including local signboards on which official regulations and communications could be posted. The general congruence of authority patterns in Japan gave village-han ties a smooth and efficient quality lacking in Russia.

In considering the weaker linkage between village and state in Russia it is necessary to distinguish between peasant villages owned by gentry and those owned directly by the state. Villages owned by the state had more direct (but not necessarily more frequent) ties with the central government because they did not communicate with it through the intermediary of the local landlord but rather through regularly appointed officials. In villages owned by the gentry, the gentry landlord represented the authority of the state in all matters.

An element of political contact between the Russian village and higher authorities lacking in Japan was the frequent need to provide military recruits. Veterans who survived the ordeal of a quarter century of service generally returned to their villages, to which they brought their long contact with the military institutions of the autocracy. This link, however, did not suffice to convince some Russians, both educated and uneducated, that the political worlds of the village and the state were as fully integrated with each other as could be desired, or that the situation was improving by the end of the premodern period.

Overall, the similarities in the allocation of power and responsibility between village and state merit stress. Operating as units of collective decision-making, villages in Japan and Russia were autonomous in many ways. In critical respects relating to fiscal authority, commerce, the maintenance of local order, and the dissemination of knowledge, however, the outside administrators could and did intervene. In the efficiency of such contacts, the two countries present somewhat of a contrast: village-state articulation in Japan was on the whole smooth and continuous, whereas in Russia it was a source of some conflict and occasional discontinuity.

Control of Conflict

As might be gathered from the previous discussion on the range of powers claimed by the state, there was in Japan and Russia virtually no concept of juridical rights directed against the civil authority analogous to those prevalent in the Roman and Germanic legal traditions of Western Europe. In both Japan and Russia customary law rather than written norms provided the chief standards for regulating affairs at all levels. Official regulations were compiled periodically, but less as abstract prescriptions to be applied to all behavior than as guidelines for state officials to enforce justice in a highly personalistic manner. In contrast with both of the main legal traditions of Western Europe, with their emphasis on advocacy and on technical court procedures to be followed by professional lawyers, Japan and Russia relied more on an ethical "natural law" that had evolved and was interpreted by the litigants themselves. This practice was particularly true in Japan, where the moralistic basis of Neo-Confucian orthodoxy militated against the development of justiciable law. It was also true of Russia, however, which functioned with few truly codified laws or trained lawyers down to the nineteenth century.

In comparing the techniques of control over conflict and deviance in the two nations, it is necessary to distinguish between intravillage conflict and all other conflict because the autonomy of the village was a central feature of the political system. Japan and Russia being predominantly rural societies, most conflict and violence occurred within the village, and on the whole such matters were settled by the villagers themselves without recourse to outside authority. As in all premodern societies, the premium placed on village solidarity—on the maintenance of local consensus—demanded that conflicts be resolved through techniques of conciliation and third-party arbitration. Severe punishments could be inflicted, but denial of cooperation was more common, particularly in Japan's labor-intensive rice villages.

If there was any conspicuous distinction between Japan and Russia in the settlement of village conflicts, it was probably in the relatively large powers of the Russian serf-owner and state official to interfere personally, and at times arbitrarily, in such matters. With the exception of some separately held samurai areas within the han, the lowest level of the han bureaucracy in Japan would become involved in internal village disputes only with the greatest reluctance, normally confining its activity to grave criminal cases. For instance, the Japanese village maintained the power to impose the extreme penalty of ostracism (*mura hachibu*) on an offender, a punishment that only serf-owners and state officials could impose in Russia. Disputes between villages, on the other hand, less personal and more important, were of major concern to Tokugawa magistrates.

Above the village level, both nations were conspicuously lacking in highly elaborated judicial institutions, for most functions of adjudication were undertaken through the administrative machinery rather than through any independent judicial system. Part of the answer to the question of why civil order did not break down in the absence of regular channels of redress for offended parties lies in the great emphasis both societies placed upon collective responsibility. Under collective responsibility institutions designed to identify individual wrongdoers played less significant roles than did the entire system of self-regulation by collective units within society. This reliance on collective responsibility was most notable in Japan, where the mixture of Confucian and feudal emphasis on hierarchy, cooperation, and loyalty worked to obviate the need for sophisticated machinery for settling disputes. The creation of small collectives, entailing mutual supervision under the direction of their elder or *starosta,* in most areas of Russian life had much the same effect.

Besides these techniques and customs, both nations did possess judicial institutions at a high administrative level for settling disputes among peers. In Japan boards of appeal operated at the top of the han bureaucracy (the bakufu called it the *hyōjōsho*), and in Russia separate courts existed for each of the corporate classes, with officers elected by the assembled members. In neither nation were juries employed.

Needless to say, ethical and judicial instruments together were incapable of resolving all instances of conflict in either society. The samurai code of honor, for example, made important allowance for the vendetta. Large-scale disruption was sporadic in both city and country in the two centuries prior to the 1860's, although the frequency of such uprisings varied. Most such disturbances were of a spontaneous nature, stemming from economic distress such as high food prices and overtaxation without explicit reference to conflict between corporate groups as such. In Russia few peasant rebellions were directed toward specific political objectives, but more frequently than in Japan such broader motives are discernible, as with the eighteenth-century peasant rebellion led by Pugachev. And the mere fact that relations between peasant and landlord and between local authorities and constituents frequently degenerated to violence, whatever the causes, placed in the hands of those seeking specific change a ready and malleable weapon. In Japan, by contrast, the only uprising with an explicit political program was the rebellion led by the former samurai officeholder Ōshio Heihachirō in 1837. Although organized expressions of discontent grew in number and size during the last century of Tokugawa rule in Japan, it is equally true and perhaps more important that the high level of personal violence that prevailed at the beginning of the Tokugawa period had been replaced by a degree of civic order and organization that astonished Europeans who visited the country shortly before the Tokugawa fell. Hence the testimony of Hugh Mitford, who noted, "We could not help being struck by the great prosperity of the country . . . a happier people it would be difficult to find."

Large-scale, sustained religious violence had almost vanished by the 1860's, the last great instances being the (nominally Christian) Shimabara revolt in Japan in 1637–1638 and the Old Believer holocausts in early eighteenth–century Russia. Yet, some violence of this sort persisted in Russia, especially in the pogroms directed against Jews in the late nineteenth and early twentieth centuries.

International Comparisons

Common to all peoples who have entered early and successfully on the road to modernization is the fact that they began with the benefits of many centuries of effective government at the national level. Though not in itself a sine qua non for success, the existence of a government capable of commanding the obedience of nearly all inhabitants of a national territory is of significant value in maintaining cohesion amidst the severe dislocations that rapid change inflicts. Moreover, the habits and techniques encouraged by a complex state administration are readily transferable to new tasks. No wonder, then, that every nation aspiring to modernize has always first to give serious attention to creating a strong government.

Among the 140 or more contemporary states, Japan and Russia rank among the very few that possessed such governments prior to the beginning of their modern transformation. With few exceptions, those in this category have all been successful modernizers, most notably England and France. The apparent exceptions—such as Turkey, Spain, and China—all lagged behind Japan and Russia in important aspects of their governmental development in the eighteenth and nineteenth century. And if Germany lacked a strong national government prior to the nineteenth century, it nonetheless possessed so many of the elements normally part of the baggage of national governments—a sense of nationality, a strong and large leadership class, administrative skills—that a national state could be quickly forged when needed.

Unlike all of the great land empires except China, Japan and Russia early exhibited a strong national identity based on a single language and a cultural heritage. All the dazzling successes of Ottoman arms and Hapsburg diplomacy could not impart these qualities to the peoples under their hegemony, nor even to the capitals, which remained culturally and linguistically cosmopolitan centers.

The leadership classes of Japan and Russia bear comparison on certain points with comparable groups in the early developing nations of Western Europe. Granted that in competence the elite of Tokugawa Japan may have been closer to that of England, France, or the German states, than was Russia's, yet both are notable for their large numbers and for the emphasis they gave to achieved qualities rather than inherited rank alone. On one point the elites of Japan and Russia differ sharply from their West European counterparts. For all the comparisons that have been drawn between Japanese and West European feudalism, the Japanese samurai, denied the right to possess landed property from which to derive independent wealth, was a far more "governmentalized" class than was the Western nobility. The Russian gentry likewise constituted a service class, and like the samurai fulfilled many of the functions associated with the lawyers of early modern Europe, in addition to its role as landlord. In their stress on service to the state rather than on rights against it, however, the two elites more closely resemble the leadership classes brought into being by twentieth-century political revolutions than the feudal aristocracies of Western Europe.

A higher degree of national unity and control is demanded of nations seeking to modernize in an environment that includes already industrialized societies than was required of the "early developers." Such nations must move on all fronts with great speed and must be capable of controlling the tensions that such speed engenders if they are not to lose their economic and even political independence. Germany gained the requisite unity only with the help of a strongly nationalist ideology and authoritarian policies. It is by no means clear, however, that even these will suffice in many developing nations today.

Well before the end of their premodern eras both Japan and Russia had forged a high degree of political unity and governmental control. To a far greater extent than the earlier modernizing states, their governmental organs were able to dominate intermediate interests and authorities. Although feudal rights and loyalties persisted in both countries, individuals benefiting from these sources of power were more beholden to the national regimes than in countries such as France to 1789 and England to 1832. In sharp contrast with most new states (India, Pakistan, Nigeria, for example) and with the Ottoman and Hapsburg empires as well, there were no territorial or tribal loyalties to be overcome (although as Russia became an empire it had again to face entrenched local loyalties). Moreover, by the end of the premodern period both Japan and Russia were free from the rivalry between ecclesiastical and civil authorities that so weakened the national governments of Spain and Portugal. And perhaps more important still, in neither country was there the sharp duality of military and civilian authority that has proven so debilitating today in such countries as Greece, Peru, Egypt, and Ghana.

Enjoying far more complete a monopoly of power than did the governments of those nations which first industrialized, the governments of Japan and Russia were effectively able to administer a significant portion of the national produce even before the modern era. Many of the tasks of national and local government in Japan and Russia were the normal functions of autonomous guilds, town corporations, or independent merchants in Western Europe and North America. Thus, however inefficient the operations of the Russian bureaucracy may have seemed to the satirists of that country, the state administration, like its counterpart in Japan, was gaining valuable managerial experience that could be drawn on later. In the context of many newly created states of the present era it is far less noteworthy that certain governmental functions in Japan or Russia were imperfectly or incompletely executed than that they were indeed executed by a long maturing administrative network.

In Western Europe and North America, competition among various corporate interest groups and between them and the government provided a source of creative friction and change that is far less evident in either Japan or Russia. Was lack of friction generated by non-governmental bodies a retarding factor in the political development of Japan and Russia? To some extent yes, but other considerations would qualify such a conclusion. Among these, the often constructive pressure imposed on Russia by its international conflicts and on Japan by quarrels between the han in the mid-nineteenth century perhaps went far to substitute for the absence of sharp conflict among corporate groups in the two societies. Furthermore, the absence of well-developed intermediate groups in both societies offered the further benefit of forcing the government to become a more consistently active agent for development and change than was the case in most premodern societies. In this respect the governments of China or, until recently, most Latin American nations need only to be considered to appreciate the dynamism inherent in the Japanese and Russian systems.

The political life of these two nations before the 1860's, therefore, combined important features that we associate with those West European states that were the earliest to industrialize, and with traits more frequently found in developing nations today. Taken together, the similarities to early modernizers far outweigh those to later developers, but the balances in Japan and Russia produced political systems that were individually distinctive. Compared with England or France, Japan's political life (like that of Germany) was relatively more developed at the local (han) level, whereas the center of gravity in Russia was more firmly on the side of the national capital. But like the Western European nations, and in contrast with those postcolonial states in which a "European" type government has been balanced precariously atop the existing village structure, the levels of political life in Russia and especially Japan were relatively more compatible with one another. That this congruence declined in Russia in the post-Petrine era may to some extent explain why in the succeeding periods Russian political development shows less outward resemblance to West European models than did Japan's.

Chapter Four

ECONOMIC STRUCTURE
AND GROWTH

MOST PEOPLE in Japan and Russia were peasants in the mid-nineteenth century, farming the land with little capital equipment and with little knowledge of scientific agronomy. For a half century or longer a rapidly widening gap had separated the economies of the already industrializing nations from those of Japan and Russia. Yet when one compares them with other premodern countries in regard to such factors as the development of markets and trade networks, specialized production, and the regional diffusion of industrial activity, Japan and Russia stand out as relatively advanced. Both countries acquired these rather advanced features for a premodern society during the final centuries before the 1860's. They came about as output per capita gradually rose, most notably through an increase in per capita grain production but also through the spread of other crops, through new rural nonagricultural production for market, and through increased urban employment. In the separate examination below of the various sectors of the economy, our primary attention will focus on the ways in which these new patterns were emerging in countries with per capita outputs estimated by 1870 at only one-fourth or one-third of the value of that in Great Britain.

Before proceeding, mention should be made of some of the major differences between the two economies. First, the differences in the physical features of Japan and Russia are fundamental causes of a number of economic differences as well as of political differences, as noted in Chapter 3. Inhabiting a nation of narrow islands, Japanese have ready access to the sea, which has long been a natural provider of relatively cheap transportation and food. Furthermore, six-sevenths of Japan's land surface is covered by mountains; thus, only one-seventh can be readily used for cultivation and habitation. Favorable soil conditions and climate, along with its close proximity to the coastline, encouraged careful use of this small amount of arable land.

The Russian situation is strikingly different. A country of immense size, its population and resources were widely dispersed by the mid-nineteenth century. It could not make use of coastal shipping. And though it does have numerous rivers, they do not naturally form a convenient transportation network. As a consequence transportation has been a major difficulty—inadequate and expensive. With land relatively abundant compared with labor, extensive means of cultivation are employed, though nature has not been exactly kind in regard to agricultural resources. In the older population centers of the north the soil is relatively infertile, with much of the region covered by great bogs. In the more recently settled areas to the south the soil is far more fertile, but because of Russia's continental climate the growing seasons are short even here. And everywhere rainfall is insufficient. As a consequence, the productivity of agriculture was and continues to be a key problem.

A second basic economic difference between Japan and Russia pertains to the size of the producing unit. The size of the production unit varied in each country (more so in Russia than in Japan), but in Japan, for agriculture and industry, it was generally small. In Russia the opposite tended to be true. Serfs were employed in increasingly large estates, often by the hundreds and sometimes by the thousands. Further, industrial factories, especially those employing assigned serfs, were by the nineteenth century often large, some of them employing more than a thousand workers.

A third difference with special relevance to their economies before 1860 relates to their experiences with the early phases of manufacturing and later with full-scale industrialization in Western Europe (see Chapter 2). Japan had practically none with either. Russia, on the other hand, was exposed to new factory organization and technology under Peter I, and continued its manufacturing development —at an erratic pace—until the 1840's when its borrowing of advanced technology reached a new peak. By 1860 Russia had already developed selected aspects of industrialized production. Not only were Russians actively engaged in foreign trade contacts with Western Europe, but the nation's leading producers were also observing and importing advanced technology, equipment, and methods, and maintaining contact with the foreign scientific community.

Growth Mechanisms

No accurate measures are available of the long-run growth in aggregate economic output for Japan and Russia from the early 1700's to 1860. Nevertheless, it may not be unreasonable to suppose that output in this period grew at less than 1 per cent a year in Japan and at a somewhat higher rate in Russia. Since population, however, was more or less stable in Japan and grew rather substantially in Russia, it is not clear in which country output per capita grew more rapidly.

Though it is difficult to provide firm quantitative estimates of the growth of national product that took place, it is not as difficult to describe the growth mechanisms at work in the two countries. At the root of their low rates of growth (by the standards of modernizing societies) was the fact that all sectors of their economies—agriculture, industry, transportation, services—were constrained by labor-intensive technologies that did not permit a rapidly rising output per unit of factor inputs. Other than this, the principal elements in the growth mechanisms in the two countries differ.

Internally, Japan's bakufu and han administrations did not use their fiscal powers in any concerted way to stimulate growth. The major income of the Tokugawa economy came from taxes, equaling 30 per cent or more of the value of output paid by the peasants to the shogun and daimyo and their retainers, and it went primarily for urban consumption. By modern standards this surplus beyond what was necessary for local consumption was not used in ways that augmented the productive capacity of the economy; rather than being invested privately or publicly, it was used to support the consumption of the samurai, as the Russian surplus supported the gentry.

The Tokugawa era should be divided into two roughly equal periods, in which different growth mechanisms prevailed. During the first period the amount of surplus in the economy was growing quite rapidly, not only meeting the increased consumption needs of a growing population but supplying the expanding demands of rulers still engaged in consolidating their retainers in urban centers. An increasing surplus did exist in the economy, and most of it was siphoned off into the cities in the form of heavy taxes borne by the peasantry. Throughout the second half of the Tokugawa era a relatively stable total population, and relatively unchanging samurai urban populations and real incomes, meant that increases in output went primarily to the direct producers and merchants. A growing surplus, which also existed in this second period, was being reemployed both in private investment and in the somewhat increased consumption of social strata other than the samurai.

The growth mechanism of Russia as it pertains to industry before the 1860's is very different. Spurts of rapid industrial growth are followed by long spells of relatively little growth of output. Another prominent feature is the dominant role played by the Russian state in industrial development. Both of these features apply to the modern as well as premodern period, although it should be remembered that industry's contribution to national product in the premodern period was tiny in comparison with that of agriculture and small in comparison with that of commerce. In an attempt to explain this general pattern, Alexander Gershenkron has put forth the following hypothesis about the growth mechanism which is observable on a number of occasions in the course of Russian economic history.

The history of Russia for the past 500 years has been dominated by the theme of territorial expansion—a sharp contrast with Japan. During the process of expansion, the Russian state frequently came into contact and conflict with Western nations more advanced and more powerful than it. Such confrontations forced upon the leaders of Russia the realization that they would not be able to attain their goals because of the backwardness of the Russian economy. In such situations, the Russian state would take on the role of initiator of economic development, especially the development of the industrial sector. The state, through the pressure of its coercive and fiscal powers, would accelerate the development of the internal economy, in order to support its foreign-policy aims, in as short a period as possible. This combustion was the cause of the fitful movement of Russian industrial development: when the military needs of the state were compelling, the economy was pressured into rapid growth overburdening the population; when a degree of power parity was reached, the need for further rapid growth subsided and the state relaxed its pressure.

This pattern is clearly seen in the period of Peter I, whose economic policies bore certain similarities to those of the Mercantilists. He was concerned with means of communication and transportation, and inaugurated construction of a number of canals and a few roads. He introduced a unified system of weights and measures. He encouraged the development of domestic industries. He imported foreign technology and technologists, offering high salaries and privileges. But there were also significant differences. The state under

Peter performed much more of an entrepreneurial function than it did in the West, or in Tokugawa Japan. The scale of industry was large, illustrating the state's ability to command. The composition of output reflected a devotion of the economy to the needs of the state: (a) little production of luxury goods, (b) great development of mining and metallurgy for military hardware, (c) increased output of linen and wool for sailcloth and uniforms. State action, therefore, deemphasized commercialization in favor of industrialization, and this early essay gave precedent for just such a policy when it was to become so important for modernization.

A sharp confrontation of foreign-policy ambitions and economic weakness such as occurred at the time of Peter I is not to be seen again until the 1850's with the Russian defeat in the Crimean War. In the interim, moderate growth was achieved, supplying the needs of a now rapidly increasing population. As the population rose, it expanded the potential market for goods and it allowed for the colonization of newly acquired, scantily populated territories, facilitating the development of a regional division of labor. Meanwhile, the state continued to stimulate factory development and serf-owners came to resemble han administrators in their search for increased revenues to support rising urban expenses.

Agriculture

By the mid-nineteenth century, both Japan and Russia had high production of grain per capita of population, easily the most important type of crop. The principal Japanese grain was rice, which was generally cultivated in irrigated paddy fields. The average Japanese peasant family cultivated a small plot using only hand tools, and organic fertilizer (night soil and dried fish). Although agricultural technology was entirely "traditional"—that is, unaffected by modern science or machinery—it was not crude. A significant number of the peasantry were literate, among whom were some who could read treatises on farm management that were widely diffused. Furthermore, the labor-intensive techniques had reached levels of considerable sophistication and incorporated hundreds of years of accumulated knowledge. Of course, individual variations did exist. There were rich peasants whose holdings were larger than one hectare and who increasingly used wage labor, but they were not numerous. In Japan peasants were not serfs, though some restrictions were imposed on their movement, on the transfer of their land, and even on the choice of crops they planted.

Grain production in Russia was more varied, including sizable outputs of rye, oats, wheat, and barley. Much of it was produced by serfs working on their owners' land in the form of three or four days a week obligatory labor (*barshchina*), but the bulk of the grain came from the plots worked by serfs on their own time and from the plots of the state and imperial family peasants. This technology of Russian agriculture was primitive: crude tools such as the ancient wooden plow were used, and many village communes employed the open three-field system in which one of the fields was left fallow each year. Furthermore, due to the egalitarian principles of the village, each household had its land distributed in many strips in different fields and within fields, in areas of differing quality. This form of allotment contributed to low levels of productivity per hectare. Where there was no guarantee that the family would retain ownership of improved strips, the periodic redistribution of land weakened individual incentive. Work animals were in short supply, though even so they were more widely used than in Japan. Because of the extensive nature of agriculture, there was little use of fertilizer. Yet these rather primitive agricultural methods did not prevent the realization of a high total output. Primarily by increasing their landholdings and the number of serfs, members of the gentry could increase the amount of production for market. To a lesser extent than in Japan, a noticeable increase occurred also in private marketing by peasants during the eighteenth and early nineteenth centuries.

Despite the slight use of mechanized tools and work animals, grain output in Japan and Russia was high—in Japan both in terms of output per hectare and of output per capita, and in Russia in terms of output per capita. In the 1860's Japanese average rice yields approximated 2.5 tons per hectare. (Yields in the rich Osaka-Kyoto region averaged 50 per cent above those in northern Honshu.) These yields are rather close to those of 1952–1963 in Malaysia, Korea, and Taiwan, well above present yields in the Philippines and India, but well below recent yield levels in Japan, which reached nearly 5 tons per hectare. Japanese agriculture at the end of the Tokugawa era was traditional, labor-intensive, and by modern standards attained only low levels of productivity. Yet it was neither rude nor primitive, and by Asian standards the levels of performance were impressive.

In Russia grain yields per hectare in 1860 were less than one-half of what they were in Belgium, Holland and the United Kingdom, where population densities were higher. Due to a great increase, however, in Russia's agricultural population and in sown area (especially in the southern black-earth regions), total output of grain had risen sharply in the eighteenth and nineteenth centuries. With 96

per cent of the arable land planted to grain and with a high proportion of the population engaged in agriculture, Russia in the middle
of the nineteenth century produced more grain per capita of total
population than any other European country, almost twice that of
Great Britain and Belgium. Although this figure is based on average
annual production, which ignores the problems of wide yearly fluctuations in output and the need to store grain for years of crop
failures, it reveals that under the living standards that prevailed
Russia, like Japan, had sufficient grain production to support a considerable rural population and, through a grain drain from the villages to the cities, a growing urban population.

Many of the Japanese han and Russian *guberniia* normally produced at least 20 or 30 per cent more grain than was consumed by
their rural population. Where, then, did this potentially marketable
surplus go? In Japan, labor services were usually trifling, but the
peasant was subject to an annual harvest tax payable to the daimyo.
There were no demesnes directly cultivated by the nobility, and in
this sense the Japanese peasant resembled the Western European serf
after commutation: his principal obligations were fiscal. Roughly
one-third of the rice crop was delivered to the han as a tax in kind or
marketed in order to obtain funds for a tax in cash. Because a great
deal of tax rice also eventually reached the market within the han or
in the large bakufu cities where the daimyo and samurai sold it to
obtain cash, there was a considerable market in grain. Even if tax
rice is excluded, the proportion of marketed crops is still quite large:
15 to 20 per cent of rice; 20 to 30 per cent of vegetables; 80 to 90 per
cent of industrial crops. Regional differences are particularly important; there were areas such as the central provinces in which
commercial agriculture predominated, and others, such as the Northeast, where cities received primary support from taxes paid in kind.
If tax rice is included, of course, a very large proportion of Japan's
agricultural output—perhaps as much as one-half—was marketed in
one form or another.

Much of the marketing of agricultural crops in Russia also did
not result from the peasantry simply delivering its surplus as a
matter of free will. Gentry landowners with anywhere from ten to, in
a few instances, tens of thousands of serfs on *barshchina* provided
much of the marketed grain in many regions of Russia. As expenses,
including a yearly tax on peasants (*obrok*) and the poll tax paid by
the gentry, were rising steadily, more marketed produce was required to obtain the necessary funds. The marketing of crops was
further augmented by relatively well-off peasants engaging more and

more in commercial agriculture and by those occupied with garden production near big cities and with industrial crops, particularly crops used for textiles.

In brief, decisions concerning agricultural production and distribution were divided in Japan and in Russia between members of an elite on the one hand, with a hereditary right to taxes and stipends, rents and labor services, and members of the peasantry on the other, with surpluses to market even after meeting various obligations. The effect of both systems of agricultural production and distribution was to reduce substantially the amount of grain that could be consumed locally. While less of the agricultural output was probably marketed in Russia, the amount involved was considerable.

Specialized industrial crops were next in importance to grain in both Japanese and Russian agricultural production and their output expanded faster than that of grain during the final premodern century. New areas were converted to the production of such crops as cotton in Japan and flax and hemp in Russia. Flax and hemp were used for textiles and as a source of fat (seed oil), and were a prime Russian export item. Up to the mid-1840's the value of hemp and flax exports was greater than the value of grain exports. But with the removal of restrictions on grain exports and with the acquisition of ports on the Black Sea during the reign of Catherine the Great, grain exports grew quickly, particularly after the repeal of the English corn laws in 1846, and became Russia's leading export. They accounted for 35 per cent of the total value of exports between 1856 and 1860. Russia's expansion of agricultural crops for foreign markets was not duplicated, of course, by Japan, which had closed its ports to commerce.

Crop failures were more frequent in Russia where in each ten-year period during the first half of the nineteenth century one severe crop failure and two partial ones occurred. Japan suffered three prolonged famines between 1700 and 1868, but the spread of superior transport conditions, improved production techniques, including the wider use of double cropping, and advances in agronomy reduced the danger of serious crop failure.

Industry

The industrial structures of premodern Japan and Russia were to a certain extent similar. Textiles and food processing dominated in each as in other relatively urbanized premodern societies. The data that are available (for somewhat later periods, but probably good indicators for 1860 too), suggest that textile manufacturing and food processing accounted for more than 70 per cent of the industrial output in Japan and more than 60 per cent of that in Russia. Mining and metallurgy were relatively unimportant in Japan, although they did show some development after 1853. These sectors, however, played a vital role in Russian industry, accounting for 28 per cent of all factory labor in 1860 and 20 per cent of the value of all industrial output in 1887.

In Japan the typical enterprise was small, used little wage labor or machinery, and frequently represented a form of rural by-employment. There were a few machines driven by water power, but steam power had not been introduced. After Perry's arrival, the bakufu and certain daimyo did set up some "Western" establishments, including silk and cotton mills, arms factories, shipyards and mines. However, these new enterprises had little time to take hold before the Meiji Restoration of 1868.

Although rural by-employment and the "putting-out" system of cottage industries were common in Russia, by 1860 the factory form of industrial production had securely taken hold. Through the eighteenth century the size of some Russian factories was quite large, though the average size of a producing unit remained small until the new wave of factory construction after 1800. In the middle of the nineteenth century, the average factory in the textile industry employed 125 workers, and between 5 and 10 percent of the factories in the cotton and woolen industries employed 500 workers. By 1866 there were 42 factories in Russia employing more than 1,000 workers—26 of them in the cotton industry alone.

Russian factory workers before 1861 were either serfs assigned to their jobs, freely hired workers still owing obrok payments to their owners, or free laborers. Assigned serfs made up over 90 per cent of the industrial labor force in the 1760's and remained important in textiles, beet sugar production, and mining and metallurgy. The use of hired workers grew more rapidly, however, and by 1860 they constituted more than half of all industrial workers.

In the use of machinery and mechanical power in certain industries, such as cotton manufacturing, Russia was far ahead of Japan at the end of the premodern period. Indeed, the Russian cotton industry, after modern spinning machinery was introduced in the 1840's, resembled that of the leading industrial nations. Outside of cotton textiles and the production of beet sugar, however, Russian factories were slow to adopt mechanical sources of power. The general level of technology in Russian industry was not very advanced by 1860, though in certain pockets of development the pace of technical growth was impressive.

Peter I's program for Russian industrialization gave great emphasis to mining and metallurgy. By the middle of the eighteenth century, the Ural region was one of the leading metals producers in the world. In 1800 Russia was first in the world in iron production; it produced one-third of the world's total and was the leading exporter. But Russia failed to keep pace with technical changes in metallurgy, and by the middle of the nineteenth century it dropped to eighth place in iron production. Its output grew, but the output of others grew more rapidly, so much so that in 1860 Great Britain's iron output was ten times Russia's.

The relative stagnation that hit the Russian metals industry in the first half of the nineteenth century did not affect the rest of factory industry so severely. The growth of cotton textile production and the increasing use of mechanical equipment were the outstanding industrial achievements of the period. By 1860 there were 1,200 cotton textile plants and they employed more than 150,000 workers. Furthermore, between 1842 and 1860 the number of large, mechanized cotton mills in Russia jumped threefold, from less than twenty to almost sixty, employing more than 40,000 workers in cities or their suburbs. The Neva factory in St. Petersburg operated 160,000 spindles at a time when the largest factory in the United States had less than 30,000. Russia also had large woolen and large linen and hemp industries, which were not nearly as technically advanced in 1860, however, as the cotton industry. Second to cotton in 1860 as one of the few modern industries in Russia was the beet sugar industry. Starting in the 1830's, large-scale beet sugar factories began to be set up on estates of great landholders, primarily in the Ukraine, using modern, foreign-produced machinery. This industry provides an example where entrepreneurs from the landholding nobility, using assigned serfs, were able to develop a modern, mechanized industry. A substantial machine-building industry in Russia began only in the 1840's and 1850's, though by 1860 Russia was producing as much machinery as it imported. Most of the leading Russian machine-building factories, however, were set up and owned by foreigners.

Japan lacked these pockets of technological growth resulting from earlier contact with the first modernizing countries. Even so, by the nineteenth century most Japanese villages were engaged in some kind of industrial-handicraft activity and specialized industrial production was taking place in the towns. The manufacture of silk and cotton textiles, including elaborate fabrics for samurai and wealthy merchants, was highly developed, and the production of metal goods and pottery, including finely finished metal and china wares, was well established. As in Russia, significant development occurred in the peasant handicraft industry, including both simple wares that circulated locally and specialized products for distant urban markets. Immediately preceding the Meiji Restoration some Western-style manufacturing was introduced in Japan, including several iron foundries and furnaces for smelting iron ore. Only at this time did modern firms first appear. The difference between the industrial sectors in these two countries should be viewed against the background that even in Russia far more people were engaged in nonmechanized crafts than in the new modern enterprises; the total value of Russian handicraft production probably exceeded the value of output of its factories.

In both Japan and Russia industrial activity was widely dispersed. Most regions, for example, produced cloth and alcoholic beverages. Specialized industrial regions appeared where production depended on certain raw materials available only in a particular region and not easily transported, as in the case of the Russian mining and metallurgical industries in the Ural region. These specialized regions also appeared where proximity to large urban centers made for heavy demand, as in the textile producing areas of the Tokyo plain and the upper central-industrial region near Moscow. Small-scale craft enterprises, common in villages throughout the two countries, showed the greatest geographic spread.

Entrepreneurs in both countries were usually merchants. In Japan, however, even before the restoration some progressive han promoted monopolies and new manufactures, which provided a breeding ground for the entrepreneurial talents of energetic young samurai. In Russia entrepreneurial activity was also undertaken by a number of groups other than the merchants: government officials, members of the nobility, foreigners, in some cases serfs, and, of special importance, members of religious minorities—Old Believers, Jews, and Skoptsy. One of the ways in which the greater heterogeneity of the Russian population manifested itself was in terms of entrepreneurial activity.

Other Sectors

Commerce, construction, and transportation engaged much of the Japanese and Russian population on a part-time or temporary basis as well as some of the urban population on a permanent basis. There were peddlers in cities, itinerant merchants who visited periodic markets, store operators, and powerful merchants engaged in bulk shipments of long-distance commerce. Typically, merchants and artisans in both countries operated as small family enterprises.

At the apex of the system of distribution in Japan were the Osaka merchant financiers, who handled conversions of tax rice and gave loans to the daimyo. Some of them accumulated vast fortunes, but their ties to the han barons were close and their wealth could also disappear when—as frequently happened—a daimyo encountered severe financial difficulties. Of increasing importance toward the end of the Tokugawa era were wholesalers (*tonya*) who specialized in the rising interregional trade between western and eastern Japan and the local merchants who exploited the increasing commercialization of agriculture. Both of these groups survived the restoration in better shape than the Osaka financiers, most of whom disappeared with their masters.

Wealthy merchants in Russia frequently specialized in foreign trade or in the supply of St. Petersburg and Moscow. These merchants or their representatives traveled throughout the year to the major interregional fairs, which were opened for two weeks or longer and produced the largest turnover of goods within the country. Fairs have often been said to be an inefficient means of conducting trade, even in a premodern society, but they continued to increase their volume of trade in the Russian Empire as commerce in general expanded rapidly in the eighteenth and nineteenth centuries. In other respects, the conduct of commerce was coming into closer correspondence with the usual expectations for a more advanced premodern society—fairs in sizable cities were less important by the mid-eighteenth century, stores were replacing periodic markets as the centers of urban exchange, and the number of rural periodic markets in many areas of the country was declining by the early nineteenth century.

Russia, unlike Japan, was a participant in international trade during the premodern period, although this trade was much less crucial than domestic commerce. Russia's foreign trade in the 1840's accounted for only 5 per cent of the world total, yet this put the country in sixth place among the trading nations of the world.

Russia's exports almost always exceeded imports. Grain, cotton goods, and, primarily, raw materials were exchanged for imports of raw cotton, foodstuffs, and luxury items. In the 1840's the value of tea imports was seven times that of machinery. The advantages to Russia of its foreign trade were reduced by the fact that almost all of the trade was in the hands of foreigners. In the middle of the nineteenth century, a Russian merchant marine hardly existed. Foreigners controlled both the ships and the trade passing through Russia's major ports, including St. Petersburg, Riga, and Odessa.

In Japan both goods and people moved rapidly by nineteenth-century standards. The Japanese achieved efficient domestic commerce without large fairs. More important for transportation than the major road arteries that radiated out from Edo was the long seacoast around Japan's narrow land mass. In Russia the necessity of relying on slower and more costly land transportation was compounded by the size of the country. Sleds could move heavy goods at somewhat reduced costs over the winter cover of snow and ice, but sleds were still inferior to the readily accessible water transportation in Japan.

From the early eighteenth century, some noteworthy improvements were effected in the transportation system of Russia. The usefulness of the river system was much enhanced by state-built canals that connected some of the major rivers and later by the importation of steamships, though animals and humans remained the predominant source of motive power on Russian rivers and canals in the premodern period. Some experiments were undertaken, early in the nineteenth century, with the construction of modern highways, particularly linking the two capitals of St. Petersburg and Moscow. Only railroads, however, could transport bulky industrial goods and raw materials over long distances at a reasonable cost and within a reasonable time—and the government was slow to build them. It was the tsar's personal insistence in the 1850's that led to the construction of the St. Petersburg-Moscow railroad under the supervision of an American engineer named Whistler (Whistler's father). By the end of the 1850's Russia had little more than 600 miles of railroads, far less than the industrializing nations and woefully short of its own immense needs. Russia's defeat in the Crimean War, brought on to a great extent by the absence of railroads and the nation's inability to supply its armies in the Crimea, made clear to the Russian government the importance of a modern transportation network.

One final sector of the economic structure of the two countries must be noted: money. Neither Japan nor Russia in this period had anything resembling a modern banking system. Nonetheless, the use of money had expanded considerably—and with it the swarms of pawnbrokers, money-lenders, and, in the case of Japan where there were 1,600 varieties of paper money in circulation, money-changers.

These individuals specialized in consumption loans at high rates of interest, and in Japan they provided short-term business loans to daimyo and samurai. In Russia, although there were no real private banks until the middle of the nineteenth century, a few financial houses (for example, Stieglitz, the "Rothschild of Russia") had developed earlier and participated in the financing of some industrial undertakings. Also, the state had established so-called commercial banks on several occasions, but they served more as deposit and mortgage banks and as state fiscal agents than they did as lending institutions for industry and commerce.

Corporate methods of raising investment capital were not used in premodern Japan or in Russia before the very end of the eighteenth century. After 1830 the flotation of new companies in Russia became more frequent, and between 1835 and 1860 about 200 new joint stock companies were established. Also after 1830 the Saint Petersburg stock exchange began dealing in government obligations and the stocks of private companies.

International Comparisons

Certain economic aspects of both countries when compared with other premodern countries are especially relevant from the point of view of future modern economic growth. First, with regard to Japan an overall loosening of state control occurred in the first half of the nineteenth century. In theory, the economic aspects of Tokugawa centralized feudalism were highly restrictive: a great deal of dictation was meant to take place at all levels, and the intent of economic policies has frequently been described as mercantilistic. Actually, as the Tokugawa era progressed, the hold of the government became less restrictive; people moved more easily, merchants gained more power, and local areas had more economic and political autonomy. All of these were promising signs, and were related to the declining economic position of the shogunate. The shogunate (and many daimyo) faced rising expenses without a sufficiently expanding tax base. One solution lay in somewhat greater economic freedom.

In Russia there was also some loosening of state control. Restrictions on the buying and selling of land and on peasant entrepreneurs were reduced and rights to engage in business activity were expanded. In a few areas of the empire serfs were freed and, even more important, many were switched from *barshchina* to *obrok*. Gentry found it easier to invest in industry. Yet state regulation with its

impeding effects of frequently unchecked centralization and cor-
ruption remained pervasive. There were continuous attempts even
to augment it, particularly in support of a rising military budget.
Perhaps because it was the economic position of the gentry rather
than that of the tsarist government that was declining, there was
less apparent relaxation of the hold of the government in Russia.

Second, it is likely that agricultural output was rising more
rapidly in both countries during the final century of this period. In
Japan this increase was the result of improving traditional technology, and it was of great importance because the growth mechanism
from the 1860's to World War I were to depend so heavily on an
agricultural surplus. In Russia greater agricultural output came
from the use of existing methods on newly cultivated lands. The
growth in production supported the rising export of agricultural
products, and also the much greater domestic needs.

Third, small-scale industries or craft enterprises had spread
widely through small cities and villages over most of each country.
To a great extent, this diffusion is analogous to the undermining of
the restrictiveness of craft guilds in Europe, and to the rise of the
cottage industry and the putting-out system. Other premodern societies lacked a large agricultural production per capita and a widely
distributed craft production involved in long-distance commerce.
The Western European countries which first modernized did have
these characteristics, however, although they were coupled with
weaker state control over the economy. Certainly these conditions
were favorable for early modernization in Europe.

China had experienced some craft specialization in villages
within certain advanced provinces by the fifteenth and sixteenth
centuries prior to similar changes in other countries, but it did not
have a qualitatively new wave of industrial dispersion in the eighteenth and nineteenth centuries as did Japan and Russia. Moreover,
Chinese population growth had proceeded at least as rapidly as
increases in grain production for more than a century prior to the
1860's. Without the aggressive assertion of state controls over the
production and distribution process, Chinese leaders could con-
fiscate wealth unprotected by government connections, but they
could not sponsor a vast expansion in the amount of wealth flowing
into the cities. China provides a contrasting example of a latecomer
that began the modernizing transformation in the mid-nineteenth
century with a vast internal trading network but without the assets
of an agricultural surplus and a widely dispersed craft production
found in Japan and Russia.

One final observation: Japan and Russia on the eve of the period of transformation faced a similar institutional problem. After the elimination of the feudal hierarchy and samurai stipends in Japan and the abolition of serfdom in Russia, they both needed to maintain the large agricultural surpluses not consumed locally. And they needed to divert these surpluses, or the considerable revenues from them, to investment purposes. Samurai stipends and serfdom were part of an earlier mechanism of growth, though that growth had been slow. They were now serious barriers in the path of modern economic growth. Unlike the barriers existing in most premodern societies, however, these could be removed by swift administrative reforms timed to capitalize on the weak capacities for resistance of elites long accustomed to extravagant urban consumption and long reliant on highly developed market mechanisms.

Chapter Five

SOCIAL INTERDEPENDENCE

BETWEEN 1600 and 1850, both Japan and Russia achieved unusual degrees of growth and mobilization in their resources. People and goods increased in number and circulated to an unprecedented degree. By 1850 merchants and artisans had proliferated in rural as well as urban settings, a large and literate elite had grown accustomed to bureaucratic administration, and peasants were engaged in an ever-wider spectrum of activities that expanded their awareness of areas distant from their home villages. The landscape filled with larger marketplaces and cities, and it became integrated into expanding networks of commercial and administrative centers. Goods streamed from villages to nearby periodic markets or fairs and on to cities of various sizes. Few premodern societies could boast of cities as large as Edo, Osaka, and Kyoto in Japan or St. Petersburg and Moscow in Russia. Rural-urban migration rates rose, and within the facade of closed social classes, intraclass mobility gained momentum. Japan and Russia had become markedly different societies by 1850—from their own pasts and from other premodern societies.

In the final centuries of their premodern pasts, how were these two countries alike and how were they different? In what strategic respects did they resemble each other by the early nineteenth century and what were the elements of continuity within each throughout these dynamic periods? Can basic similarities be suggested in the forms which social interdependence took that might distinguish Japan and Russia from other premodern societies and that might eventually have exerted a crucial impact on the period of transformation?

Human Resources

Similar dramatic changes occurred in population and skills in Japan and Russia. As in measures of urban development, Japan preceded Russia by about 100 years in entering a period of sudden, accelerated population growth. By the 1720's, after more than a century of growth, Japan's population had almost doubled to about 30 million. Meanwhile, Russia's total was beginning to rise even more swiftly, reaching the 30-million level near the end of the eighteenth century. By this time, the populations of the two countries were roughly equal, each constituting about 3 to 4 per cent of the world's total.

These large populations had become increasingly differentiated to an extent rarely found in premodern societies: peasants found new opportunities for nonagricultural income through crafts, trade, and hired labor; merchants and artisans grew steadily in number; and a service nobility became more and more bureaucratized. Rising literacy rates promoted a national awareness of the skills that made improved conditions of living accessible and new modes of urban life possible.

In other respects the development of the population of the two countries represented alternatives between numerical expansion and improvement in skills. While Japan was practically standing still in total population during the final one and one-half centuries before the 1860's, Russia's population climbed steadily, spurred in part by territorial expansion. Literacy, however, was spreading much more quickly through Japan. As measured by the dissemination of skills among large numbers of people, Japan's resources were concentrated—not through deliberate strategies but through a combination of circumstances—more on improving the quality of the population. Within the context of the premodern setting, then, Russia's development can be seen in terms of quantity and Japan's in terms of quality, despite great strides in both respects in both countries.

The development of human resources as evidenced by population growth occurred at different times in Japan and Russia. Both nations were constantly gaining in population with sporadic jumps. In some centuries the total number of people would climb by 50 per cent or more; in other centuries there would be relative lulls in which the population would grow by less than 20 per cent. Yet until the final 75 years of the approximately 1,000 of recorded history before the 1860's, Japan was more populous than Russia. As late as the eighteenth century Russians numbered only about half as many as the 30 million Japanese. Then, as the Japanese figure remained almost constant, the larger country moved into the lead with 39 million people in 1800 and thereafter steadily widened its lead. By the 1860's the 60 to 70 million inhabitants of the Russian Empire were twice as numerous as the Japanese.

Studies of the causes and consequences of premodern population growth are still in an early stage. One obvious factor in population growth is the availability of land. While the Japanese were intensively cultivating nearly all arable land on their principal islands by 1700, Russians were being redistributed to sparsely settled areas. Furthermore Russia's reclamation of marginal lands continued, and the empire benefited from the acquisition of already settled areas. Yet, although dramatic increases in Russia's population were accompanied by vast territorial expansion, most of its population growth cannot be attributed to annexations. Nor did it occur on newly acquired lands. As can be seen in Table 5.1, the number of people within the territory of Russia at the time of the first enumeration in 1719 jumped threefold by the time of the tenth enumeration in 1857. Even in the central part of the country, the population of the various regions rose by a minimum of 60 per cent and a maximum of more than 300 per cent.

The new levels of national integration achieved through the further development of commerce and through administrative reforms—initiated in part by Tokugawa Ieyasu around 1600 and Peter I around 1700—undoubtedly contributed to the sudden spurts in population growth. But the divergence in growth rates that ensued must also be explained. It is likely that in comparison with other premodern societies, population control in Japan was practiced on an unprecedented scale during the second half of the Tokugawa period. Regional variations make generalization difficult. Nonetheless, there was a tendency among the Japanese to prefer higher standards of living and rates of saving. The Russians, however, practiced less population control and were, perhaps, left with the means to support more children. As agricultural production increased, primarily through an expansion in cultivated acreage, Russian population growth persisted into the nineteenth century.

Of course, total population is an inadequate measure of human resources. A completely illiterate people among whom skills have scarcely been differentiated is no match for an equally large community with diverse specialists. How skills are distributed among a

T A B L E 5. 1. The Premodern Population of Japan and Russia

	(in millions) 1600	1700		1800		
Japan	18	25	30	30	31	32
Russian Empire	11	15	18	39	52	59
Territory of Russia in 1719		15	18	28	40	46

population and how social groupings are organized is in most contexts as telling as the population figure. In the discussion that follows, therefore, the changing distribution of people in each social class will be examined along with the ways in which governments controlled to their own advantage the increasing specialization of the population.

At the top of the social hierarchy in both countries was a service nobility, a term used here to refer to both the Russian gentry and the Japanese samurai. Over several centuries a small number of aristocrats (*boiars* in Russia and *kuge* in Japan) who had exercised considerable freedom in governing their local areas were superseded by the much larger and more dependent groups of gentry and samurai, groups rewarded partly on the basis of the service they performed. These new groups, both as the military elite and as skilled administrators, became the bulwark of increased government control over members of other social classes—and the main beneficiaries of that control. Sharing the exclusive privileges of possessing serfs and estates in Russia and of receiving fixed stipends in Japan, and free from personal taxes, from many obligations, and from corporal punishment, the service nobility in both countries acquired great wealth, though it was distributed among them very unevenly.

The gentry of Russia lived in a style markedly different from that of most other Russians. Many wore Western European fashions and some even conversed regularly in French. Few in other classes attempted to emulate them or had the wealth to do so. The samurai of Japan also had higher status and usually greater wealth than other Japanese. But in contrast with the Russian gentry, the code of conduct these Japanese warrior-administrators were expected to follow gradually permeated the outlook of those in other classes. Even persons who were not expected to live by it came to admire and respect the samurai code as a semi-utopian ideal.

The distances between classes as measured by the permeation of life-styles may have been narrower in Japan because of the greater size of its elite. During the first third of the eighteenth century, nearly twenty-five times as many Japanese as Russians (2 million versus 80,000) can be properly labeled members of service nobility families. Though this ratio of elites subsequently fell, Russian elite figures of about 2 per cent, including a disproportionately large number of gentry on newly annexed lands in the West, never approached the Japanese service nobility figure of 6 to 7 per cent of the total population. This sizable elite in Japan was separated from villages, converted into an urban administrative force, skillfully utilized, and deprived of independent sources of income. All of these trends were apparent in Russia, but in weaker form. And some were diluted or reversed by decrees such as the one of 1762 that freed nobles from service obligations, thereby encouraging them to take up residence on their local estates. The two countries were similar in the increased reliance they placed on a service nobility. But they differed in the size of their elite, in the elite's ability to serve as a model for other classes, and in the way in which the elite's duties were defined and executed.

Two small, but growing, social classes in each country were the merchants and the artisans. By 1800 full-time members of these classes were joined by numerous part-time and temporary colleagues still officially registered as peasants. Prominent groups with commercial employment came under close regulation. They rarely challenged the government authorities who had granted them monopolies over certain products and areas of trade. Those excluded from these monopolies generally operated on a small scale, but on occasion groups succeeded in expanding their operations to a point that challenged and even caused a change in the rules guiding commerce. Even more circumscribed in their activities, peasants who entered these professions were limited to the fringes of the formal associations to which monopolies were granted.

Japan and Russia resembled each other both in the rapid growth of a commercially active population and in the close regulation of it. In each country artisans and merchants, once dependent on specific aristocratic households, gradually became directly responsive to the demands of government administrators. In the Japanese setting in which government contact with merchants (who ranked at the bottom of the ideally perceived hierarchy of social classes) was so quickly corrupt by Confucian standards, the walling off of their class status gave them some critical advantages to operate independently. In Russia centralization of administration proceeded without as much mobilization of artisans and merchants for state purposes—

yet with more likelihood of harmful interference. By the nineteenth century most of the expanding small-scale commerce in both countries escaped regulation. Government controls remained, however, on merchants and artisans concentrated in cities.

The direct impact of the Russian state on the commercial population was limited in three ways. First, rich merchants were not held permanently accountable (as were the merchants in Japan), but instead some found opportunities for themselves or for their children to attain the style and titles of noble life. Second, many of those engaged in nonagricultural activities in the large Russian cities were serfs and state peasants allowed to earn money there for varying periods of time by owners who received a share of their earnings. Only in the 1830's in Moscow did the proportion of those officially registered not as peasants but as merchants and artisans rise from the previous level of 12 per cent to near 30 per cent. And third, settlements of full-time Russian craftsmen who belonged to a serf-owner persisted even into the nineteenth century. Despite a greater proportion of merchants and artisans in the total population, Japanese administrators maintained firmer direct control over them.

Growing commercial involvement and occupational specialization among peasants, as among those in other classes, were also evident in Japan and Russia in the centuries before the 1860's. The imposition of serfdom in Russia and the drawing of clear boundaries to separate classes in Japan did not prevent the continued division of labor in villages or the appearance of new opportunities for wealthy and enterprising peasants. Not only were there growing possibilities for employment outside of the village in transportation and in urban commercial pursuits, but even within villages specialization for a distant market increased. In both countries, new forms of mobilization of the service nobility and a gradually rising commercial exchange still permitted close control over peasants while contributing to the reasons that motivated their continued advancement.

That Japan through its han administrators was more attentive than Russia to the even-handed exercises of local control presumably contributed to less violent conflict. The Russian gentry maintained considerable freedom to make arbitrary decisions affecting serfs, even to the extreme of dividing families or of sending a serf to jail. The Japanese peasant, albeit with some difficulty, was able to move to a city without a passport setting a time limit on his stay outside the village, was in control of the land he farmed as well as the time he spent farming, and was not threatened with the terrible fate of conscription for 25 years. All these factors would seem to have given him a greater incentive to better his conditions.

Omitted from the above description of the social ladder were Japan's outcasts, consisting of about 1.5 per cent of its population, and Russia's much more numerous, and for the most part geographically autonomous, ethnic minorities. These groups were not similar in many respects, although persons from certain ethnic minorities in Russia, like Japan's outcasts, were also denied access to the dominant society. Small communities of outcasts scattered throughout Japan were not a serious threat to the preservation of order, but the large non-Slavic minorities posed a continuing problem for Russian authorities; they were concerned with the danger of alliances between the non-Slavs and neighboring foreign powers and with the repetition of large-scale peasant rebellions. At times demands for religious conversion and russification sought to impose a greater degree of homogeneity, and such programs, of course, stirred discontent. In obvious contrast, Japan preserved an extraordinary degree of homogeneity despite the division of the country into han.

Ideally, in each of these virtually closed societies an immobile peasantry guided by a service nobility tolerant of regulated merchants and artisans would have provided a stable foundation for the gradual expansion of production. In practice, however, Japan achieved greater stability based on a larger elite, a larger corps of artisans and merchants, greater freedom for villagers, and no troublesome ethnic minorities. Russia, rapidly expanding in population and settled areas, was in a greater state of flux in class relations. Peasant uprisings were more turbulent, and rivalry among gentry and at court detracted from joint efforts to solve local and regional problems.

Because most job training occurred within the family, the widespread practice of primogeniture and of meritorious adoption in Japan meant that the heir to an occupation there had greater familiarity with future tasks. Evidence is scanty, but it is likely that Japanese urban administrators, merchants, and artisans were better prepared for their jobs than their Russian counterparts because of higher literacy, longer experience in cities, and greater opportunities to observe role models. Similarly, Japan was ahead in the extension of skills and knowledge to rural areas. In short, whereas a favored few Russians benefited from contact with externally generated knowledge, more rudimentary skills and knowledge penetrated further in Japan. Despite these differences, a fundamental similarity obtained between them in the steady movement toward a population better equipped for technological change.

Not only were members of each social class acquiring more skills and knowledge, they were also enjoying improved levels of living, although this long-term trend may have been interrupted in Russia for a time in the nineteenth century. Of course, as in other pre-modern settings severe natural disasters, possibly exacerbated by improper administration, resulted in famine. Japan was devastated by three famines, in 1732–1733, 1783–1787, and 1830–1834. Yet the means became widely available to reduce the severity and frequency of famine. Though the majority still lived in small wooden houses and subsisted primarily on grain diets, growing numbers in both countries were becoming accustomed to multiroom dwellings and to varied diets. Sharply increased taxes imposed serious hardship on some, but they did not deprive most of improved living conditions.

The growth of human resources in Japan and the Russian Empire can be measured by comparing conditions in 1600 with those in 1850. Other societies that were also not in close contact with the industrial revolution lacked the same dynamism of Japan and Russia during this period. Even China, which experienced considerable population growth, was not as vigorous in other respects. In 1600 the population of Japan and Russia together totaled only about 30 million; by 1850 that figure had almost tripled. In 1600 rural merchants and artisans were scarce, a service nobility was just beginning to appear, and peasants had little opportunity to acquire new skills. By 1850 networks of merchants and artisans covered the landscape, a large service nobility specialized in administration, and the horizons of peasants had expanded to encompass new patterns of urban consumption. The population of Japan grew by roughly 75 per cent in these 250 years, and it improved considerably in skill and knowledge. The population of Russia skyrocketed by more than 500 per cent, in part because of territorial expansion, and it also acquired the attributes of a more advanced people, although these attributes penetrated less deeply among the masses. By the standards of pre-modern societies, Japan and Russia in the 1860's consisted of large-scale, relatively educated and skilled populations.

Important as these similarities are, it must be remembered that Japan was practically standing still in total population and in the number of its elite in the 150 years before the 1860's, a time when the corresponding figures in Russia were climbing steadily. True, Japan had reached the eighteenth century with impressive leads, and its rising rates of literacy indicate that it continued to forge ahead in this measure of the quality of its population. Indeed, although spurting ahead in population, Russia never succeeded in catching up to Japan's higher proportion of service nobility.

Patterns of Settlement

An essential step in determining the import of the foregoing comparisons of human resources is to examine patterns of settlement. In both Japan and Russia sharp rural-urban dichotomies existed, with two or three central cities standing out in total population and as centers of conspicuous consumption. By the end of the eighteenth century each country had a few hundred cities with a minimum of 3,000 inhabitants, and most of these cities were designated administrative centers. At the bottom of the hierarchy of settlements were nucleated villages in which more than 80 per cent of the population lived. Yet these similarities should not obscure the fact that Japan, favored by easier accessibility to water transportation, was approximately twice as urban. While both countries exceeded world averages for urban population in 1800, as seen in Table 5.2, Japan was considerably ahead of Russia and its urban population was considerably more concentrated in large cities.

In both Japan and Russia momentous changes in village organ-

T A B L E 5. 2. Estimates of World Urban Population in 1800

AREA	TOTAL POPULATION (MILLIONS)	URBAN POPULATION[1] (MILLIONS)	URBAN POPULATION (PERCENT)
Europe (except			
Russian Empire)	160	(20)	12–14
(England and France)[2]	(35)	(7)	(20)
North and South America	31	(2)	5–8
Africa	107	(3)	2–4
Russian Empire	39	3	8–9
Japan	30	5	16–17
China	300	18	6–7
Asia (except above)	310	(12)	3–5
Totals	950–1,000	60–66	6–7

[1] Definition of urban population: the number of people in settlements of more than 3,000 in which there are periodic or daily marketing activities, plus one-half the number of people in settlements of less than 3,000 in which there are intermediate marketing activities or administrative centers or both.

[2] England was more than 30 per cent urban when its figures were already reflecting a rapid increase in city residents associated with initial modernization after 1750. France remained well below 20 per cent urban in 1789, but its city population was also beginning to increase sharply by 1800. These two countries are singled out because they began their urban transformation before 1800.

ization accompanied administrative reforms during the seventeenth and eighteenth centuries. Careful land surveys in Japan, together with the removal from the village of nearly all people with independent sources of power (the samurai), produced a readily tapped source of land tax revenues. Subsequently, as labor became divorced from kinship and pseudokinship ties, farming became more efficient and rural labor shifted to by-employment. The Russian village matured later, partly as a result of the introduction in 1724 of a uniform poll tax, which was levied on every adult male but apportioned on a village-wide basis, and partly as a result of the growing attention given to local administration during the eighteenth century, which increased collective responsibility. By the mid-nineteenth century the Russian village commune experienced a periodic equalization of land distribution, in an effort to maximize the potential for meeting rising tax obligations. It was a practice also employed on occasion in Japan. Even those who earned cash through outside employment had to contribute to the village quota and remained under the supervision of village authorities.

In addition to these changes in village organization, changes in village structure occurred through government planning and through altered economic conditions. Not surprisingly, villages were usually smaller and more scattered in Russia. By the mid-nineteenth century its more than 200,000 villages contained barely twice the population of the 65,000 villages in Japan. An unusual degree of explicit planning led to the strengthening of the village unit in both countries. Village authorities were given tax quotas to distribute among resident households. And though it took longer for the Russian village to be placed under firm administrative control because of the presence of local serf-owners, the spread of land redistributive practices based on household size provided fundamentally greater village-wide controls than in Japan.

It should be remembered that the strengthening of serfdom and the inauguration of communal land redistribution in Russia, like the removal of the elite from rural areas and the securing of village wide mutual responsibility to lords in Japan, were steps taken in advanced premodern societies that continued to develop commercialized agriculture. They were responses to and at the same time stimuli for further commercialization. Despite the various methods of village control, peasants in both societies had many opportunities and incentives to increase their incomes. The integration of the village into a subadministrative system was premised on the commercial integration of local areas. Success in both Japan and Russia in creat-

ing a highly organized village unit in which most of the population
was subject to control, paid taxes, and cooperated for mutual benefit attests to the achievement of a stable system with considerable but
carefully limited village autonomy.

In glittering contrast with the settlement pattern of the unob-
trusive village were the three central cities of Japan and the two
capitals of Russia. Kyoto and Moscow had reigned for centuries as
great cities of 100,000 or more inhabitants. The sudden burgeoning
of urban populations in central cities during the seventeenth and
eighteenth centuries, however, marked a sharp break with the past
in both Japan and Russia. Together Edo, Osaka, and Kyoto reached
a total of roughly 1.8 million people. Edo alone probably became
along with Peking one of the two cities in the world with as many
as one million inhabitants. St. Petersburg and Moscow grew to
roughly one-half million people by 1800 and continued to increase,
together reaching almost one million by the 1860's. Russia was
slower to acquire a huge national administrative center; after the
transfer of the court to St. Petersburg, this newly planned city
added both civilian and military bureaucracies and steadily overtook
Moscow in population during the eighteenth century. A higher proportion of city residents in Japan lived in the central cities. Although
both countries had achieved great urban concentration, Japan was
able to move more resources into its principal cities, thereby creating
a powerful demonstration effect through new patterns of consumption that were emulated in local areas.

The shift of the respective national centers under the strong
leadership of Tokugawa Ieyasu and Peter I—to Edo shortly after
1600 and to St. Petersburg shortly after 1700—ushered in new eras
of less impeded administrative direction and of rising consumption
in central cities. The Osaka-Kyoto area and the Moscow region, the
former centers of administration, prospered now as the centers of a
national market. Vast amounts of goods were forwarded to Edo and
St. Petersburg, where the service nobility, and in Russia also the
court, became accustomed to high levels of consumption. That the
number of samurai in Edo exceeded 400,000 while the figure for
St. Petersburg's gentry as late as 1811 remained near 25,000 gives
some indication of a basic difference between the two cities. The
system of alternate-year residence for lords throughout Japan, which
required them to leave large retinues in Edo, promoted the centralization of resources in this one city.

At all levels urbanization proceeded more swiftly in Japan. When
Russia pulled slightly ahead of Japan in population, it contained
only three or four cities in the 30,000-to-150,000 range and thirty

cities in the 10,000-to-30,000 range compared with Japan's twenty cities in the higher range and some sixty in the lower range. Altogether, as much as 12 per cent of the Japanese population lived in cities with more than 10,000 people as opposed to only 4 per cent of the citizens of the Russian Empire. Even if a lower cutoff point for calculating urban totals were chosen, Japan would appear roughly twice as urbanized. Russian urban figures by the mid-eighteenth century were already well above world averages, but they still had reached only slightly more than half of Japan's proportions. Each country showed dramatic urban increases before 1750, though the proportion of population in cities changed little during the final century before 1860 despite the continued dynamism of the two societies.

Numerous cities in both countries were noted as administrative centers. Nearly all cities of more than 10,000 people were castle towns in Japan and at least 100 smaller castle towns, also with large proportions of samurai inhabitants, functioned as the centers of small- and medium-sized han. Generally, about 10 per cent of the population of a han resided in the centrally located castle town. Russian administrative centers increased with the establishment of fortress cities in newly annexed territories and with the addition of administrative divisions in 1775 requiring the upgrading of local settlements as county seats. There were more than twice as many county seats as castle towns, but the Russian centers were meagerly staffed. The fact that the Russian service nobility was much smaller and less urban in residence meant that there was a smaller core of large-scale consumers in Russian cities.

Lively commerce was essential to the prosperity of all cities, administrative and nonadministrative alike. Goods flowed up a hierarchy of settlements from villages to nearby periodic markets, and frequently in Russia to fairs, and on to small and large cities. At the bottom of this hierarchy of marketing centers in Russia there were roughly 1,400 weekly markets by 1800 and thousands of small annual fairs; in Japan there were approximately 1,600 periodic markets, mostly meeting once or twice every ten days. Huge annual fairs also supplemented the exchange of goods in Russia. In contrast, small fairs were relatively insignificant in Japan and large fairs were absent altogether. The larger number of settlements and the more extensive area of Russia required more markets and fairs to be properly serviced, but more efficient organization of transportation and commerce in densely settled Japan must have facilitated the flow of goods from a smaller number of local gathering points to a far greater number of urban consumers.

The rapid spread of periodic marketing and of fairs from the thirteenth century in Japan and the fifteenth century in Russia provided a foundation for national commercial integration and substantial urbanization. By the early nineteenth century, however, daily shopping in stores had become so prevalent in both countries that periodic marketing began to decline, at least in the most advanced regions. Replacement of periodic marketing was a sign of the continued development of both countries, revealing the improved efficiency in moving goods directly to cities with daily commerce.

The dynamism of these two societies, evident in the previous section on human resources, was no less present in settlement changes from 1600 to the 1860's. Villages proliferated, gaining in internal organization and in connections with emerging local markets and administrative centers. Tiny periodic markets and fairs became joined through commerce to distant bustling cities. National administrative centers topped a panoply of hundreds of local administrative cities. Both Japan and Russia gained urban populations in a spectacular fashion. From initial totals of about one million city residents in Japan and barely a few hundred thousand in Russia, the two countries had each climbed to roughly 5.5 million in cities by 1860. And through the unusually urbanized pattern of settlements the greater concentration of resources in Japan can be seen.

Organizational Contexts

In what ways were these people organized? Of primary importance was the family, the major unit of production, consumption, recreation, and socialization. Both countries placed an emphasis on the perpetuation of the family, normally under the leadership of the oldest male. Marriages were arranged by parents in order to further the aims of the family as a whole. The weakness of clans and large extended families, even as an ideal to which households should aspire, tended to isolate the individual stem family where one son remained at home to perpetuate the line. In short, both Japan and Russia were patriarchal societies in which stem families provided the context for most behavior.

There are several reasons for thinking that the family was a more stable unit in Japan than in Russia. First, the prevalence of primogeniture attenuated by concern for merit in Japan contrasts with its general absence unless only one son survived in Russia.

However, primogeniture was less common among Japanese peasants than samurai and in Russia there was also an effort to persuade the gentry to practice primogeniture. Second, younger sons were often adopted out to families with no male heirs, enhancing the continuity of household planning in Japan. Third, ancestral tablets reinforced the awareness that the Japanese family persisted for many generations. By contrast, in the conditions of growing population and periodic villagewide repartition of lands in Russia, it was more difficult to maintain family continuity. Furthermore, imported ideologies brought individualism and romanticism earlier to Russia, subverting through love marriages and adulterous relationships some existing family patterns of the elite. This pattern contrasted with the development of a Confucian family-centered ethic in Japan. Greater continuity in family property, inheritance of position, and the Confucian ethic of the elite certainly helped preserve the stability of Japanese family life. Indeed, the potential for long-range planning of the household economy may have emerged as a factor in limiting aspirations for more children in Japan.

Authority over the conduct of household heads, who were responsible for the actions of family members, rested with village leaders. Some tens of thousands of households frequently were located in a single administered area—a *uezd* in Russia and a han or an area assigned to a *daikan* or *bugyo* in Japan. In Japan, the goningumi, or units of five households, were held responsible for individual misbehavior whereas in Russia serf-owners were expected to control most of the rural population—and forward its taxes. Yet controls within single settlements were insufficient to fill the wide hiatus in the society between distant administrator and household head. Local priests and monks gave some direct guidance regarding personal conduct. A difference between the impact of religious personnel in the two countries was that whereas Japanese religious bodies had long before been divested of most land holdings and lacked a clear hierarchy of priests, the Orthodox Church in Russia remained important as a pyramidal organization of clergy whose heads commanded considerable funds and, until 1764, large estates with serfs. Approximately 1 to 2 per cent of Russian city residents were in clergy families, a proportion far greater than that of Japan.

Groupings of men engaged in craft and commercial production also provided a critical organizational focus in both Japan and Russia. These guilds and related associations were generally established through government initiative. In both countries production was atomized with only a small proportion of commercial enterprises employing more than five or ten workers. The establishment of associations in which operators of relatively large enterprises were selected as leaders provided the state with a structure through which to exercise control and in return gave privileges and monopolies to the merchants and craftsmen involved. Close regulation combined with acceptance of the priority of the service nobility's interests accompanied the expansion of trade and handicraft production.

Despite these basic similarities, some major differences existed in the organization and regulation of trade and crafts. Most Japanese monopolies were centered in local castle towns, permitting diversity and responsiveness to local needs. Merchants might be thought of as allies of the local samurai and daimyo in a joint effort to improve the economic position of the han within the nation, an effort that at times resulted in struggles against bakufu-designated monopolies. In Russia, by contrast, class interests of merchants and gentry were more opposed. Merchants were engaged in a struggle to free themselves from the restrictions of a serf society. Change in the eighteenth and nineteenth centuries came more quickly in Russia as officials granted some successes to struggling merchants.

Nonetheless, in both countries the general pattern was for commercial interests to be allied with administrative ones and for those who prospered as merchants to become co-opted into service to the government. The system of basically closed classes may have been a principal cause in both countries for the spread of an achievement ethic among merchants. Merchants who lacked the opportunity to pull their capital and the talents of their sons out of commerce into elite status were more likely to concentrate on the long-run implications of investments and entrepreneurship. The fact that government leadership was normally hereditary in Japan and Russia may have given the elite more assurance and flexibility in confronting the challenge of modern societies. Given these conditions for merchants and administrators, it appears that relatively closed class systems constitute a better basis for quick and smooth transition to modernizing societies than open class systems generally. In short, there are settings in which a closed class system as well as a Protestant ethic can give rise to radical this-worldly asceticism.

Rural and urban administrative and commercial organizations were part of the context in which families operated. The individual family head was constrained and guided in his judgments about how to utilize the resources of his family by a variety of sources. Urban guilds and rural landlords, neighborhood and village organizations, priests, friends and relatives, all influenced personal decisions in these two countries, as they did elsewhere. But in Japan and

Russia even further restrictions on many forms of behavior and a broader direction of resource accumulation were extended to far corners of the society. The replacement of autonomous local authorities with representatives of the central authority—or at least with men subject to continuous regulation from the center who shared common approaches toward resource accumulation—was a process under way for many centuries and had great implications for all organizations. By the mid- or late eighteenth century daimyo, serf-owners, and other local authorities had devised new methods as part of a regularized pattern to mobilize local resources.

Japan and Russia, before the 1860's, faced three problems in connection with this increase in bureaucratic administration. First, in such basically ascriptive societies how can incompetents born to high nobility be prevented from misusing power? Although neither country completely resolved this question, both provided some means for talent to leapfrog birth, offering opportunities for future officials to receive an education and then to rise in the bureaucracy. Japan was probably more successful in this regard because it did not leave considerable areas of local control in the hands of nobles who were not part of any bureaucracy. Russia, however, had the advantage of one national administrative apparatus that could utilize talent, including the talent of those who were not born to the gentry. It was not hamstrung like Japan with many separate and often uneconomically tiny bureaucracies drawing only from one class, the samurai.

A second potential problem was the difficulty of maintaining firm central control. Neither country had the potential for achieving the kind of centralization that has appeared in modernizing countries. Most people in Japan were under local han governments and in Russia roughly half were under nobles responsible for taxes and order. These locally based service nobility and national authorities were in agreement that local resources should be withdrawn more efficiently and concentrated in the large cities without impairing long-run productivity.

Finally, there remained the problem of conflicting military and civilian organizations. In Japan samurai were both warriors and civilian administrators; there was no need for additional soldiers. In Russia, however, the military was separated from the civil service; both drew personnel from the gentry and both made rival claims on state revenues. Frequent wars prompted continued efforts to strengthen the army and navy. Moreover, conscription of serfs into the severe life of common soldiers—a fate which those with means

sought desperately to avoid—contrasted with the prestige and rewards gained by even the lower samurai who were trained for combat.
Also, the kind of grave national and personal problems caused by
military actions in Russia aroused scarcely any attention in Japan,
where no wars had been fought for more than 200 years.

The general impression to be obtained from a comparison of
organizations is that Japan achieved an extremely firm pattern of
social structure and maintained it for 150 to 250 years. Stable family
patterns, closely regulated commercial organizations, and large
samurai staffs able to exert a direct impact on the lives of commoners
reveal a picture of essentially unchanging organizational structures,
although there were, of course, some minor readjustments. In Russia
during these same centuries organizations were sharply in flux. New
decrees every few decades brought marked changes. Lines of authority appear to have been ambivalent. Artisans and hired laborers in
cities remained in an uncertain state. Loyalty to the tsar meant
that the judgment of subordinates could easily be questioned by
appeal to the tsar's declared or real intent. There was greater convergence of authority patterns in Japan, while in Russia, family
heads, village leaders, serf-owners, clergy, and local officials all
claimed to guide the peasant in his behavior. This divergence between organizations in Japan and Russia can be symbolized by the
difference between loosely organized gentry scattered in estates over
the Russian countryside and highly organized samurai united in bureaucracies within the castle cities of Japan. Both societies were mobilized, but Japan was more mobilized.

Redistributive Processes

In any society, there are always three redistributive processes:
social mobility—the movement of people between and within social
classes; migration—the geographic movement of people; and marketing, rents, usury, taxation, and welfare—the movement of money
or goods. How these processes occurred in Japan and Russia provides
further material for comparing them.

Classes in these two countries were in theory closed, although
there was less rigidity in occupational mobility than in the formal
transfer from one class to another. The most fluid ladders for occupational mobility were merchant and artisan occupations, which
swallowed up a continuous diet of peasants though some also returned to farming occupations. Movement to and from the service
nobility was much more restricted. A bright young Japanese man

might be adopted into a family of this class, a merchant daughter might be chosen as a bride, a second or third son of a samurai family might fall to commoner status, but these were rare exceptions to the closed character of Japan's middle and upper samurai. Only the lower ranks of the samurai revealed notable fluidity. Because the Russian bureaucracy did not consist entirely of nobles, there was some opportunity for commoners to rise through service to nobility status. Moreover, impoverished nobles were in danger of losing their lands and serfs and of eventually falling from this class. A basic contrast between the two countries was that Russian merchants and artisans in theory ranked above peasants, whereas the opposite was true in Japan, although wealthy members of these classes did enjoy many opportunities unavailable to peasants in Japan. The practice of separating individuals registered as city residents from serfs and state peasants caused those Russians fortunate enough to be listed as urban to cling to this identification. Occasional efforts to return recent arrivals in the city to their native occupations complicated the struggle to succeed as a merchant or an artisan in Japan. Even greater barriers, however, were placed in the path of those seeking to escape farming in Russia where peasants were required to carry a passport in a city and continued to feel the restraints of serf ownership. Large numbers of persons formally registered as peasants in certain regions of Russia actually were engaged in nonagricultural activities often away from home, but it was almost impossible for them to register in another class. In comparison with Japan, there seems to have been greater rigidity regarding interclass movement in Russia, except for the service nobility.

Intraclass mobility, on the other hand, encountered fewer barriers in either country. Facing obstacles to investment in rural land, and often in urban real estate too, merchants were obliged to forego efforts to rise into the service nobility. Instead, they concentrated their resources on building up family commercial fortunes. From the seventeenth to the nineteenth centuries, certain merchant families acquired vast wealth, which served in part as a source of loans to members of the service nobility. Intraclass mobility, except through adoption, was most difficult for samurai. Inheriting stipends which they had little chance of changing, first sons generally performed duties roughly commensurate with their ascribed pay. (Only in certain offices could their stipends be augmented by special payments.) Attention was given, therefore, to placing second sons and daughters with families whose stipends were not much lower. Yet there were many elements of a meritocracy whereby talented samurai could rise in the various bureaucracies across Japan. If the samurai of Japan

had one main source of income, the gentry of Russia received cash
and goods in kind from such varied sources as military or civilian
service, personal serfs on village estates, urban real estate, and even
serf labor in factories. Partly as a result of these more varied means
for altering one's income, and partly as a result of the ramifications
of frequent changes in policy and in court favorites, gentry families
in Russia had a greater chance to change their position vis-à-vis
other gentry.

Among peasants, understandably enough, competition for survival and wealth was keen. The elimination of samurai from villages,
the strengthening of stem families, and the growth of marketing produced a fluid situation in Japan. The continuation of serf ownership
hindered a similar process in Russian villages, but widening opportunities also materialized for peasants to use their labor and, at
times, their savings to alter their family's position. Especially in the
final century before the 1860's, a rising intensity can be seen in both
countries, but particularly in Japan, in the competition among villagers to increase landholdings and to profit from more commercialized agriculture.

At least three kinds of migration can be distinguished. One is
the movement of people to sparsely settled lands. To some extent
this movement occurred in seventeenth-century Japan as marginal
lands or newly irrigated lands became cultivated. In this tiny country,
though, new villages were typically founded only short distances
from previously settled ones. No major redistribution of people
occurred between 1600 and the 1860's. In contrast, vast territories in
the south and east of the Russian Empire were settled during these
centuries. With soldiers and traders leading the way, serfdom was
successively extended to the newly acquired areas of the empire. By
the eighteenth century the Ural Mountain region had become the
center of mining and metallurgy, more distant Siberia was emerging
as the route of a flourishing trade with China and the source of
valuable furs, and the south's recently developed areas of rich soil
were becoming noted as the breadbasket of the empire. Even before
the large-scale migrations to the West by Americans, and to Manchuria by Chinese, the migration of Russians was in progress. The
persistence of serfdom undoubtedly limited the liberating effect of
moving to a frontier area, yet the mood of adventurism also left its
mark on Russian social structure.

A second kind of migration is the regular movement of people
within a region, often from one type of settlement to another. In
both Japan and Russia there was considerable geographical mobility
of labor, with this movement taking a more seasonal character in

Russia. Those engaged in certain mobile occupations—merchants, transport workers, soldiers—were likely to change their place of living. The conscription of serfs as soldiers produced greater migration in Russia. Since the population of the two or three principal cities in both countries was at least for a time two-thirds male and mainly of working age, regular male migration into and out of cities clearly occurred at definite points of the life cycle.

A third form of migration is the periodic movement from one area to another. This kind of movement was typical of the service nobility, many of whom maintained two residences. Their trips between local areas and the national administrative centers provided an exchange of observations and customs that was critical to the integration of the two societies. Migration to and from Edo was closely regulated and even larger in scale, aiding in the greater integration of Japan.

There was a disciplined quality to the movement of both the service nobility and peasants into the administrative centers of Edo and Saint Petersburg. These individuals were identified with specific local areas, to which most of them would return. Japanese authorities paid closest attention to the movement of the samurai, whereas Russians controlled more closely the movement of the serfs. In both cases the urban instability and excessive regionalism that might have been expected to occur during the late premodern period did not.

Changing patterns of marketing and taxation facilitated intraclass mobility. The individual peasant family increasingly channeled its resources into markets for hired labor and for agricultural and craft goods. Villages and even provinces became noted for special products or as sources of labor for transportation along a road or canal or for emigration to a city. And taxes, which became more regularized and predictable, increased.

A slight contrast should be made between the importance of the systems of marketing and taxation in Japan and Russia. In Japan what mattered was an impersonal, well-regulated system of marketing and redistribution of tax revenues, successfully joining more than 250 separately administered areas. This system with a set of universally observed rules supporting a market mechanism flourished through the emulative consequences of each han striving to keep up with other han in the bakuhan system. This degree of impersonality was not as fully accepted in Russia. Serf-owners were directly responsible to the government for the taxes owed by their serfs. Private contacts between neighboring nobles or between nobles in two regions could proceed in Russia as a personal basis for linking those in two areas, but not in Japan. Furthermore, because it did not have a system of direct payment of rents or labor services to individual nobles, Japan relied more on just two forms of redistribution out of villages, taxes and marketing. Local and national integration based on these two pillars contrasted with the importance of personal bonds in Russia. Yet the extent to which the state was also the impersonal overseer of peasants in Russia should not be ignored, including those who were serfs as well as the nearly 50 per cent who were directly controlled by the state.

Redistribution in its various forms had changed considerably in the centuries before 1860. The primacy of loyalties owed to lords rather than to families facilitated the emergence of highly organized groupings with clear lines of responsibility between them. While opportunities for interclass mobility were narrowly circumscribed, new channels of intraclass mobility became widely used. Rural-urban migration rates increased as urbanization rose, and at the same time migration to major cities was in various ways regulated. Improved marketing was instrumental in national integration and in the breakdown of village self-sufficiency. In Japan a tremendous flow of resources was necessary to support a high level of urbanization. In Russia the rapid growth of exports had an impact on nearly all areas of the empire. Yet in neither country were these changes completely consistent. In Japan intraclass mobility among the samurai seems to have slowed after the mid-eighteenth century, although constant movement in and out at lower levels persisted. In Russia bonds of serfdom constrained peasants. The overall impression is that rising mobility, migration, and marketing were remarkably undisruptive to the preservation of order in the two countries.

Personal Relationships

Sociologists have compared modernized and nonmodernized societies in terms of personal relationships, arguing that the patterns found in modernized societies improve the capacity of individuals to interrelate in order to achieve the ends being sought. Productivity in units of high specialized production or of administration, for example, is improved by choosing personnel on the basis of relevant abilities and by confining most mutual expectations to specific functions essential for production. While no nonmodernized peoples take these universalistic criteria and functionally specific patterns for granted, they were more widespread in Japan and Russia than in most societies prior to 1800. If these aspects of personal relationships are not thought of as dichotomous, but as a continuum, then Japan and Russia can be compared with other societies along the nonmodernized end of the continuum to determine basic similarities and differences.

A list of relationships in which important differences among premodern societies might be found includes the following: landlord-tenant, employer-hired laborer, merchant-customer, administrator-subject, and official-official. In both Japan and Russia a growing impersonality and specificity in all of these relationships can be observed. A decline of kinship and pseudo-kinship ties in units of production was particularly noteworthy in rural Japan. Similarly, the continuation of serfdom in Russia cannot disguise the growing impersonality of landowner-serf relations. Despite the strengthening of a system of assigning state peasants to specific factories, a market of hired labor was expanding rapidly in Russia. In both countries the proliferation of stores and commerce was a tremendous force for increasing the specialization of productive activities, especially among urban craftsmen, and for increasing buyer-seller relationships. Changing administrative practices and the bureaucratization of administration also point to the conclusion that Japan and Russia developed advanced forms of interaction in comparison with other premodern societies.

Even when the explicit ideals of inheritance and closed classes seemed to close off a meritocratic approach in Japan, special devices developed. Among the samurai there operated a sort of civil service by adoption that frequently put able young samurai in positions they would never have attained without adoption. Special appointments and power through loans to daimyo similarly gave able merchants roles in the han and even bakufu administration.

A somewhat different conclusion seems likely when the goal-orientation aspects in Japan and Russia are compared with conditions elsewhere. Individualism was weak in both countries. In comparison with other advanced premodern societies, even individualism by default was relatively absent; persons away from their families were still firmly bound in group affiliations. Groups of families or an entire village were jointly responsible for criminal acts, for tax arrears, and, in Russia, for runaway serfs. There was a large degree of collectivism, to the extent in Japan that some posts were held alternately by two or three men who were jointly responsible.

Underlying this collectivistic framework was a stress on unconditional loyalty to the tsar in Russia and to one's lord in Japan. The chain of command in Japan was direct and unambiguous. In theory, any decision of a samurai was perforce the collective decision of all below him in the hierarchy of power-holders and could not contradict a decision of his superior. Clear lines of authority made unconditional loyalty a living force that could be activated quickly. By contrast, in the mind of a Russian serf a gap often existed between the tsar's intent and the action of local gentry. Gentry in Russia received nearly unlimited legal support for their treatment of serfs. Loyalty to a distant, often symbolic, presence remained a powerful force, but one that could not always be conveyed as the source of a specific directive.

The weakness of individualism, restricted as it was by an emphasis on loyalty and collectivism, may have been an asset in subsequent modernization. The great stress on individualism so characteristic of the firstcomers to modernization by no means conferred the same sort of comparative advantages on latecomers. The transition from one set of responsible orientations to a *different* set of responsible orientations not only minimized problems of control but also divisive problems of suspicion and distrust. Village collectivism, direct and unambiguous hierarchies of power, and the potent symbolism of emperor and tsar cemented the orientation toward responsibility in diverse personal relationships.

International Comparisons

The specific focus of this section is the distribution of social classes. The majority of people in premodern societies were peasants, with the exception of those small-scale societies made up of sparse and mobile clusters of pastoral nomads or hunters and gatherers. Engaged in farming or supportive household tasks, most individuals resided in villages. Ordinarily the individual peasant's participation in productive activities took place primarily within the family context, and varied in a predictable fashion according to sex, the life cycle, and the agricultural season.

For the purposes of comparison here, the social strata to be singled out in peasant societies are not the majority with regular schedules of agricultural activities nor the small number of additional primary producers such as fishermen. Rather, our focus will be on the residual minority population whose schedules were to a considerable extent independent of the agricultural cycle. This minority includes the elite, officials, soldiers, clergy, noncultivator landlords, merchants, artisans, hired nonagricultural laborers, servants, serf factory and household laborers, and nonfarming outcasts. Not all of these categories were necessarily found in a given society, and additional categories might also have been present. Nonetheless, this list is clearly indicative of the range of groups that in varying ways secured and consumed agricultural production without producing it, except, perhaps, in garden plots. Freed from the rhythm of peasant life, individuals in these categories were generally more mobile geographically and socially. In various ways this critical minority formed the basis for the emergence of a modern sector of society during the transitional period.

Societies can be distinguished according to the percentage of the total population in each of these categories as well as the sum of these nonagricultural populations. Among the large societies before 1800, some had small elites of fewer than 1 per cent. Others had large elites of at least 6 per cent of the total population. Some officials, soldiers, clergy, and noncultivator landlords might customarily be members of the designated elite. The number of merchants and artisans had a similar range. Figures as high as 5 to 10 per cent of household heads are indicative of a rare degree of development of these occupations. Hired or serf nonagricultural laborers could also tally at least several percentage points of the total population. Altogether, societies seemed to have ranged from a few percentage points to more than 20 in these residual categories.

Comparisons of societies also reveal that these strata could vary in hereditary urbanness. Officials, landlords, artisans, merchants, and others were to a varying degree self-perpetuating through inheritance. Where examinations were used to determine access to official positions, where land could be bought and sold freely, where commerce and crafts were open to all who were venturesome or desperate, and where migration was not restricted, the conditions existed for open classes and considerable upward and downward mobility, at least ideally speaking. Even where these conditions were absent, widespread, intraclass mobility could occur or well-traveled occupational channels could develop through which merit was rewarded. While all of these strata were disproportionately urban, the leisured elite and noncultivator landlords were the ones who had the option of living in cities or villages instead of being obliged by the nature of their work to reside in a particular type of settlement. The distribution of these strata among cities of varying sizes is a further basis for comparing societies.

Japan and Russia, with collectively one-fourteenth of the world's population in 1800 and roughly one-seventh or one-eighth of the urban inhabitants, each had from 10 to 25 per cent of its population in these residual nonagricultural categories. In part because of its much more numerous urban elite, Japan was twice as urban as Russia and probably had nearly twice the nonagricultural population. Yet these obvious differences should not obscure the important similarities between the two countries.

The many parallel shifts in the distribution of social classes experienced by Japan and Russia between 1600 and 1860 have already been noted. Although a large and highly urbanized elite appeared first in Japan, the Russian gentry grew rapidly from the early eighteenth century, and especially the wealthy gentry that increasingly came to reside in St. Petersburg and Moscow. By the 1800's hereditary elites in each country maintained lavish residences in one or two great cities and kept houses in local areas. Roughly 20 per cent of the samurai, including all the daimyo, lived in Edo or regularly migrated there to stay for at least a year at a time. The geographical mobility of the Russian gentry, followed by a retinue of house serfs, often took the form of spending summers at rural estates. The large-scale movement of goods to market, in order to support the costly life-style in Edo, St. Petersburg, and Moscow, was a necessary consequence of these continuous and regular interval migrations by individuals who had the greatest control over local resources. A common denominator in the development of these two countries was the existence of large, circulating service nobilities who were unchallenged in their control of local resources and who came together regularly in one or two national centers where they were directly subordinate to a central administration that also controlled huge areas of land. The elements of similarity between the two countries include the sharp differences between life in a few cities and life elsewhere in the country, a system of alternate residences, relatively closed classes, and an increasingly literate elite experienced in administration but dependent on local bases of support which it was free to administer in more efficient ways.

Most premodern societies were considerably less urbanized. Even where at least 5 per cent of the population lived in cities, as in Japan and Russia in the sixteenth century, the early dependence on administrative centralization often had not yet given way to predominantly commercial centralization with a corresponding growth in the number of merchants, artisans, and hired laborers in cities. In other words, early nineteenth-century Japan and Russia can be immediately distinguished from many societies in which the size and distribution of social classes were less complex.

One society roughly a century ahead of Japan and Russia was England. The implications of London's growth from 1600 to 1750 were strikingly parallel to the observations made for Japan and Russia before the 1860's. As a growing center of consumption, London attracted a great number of wealthy English migrants who continued to be supported by scattered estates. As E. A. Wrigley has written, "The demonstration effect of London's growth played an important part in engendering changes elsewhere."

Outside of Europe at least one other society had achieved considerable commercial development, a level of urbanization of at least 6 per cent, and corresponding diversification of social classes. China was one of the exceptional examples of advanced premodern societies. By 1800 it had about 30 per cent of the world's urban and total population. In many respects, however, China was different from Japan and Russia. First, Chinese classes were open, not closed. Membership in China's elite of scholarly degree-holders was fluid, though access was confined primarily to those who had passed an examination. Second, the elite was exceptionally rural. Individuals generally remained in their places of birth, except during visits to the cities in which examinations were held and except during periods of appointment for the select few to official positions. Some local landlords chose to live in cities, but these cities were typically nearby county seats. China did not have a large, urban self-perpetuating elite. Similarly, there was no mobilization of other social strata in urban areas either by lords, as in Japan, or by gentry, as in Russia. In other words, no special force in China set in motion the chain of circumstances that could be found in Japan or Russia.

Until further comparisons are carried out, it is possible only to hypothesize that basic differences existed between social mobilization in Japan and Russia on the one hand and in other premodern societies on the other. Dividing all societies before 1800 into stages of urban development, we find that the simplest pre-urban societies gave way to societies with increasingly complex networks of administrative centers mainly reliant on taxes and rents, societies that in turn were eventually transformed into commercially integrated societies. Japan by the early seventeenth century and Russia about a century later had joined the ranks of the advanced commercially integrated societies. The dynamism of these two countries accelerated at this point, however. The new demands on the samurai and gentry formalized by Tokugawa Ieyasu and Peter I, and then fully worked out during the subsequent century, precipitated other dramatic and essentially similar changes in Japan and Russia.

Changes in human resources, patterns of settlement, organizational contexts, redistributive processes, and aspects of personal relationships were all part of this final premodern transformation.

Japan and Russia were unique outside of Western Europe in the degree to which social mobilization anticipated the period of the modernizing transformation. Tens of thousands of samurai household heads plus some of their families moved to and from Edo, while their local areas under the close supervision of the daimyo's staff supplied the money for their needs through shipments to Osaka and Edo. Similarly, thousands of serf-owners, together with their families, and trailed by large numbers of serfs, spent at least the winter months in St. Petersburg and Moscow. In the summer they returned to supervise personally the productive activities on their local estates from which they derived their support. The emergence of a civil service in Russia, including officials who were not part of the gentry, paralleled the strengthening of urban bureaucracies in Japan. In both countries this interpenetration of the center and the province and of urban and rural is likely to have had an important impact on conditions experienced by the majority of the population within villages.

Chapter Six

KNOWLEDGE AND EDUCATION

BOTH JAPAN AND RUSSIA had by the 1860's made substantial and increasingly faster progress in replacing the informal, family-based means of transmitting knowledge and values with formalized institutions of education and impersonal systems of communication. A good deal of this development occurred in the private domain. Even so, it was the public authorities in both nations who took the major initiatives, particularly in formal education, and who determined, whether by example or edict, the broad guidelines for the content of education and the production of new knowledge.

As early as the seventeenth century in Japan and by the mid-eighteenth century in Russia, religious authorities no longer accounted for any important, independent initiatives in the definition or control of education. This early secularization of education is a characteristic that was not shared by the firstcomers to modernization, much less by the great majority of the latecomers, and it may have been of critical advantage to Japan and Russia in subsequent modernization.

In three specific educational areas—elite education, commoner education, and publishing—Japan and Russia were by the 1860's similar in the *kind* of development experienced but strikingly different in *degree,* with Japan in each respect far more advanced. More specifically:

Elite education: Formal education in the two countries was thought of by the political leaders primarily in terms of training in the skills and values necessary for public service on the local or regional (particularly in Japan) and national level. By the nineteenth century formal education came to be considered a proper and, indeed, an essential qualification for political leadership. Though

Japan preceded Russia by a substantial margin in stressing the importance of formal schooling, and was probably more advanced in the average level of elite education, both nations by the 1860's had nevertheless achieved the goal of a well-educated and wholly literate elite.

Commoner education: The number of Japanese and Russian schools for commoners multiplied in the first half of the nineteenth century. The rate of expansion in Japan, however, was far above that in Russia. In Japan the estimated national level of male literacy was more than 40 per cent, versus an increasing but still minuscule overall percentage for Russia.

Publishing: To cater to the growing numbers of the literate, new and diverse publishing establishments were founded in both countries by the end of the premodern period. Japan's substantially higher rate of commoner literacy put it far ahead of Russia in popular publishing and, hence, in the total volume published.

Finally, neither Japan nor Russia possessed indigenous intellectual traditions that were particularly well-adapted to modern scientific inquiry. Yet neither were they beset with priestly elites in a position to oppose such inquiry. And both shared the highly developed traditions of craftsmanship and technology that provided a basis for the easy introduction of practical knowledge from the West. By virtue of earlier and far more intimate contact with nations beyond its borders, Russia was, of course, already far ahead of Japan by the mid-nineteenth century in the process of borrowing and absorbing Western science and technology.

The Secularization of Education

Japan and Russia until the 1860's were little different from other premodern societies in that the transmission of knowledge from generation to generation was accomplished for the greatest part informally within the family. Even in the more mobile urban environment, traditions of apprenticeship training among merchants and artisans provided a family-like context for learning both skills and values. The preponderance of family-based education in both countries, however, should not obscure the rapidly expanding systems of formal education outside the family which were developing by the end of this period. This area of formal education will be given the most attention here, particularly since family-based education alone cannot provide the basis for achieving the levels of national control and coordination necessary for modernization.

Before considering the levels and extent of formal education, however, it is necessary to address the more basic question of how formal education was conceived in both countries. What were its goals and how were they to be achieved? The central issue here, as in other premodern societies, is the conflict of religious and secular conceptions of education. At one extreme, education may be conceived as purely a means for achieving personal spiritual salvation, with the church as the only appropriate authority. At the other extreme, education may be conceived solely in terms of its political utility, with political authorities taking direct responsibility for its content. Within the context of all premodern societies, Japan and Russia were exceptional in the degree to which they had, by the nineteenth century, come to develop a highly secularized system of formal, elite education, one run or controlled to a considerable degree by public authority.

The secularization of education in both nations occurred from the sixteenth through the eighteenth centuries. Before that period, Buddhist priests in Japan and Orthodox Christian clerics in Russia had a monopoly on the major sources of higher learning; literate academic traditions were preserved and developed within temples and monasteries, and virtually no attempts were made to spread knowledge outside these institutions until the seventeenth century. Little conception existed in either country of education in the sense of formal schooling.

From the sixteenth through the eighteenth centuries a crucial change occurred in both Japan and Russia, one that distinguished them from most other premodern societies. The church receded in importance as a major independent force in formal education, with the result that political authorities were given a free hand in the encouragement of and control over education, both at the elite and commoner levels. This parallel change in the two countries is of great importance and deserves closer analysis because it contrasts so vividly with the experiences of the first modernizers.

The establishment in the first half of the seventeenth century of Neo-Confucianism as an officially sponsored ideology provided the basis for the secularization of education in Japan and its spread in the next two centuries. Neo-Confucianism was established by both the bakufu and han. Education in the Confucian scheme was conceived of as training in the art of governing self and society, and it consisted of reading classical texts. This tradition, adopted from China, thus established in Japan a view that education must be useful for the community. It was a view that came to dominate not only the education of the elite but that of commoners as well.

In Russia education in the eighteenth century came to be actively promoted and dominated by secular authorities under the strong influence of West European models. It was a time in which the Russian state sought to enforce regular and systematic training on the gentry class. Here, as in Japan, education was appreciated primarily for its political utility. In contrast with the Confucian emphasis on the inherent desirability of education for the sake of a stable social order, however, Russia's underlying concern was whether education could help increase its military strength to match foreign rivals.

Japan and Russia were alike not only in the vigor with which political authorities encouraged education, but in the relative absence of opposition by religious establishments to this assertion of political control. The probable cause of this lack of opposition was that in neither country was there any concept of the duality of church and state of the sort that characterized Western Christendom. Russian Orthodox Christianity, like Byzantine Orthodoxy of which it is a part, is caesaropapist; it stresses the common concerns and indeed the interrelation of church and state. In Japan, likewise, Buddhism from the time of its import from China in the sixth century was considered a crucial part of the polity as a talisman and unifying force. The indigenous Japanese religious practices, which came to be systematized as Shinto, performed a similar unifying function at the village level, providing the basis for a future nationalistic symbol.

Hence, in both nations the church served to give important nationalistic sanction to the state without becoming an independent threat, either politically or in the propagation of values. Clerics were responsible for conducting an important segment of formal education, particularly among commoners, but they performed this function no less in their capacity as educated men than as propagators of the faith.

Elite Education

The political authorities of Japan and Russia were thus freed from the threat of any independent educational initiative by religious leaders. They were left unimpeded to develop educational institutions for the indoctrination and practical training of the elite class. The training of the service nobility was the object of calculated efforts by political authorities in both countries. By the end of the premodern period, therefore, all members of the elite class likely to engage in public life were thoroughly literate and trained in the skills necessary for their duties in the bureaucracy. Precedents for the political uses of education were to be of great importance in the transitional period. In addition, and particularly in Japan, training in military skills was considered an integral part of the education of the elite.

The achievement of the goal of a literate and well-trained elite differed in the two cases in both timing and techniques. Japan was about a century ahead of Russia in making an initial commitment to the formal education of the elite class, with the bakufu and several han providing schooling for their retainers from the beginning of the Tokugawa period. It was only in the last century of Tokugawa rule, however, that such education became universally effective for the samurai class; the number of official han schools jumped from 31 in 1750 to 219 at the time of the Meiji Restoration. In the same period, samurai education under private auspices in the private academies (*shijuku*) also expanded dramatically.

In Russia formal education for the gentry class was first promoted by Peter I in the early 1700's, with renewed efforts made under Elizabeth at mid-century. Gradually the state gained the power to make formal education mandatory for all members of the service nobility. Initially, the accent was on technical institutes at the highest level as a means of incorporating Western knowledge. But over the next century a variety of schools treating diverse specialties was established. Simultaneously, new seminaries were created to give the clergy a "modern" classical education.

It bears underscoring that in Russia all of these schools were modeled on Western European institutions. Pedagogical ideals and even many of the teachers were brought in from the West—usually Germany—endowing the Russian intelligentsia with a thoroughly European cast by the late eighteenth century. Partly as a consequence, the Russians would face fewer of the problems of conversion during the period of transformation than would the Japanese.

One result of this pattern of educational borrowing in Russia was to diminish the links between the elite and other social classes. As the elite became an island of Western influence, the values and outlook of the various social classes diverged. In contrast, Western learning in Japan was developed by lay scholars, usually samurai or doctors, in the service, or hoping to be in the service, of political authorities. Thus, the spread of Western influence in Japan did not threaten social solidarity.

In Tokugawa Japan elite education developed without foreign examples, although the pedagogical ideals had been overwhelmingly influenced by the Chinese Confucian model. This model had been adapted to the needs of Japanese society by a heavy stress on loyalty, martial values, and reciprocal obligations inherent in a feudal society. Education was to be education not only in the art of governing but also in discipline and obedience. It was this peculiarly Japanese emphasis that provided for the easy spread of schooling to the other classes. In the process the samurai evolved as the ideal ethical type for all classes, and the kind of gulf between elite and commoner education that manifested itself in Russia was not only avoided but actively bridged.

A further contrast in elite education between Japan and Russia lay in the greater receptivity of the Japanese samurai to educational opportunity. That the samurai were more eager than the Russian gentry to capitalize on educational programs was particularly true by the end of the Tokugawa period, when education had become the key channel for what limited mobility was afforded samurai, particularly those in the lower ranks. In Russia the first efforts at making education a prerequisite of the service gentry met with suspicion and resistance of a sort inconceivable in Japan, where literary traditions were deeply rooted in the aristocratic classes. Once it was realized that educational requirements, far from serving as a device for weakening the Russian gentry, could actually strengthen it, their initial resistance quickly disappeared and formal education was assumed to be a necessary and natural part of elite qualification. Thus, by the 1860's both Japan and Russia had in common the crucial similarity that their elite classes had received a thorough and uniform education both in basic skills and in handling practical matters.

Commoner Education

In the field of commoner education, Japan was far in advance of Russia. In the scale of formal education in the basic skills of reading, writing, and arithmetic for commoner classes, there was no comparison between the two countries. By the time of the Meiji Restoration, an estimated 40 per cent of the male population and 10 per cent of the female had achieved some degree of literacy. In the cities the figures were much higher, an estimated 75 to 85 per cent of the population of Edo being literate by the end of the Tokugawa period.

Japan's exceptional rate of literacy seems most directly related to the lack of any hostility on the part of the elite to the spread of education among commoners. On the contrary, the elite had a distinct sense that the more people who were educated the better, in clear distinction with the widespread suspicion in Russia toward commoner education. This attitude may in part have stemmed from the fact that education in Tokugawa Japan was conceived of primarily as ethical education, and indeed the bulk of commoner education leaned heavily on Confucian ethics and Buddhist homilies. The primary institution for commoner education in Tokugawa Japan was the *terakoya* (literally "temple school," after the origins of the institution in early Buddhist temples, although by the end of the Tokugawa period the schools had no connection with religious institutions per se). For the most part, the spread of the terakoya occurred after 1800.

One important effect of the spread of commoner education in Tokugawa Japan, and its encouragement by the political authorities, was that it reinforced an increasing homogeneity between elite and commoner values. By the end of the Tokugawa period Confucian notions of order and class were diffused through the education of all classes, creating a very strong ethical base for the building of a modern state. The general lack of any modern scientific training in the educational system may well have been a minor disadvantage in comparison with this strength. In Russia, on the contrary, a gap continued to exist between elite and mass values, a gap that was to be spanned only in the twentieth century.

Literacy among the Russian serfs was practically nil. This did not mean, however, that no educational opportunities were available for the nonelite in Russia. From its founding in the mid-eighteenth century, Moscow University included a section for commoners, and many commoners were able to gain access to the elite through such education. Moreover, serfs were frequently trained as estate managers, craftsmen, composers, and so forth, which offered a channel for advancement for some small numbers of the peasantry. Though rural literacy was negligible, literacy did begin to grow quickly in the Russian towns from the eighteenth century, as the popularity of wood-block prints with simple writing attests. While the numbers involved in such advances account for only a tiny percentage of the total commoner population in Russia, educational opportunities did exist for the nonelite and provided a basis for further expansion.

Literacy and Publishing

Language itself presented certain obstacles to the achievement of literacy in Japan, and to a lesser extent, Russia. It created challenges that would continue to demand attention into the years of modernization. The Japanese were burdened by a writing system of devilish complexity, a confused amalgam of ideograms borrowed from China and phonetic symbols. Even in contemporary Japan, where the system of transcription has been drastically simplified and standardized, it requires from two to four times as many hours for the Japanese child to master the reading and writing of his own language as it does any of his Western counterparts, including Russians.

The Russians with a simple alphabet faced no particular problem in their writing system. They were beset, however, with the linguistic diversity of their empire as a whole and with the growing schism between the traditional written language of Church Slavonic and spoken Russian. Even so, during the premodern period the problem of linguistic minorities was relatively insignificant, and with the creation in the eighteenth century of standard modern literary Russian the written and the spoken languages of the majority population merged.

The difficulty of the Japanese writing system seems not to have been an overwhelming obstacle in the spread of literacy. Japan in the first place shared with the rest of the East Asian cultural zone a boundless respect for the written word and for scholarship. One may further surmise that the very difficulty of the Japanese writing system made it a great challenge, and hence desirable, while at the same time it provided a level of discipline and patience in the acquisition of literacy that doubtless had positive effects in the realm of social stability. Writing in particular was a highly refined artistic tradition, so much so that all artistic production in premodern times was intimately associated with the written word. In Japan literacy received an aura of prestige far greater than it did in Russia.

Both Japan and Russia saw the beginnings of regular publishing in the late sixteenth century, although the Japanese had behind them almost ten centuries of experience with wood-block printing of Buddhist passages. The introduction of movable type into Japan from Korea in the 1590's was an important element in this growth, parallel to the similar import into Russia from Central Europe in the 1550's. The Japanese later abandoned movable type and reverted to wood-block printing for technical reasons related to their far more difficult writing system, but the pace of publishing continued to grow unabated in response to the demands of the increasingly literate urban classes.

Publishing in Russia expanded in the same period, but at a far less dramatic rate than in Japan. After the introduction of printing in Russia the quantity of titles produced scarcely rose over two centuries, though it thereafter soared to an average of some 400 titles a year in the 1780's. Japan in the same period was publishing in excess of 3,000 titles annually. These figures indicate a striking difference between Japan and Russia in the levels of achievement in literacy and publishing.

The spread of literacy in both nations enabled the government to exploit it for official communication. In Russia by the mid-nineteenth century, all laws were published, printing was a primary mode of governmental communication, and nongovernmental printing was effectively controlled through censorship and regulation. In Japan laws were not actually published, but this fact was less important because of the widespread use of public signboards to communicate the will of the shogunal and domain authorities. Such signboards were striking symbols of the increasing reliance on the written language in the political system of Tokugawa Japan.

In both nations scholarly publishing had considerable consequence by the 1860's, with increasing attention given to the translation of foreign books. Russia's systematic import of Western knowledge through translation was well in advance of Japan's by virtue of proximity, minimal linguistic impediments, and an earlier commitment, even prior to Peter I, to such a policy. Indeed, by 1800 most landmarks of contemporary West European literature, as well as most classical texts, had appeared in Russian translation and had a profound impact on Russian letters and thought. But although Japan did not translate Western works until much later, and was beset with far greater language difficulties, a huge increase of translated and original books dealing with the West did occur in the decades immediately before 1868. Fukuzawa Yukichi's *Conditions in the West,* for example, is reported to have sold 150,000 copies in its first edition in 1867.

Science and Technology

Japan and Russia in the eighteenth century both began to catch up with the advances in Western science made in the previous two centuries. Neither country seemed to offer fertile ground for the indigenous evolution of the techniques of experimentation and observation that were central to the scientific revolution. Russian religious culture was intensely otherworldly, and lacked the strong Aristotelian tradition that enabled the Catholic Church to patronize scientific inquiry at certain times. The Japanese were on the whole more this-worldly in their religious concerns than the Russians, but the primary focus on human relations and statecraft in the Confucianism that dominated the Tokugawa intellectual scene similarly offered little open encouragement to the investigation of the physical world.

Despite such unpromising epistemological traditions for the development of experimental science, both Japan and Russia had always shown an exceptional interest in technology, that is, in the uses rather than the underlying principles of things. This interest was buttressed by strong craft traditions, although the general level of craftsmanship by the nineteenth century seems to have been considerably higher in Japan than in Russia. By 1700 the Russians had cast the largest bell and the largest cannon in the world, while the Japanese had since medieval time developed extremely sophisticated techniques of sword-making, irrigation, surveying, and castle construction.

The development of modern science in Russia began under Peter I with the establishment of the Academy of Sciences in 1724 along lines of Central and West European academies. From that point on Russian science was directly and heavily sponsored by the state and was conducted exclusively in the Western pattern, giving Russia a sound advantage over Japan. Most of the early members of the academy were Germans, and it was only in the nineteenth century that native, first-rate scientists began to appear. By the second half of the nineteenth century Russia possessed a small but extremely fine scientific establishment, whose personnel were full-fledged members of the Western scientific community. Russia had produced several scientists of world renown: Lomonosov, the eighteenth-century father of physical chemistry, and Lobachevsky, the early nineteenth century mathematician, to name but two. In addition to the Academy, Russia had research libraries, several universities of the most contemporary structure, museums, and the world's largest observatory.

The Japanese process of catching up with modern science may be dated from roughly the same time as the Russian—with the relaxation in 1720 of the ban on the importation of books connected with the Jesuits, a prime source of information on Western science. But progress remained extremely slow. Not only did tremendous barriers of language have to be overcome, but Japanese practitioners of the "Dutch Learning" were not given the level of organized state support enjoyed in Russia. Whereas the Russians were permitted to employ famous Western scientists, the Japanese could only learn from the sporadic and not always well-informed accounts of the Dutch traders and physicians at Nagasaki and the books they brought. But slowly throughout the last century of the Tokugawa era, Japanese knowledge of Western science increased and the barriers were broken down. Equally important was the breakdown of the tradition of *hiden,* the "secret transmission" of knowledge within closed crafts and professions which prevented the free exchange of information necessary to the development of modern scientific knowledge.

From the 1850's the Japanese began to move in the direction the Russians had taken in the eighteenth century. Official sponsorship of scientific research increased and foreign experts were welcomed. As in the past, the overwhelming interest of the Japanese was in the practical aspects of Western knowledge rather than in the fundamental principles, so that the earliest areas to develop were gunnery, cartography, and medicine. Virtually all of these achievements were soon outdated with the arrival of well-trained Western experts in the 1860's and after; however, these earlier experiences established the precedents of state encouragement of science and the willingness to learn from abroad, both of which would enable the Japanese to create a Western-style scientific establishment in a very short time.

International Comparisons

Despite the important contrasts in overall quantitative achievements in education between Japan and Russia, the two nations had in common two characteristics that set them apart from most other latecomers to modernization. In the first place, in both states formal education became a requirement for participation in the political elite. Japan accomplished the task earlier and with less resistance than Russia experienced, but by the end of the premodern period the ruling classes in both Japan and Russia were fully literate. It is doubtful that any country outside of Europe, with the one exception of China, had reached this level by the mid-nineteenth century.

Second, neither Japan nor Russia were beset by the tension between church and state as they competed for control over formal education, a tension that plagued both Catholic and Protestant nations. The general secularization of academic traditions in science and technology was particularly beneficial, for it meant that there would be little opposition by a threatened priestly elite to imported modern knowledge. Both the ease and eagerness with which the state sponsored formal education in Japan and Russia were advantages that not all European and few non-European nations have possessed.

Among other latecomers, the nations bearing the strongest similarities to Japan and Russia in these respects are those of the East Asian cultural sphere, particularly China. Indeed, it might be argued that China was even better endowed with these advantages than Japan and, certainly, Russia. China had for centuries been largely governed by an elite secular class that was actually defined by educational achievement through civil service examinations. Even in the realm of commoner education, China appears to have been well ahead of Russia prior to the nineteenth century, even if levels of mass literacy were beginning to lag considerably behind those in Japan.

The major differences in the Chinese case seems to lie not with the type or levels of education offered under traditional society, but rather with the *direction* of change at the point of contact with modernizing peoples in the first half of the nineteenth century. The Chinese examination system, far from enjoying the vigorous growth characteristic of elite education in Japan and Russia in the century prior to the 1860's, had hardened into fixed and inflexible forms that proved resistant to change. The very success of the system over such a long period of time made the Chinese less eager than either the Japanese or the Russians to experiment with new systems of elite education. In the realm of commoner education, there likewise appears to have been stagnation rather than growth in the nineteenth century, suggesting that the demand for literacy among commoners had reached a plateau in China just when it was beginning to rise in Japan and Russia.

Chapter Seven

CONCLUSIONS: THE HERITAGE
OF THE PAST

THE PRINCIPAL CONCLUSION that can be drawn from our consideration of the heritage of the past of Japan and Russia is a truism: The capabilities that account for the rapid modernization of these two countries were to a compelling degree present in their premodern societies. But not all truisms are irrelevant. While we are all committed in some sense to the idea that the future is writ in the past, two elements are added here. One is that the peculiarities of the introduction of elements of modernization do not account for the swiftness of the process in the case of Japan and Russia. The other is that the elements in their histories that are critical are rare combinations for all the latecomers faced with modernization problems. All modernization is a radical conversion of historical heritage, but most latecomers, if indeed they are to escape the limbo of modernization, seem to be in for a double conversion. For most, the first conversion forms those preconditions found ready to hand in Japan and Russia. The second, if it takes place, builds on that first, if that has taken place.

Just as the historical experiences of England and France before the eighteenth century gave rise to indigenous modernization, so also the experiences of societies that were to become latecomers to this process provided them with certain comparative advantages. A detailed list of preconditions advantageous to future modernization is beyond the scope of this study. Nonetheless an attempt has been made to specify the assets of Japan and Russia that distinguished them from other premodern societies. These comparisons of the similarities between Japan and Russia and differing conditions elsewhere may serve as a starting point for the study of the preconditions of modernization.

Looked at from the point of view of the subsequent period of transformation, the premodern experiences of Japan and Russia made them to an important degree receptive to radically new foreign influences. They prepared them to accept leadership of a centralized administrative system embracing large populations, and in the Russian case numerous peoples in a vast territory; they accustomed them to accumulating exceptional savings from current production; they demonstrated the advantages of channeling large amounts of resources into cities; and, finally, they familiarized them with educational institutions designed to perpetuate a growing body of knowledge and a complex system of values. Furthermore, the state of their governments was such that they were not overwhelmed by contacts with modernized peoples. Thus, these internal social developments prior to the 1860's provided a basis for radically increased coordination and control—a basis relatively invulnerable to the other accompanying changes—and they resulted in a population with skills, attitudes, and experiences relatively receptive to the new demands encountered as modernization began.

Most other latecomers to the process have lacked most or all of these preconditions, factors we think were strategic for the subsequent process of modernization. Some had not experienced a period of independent borrowing from a foreign model, but had instead retained a fierce pride in deeply rooted beliefs that they saw as superior to all foreign influences. Some had not known independent rule with elaborate systems of administration, or possessed only nominally centralized bureaucracies that, in fact, did not penetrate deeply into the countryside or control a large amount of national production. Some did not have high levels of commercial production and village crafts specializing for distant markets. Some were not under pressure to find new sources of revenue to meet needs in the central cities, as Japan and Russia were to support their elites circulating between local areas and cities. Some lacked an educational system capable of staffing an increasingly bureaucratized administration. By singling out factors that seem to have been of help in the subsequent modernization of Japan and Russia, but which were absent in most nonmodernized societies, we can improve our understanding of what must be done during the transitional period to make up for the lacking elements.

Among latecomers slow to modernize, China stands out for the precocious achievement of some of the traits identified as strategic in the premodern experiences of Japan and Russia. For that reason we have paid particular attention in the international comparisons to explaining what was different about China. With regard to each of the five headings in terms of which preconditions have been discussed, we have drawn attention to distinctive similarities of Japan and Russia not shared by China. At the same time we should be aware that until the eighteenth century China was politically unified in ways other countries were not, and that while basically closed classes may have spurred the achievement ethic in Japan and Russia, an open class system in China led to a high development of the achievement ethic. In addition to the factors already mentioned, Chinese premodern development encountered unique problems of scale. With eight to fourteen times the population of Japan and Russia during the century before the 1860's, China encompassed vast regional variations and multicentered commercial networks. This diversity allowed more outlets for achievement outside home areas, but it also inhibited the penetration of new patterns. Overextended central control over this enormous mass probably reduced coordination and stifled initiative at the very time that opposite forces prevailed in Japan and Russia.

International Context

The comparison of Russia and Japan suggests that their historic experience of borrowing extensively from influential foreign models, without loss of national identity, was important in facilitating the acceptance of modern knowledge. Although the Muscovite and the Tokugawa regimes were essentially hostile to the modernized countries—the Tokugawa well into the nineteenth century—the leaders of both societies were well aware of and not averse to the precedents in their histories of large-scale borrowing from abroad. Byzantine and Chinese influences were sufficiently all-embracing to exert a considerable impact on various aspects of social structure. In the modern era Russia and Japan turned to the West for new developments in science and technology, initially as a means of defending their institutional heritage, and only later as a basis for fundamental transformation of their societies.

It is significant that the European countries were similarly open to foreign influences. The rediscovery of the classical predisposition to intellectual curiosity that characterized the renaissance in Europe was the first essential step in the inauguration of the modern era.

For all nonmodernized peoples the horizons of the possible have been limited and close to hand. For the firstcomers to modernization there was a gradual expansion of these horizons, but for the late-comers these are thrust open abruptly. It is at once a casket of jewels and a true Pandora's box.

Elsewhere the leaders of societies were less prepared to borrow from foreign models. China is an outstanding example of this resistance to the influence of the scientific and technological revolution. Political leadership in China was in the hands of scholar officials who had a vested interest in maintaining the classical Chinese culture. When they were confronted with the technological expertise of the powerful nineteenth-century countries, they reacted with a marked ethnocentrism, influenced by their confidence in traditional Chinese culture. The integrity of Chinese culture in a sense mattered more to them than the integrity of Chinese power.

A similar reluctance to borrow from Europe also characterized the leaders of the Ottoman Empire. Islam's antipathy to innovation based on foreign models was enhanced by the success of Ottoman statecraft. From the fourteenth to the seventeenth centuries this statecraft expanded the empire's position in Europe at the expense of Christian peoples perceived as infidels inherently inferior to Moslems. Later political and intellectual leaders gradually overcame their sense of innate superiority and became curious about the modern West, but it was not until the twentieth century that modern-minded leaders came to full ascendancy in Turkey.

Looking backward at the intense feelings of national pride and at the times of suspicion of foreigners present in Japan and Russia during the past half century, we note that the peoples of these countries were prepared to borrow intensively but under their own steam and at their own pace. Japan as long ago as the seventh century began with an unprecedented effort to model its institutions after those of China, and it ended the premodern era with a self-imposed sentence of solitary confinement. Correspondingly, Russia borrowed extensively from Byzantium, and Peter I implanted the modern bureaucratic procedures of his day. During the transitional period the script was being replayed in a modern guise. Japan began with a new wave of wide-ranging borrowing, and ended with a call for the "co-prosperity" of East Asia under Japanese hegemony; Russia changed its approach to borrowing from abroad after the revolution, seeking rather autarky and the development of an independent socialist bloc.

Political Structure

Policies of administrative consolidation and integration likewise had deep historic roots in Japan and Russia, perhaps even more than in the early modernizing Western societies. Both Japan and Russia had known a long historic continuity as independent, integrated states, and by the nineteenth century their governments had developed an impressive capacity to mobilize skills and resources on both a regional and a national scale. The role of ruling houses was strengthened with mystical and theocratic claims, but since in Japan actual administration was delegated to others this imperial aura mattered chiefly for its future utility in unification. Japan's baronial divisions in Tokugawa times did not conceal impressive steps toward political and economic centralization in which a sizable service force gained experience in the arts of practical administration. In both Japan and Russia, stable authoritarian political systems were without major challenge by autonomous interest groups. In both societies important regional centers of power survived, but the existence of uniform and integrated political hierarchies within those regional structures suggested the possibility of early and effective unification. Above all, in the case of both Japan and Russia, loyalty to hierarchy over and beyond family interest or local interests was taken for granted.

This precedence of outside loyalties is not generally the case in relatively nonmodernized societies. Before the modern era, only the presence of charismatic leaders or the actual use of power has placed more remote interest above much more localized and, in the last analysis, family-based concerns. In the premodern world, political structures with the capabilities Japan and Russia showed were rare, and it is probably most appropriate to look to the absolutisms of early modern Europe for analogous situations in which monarchs advanced central rule with the aid of secular and increasingly professional bureaucracies. But it is also probable that in important respects these European political systems were less centralized and less independently legitimized than those of Japan and Russia. In any case, however, it is also true that early modernizers required less centralization because their changes took place over a longer time span. England may even have required certain laissez-faire characteristics that would have been detrimental in later modernizers.

The European monarchs had to contend with local authorities and often with clerical power, and did so by allying with rural gentry and urban merchant interests that soon constituted new limitations on their powers. In Japan the institutional power of the Buddhist temples had been broken by the late sixteenth-century leaders in the unification effort, and in Russia that of the Orthodox Church was absorbed by the theocratic claims of the throne. Commercial and merchant power in Japan, though considerable, was never dignified with independent or legal rights under the Confucian and samurai codes of values, and in autocratic Russia it relied upon the protection of the state. As a result, both the Japanese and Russian governments were relatively free from limitations imposed by privileged strata, and able to pursue policies called for by the national interest as they perceived that interest. By the nineteenth century they were also able to achieve high levels of conformity with relatively low levels of coercion.

China, particularly during its last dynasties, was a centralized bureaucratic empire. Nevertheless, in several respects there was less control over the distribution of power and resources in China than in Japan or Russia. Tax revenues were collected without adequate administrative guidelines, central government controls did not penetrate to the village level, and bureaucratic structures were not revised in response to the growth of commerce and the drastic increases in population. The Chinese administrative system was also perceived as cyclical in nature, so that the state of disarray to which it had fallen by the late nineteenth century was presumed to be amenable to time-tested reforms intended to reinstate virtuous government. China's size and relatively diffuse administrative structure also operated to limit the perception and impact of the foreign threat.

During the transitional period the Japanese and Russian governments maintained tight villagewide controls while strengthening central power at the expense of regional forces. The roots of these transitional political controls can be traced back to stable and autonomous village institutions of the premodern periods responsive to outside directives and to the diverse state powers that were concentrated at regional and central levels and could be converted to more highly concentrated national powers. The lesson that might be drawn from these experiences is that a country that succeeds in the conversion from decentralized village autonomy and local self-sufficiency to a system of more centralized power has a valuable foundation for modernization. In most countries enormous efforts have had to be expended in unification and in the extension of new techniques of control and coordination to local levels. The newly needed degrees of coordination and control must first cause and then survive the demise of the previously more decentralized forms.

Economic Growth

By premodern standards, Japan and Russia also shared in certain unusual features of production and accumulation. Both had high and increasing amounts of per capita agricultural production, although in Russia this fact was not a sign of much improvement in productivity per acre. In Japan rising per capita figures were a result of high productivity per unit of land together with a long period of population stability. Increased regional specialization and the spread of nonagricultural pursuits were factors in the overall growth of per capita national production before the 1860's. In Russia land yields were lower, but population densities were also much lower. As in Japan rising output was funneled into a considerable growth of domestic trade, but unlike Japan into foreign trade as well.

The accumulation of goods for long-distance commerce can be divided into two forms in each country. Most domestic trade in Russia originated with either the gentry or directly with the peasants, and in Japan with either artisans and merchants providing for the needs of urban-based samurai in exchange for their rice or currency stipends or directly with the peasants. In comparison with other premodern countries, a good deal of the agricultural production reached the market. The high rate of outflow from villages for premodern times was achieved partly by mobilizing the elite (gentry or samurai) and groups of merchants to reorganize the flow of local commerce, to take a more active part in generating that commerce, and to stimulate direct peasant participation in commercial pursuits. Increased taxes and urban expenses had stimulated the development of various methods for pumping much of the rural surplus out of the villages.

Methods of commerce evolved in Japan and Russia resembled those that had previously appeared in England and France. For instance, the beginning of the decline of small periodic markets within relatively urbanized regions of both Japan and Russia occurred within about a century of the same phenomenon in England and France. In other countries, such as China, it was not until the transitional period that the flow of commerce began to bypass such marketing centers.

Furthermore, new factory and craft enterprises in rural settlements and in small central places point to a stage of decentralization of artisan activities and the earliest industrial forms in Japan and Russia from about the mid- or late eighteenth century. Again, a comparable stage can be identified as having begun somewhat earlier in late premodern England and France. Most likely the dynamism of expanding commerce enabled local crafts to serve a much wider market. Other societies that were to become latecomers appear to have lacked this dynamism.

Social Interdependence

The clearest indications of an evolutionary developmental structure are seen in the measures of social integration. Among these measures most attention has so far been given to patterns of settlement.

Premodern countries range from small-scale entities without any cities, to societies with a network of administrative centers but without separate periodic marketing settlements, to large-scale societies densely packed with a network of cities and small marketing places. Comparisons of the rate of expansion of these urban networks reveal an unusual dynamism in Japan and Russia, which were surprisingly similar in their development from century to century over 1,000 years. Japan preceded Russia by about two centuries in the initial establishment of cities (seventh versus ninth) and in the initial proliferation of periodic markets (thirteenth versus fifteenth). In the final centuries, however, Russia's premodern network was completed more quickly. With the growth of St. Petersburg only 100 years after Edo's development, Japan's lead narrowed to only one century, and by 1800 the two countries were about even as daily commerce gradually began to replace periodic markets in advanced regions.

By the late eighteenth century, Japan and Russia were the two largest societies that: 1) exceeded the average level of urbanization in the world, 2) had sharp rural-urban dichotomies, and 3) boasted large circulating elites. West European countries were not as populous, and more populous countries lacked the other three characteristics. Related to these patterns of settlement was the existence of exceptional service nobilities, relatively skilled populations, and delimited impersonal relationships based on achievement.

In these respects Japan and Russia again resemble England and France, but stand apart from China and the half of the world that was less urbanized than China. During the three centuries before the 1860's, Japan and Russia had shown unusual dynamism in many aspects of social interdependence. They had surpassed China, which as late as the sixteenth century was probably the world leader in urban development, and had revealed many of the signs of rapid change seen in England and France. The rise of the new city of Edo as the world's largest and of the new city of Saint Petersburg as one of Europe's foremost signify the break with the spatial patterns of the past.

Among late eighteenth-century societies, those of Japan and Russia had an unusual concentration of people in cities. In Japan a large number of the samurai were required to alternate residence in the national administrative center and in their local castle town. In Russia uniform governance of local areas at the county level was accompanied by free migration of the gentry into the two national urban centers. The emergence of a large circulating elite came later than in Japan, but it was likewise based on an impressive capacity to support distant cities. In turn it stimulated the diffusion of patterns typical of the largest cities to the country as a whole. In both nations the presence of a large circulating elite was evidence of an advanced stage of development and an exceptional capacity for control and coordination.

Many of the factors of social interdependence singled out as distinctive similarities between Japan and Russia required the presence of circulating service nobilities. Large cities thrived through their demands for consumption and villages increased outflow in response to their requirements; in the national centers and in local areas these elite figures shaped new social conditions. Other societies such as China lacked a disciplined, mobilized elite on this scale. Indeed, Russia never overtook Japan in the proportion of urban residents and elite members and in the disciplined service offered by the samurai.

Knowledge and Education

Japan and Russia stand out also in various aspects of education. In both countries new schools were founded initially as an effort to expand the education of the service nobility. Accompanying the development of a meritocracy, members of the service nobility were expected to demonstrate their abilities first by becoming literate and then by carrying on their education in specified ways. In the case of Russia valuable contributions in science and literature testify that education had caught on among the elite by the mid-nineteenth century. In the case of Japan, schooling spread to other social classes, resulting in an exceptional rate of literacy. Although the most striking changes in Russia occurred at the highest levels of education, as in the introduction of the academy system, and in Japan at the lowest levels through the spread of village schools, both countries were exceptionally innovative.

Among the early modernizing countries, important educational developments also had preceded modernization. In China, by contrast, where many years of study had long been required for entry into the elite of degree-holders, stability in the form and content of education, and possibly a proportional decline in popular education, seem to have characterized the final centuries before contact with Western modernizers.

We have taken twin paths to our comparative conclusions. The first path deals with the general problem of social control. Greater receptivity to foreign models and less vulnerable bases for coordination and control in Japan and Russia are both seen as related to unusual mechanisms of social control. The Russians and Japanese generated an unusual set of political insulations. Each had, in common with all relatively nonmodernized societies, allocations of power and responsibility that were extremely decentralized, and, by preference, life at the local levels was concentrated on maximizing local degrees of self-sufficiency. Yet each country also managed to construct a system in which the devices of coordination and control at centralized levels were relatively impervious to changes in either the kinship or village structure. In the case of the Japanese this system was a peculiar form of "feudalism," one that lacked the intervening range of landed vassals characteristic of other feudalisms, and one that usually fixed loyalties directly on a single overlord who was prominent and far away. In the case of the Russians this system was a central administrative network with semiprofessional role players rather than intervening vassals, and with loyalty focused directly on the system itself rather than on intervening allegiances. Both administrative systems were reinforced by an overwhelming loyalty to and focus on a state capable of providing the growing requirements for coordination and control necessary if modernization was to take place quickly and effectively. Above all, both had systems that were remarkably invulnerable to the shifting roles of family and village authority that always accompany changes in the direction of modernization. Finally, in Japan and to a lesser extent in Russia there were leaders who seemed to understand these conditions and who took explicit advantage of them.

This state of affairs with regard to the structure of control is exceedingly uncommon in the history of nonmodernized societies. For most nonmodernized societies, family loyalties and village loyalties are transmitted only link by link to more central focuses, if, indeed, the occasion for such transmissions ever takes place at all. All such systems are especially vulnerable to the erosion of the patterns of coordination and control over families and villages, and in the process of modernization the families and villages themselves are always disintegrated. All latecomers bereft of these conditions for easy centralization go through the revolutionary (in terms of their pre-existing social structure) establishment of a basis for radically increased coordination and control. It is exactly this type of political integration that seems to be occurring successfully in China at the present time; it is still very far from being achieved in most of the other latecomers. Japan and Russia are illuminating precisely because they point to a set of conditions that no other latecomers have achieved or are likely to achieve without a transitional period that itself seems to be a special function of the travail of modernization.

The second path to our conclusions, which directs attention to certain preconditions advantageous for modernization, is based on the notion that the development of productive techniques, commerce, cities, and a skilled and literate population in premodern societies generally follows a linear path of evolution. The ability to extract resources from villages, the development of mobilized elites, and the institution of educational innovations visible by the nineteenth century in Japan and Russia were the culmination of centuries of change. These two countries had not been exceptional in commercialization, urbanization, or literacy as late as the sixteenth century, yet by the nineteenth century they were probably closer to West European standards than any other nonmodernized societies. Their capacity for a modernizing transformation was derived from various preconditions that were signs of the advanced premodern societies found in Japan and Russia by the nineteenth century.

Part II

Transformation

From the 1860's to the 1940's Japan and Russia underwent the fundamental transformation from premodern to modernized societies. Our discussion of this long and complex period is concerned primarily with a consideration of how these countries achieved their goals in this process. By way of contrast, it is also necessary to suggest reasons why similar transformations did not happen in other countries. A brief attempt is also made, based on the similarities in the transitional experiences of these two countries as compared with other countries, to consider the extent to which the processes and policies characteristic of Japan and Russia have more general implications. Although the identification of requirements for modernization, that is, what must be done to bring it about, is not as novel an undertaking as the identification of preconditions for modernization in Part 1, this comparative study of Japan and Russia in the act of transformation should provide the basis for a new approach to the study of the modernization process.

If we start with the notion that societies on the eve of initial modernization vary in the degree to which preconditions for modernization are present, it follows that the societies in which these preconditions are more developed are better able to realize the conditions necessary for modernization, and especially those of allocation and control. In addition to indicating the strategic similarities between Japan and Russia in this period, it is also desirable to show how these similarities relate to others of the premodern period and to ask whether, in the absence of some or all of the preconditions in other countries, they might be realized through other means or in other forms.

From this conceptualization of the relation between preconditions and requirements of modernization, it follows that two basic processes of innovation are at work in the period of transformation: conversion—the adaptation of qualities already present in the premodern period; and borrowing—the introduction of new institutions and values from other societies. Any specific case of large-scale change is likely to involve both processes. Conversion occurs in a context of newly created or borrowed patterns, and borrowing occurs in a context of existing patterns. Where the chief preconditions for modernization were present, as in Japan and Russia, conversion could be relied on to a great extent. In the absence of certain preconditions, the opportunities for conversion were lessened and the corresponding necessity for borrowing was heightened. The cases of Japan and Russia are instructive because substantial elements of the premodern patterns were convertible to or served as a basis for the transition to modernization. Their histories are likely to be less relevant to nations without such preconditions, through even here a study of the relationship between the preconditions and requirements for transformation of these two latecomers should be useful as an illustration of the complexity of the interconnection between conversion and borrowing.

Though the emphasis up to this point has been on continuities with the past, it is well to keep in mind that in general modernization does not come about through sudden revolutions in social relationships. The most dramatic transformations are caused primarily not by the conversion of existing relationships but rather by the introduction of new relationships. The major effect on existing relationships is frequently a function of the fact that the introduction of new relationships alters the context in which the old relationships operated. For example, the most revolutionary changes do not ordinarily occur by virtue of the direct conversion of family relationships on a farm. They take place principally through the introduction of new forms of employment, usually urban employment. The opportunity people see of working in these new contexts gives them degrees of freedom from the old dependencies and thereby shatters the ability of their elders to control their behavior. The existence of alternative forms of employment on relatively objective grounds is the revolutionizing force, not the direct conversion of the conditions of work on a given farm plot.

This development of new contexts holds true in every sphere of social behavior save one, government. In government a direct conversion of relationships from old to new must occur. The government must develop a new kind of central coordination and control with regard to social mobilization for the people as a whole. Thus, the one sphere par excellence in which there is a built-in strain toward revolution under modernizing conditions is the governmental sphere. In very few instances are latecomers to modernization capable of reaching the degree of organization needed for the new social processes, let alone the degree of organization needed to carry out a revolutionizing of the governmental sphere itself without the loss of stability and control. Here there are also important contrasts between the Japanese and the Russian experience. The problem of social control, which was maintained with unusual continuity in Japan, has special relevance for the Bolshevik Revolution, and it is one of the recurrent themes in the chapters that follow on the period of transformation.

Chapter Eight

INTERNATIONAL CONTEXT

THE EXPANSIVE INFLUENCE of the Western countries that had pioneered the scientific and technological revolution presented a critical challenge to Japan and Russia after the 1860's. It was a challenge to which they responded by drawing extensively on Western institutional models. The revolutionary innovations inaugurated by the Meiji Restoration (1868) and the Great Reforms (1860) marked the beginning of rapid modernization in both Japan and Russia.

Some close parallels obtain between Japan and Russia in regard to their nineteenth-century response to Western military challenges, the process by which they sought to reconstruct values and institutions on the basis of European models, their perception of the particular adaptability of German and Austrian institutions to their needs, and their extensive reliance on Western technology. Also, in the years between the world wars both countries saw the international system as essentially hostile to their interests, and were inclined to associate with and to draw assistance from a similarly alienated Germany—Russia particularly in the 1920's, Japan in the 1930's.

There were also striking differences in the impact on Japan and Russia of the wars in which they participated. In both the Russian-Japanese War and the First World War, Japan emerged as a victor with heightened prestige and a confirmation of its policies of cautious reform at home and expansion abroad. In 1905 and 1917 Russia was defeated, however, and each defeat was followed by revolution. That of October–November 1917 was more radical than any in history in the changes it sought to achieve. During this period Japan, by contrast, experienced a remarkable continuity of elite leadership. In consequence, especially for those influenced by the Marxist-Leninist world view, Japan and Russia came to be seen as having antagonistic "capitalist" (or, later, "fascist") and "socialist" economic and social systems.

Western Influence on Domestic Reforms

The defeat of Russia in the Crimean War (1853–1856) had consequences similar to America's successful demands for the opening of Japan to foreign trade (1853–1854): it upset the existing balance of power within the ruling elite. Within a few years reform programs were adopted that borrowed Western institutions that had been developed after the 1600's under the impact of the scientific and technological revolution. The change was less abrupt and the reforms were less drastic in Russia because its institutions and values had already followed Western models from the time of Peter. The much more radical changes undertaken in Japan were facilitated by its relative distance from the centers of Western military power, the weakness of its East Asian neighbors, and the absence of a direct military threat.

The timing, nature, and consequences of the humiliation of the two countries at the hands of the technologically more advanced Western states were remarkably similar in form but considerably different in substance. The process of adapting domestic institutions to the standards of performance developed in the West had been national policy in Russia from the beginning of the eighteenth century, and as a result Russia had become a major participant in international relations as a European state. Russia's role in the defeat of Napoleon and its relative stability during the revolutions of 1830 and 1848 in Western Europe had given it a sense of strength and self-confidence, and it was natural that the influence of bureaucrats and public figures who favored the status quo outweighed that of potential reformers. The defeat in the Crimea was a relatively minor setback in terms of Russia's international position. Nonetheless, this demonstration of Russian weakness had the effect of tipping the domestic political balance in favor of those who demanded a more thoroughgoing reconstruction of Russian institutions along Western lines. Without political violence and through the manipulation of existing institutions and procedures, the forces that had struggled for reform with only modest success in the first half of the century came to dominate the political scene.

Japan did not suffer a military defeat in 1854, but the failure of the faltering shogunate to prevent the opening of Japan to trade led ultimately to the collapse of Tokugawa rule in 1868. The new government was dominated by young samurai who understood that Japan would be at the mercy of the West if it could not match its technology and who committed their own leadership position to the speedy acquisition of national strength. The Japanese reforms represented a sharper break with continuity than the Russian because Japan's prior contact with Western influence had been limited and tenuous. Yet the Meiji decision, though compressed into a very few years, had been anticipated by the turn of events during the last decade of Tokugawa rule after the opening of the ports in 1859. In the 1860's the shogunate and several of the han had sent student groups to the West; they had hired a number of foreign experts; they had utilized as learning missions the embassies they sent to the West to ratify treaties; and, in its last years, the shogunate had turned to the France of the Second Empire for military, technological, and organizational assistance.

In both countries the challenge of a more developed West was met by looking to European models as the basis for change. In Russia it was an accustomed road to reform. In Japan it was an experience for which the only precedent lay in relations with China a thousand years earlier. For Russia, the more immediate precedents had been those developed by Peter I, and involved the appointment of government missions to study those foreign models deemed to be most appropriate to specific Russian needs. Japan's approach to Europe was to some degree made legitimate by the memory of its earlier relations with China; its rejection of China in the Meiji period, however, was facilitated by the cultural nationalism of the eighteenth century. Japan's growing interest in its history and tradition had produced an awareness in the popular consciousness that the nation had moved in very different directions since the seventh century from those of the Middle Country. Advocates of centralization and of a more open society ("rule by those with ability") could cite Chinese as well as Western examples, however, to argue that Japan was out of step with everybody.

In both Russia and Japan, the principal institutional models came from Central Europe. The examples of the German and Austrian bureaucratic empires seemed to be more adaptable to Russia and Japan than those of France or Britain; as "late modernizers" within a European context, they had developed military strength on the basis of central controls. By the 1880's the success of a Germany that was looming as the dominant power in Europe gave it unique prestige as the most appropriate model to follow. The terms of the

Russian emancipation act of 1861 were based primarily on the Austrian agrarian reforms of 1848, the juridical reforms of 1864 followed general European principles of jurisprudence, and the army reform of 1874 followed German precedents. The political and economic reforms sponsored by Witte and his colleagues at the turn of the century—including the October Manifesto of 1905, which established a limited form of parliamentary government—drew primarily on Austrian models.

Japan made use of a wider range of Western institutions than did Russia. American expertise was used in early educational reforms and for the development of the north, where Hokkaido was settled to provide a firm limit to Russian pressure. French advice was used in planning centralized banking, and English influence predominated in naval and maritime affairs and in industry and railroads. But when it came to military and political institutions, Japanese leaders too found German and Austrian models particularly congenial. Like their Russian counterparts, they also sought to adapt these models to their own society and tradition, and the final product seldom matched the expectations of the foreign advisers.

Both countries relied extensively on foreign personnel, but they employed them in contrasting ways. Russia, as a European state, could readily assimilate advisers from the West and many became citizens and permanent residents. An untold number of foreigners entered Russian service in public and private capacities in the eighteenth and nineteenth centuries. Many top officials were also Baltic Germans and Swedes from Finland—Central European in education and outlook even though they were citizens of the empire. Westerners in this broad sense not only served as advisers but occupied the highest government positions for long stretches of time. It has been estimated that of some 2,900 persons holding the highest government positions in the period 1700–1917, more than 900 had names of Western and Central European origin.

No comparable phenomenon occurred in Japan. There was no question of the assimilation of Europeans there, but foreign employees were expected and encouraged to depart after they had fulfilled their tasks. During the Meiji period some 2,000 foreigners were hired, mainly in the first three decades after 1870. English was the principal language used by advisers of all nationalities, except in the military. After the 1880's most advisers were privately employed. Generally, they remained for a relatively short time and they were never nationalized, for their expertise was rapidly internalized by the Japanese. This experience serves to underline once again the importance of insularity and homogeneity in the Japanese experience. In the long run the thousands of Japanese who were sent overseas as students were far more important. This tide was at first strongly toward America and England, but the German language and experience gradually became more important.

The two countries also relied heavily on Western technology in this transformation period. A modern Russian industry had been developed for some two centuries; in the eighteenth century it had attained considerable advances in certain fields, but by the mid-nineteenth it was no match for the West. The techniques of mining and metalworking, and the machinery for the electrical and chemical industries, were brought in for the most part by foreign entrepreneurs, who also contributed the initial managerial skills. Russian businessmen retained control over these developments with state support, however, and by the eve of the First World War the new technology had been largely internalized.

In Japan's case the initial reliance on foreign technology was far greater, because modern industry was virtually unknown in the 1860's and an entire industrial plant had to be built. The Japanese reliance on the West was almost total at the start, but the process of learning was faster than in Russia, and by 1914 production and management were more exclusively in native hands. In contrast with Russia, where by 1900 about one-third of the investment in industry and almost one-half of the capital in banks was foreign, Western capital played a relatively small role in the industrialization of Japan.

The Age of Imperialism

In the nineteenth century success in war was regarded by some as a more valid test of modernization than civic achievements. Both Japan and Russia placed a very high priority on the development of land and naval forces. The tax burdens that militarization imposed on both populations were heavy, and also comparable. Part of the challenge each faced was provided by the awareness of mutually conflicting interests. As competitors, Russia and Japan appeared to contemporaries in the nineteenth century to be unevenly matched. In the second half of the nineteenth century Russia expanded its vast territories by acquiring Amur and the Maritime Province from China (1858–1860), the Caucasus (1859), the khanates of Bokhara and Khiva (1864–1865), and from China (1896) the right to build the Chinese Eastern Railway across Manchuria and, two years later (1898), the connecting South Manchurian Railway to Port Arthur, which it had leased for a naval base. The next step was a struggle with Japan for the control of Korea.

Japan, for its part, had been expanding its territory by annexing the Ryukyu (1874) and Ogasawara (1875) islands, and by negotiating a boundary treaty (1875) that gained the Kurile Islands for Japan and assigned Sakhalin to Russia. Japan opened Korea to trade in 1876 by gunboat methods modeled closely on those originally used against Japan by the West, and in 1895 it gained European recognition as a modern state by defeating China and annexing Taiwan. In 1894 Japan had finally been able to end the humiliation of its "unequal treaties" with the West, but her inability to retain her war gains in Port Arthur and Dairen against the disapproval and "Triple Intervention" of Russia, Germany, and France rankled. Shortly afterward Russia secured the South Manchurian concessions for itself, and after the Boxer Rebellion of 1900 in China its armies occupied all of Manchuria and threatened Korea. Japan's alliance with England in 1902 marked its acceptance for the first time as a partner with a European state, and permitted the Japanese leaders to turn their attention to the Russian threat in Manchuria and Korea.

The inequality of Japan and Russia as they faced each other across the Yellow Sea at the turn of the century was more apparent than real. Japan was only a fraction of Russia in size, with an area of 165,000 square miles and a population of 46 million, as compared with Russia's 8,660,000 square miles and 129 million. Its sovereignty had been limited by the unequal treaties with the Western powers which guaranteed extraterritoriality for their citizens; even by the schedule worked out in 1894, Japan was limited in the duties it could levy in imports and exports until 1911. But the fact that the Russian-Japanese War was fought close to Japanese territorial waters, and that the Japanese had better equipment and better led and better motivated forces more than compensated for other inequalities. Within sixteen months after its initial attack on Port Arthur (February 1904), Japan had defeated the Russian forces and sunk much of the Russian Navy. At the 1905 Treaty of Portsmouth Japan received the southern half of Sakhalin Island, Russian holdings in South Manchuria, and a free hand in Korea. Five years later it annexed Korea.

The domestic impact of war on the two countries reflected the nature of its outcome. In Japan the victory served to justify the policies that had given first priority to national strength, and thus encouraged the trend toward a vigorous role on continental Asia. Within Russia its effect was similar to that of the defeat in the

Crimean War in that the government's failure to meet a foreign test led to a weakening of the forces favoring the established order. Once again the essential lesson was that Russia was not keeping up with its rivals, and that more drastic defeats would lie ahead if it did not make greater efforts to industrialize and improve education and the public welfare. For most Japanese the victory over Russia, like the earlier one over China, was proof of the effectiveness of modern, and especially constitutional, institutions. In Russia the educated public recognized this need, but the emperor and many of his leading officials did not. More directly and more violently than in the 1850's, the defeat in 1905 led to a revolution that could only be satisfied by political concessions. The concessions were limited, however, and were to a substantial degree withdrawn within a few years. The Russian commitment to constitutionalism was never as voluntary or as full as that of the Japanese leaders, in part, no doubt, because Russia's inequality with the West had never been as marked.

The First World War affected Japan and particularly Russia much more profoundly, but again in markedly different ways. Both countries fought Germany as the principal enemy, but not as allies and for very different reasons. Japanese leaders saw the European conflict as an opportunity to gain ascendancy in East Asia by displacing Germany's influence there, and in this ploy they were successful. In the Twenty-One Demands on China in 1915 they tried to consolidate their hold on Manchurian and Chinese concessions, and after the fall of the Russian Empire in 1917 they succumbed to the temptation to score new advances to the north. Yet of more lasting importance was the fact that the wartime interlude of freedom from European competition allowed Japan to make economic advances that produced dramatic growth in industry and accelerated social change. With the passing of the Meiji emperor (1912) and the first generation of modernizing leaders, however, there was no longer as cohesive a pool of administrative leadership. Japan began to experience divided councils of civil and military, political party, and business-industrial interests.

The war that brought prosperity to Japan led to collapse in Russia, and when elements of the army mutinied in Saint Petersburg early in 1917 the emperor was persuaded to abdicate. In its nine-month existence, the successor Provisional Government enacted a series of reforms based on European liberal models, but its determination to continue the war effort, using the shattered army and bureaucracy that survived the empire, prompted its overthrow. As conditions became increasingly chaotic in the course of 1917 the

Bolsheviks under the leadership of Lenin seized the opportunity to gain power. Opinions differ regarding the relative importance of the war effort and domestic problems in bringing down the empire, and shortly thereafter the Provisional Government, but few deny that the strains of the war were a key factor in generating the revolution.

The breakdown of the European order provided Russia and Japan with new opportunities to pursue independent policies, although with singularly different aims and results. The war greatly undermined the influence of the European governments in East Asia, replacing it with that of the United States. Japanese policy for the next two decades was to be dominated by its efforts to adjust to these new conditions, and in this sense changes in the international environment had a determining effect on Japanese development. Ultimately, surging Chinese nationalism came to seem a threat to Japanese interest in Manchuria and persuaded the Japanese military to advocate and implement policies of continental advance.

The new Russian leaders also saw in the failure of the European order an opportunity for new policies, and Lenin's analysis of the revolutionary situation in 1917 was strongly colored by the international environment. Not only was his Marxist ideology of West European origin and concerned with the worldwide development of societies, but Lenin's interpretation of Marxism was one that related events in Russia directly to the European-wide crisis. His belief in the possibility of revolution in Russia was based on the assumption that it would be part of a general European revolution resulting from the war. When in the end the revolution succeeded in Russia but failed to materialize elsewhere, Lenin concluded that the proletariat from the "bourgeois" countries had at least prevented their governments from undertaking a successful counter-revolutionary intervention in Russia. This question soon became academic, but it is significant that Lenin would in all likelihood not have undertaken to overthrow the Provisional Government had he not believed that the Russian Revolution would be part of a European-wide revolutionary movement championed by countries he considered to be at a more advanced stage of development than Russia.

The Interwar Period

The relation of Japan and Russia to the international environment in the interwar period was marked primarily by contrasts. The

Soviet Union developed in relative isolation from the outside world, partly because of ostracism by its traditional partners in politics and trade, but also in considerable measure because it had to set its own house in order. The ravages of war, revolution, and civil strife had to be overcome before it could compete again in the international arena. Japan, on the other hand, came out of the war as a far more vigorous participant in international affairs. Soviet foreign trade declined drastically after 1917 and did not regain its prewar volume in the interwar period, whereas Japan's trade continued to expand rapidly even during the years of the Great Depression. In the peace settlement Japan acquired as mandates Germany's Pacific territories; it retained (until 1922) Germany's rights on China's Shantung Peninsula, and it received, as one of the five great powers, a permanent seat on the Council of the League of Nations. Russia, however, lost extensive territories as a result of the war and did not participate in the establishment of the League.

Despite these differences, a few elements of similarity are apparent in this period. Both countries continued to depend extensively on foreign technology for their economic development. Japan's borrowing was essentially private, as individual enterprises sought to improve their position in the international market. The import of foreign technology in Russia was, by contrast, a matter of state policy. The fastest growing sectors of Soviet industry under its five-year plans relied heavily on American, German, and British technology acquired chiefly through technical assistance agreements between state enterprises and individual foreign companies.

Russia and Japan also continued to share to some extent an orientation toward Germany as a model for development. For Russia this was natural; Germany had been regarded in the early postrevolutionary years as the country most likely to lead Europe, including Russia, in the construction of socialism, and most Russian economists and engineers were trained in the German tradition. German was, in fact, the principal foreign language with which the new generation of Soviet technicians was familiar. The German wartime experience with economic planning also had a large influence on the economic views of Lenin and his successors. The Russian orientation toward Germany was further encouraged by the ostracism of the two countries, which caused them to seek each other's support. The conclusion of the Treaty of Rapallo in 1922 was a dramatic indication of this common interest, and it was followed by a rapid expansion of Russian-German trade. These years also saw secret military collaboration between the two countries under agreements that permitted Germany to evade its disarmament obligations by developing weapons on Russian soil in return for sharing its military technology with the Russians.

Japanese popular culture was more strongly influenced by the United States in this period, but in intellectual, medical, and technological realms German influence remained strong. Japan also came to share with Germany a frustration with the peace settlement —Japan because its desire for a statement of racial equality had not been met, and Germany because of the harsh terms of the Versailles Treaty. In 1922 the Washington Conference saw Great Britain terminate its alliance with Japan and join with the United States to limit Japanese naval strength. Henceforth, the United States and Great Britain would be the principal obstacles to Asian leadership for Japan. Two years later America's Oriental Exclusion Act greatly weakened the position of pro-Western circles in Japan. Despite marked differences in their domestic political systems in the 1930's, both Japan and Germany also saw the rise to influence of a "radical right" allied to the military. In both countries the traditional political parties gradually lost prestige, and new systems were established that looked toward total mobilization of national strength for an anticipated military solution to international problems. These were essentially separate and parallel developments, but they had roots in similar circumstances and found at least a symbolic common expression in the Anti-Comintern Pact signed by the two countries in 1936. This pact reflected not only their antagonism to communism but also, more generally, their discontent with the existing international order.

To a greater extent than before the First World War when the contacts had been political and military, Japan and Russia now also exercised an important influence on each other. Japan's leaders saw in the Russian Civil War an opportunity to reinforce the position of their country in East Asia, and until the consolidation of Soviet power made its position untenable they maintained an expeditionary force in Siberia between 1918 and 1922. The withdrawal of Japanese troops resulted in the establishment of diplomatic relations in 1925, but within a few years Japan's expansion into Manchuria again brought about a political confrontation. The Japanese military threat to the Soviet Far East was not matched by political or ideological influence, however, and the impressive development of the Japanese economy and society in the 1930's went largely unnoticed in the Soviet Union.

The reverse was not true. Marxism in general and the example of Soviet developments in particular played a substantial role in the thinking of radical critics in Japan. A Japanese Communist Party was founded in 1922, and Marxism-Leninism had a strong appeal among revolutionary students and intellectuals throughout the 1920's. Even so, communism did not sink deep roots in Japan, and both factionalism and police measures contributed to the decline of the movement in the 1930's.

On the eve of the Second World War, the immediate needs of national security proved to have more weight than two decades of strife. The Nazi-Soviet Pact was supplemented by conciliatory Russian moves toward Japan, despite two severe conflicts in 1938 and 1939 at points on the Manchurian-Soviet frontier. The Russian-Japanese neutrality treaty of 1941 served to protect their common frontier in East Asia while they concentrated their efforts in other directions. When Japan prepared to surrender in 1945 it hoped for Soviet mediation with its Anglo-American antagonists, but the Russians declared war instead. Active hostilities between the two countries were nevertheless limited to one week in 1945.

International Comparisons

From the 1860's to the 1940's the course of modernization in all parts of the world was profoundly affected by the preeminent role of the West European countries, by virtue of their level of political and economic achievement. Although Europe was seriously weakened and divided by the First World War, it retained an important position until 1945. This role of leadership served as a challenge to other peoples. The offshoots of Europe in North and South America and in Oceania received an unprecedented flow of immigrants from the Old World, and in some cases overtook and surpassed Europe in industrial productivity by the middle of the twentieth century. Many of the peoples of Asia and most of Africa submitted to European rule, and remained in a colonial status until after the Second World War. The Ottoman, Chinese, and Persian states, though weakened by Western pressure, survived until the First World War as independent polities and initiated programs of modernizing reforms after 1918. Siam and Afghanistan maintained a degree of freedom by balancing off rival pressures. Only Russia and Japan met the challenge of the more modern West by undertaking a thoroughgoing transformation of their political, economic, and social institutions. In doing so they forced their way into the front rank of industrial and military powers.

The humiliation of Russia in the Crimean War and of Japan over the enforced "opening" under Perry disrupted the relatively isolated and secluded elites of these two nations. Russia's defeat brought into positions of authority advocates of institutional change, and Japan's loss of countenance resulted in the overthrow of the Tokugawa government and its replacement by a samurai elite committed to modernization as a means to national strength. Both were processes of reactive, or defensive, modernization, but both moved well beyond the steps their leaders had initially thought of as desirable or necessary. This success made it possible for Japan and Russia to join their efforts to those of early modernizing nations in forcing their attentions on less developed neighbors. Russia played its part in crippling the Ottoman Empire and the Ch'ing Empire, and Japan played its part in the "opening" and closing of Korea and in the oppression of China after 1895.

These developments took place in a setting dominated by Western technology and imperialism. China was battered by a series of wars between 1839 and 1895 and all but disappeared as a political entity during the Boxer Rebellion in 1900. England completed its control over the Indian subcontinent, and Holland over the Indonesian archipelago. At the century's end, Africa too was divided among the European powers. Japan's response to these events was particularly sharp. Its leaders saw their country's independence threatened; they saw colonialism as contributing to ever greater strength for their rivals; and they became obsessed with the urgency of winning for themselves areas that might remain available. The international environment dictated the Japanese response.

The same environment also prompted Japan and Russia to take opposing roles in the alliance system on the eve of the First World War. The Russian move into Manchuria preceded the Anglo-Japanese alliance, but after Japan's victory over Russia in 1905 these tensions were gradually resolved in a series of agreements that culminated in the Russian-Japanese alliance of 1916. Japan's new power, and its drift into a position of adversary with the United States, caused Great Britain to seek to replace the Anglo-Japanese alliance with the Washington order of treaties. One of the reasons that structure failed was that it made no allowance for Russian participation.

The First World War destroyed the old system of alliances and most of the empires that had inspired it. Without the Russian alliance Japan tried to work out its own security in Northeast Asia, and without the English alliance it experimented with unilateral tactics in Republican China. In the 1920's both Japan and Russia sensed the international environment as unfriendly to them. The Russians were excluded from international councils. The Japanese found that the empire they had so recently acquired was now viewed with disapproval. Both tried to advance their interests in China, the Russians through establishment of a Communist Party and help to the Nationalist Government, the Japanese through support to anti-Nationalist warlords. Diplomatic relations between Japan and Russia were reestablished in 1925, but military leaders in both countries prepared for war. Japanese hard-liners pointed to the "Crisis of 1936" as a date when Soviet economic planning would have borne military fruit guaranteeing superiority.

The international environment of Japan and Russia, dominated as it was by the consciousness of isolation and second-class status, made a distinct contrast with the multi-state climate of most of the West, in which prior development of industry, secure membership in the bloc of "advanced countries," and access to raw materials produced radically different views. Germany, which had had to fight its way into the international order, provides some parallels, which perhaps help account for the attraction of its institutions for Japan and Russia. But even so, its central geographic position, international consciousness, and advanced intellectual role generated less of the alarm about the menace of the outside world that characterized Japanese and Russian thinking. The United States, which lacked neither security nor raw materials, provides an even greater contrast with Japan and Russia.

The Ottoman Empire's circle of predator states, on the other hand, was far more menacing than anything either Japan or Russia experienced, and its internal cohesion was also less. Its successive disasters and early disappearance as a multinational state reflected this hostile environment. China's environment was also less favorable than Japan's. The Western powers came sooner to China, their expectations were greater, and their control on its periphery was tighter. Ironically, the most troublesome of those powers for China proved to be Russia, which had territorial goals to the north, and Japan, which added new advantages for all the powers through the commercial and manufacturing privileges incorporated into the Shimonoseki Treaty of Peace in 1895, and then went on to develop territorial goals as well.

In the vast area of the world controlled by the imperialist powers, independent political response by other states was limited and the modern sectors that developed were usually complementary to and restrained by the imperialist powers themselves. The First World War saw the first strains in that system, however, and thereafter nationalist movements in the colonies profited from the growing anti-imperialist climate in the West.

As the influence of the European states waned in the wake of the world depression, the U.S.S.R. and Japan came to be recognized as the most likely candidates among the less developed states to achieve an advanced level of development. Again a world war proved to be the critical test of institutional vitality. Both the U.S.S.R., which won and had to generate its own institutional change over the next quarter century, and Japan, which lost and experienced another round of sweeping reforms under foreign guidance, survived the test to achieve an enhanced international status as modernizing societies.

The international environment in which Japan and Russia underwent transformation was thus characterized by the growing power and influence of the Western world. This influence brought with it the need for constant military preparedness and participation in the shifting alliances of the late imperialist period as both Japan and Russia struggled to free themselves from the disadvantages of being late starters in the international competition. Their struggle for position in countries along their borders found them relatively hindered by shortage of capital and disposed to require and demand preferential positions, a policy that brought them into conflict with the better financed trading giants of the Western world. What was special about Japan and Russia was the speed with which their leaders, responding to the Western model of fiercely defended sovereignty, concluded that special priority should be accorded military needs and the supporting strength that this priority required. Both countries quickly became pivotal units in alliances with the early modernizers of the West as well as competitors for foreign favor and protection, and both sought to advance their economic and political security through increased involvement with the nations on their borders.

Chapter Nine

POLITICAL STRUCTURE

THE POLITICAL HISTORY of Japan and Russia from the 1860's to the 1940's is dominated by themes of crisis, revolutionary innovation, and the conversion of older patterns to meet new needs. Fundamental change swept both systems as the two governments came to control the expenditure of increasing percentages of the total national product. Scores of institutions were created either on the foundation of old ones or by the introduction of foreign examples. All of these changes were effected with dazzling speed, and they altered the styles of public life almost beyond recognition.

Political life was transformed. In Russia the autocracy first became a European type of grand monarchy and then gave way to the first socialist state. In Japan the development from a parochial and decentralized realm to a centralized constitutional state occurred within the first two decades after 1870. Even though the new systems assumed dangerous and unstable forms in the 1930's, all the principal elements of the contemporary political order of Russia and Japan were present in each state by 1941. In both the changes proceeded in very different forms, sometimes so much so as to make all search for similarities seem strained. Yet important differences should not be allowed to obscure certain basic similarities.

In Japan the period of transformation began in 1868 with a series of fundamental reforms known as the Meiji Restoration. Designed as a means of achieving parity with Western powers according to the slogan "Rich country, strong military," the reforms ultimately embraced nearly every sphere of national life. Because Japan's prior experience with the West was more shallow than Russia's, some of these reforms—the adoption of the Western calendar, sending students to the West, the introduction of new types of clothing—

are analogous to the changes introduced by Peter the Great long before. But the proper comparison is with the Russian "Era of the Great Reforms" (1861–1873), with which they were also contemporaneous.

The scope of the Meiji reforms can be suggested by enumeration of the intentions made public in the "Charter Oath" of 1868, a document sufficiently comprehensive to be invoked again as justification for Japan's reforms after World War II. It incorporated five general subjects. The first was political centralization. Soon the several hundred baronies were placed under central rule and consolidated into seventy-five, then into fifty prefectures, and the top feudality was pensioned off. The oath contained a promise of "councils" and assurance that state matters would be decided on the basis of some general agreement. Social equality was a second issue. All Japanese were assured the opportunity to achieve their "aspirations," and class lines were soon restructured to disestablish the samurai, replace them with a commoner army, and provide the commoners with opportunities for education. Farmers received the dignity of family names and title to their lands. Learning was to be sought "throughout the world," and soon hundreds of students were overseas and numerous foreign teachers were in Japan. Government leaders traveled to the West on "learning missions." Finally, "absurd customs" of the past were to be abandoned, the impracticalities of feudal autonomy were to be eliminated, and the inefficiency of the feudal class and sumptuary legislation was to be terminated.

Russia's "Great Reforms" were less sweeping and innovative. But the entire servile population was emancipated in 1861–1864; new local assemblies (*zemstvos*) came into being, as in Japan; the court system was entirely revamped, the jury system introduced, and a legal profession brought into being to operate the new judicial apparatus; military institutions were reformed after German models; new regulations were introduced governing higher education; and new measures to encourage—and control—the dissemination of news and information were issued. The Meiji Diet preceded the Russian Duma by only sixteen years.

The Meiji reforms surpassed in their impact the Russian reforms of the same period, and can with justice be called "revolutionary." The Russian reforms followed a century and more of Western-oriented measures, and had simply to add new institutions to an existing pattern. Consequently, many earlier practices, though not legal bondage, were left intact and in some cases even strengthened. The Meiji pattern of institutions, crowned by the constitution, education rescript, and a civil code in the 1890's, constituted a synthesis that endured in most respects to 1945. Russian attempts between 1861 and 1917 to create a comparably durable synthesis, similarly congruent with the dominant political heritage, proved unsuccessful. The constitutional and parliamentary experimentation that occupied reformist leaders in both countries from the 1890's to the World War assumed an antiregime character in Russia, whereas in Japan it was for the most part supportive of the prevailing system. The Japanese synthesis gained in strength and became increasingly sacrosanct as education took hold: the attempted Russian synthesis, however, was subject to the criticism of the educated intelligentsia.

The October Revolution altered fundamentally the institutional forms and the social basis of politics in Russia. Marxism-Leninism sees the revolution as an event of transcendent importance not only for Russian history but for the history of all societies because it created the first socialist state and in so doing set a pattern other societies would inevitably have to follow. A new leadership group appeared with a strongly voluntarist form of Marxism that justified its efforts to serve as the agent of historical change by intervening in the process of modernization. This group exercised its power through institutions bearing little outward resemblance to earlier forms in Russia or, for that matter, to those of the developed nations of Western Europe. The October Revolution opened a deep gulf between subsequent developments in Russia and Japan.

Notwithstanding this break, the Japanese as well as the Russian state became preoccupied with the problem of creating new centers of authority in the late 1920's and 1930's. By that time the oligarchy that had dominated Japanese life during the half century of the Meiji era had died off, leaving a struggle for power among rival interests—a struggle from which the military eventually emerged triumphant. The revolution in Russia, meanwhile, had solved the question of authority de jure but not de facto. The rise of Joseph Stalin and his reconstituted Communist Party to a peak of totalitarian power was, to say the least, an effort to resolve this issue. Yet in neither Japan nor Russia did the solutions of the 1930's long outlast the lives of those who devised them.

Changing Conditions and Common Responses

Throughout this transformation period, certain general conditions came into being in both nations to which any government in power would have had to respond. In the first place, as has been described, both nations found themselves in an international environment in which isolation was virtually impossible and global involvement all but unavoidable. In this circumstance large military budgets prevailed throughout the period and gave the governments a leverage in the economy and a claim on loyalty that they might otherwise have lacked.

A second condition that defined the sphere in which both governments moved was the rise of industrialization and urbanization and their social consequences. These forces combined to increase vastly the tax base and to place the entire populaces of the two nations within the direct purview of public policy. The greater geographical concentration of the populations made new degrees of control possible and even necessary. Broader participation in and, the leaders hoped, assent to public decisions was also called for by the facts of the situation. Universal suffrage, proclaimed in Russia first by the Provisional Government and then by the Bolsheviks in 1917 and in Japan (for males) in 1925 was but one means of achieving this end.

Related to the rise of industry was the expansion of modern technology and its application to communications through railroads, and postal, telegraph and telephone systems. Both nations relied heavily on rail communications, but the compactness of its territory permitted Japan to have the better network. In both domestic telegrams per capita and number of telephones per capita, Japan's communication system was more advanced by 1914 than Russia's, growth rates in Japan being such that by 1939 it had approximately three times as many telephones and twice as many telegrams per capita as the U.S.S.R. Radio ownership and automobile travel showed similar and growing differentials.

Geography always played a crucial part in the priorities of these two nations, of course, but in the transformation period the far greater diversity of the population in the enormous area ruled by Russia intensified the need for an expanded communication network as an aid to national integration. To the extent that communications technology advanced with greater speed in Japan, its government would seem to have had less need to pursue national integration through administrative policies. Yet for a generation and more the Meiji leaders placed national integration and consciousness at the top of their priorities. Only thus, they reasoned, could the country be made strong. The U.S.S.R., meanwhile, deliberately employed communications, administration, education, and economic development as means of achieving national integration.

A fourth condition that any government in either nation would have had to take into account was the rapid growth in the size and complexity of managerial systems at all levels. The growth and concentration of populations demanded governmental action, as did the expansion and complexity of the industrial establishments. In Russia the government was particularly expeditious in stepping into this situation, for as early as 1900 the state budget (per capita) was 70 per cent larger than in Japan. Nonetheless, the growth of large industrial combines in both nations before the First World War provided a strong impetus toward complex forms of administration, an impetus further accelerated in Russia after those organizations were absorbed by the state.

Both governments performed unusual feats of social engineering in forecasting and planning for these changes. Judged by the standards of their time, when there were still no real precedents for national planning, this factor alone sets Japan and Russia apart from most other nations. Their governments saw these changes as desirable, and they did what they could to speed their realization. Even when resort was made to ideologies that gave scant attention to some of these developments, the objective of state activity was to promote the rationalization of life that these changes furthered.

In some efforts the national governments themselves assumed the central and often dominant role. The manner and extent of their direction differed considerably, particularly after 1917, but basically both societies accepted the idea that the government should oversee and direct the development process. In Japan the scarcity of resources and skills required central guidance. The early Meiji state established such industries as cement, glass, and machine-tool factories; it also extended credit, subsidies, and technical aid to the private sector, and in 1884 adopted a ten-year plan for expansion of industry. Government sponsorship of individual freeholding of land was also an aspect of state direction. In Russia the state emancipated the entire serf population and later, under the ministry of Stolypin, it also proposed to change the system of landholding to individual tenure. Though the early Meiji years had seen equally sweeping reforms in Japan, the Russian state persistently tried to change the structure of society and often seemed to surpass Japanese policies in range and effort. Once the pattern of the Japanese economy was set the state refrained from taking measures to control tenant or factory conditions, probably because of a reluctance to upset the balance of societal forces that had been created with the restoration. By contrast, the Russian state grew ever more active, and after 1917—and particularly during the First Five Year Plan (1929–1932)—undertook to liquidate the property basis of whole segments of the population, notably the peasant freeholder, in favor of groups it was patronizing.

In both countries these efforts could be justified by the notion that they brought nearer the day when Japan and the U.S.S.R. would achieve economic and military parity with the more advanced states of Europe and North America. This striving gave unity to the political experience of both nations through the entire transformation period. Perhaps more than any other element, a shared goal of national equality and strength stands out as the most prominent feature in government policy-making during the generations between the mid-nineteenth century and World War II.

Yet the willingness of the Russian and Japanese governments to take on roles of leadership does not set them off from most other late modernizers as much as does their ability to produce a bureaucracy capable of leading such innovations without stifling them. In Imperial Russia and Meiji Japan government leaders worked closely with leading entrepreneurs and industrialists, and saw no bar to the substitution and delegation of roles. As a consequence the two governments rarely took on more than they could handle, and remained relatively free from serious charges of scandal, at least in the area of economic development. The arrogation of all functions to itself by the Russian state after the Bolshevik Revolution gave rise to serious problems in the managerial area, but within a generation a new and reasonably effective managerial class had been brought into being.

Leadership

Russia and Japan were distinguished throughout the period under review for the vigor and unity of purpose of their leadership groups. In Japan this leadership characteristic was particularly true of the Meiji oligarchy and the first several generations of bureaucrats it led; in Russia it was increasingly the case after the revolution, as modern schools and party structure began to produce a managerial elite. In both countries formal structures of participatory institutions—Diet, Duma, and Soviet—were less vital in decision-making than the consensus of the managerial (and in the U.S.S.R., party) elite. In Russia more than in Japan, strong individual leadership played its role. In both countries, however, there was profession of deference and loyalty to higher authority—*tennō*, tsar, and later party—and affirmation of the importance of consensual and group leadership, operating through accepted and effective mechanisms to manage political life.

The central decision in the evolution of both Japanese and Russian politics was the adaptation of the respective heritages of imperial authority to meet new needs in a transformed social and institutional setting. In Japan the Meiji leaders, whose rise to power had been under slogans calling for the restoration of power to the throne, were committed to efforts to revive the imperial office. This objective they accomplished by calling attention to the *tennō* as a symbol of national unity and by moving his court from Kyoto to Tokyo, legitimizing the new capital and uniting ritual and administrative functions. But although an "Enlightened Reign" (Meiji) was proclaimed, the monarch did not rule. His name sufficed to endow the bold departures of his government with a legitimacy they might not otherwise have possessed—the constitution was his free gift to his people. At the same time the imperial office remained identified with policies but not with any particular politics, down to the end of the period.

By contrast, the Russian tsar ruled but by doing so came decreasingly to reign as a symbol of national unity. All acts of state were issued by him, including the manifesto of October 1905 creating the Duma, whose members later took the lead in urging him to abdicate. The union of symbolic and executive roles was not entirely broken by the revolution. Whatever Lenin's own intentions may have been, the demands of the Civil War era, the small numbers of Bolsheviks with the training necessary to run the machinery of society, and his own personal prestige combined to perpetuate into the postrevolutionary era certain elements of the Russian autocratic tradition. It remained for Stalin to recombine these elements during the late 1920's and the 1930's and to place them at the core of a system that for years concentrated all political power in his one person. Since this authority was personal and not institutional, however, the man who possessed it had at every turn to defend it against real and supposed dangers. For the same reason, succession remained an acute problem in the U.S.S.R. but not in Japan.

As government became more complex, the importance of top leadership grew apace. The challenge both nations faced was to encourage the growth and diversification of elites while simultaneously maintaining a high degree of unity and internal harmony. Taking the period 1860–1941 as a whole, it can be said that Japan achieved these ideals most fully in the late nineteenth century and that Russia most closely approached them after 1917, and then only with the application of enormous force during the 1930's.

Whatever the formal structure of Japanese government, in practice it was an oligarchy of gifted leaders down to the turn of the century. The office of premier assumed great stature, but its occupants were themselves part of the oligarchy. The homogeneity of this group was rooted in the common geographic origin of its members (the han of Satsuma and Choshu), their similar age (most were young men at the time of the restoration), their origins from the ranks of minor samurai, their shared memories of the heroic days of the early Meiji era, and their consciousness of themselves as a privileged and experienced elite.

In these same years Russia could boast of no such group. In Japan the disestablishment of the feudal aristocracy had eliminated older forms of privilege, but the statesmen of late Imperial Russia included landowners, courtiers, career bureaucrats, and even one railroad specialist. "Politics" became the task of harmonizing the divergent interests within this group and squaring them with the views of the tsar. The rise of the Bolshevik (later, Communist) Party, and to a great extent its character, was an effort to introduce into Russian life a more homogeneous and disciplined elite. The massive educational efforts of the 1920's and 1930's were addressed to this problem, as were Lenin's theories of party discipline and democratic centralism, not to mention the periodic purges through which discordant elements were winnowed from the party, often with great brutality. Gradually, though, a homogeneous, dynamic, and effective elite was molded and assumed complete control of Soviet politics.

In both nations the top elites gained support from a large and expanding circle of like-minded men and women in industry and the expanding professions who were the products of national institutions of higher education. In Russia leading figures of this group were systematically recruited into the Communist Party, thus linking it more closely with diverse walks of life. The involvement of these people in the affairs both of the party and of their professions enabled them to serve as transmitters of party policy to their respective fields and institutions and as sources of information from these bodies to the party. People prominent in Japanese industrial and professional life in the Meiji period, however, were closely tied to political leaders through family and friendship, and they shared a close community of interest within the national leadership as a whole. Thereafter the graduates of the new educational institutions became a remarkably homogeneous elite for all sectors of public and private life.

The structure of leadership in both nations gained strength from the continuing system of patronage. Patronage assured that links between various levels would be strong and that a proper relationship between service and rewards would be maintained. But if it helped create loyalty in Russia, the prevailing instability there discouraged risk-taking by subordinates even at the pinnacle of the system, whereas in Japan personal relations and patronage permitted the oligarchy to draw on the talents of men from all parts of the country without also sapping their initiative. For both nations the Japanese maxim "To move into shade of a large tree" contained a truth that aspiring leaders would have been ill-advised to ignore.

The Interests

In both Japan and Russia the skein of interest groups with which national leaders had to work became steadily more complex during the transformation period. Not only did the principal interests grow more numerous, they also became better organized. Yet, with the exception of the military, in Japan the interest groups did not develop a strong and exclusive esprit de corps, nor did their rise result in the breakdown of the prevailing pattern of authority. The growth in number and strength of interest groups in the intervening period did, however, increase problems of conflict management just at the time the original oligarchy passed from the scene. It has been said of each country that the interests became "governmentalized" in the twentieth century. This is true, but imprecise. Rather, it should be said that in both Japan and Russia that part of the national value systems that denied legitimacy to any purely "private interests" retained its vitality. Throughout the period, all separate groups within society felt compelled to legitimize themselves in terms of the national interest.

A particularly clear example of this phenomenon was the behavior of political parties in the two countries. In both cases, the parties came into existence prior to the parliaments (Diet and Duma), and they carried on a semilegal or informal existence for years before their parliamentary debuts. Heroic expectations of the unity that effective parliamentary representation would bring inclined them toward a speculative and totalistic approach to politics that was only slowly overcome in Japan and never in Russia, where the parties proved all but incapable of exercising executive leadership before World War I. In Japan prefectural assemblies co-opted the local elite and plutocracy after the 1870's and prepared the parties for the restricted franchise of the Diet. In both countries the only groups capable of gaining direct influence on policy were those willing to enter into working alliance with the state. As a result, twentieth-century political parties inevitably became more bureaucratic in structure and orientation.

After the First World War the fate of parties in Japan and Russia diverged. The Communist Party abolished the parliamentary system and took sole command of the Soviet state, while the Japanese parties gained considerably greater responsibility and power within the parliamentary framework. In neither instance did this situation last, however. The military in Japan and the "Cult of Personality" in the U.S.S.R. intervened to impose more decisive policies than the parties had been able to effect.

One source of the relative weakness of parliamentary rule, particularly in Russia, was the opposition of the civil bureaucracies. Far more experienced than the parties, these organizations spread quickly and came fully to embody the principle of promotion through merit. In its utopian phase the Russian Revolution was staunchly antibureaucratic, but in the absence of other social forces, the state *apparat* (and even many of the former bureaucrats known as *apparatchiki*) came once more to assume great importance in the 1920's. In Japan the strong institutional loyalties present within the bureaucracy assured for that body an eminent role in civil life. Both bureaucracies viewed the parties—and most other interests, for that matter—with suspicion and sought to supervise them through the instruments of control at their command.

Even so, neither bureaucracy ever acted as a fully autonomous force. Both became thoroughly politicized during the 1930's, in Russia through the replacement of personnel with political appointees, and in Japan through the increasing tendency of the parties to seek leadership from experienced bureaucrats. In their political roles, civil servants could exert tremendous influence in behalf of the reigning powers, but as groups they showed neither the desire nor the capacity to assume an independent stance. Furthermore, the politicization of the bureaucracies caused marked declines in levels of performance because it gave stress to factors other than merit in promotion decisions.

One remarkable similarity between the evolution of interest groups in Japan and Russia is the ineffectualness of labor unions and the strength of industrial groups. The Japanese union movement dates from the turn of the century, but until World War I it failed to enlist substantial numbers of workers. Only in 1923 were unions legalized, at which time they began gradually to expand to a prewar peak of about one-half million members in 1936. Even this figure represented only about 8 per cent of the Japanese labor force. Russian unions achieved prominence during the Revolution of 1905, having been preceded in labor organization by radical and illegal groups and labor-oriented political parties that had begun work some decades earlier. Until February 1917 union activity was limited, but thereafter unions were encouraged as a means of maintaining proletarian pressure on the largely prerevolutionary managerial and technical elites. Lenin, suspicious even of this degree of labor autonomy, had branded the union-based "workers' opposition" movement as anarchic long before it was actually suppressed. Also impairing the union movement in Russia and Japan was the fact that large numbers of workers never really came to consider themselves members of an urban proletariat but long remained, as it were, with one foot in their rural villages.

By contrast, industrialists and other managers of the two economies assumed prominent positions in the formulation of national policy. Due to the differing development of the Japanese and Russian political systems, however, such influence was exercised in Japan from an independent position and in Russia increasingly through the state and by the state. In both nations members of the industrial leadership were intensely nationalistic in outlook, and placed great importance on establishing close relations with their governments. Such a relationship was created early in Japan by the close ties linking heads of the large industrial and trading conglomerates with the new Meiji leadership. At times the competition between firms like Mitsui and Mitsubishi became a dimension of intragovernmental struggle. Such ties were by no means absent in prerevolutionary Russia, where industrialists of all stripes looked to government for protection. Lacking direct access to power, Russian industrial groups showed keen interest in the new Duma, in which their party, Octobrists, came to assume a prominent role in the years before 1917. But even in their parliamentary activity Russia's industrialists did not abandon the hope of more directly influencing the government by working in close consort with it, and through their national organization they were the first to call for national economic planning.

After the First World War and the October Revolution the power of industrial spokesmen increased in both nations, although along lines commensurate with the two political systems. In Japan the growth of great combines (*zaibatsu*) proceeded apace, and in the new political climate they forged close connections with the political parties, as they had earlier with elements of the bureaucracy. In Russia, after a transitional period during which political control took precedence over production, industrial growth once more became a top priority. Now, though, the Soviet state itself championed and directed industrial interests, placing the industrial managers in a powerful yet more dependent position. Thus, the 1930's saw industrial spokesmen reach a peak of importance in both nations; in Japan they were independent industrialists whereas in Russia they were managers with party connections whose interests were merged with those of the state.

In few areas do the contrasts between the political life of Japan and Russia during the transformation period stand out so vividly as they do in the role of the military. In both nations the military consumed a large portion of the state budget—from 21 per cent to 48 per cent in both countries between 1860 and 1913—and vast quantities of local resources, particularly in Russia. To utilize the potentials of modern technology, the armies and navies became patrons of science and industry, and in order to make soldiers of peasants they of necessity became major educational establishments. In Russia all of these functions had been executed on a national scale from the time of Peter I and earlier. Formed by strong political leaders, the armed services were firmly subordinated to state authority, a tradition that survived 1917 and was transferred to the new revolutionary regime. Only when the state itself was in chaos—as during the turmoil of 1905 and at the time of General Kornilov's attempted coup in the summer of 1917—was this subordination weakened, and then only briefly.

In structure and outward appearance the Japanese military resembled Russia's, primarily because both were reformed in the 1870's according to the same Germanic principles. In the Russian case, however, the foreign model was modified to the extent that the officer corps remained in a role clearly subordinate to political leaders and rarely aspired to a more independent status. Unlike the Russian military, Japan's enjoyed special constitutional privileges of direct access to the throne. Moreover, its officers formed a caste that was increasingly separated by training and outlook from other interest groups. As political life became more diverse, groups within the military came to view the army not merely as the defender of the nation but as the exclusive bearer of the principles underlying it. Officially committed to a role "above politics," they simultaneously

denied the validity of political constraints on the military, and ended
by militarizing many aspects of civilian life. For the whole period
approximately 28 per cent of all Japanese cabinet officers were drawn
from the military, and during the 1930's alternate centers of power
were sufficiently uncoordinated for military officers to be able finally
to surface as the strongest interest group in the state. Their activities
could not be effectively regulated from the time of the Manchurian
Incident (1931) to the end of World War II.

The Collectivist Traditions and Ideology

If Japanese and Russian society did not break down completely
into contending interest groups during times of most intensive
change, it was due in great measure to the strength of their collectivist traditions, which placed the interest of the communal whole
over that of the parts, be they groups or individuals. Related to this
circumstance was the perpetuation of patriarchal or hierarchic forms
or organization, which in each society had long coexisted with the
collectivist ethic.

These principles found their home in the village. Both societies
were torn between developing the village as a classroom for the new
society and maintaining it as a source of stability amidst change.
In the end, they followed both courses at once. Thus, Japanese villages were amalgamated with one another and placed under new
elective councils (1878–1888). But because only 5 per cent of the
rural populace was initially enfranchised, and because numerous
concessions had been made both to the general notion of group
responsibility in local affairs and to the traditional institutions in
which that general notion was embodied, old attitudes were perpetuated through the new legislation.

Russia's village communes and the attitudes they fostered were
perpetuated by the emancipation legislation of 1861–1866. Two
generations later, Stolypin's reforms sought to sap the foundations of
communal institutions in favor of individual land tenure. This
tendency continued through the revolutions, only to be reversed
by Stalin's collectivization campaigns of 1929–1932. However staggering the human cost endured in their creation, and however
marked their economic weaknesses, the collective farms created by
Stalin had the effect of reviving the collectivist tradition and placing
it at the service of Soviet policy. Thus, down to the end of the period
most rural migrants to the cities brought with them the political

outlook of the village community rather than that of "modern," individuated farmers.

The combination of collective and hierarchical principles of decision-making was reflected in the procedures of numerous organizations in Japan and Russia. In Japanese business and government the practice of *ringisei* manifested these procedures, whereas "democratic centralism" embodied these notions in Russia. The ringisei system of drafting policies called for a document to be approved successively at all administrative levels from bottom to top before being promulgated; it assured a high degree of consensus toward the final statement, which the most senior officer would then release. Democratic centralism, adopted as the procedural guide for meetings of the Communist Party, called for debate prior to making a decision, but the decision itself had to be a collective one, that is, unanimous, with dissident elements joining in the majority position. In both nations such procedures were general in political, administrative, and industrial agencies by the end of the transformation period, though the rise of Stalin meant that most top decisions of state in the U.S.S.R. were taken on his advice rather than after collective debate.

The collective and hierarchic traditions also found expression in the ideologies of the two nations, which, with ever greater intensity through the period, stressed the importance in national affairs of unity and group effort. Such a belief was, of course, to be expected of nations that modernized under the threat of foreign military pressure. But in Japan and Russia it survived the parliamentary experiences of each and came to permeate such otherwise different ideologies as the militarism of one and the communism of the other. Russian communism stood first for urban workers, whereas Japanese militarism was strongly oriented toward agrarian interests; history for the Communist moves deliberately toward a goal in the future, whereas for the Japanese agrarianist it moved away from a golden age in the premodern past. Yet for all their differences, both movements in the 1930's placed great stress on a collectivist ethic dedicated to nationalistic and even messianic objectives, and this notwithstanding the hostility to nationalism in classical Marxism and the parochialism of traditional Japanese thought.

These ideologies formed the core of political life in Japan and the Soviet Union, particularly in the decade before World War II. They were promoted through the mass media, the army, and civic and educational organizations, though with far greater vigor and single-mindedness in Russia than in Japan, where most urban intellectuals and workers were never asked to give agrarianism and militarism more than passive assent. Not only did ideology justify specific policies of the respective governments but, perhaps more important, it rationalized the means by which those policies were set.

Dissent, Opposition, and Crisis

Strong as were the collectivist traditions in Japan and Russia, their influence did not prevent incidents of conflict and even widespread violence from occurring. Both nations adopted new court systems at least once during the period as the means of settling conflicts; they even experimented with (and ultimately rejected) English-style jury systems. The benefits of formal judicial mechanisms should not be underestimated, but they did not prevent most of the key changes in the political systems of the two nations from being accompanied by, if not caused by, civil disorder.

Before the Second World War, assassination attempts occurred frequently in both countries, though they had been infrequent earlier. In Japan these peaked during both the first decade, 1868–1878, when many Meiji leaders fell victim to assassins and Ōkubo, the most powerful of the oligarchs, was cut down, and the last decade, 1931–1941, when a number of leaders of political and industrial life fell to military and fascist plots. In prerevolutionary Russia violence was aimed at the throne and the ministers close to it; in 1881 Tsar Alexander II was killed by a bomb, and in the years following 1903 a number of highly placed leaders were murdered. Elections in Japan and poor factory conditions in both nations occasioned turmoil for a generation after 1890, and the Russian-Japanese War called forth a revolution in defeated Russia and riots in Japan in which a thousand police and demonstrators were injured in Tokyo.

To stem disorder the two governments employed West European techniques for stifling expression. Censorship was in use in Russia through the entire period except during the 1905–1914 interval, and was introduced for the first time in Japan in 1875. Martial law was also frequently proclaimed by the Russian government, while the Japanese government had available a number of legal controls over political activity, such as the Peace Protection Law of 1887. Both nations reconstituted their centralized police forces in these years. The Bolshevik and other radical parties were suppressed in Russia long before 1917, while after 1917 the new regime directed even more severe campaigns against non-Bolsheviks. The task of these regular security forces was to see that school, army, and enterprise were on the lookout for "dangerous thoughts." Left-wing groups particularly felt the brunt of suppression. In Japan arrests of Communists reached 14,000 in 1935, and in Russia the eradication of the old left began tentatively in 1921 and culminated in the mass purges of the 1930's.

Violence occurred in both nations, but with far greater frequency in Russia and the U.S.S.R. than in Japan. The Revolution of 1905 caused bloodshed on all sides, and it was followed a decade and a half later by the Civil War, one of the most devastating internal wars of the twentieth century. Further, Russia is probably unique in the extent to which its government employed violence as a policy of state. The extensive pogroms encouraged by the tsar's government in the years 1902–1905 testify to this policy, as do the several million peasants killed during collectivization and the terror of the purges in which millions perished. Particularly conspicuous was the manner in which violence was used by proponents of modernization. The collectivization of agriculture and forced-march industrialization under Stalin are but two of the most glaring examples of this pervasive phenomenon.

The overall level of internal conflict in Japan was considerably lower than it was in Russia and the U.S.S.R., which can be attributed to at least three factors. First, the range of conflicting interests was narrower in Japanese society, due both to the absence of diverse national groups and to the disestablishment of the old samurai elite by the government of the restoration. The Satsuma Rebellion of 1877 in Japan marked the last effort of the samurai to assert their power. Russian politics down to 1917, on the other hand, felt the strong and divisive efforts of rural lords to regain lost prerogatives.

Second, Japanese political practice placed a much higher value on compromise than did the Russian, where a particularly strong urge toward totalistic solutions was exhibited by all parties and factions throughout the period. Such differing attitudes, so difficult to measure, may have been the result of the earlier condition of the two nations, with the Japanese long enjoying the security of isolation while the Russians had always to present a unified front against threats from the outside.

Third, some of the violence of Japanese life during the years 1860–1941 was not so much quelled as exported through foreign war and colonial exploitation. After the conquest of Korea and the movement into Manchuria, the expanded Japanese Empire became the theater in which much of the psychological and social tension infecting Japan's domestic life was released. Had so much violence not been siphoned into Japan's Asian adventures, the degree of domestic violence could well have been much greater than it was.

International Comparisons

The principal task facing the polities of all nations during the transitional phase of their development is to bring to power leaders and elites dedicated to transforming economies and social structures by means of public policies that are actively supported by a substantial part of the entire populace. The forms of leadership may vary, the specific modes of transforming the economy and society are bound to differ in each context, and a broad range of workable methods exists for mobilizing the public behind change. But by one means or another each of these processes must take place before a society can fairly be said to have arrived at the threshold of modernity.

Only a very few of the early developers—notably England, France, and the United States—have accomplished all of these processes without being subject along the way to overwhelming pressures from beyond their borders. Far more common has been the experience of colonial and semicolonial territories, which have found themselves thrust into an extremely demanding international environment for which they were inadequately equipped to plan independently. Many such nations are now beginning to pursue economic development through the medium of regional or ideological political alliances and federations; others have at one time lost and conceivably could lose again their political autonomy. Japan and Russia are all but unique in their intermediate position between these two groups of nations. Like the low-income nations of the present era, both entered the transitional phase of their development under duress—as a means of preserving their identity in the face of outside pressure. But both were successful in this effort, as demonstrated in their ability to convert pressures generated by the early "superpowers" into positive stimuli to change and national unity. It is not surprising that both Japan and Russia came to idealize the political methods and experience of Germany, the only other nation at that time to succeed conspicuously at the same task. Similarly, during this period leaders of public opinion in both nations evinced particular contempt for those old empires like China, Ottoman Turkey, and Persia, which seemed to be incapable of maintaining control over their own destinies.

In comparing the political systems of Japan and Russia to those of the early developing states at corresponding periods of evolution, both the differences and similarities stand out: Russia breaking from the pattern of European development by creating the world's first Communist state in 1917, and Japan gradually building a blend of oligarchy and constitutionalism. Lest the contrast between Russia and the early developers be exaggerated, however, it is well to recall that the polities of England, the United States, and France all assumed revolutionary forms on the eve of their initial transformation, just as China's has done at the present time. Japan and Russia stand out as distinctive in comparison with the earlier developers in the enormous and sustained efforts they directed toward adapting their strong traditions of collectivity to the needs of a changing society. For all the stark differences between Stalin's version of Marxism-Leninism and Japanese militarism, they were both uncompromisingly hostile to individualism, affirmative of the national heritages of collective labor, and based upon a nationalism that encompassed the emerging social orders of their respective nations. A consciously articulated national ideology had played a strong part in the mobilization of the United States, France, and other early developing states; indeed, the ideologies of the French Revolution and of German nationalism and socialism long served as models for other nations aspiring to modernize, including the two under study here. But it was precisely in the nations that entered the process somewhat later that ideology figured as so crucial and persistent an aspect of the entire process, because of the necessity to affirm both the current "backwardness" of the nation and the expected brilliance of its future. Stated differently, the political ideologies of Japan and Russia were more successful than those of any earlier developing nation, including Germany, in justifying sacrifices for the sake of future benefits. Mao Tse-tung's version of Marxism-Leninism may prove to be no less successful in promoting the same end in China, but none of the military regimes formed in the past decades come close. With the possible exception of China, the Japanese and Soviet systems were unequaled in their ability to enforce and justify non-consumption during the period of transformation.

On the institutional level, the ideologies of both nations affirmed the necessity for a greater degree of state direction of the modernization process than had existed in any of the nations to develop earlier. Governmental intervention in the economies and social orders of Japan and especially of Russia exceeded even the levels attained by the baroque monarchies in the seventeenth-century West. No nation has been transformed politically without widespread coercion, violence, and even civil war, and Japan and Russia were no exceptions. Comparative statements must remain little more than guesses, but it would appear that Russia in the twentieth century exceeded all prior instances in this respect.

Among the victims in both Russia and Japan were those elements of pluralism that survived the development process in the nations of Western Europe and North America. Labor unions were far weaker in Japan and Russia, professions more closely integrated with state institutions, and contending political parties far less prominent a feature of political life than in all those West European and North American states that developed in the eighteenth and nineteenth centuries. In their place was an overwhelming emphasis upon the formation of a single, national elite extending across all fields. To be sure the Japanese military, like that of Germany, attained considerable independence within that elite, as the military did not succeed in doing in Russia or the Soviet Union. But allowing that the Soviet Union far surpassed Japan in its efforts to forge a unified elite, it appears likely that among large nations in the twentieth century only China, after 1949, moved as vigorously and successfully toward the formation of a homogeneous corps of leaders as did these two. The failure of Atatürk to achieve this end in Turkey may be one of the chief causes of that nation's more retarded rate of development.

The improved communications created by modern technology gave Japan and Russia advantages in their political transformation that were unavailable to states that had entered upon the modernization process earlier. Notwithstanding Russia's notoriously bad roads, it was easier to send a message or move physically among its major centers in 1917 than it had been in England, America, or France at the time of their revolutions. Japan's high literacy rate and its unusually extensive reading culture throughout the era of transformation insured for that country a more broadly based national discourse on public issues than had been possible at analogous periods in the history of earlier developing nations. Without exaggerating the importance of communications, it can readily be seen that they would come into play quite differently in the emerging nations of today. On the one hand such nations have powerful instruments for propaganda and control, but on the other they can lose their own identities amid a flood of information generated and transmitted from beyond their borders.

Chapter Ten

ECONOMIC STRUCTURE
AND GROWTH

AT THE BEGINNING of the period of transformation Japan and Russia were both underdeveloped and premodern economies although Russia, with a longer and closer relationship to Western European capital and technology, had more industry and more international trade. In both countries the decades after 1860 were dominated by administrative reforms that created the conditions for the changes to follow. After the mid–1880's industrial development accelerated. Japan's industrial growth was speeded by its success in foreign wars in 1895 and 1905, while Russia's was interrupted by wars and revolutions. The premodern economies in each case supported the industrialization drive by providing an agricultural surplus; in Japan this was achieved by more intensive exploitation of land in use, in Russia by enlarging the sown area. Although Russia developed a "command economy" while Japan maintained a market economy (other contrasts between the two are also noteworthy), the most startling similarity is the evidence of comparable results, e.g., per capita output at the end of the period of transformation.

This enormous economic transformation achieved by Japan and Russia between 1860 and 1940 is shown by the data in Table 10.1. It is difficult to have full confidence in figures worked out for gross national product (GNP) before 1900, but in all probability the Japanese economy expanded at an annual rate somewhat above 2 per cent for the entire period. The data are more reliable after 1900, and Table 10.1 records them separately. Between 1902 and 1940 Japan's rate of expansion averaged 3.4 per cent per year. In other words, Japan's real GNP practically quadrupled during the first

161

forty years of the twentieth century—an impressive figure inasmuch as its population growth rarely exceeded 1 per cent.

For Russia, the rate of growth of national product was about 2.5 per cent for the period 1860–1913. Years of war, defeat, revolution, civil war, and foreign intervention, however, brought a sharp decline in its growth rate. Russian national output in 1928, after a program of reconstruction under the New Economic Policy (1921–1928), was only a little more than 13 per cent above that of 1913, or an annual average rate of growth for these fifteen years of 0.8 per cent. The rate of growth during the time of great structural change, 1928–1940, involves serious problems of statistical interpretation; depending on the statistical weighting system employed, it was either 5.1 per cent or 9.3 per cent per year. If 5.1 is used, the growth rate between 1900 and 1940 works out to 2.7 per cent per year, which implies almost a tripling of output; if 9.3 is used, Russia's growth proves similar to that of Japan's: 3.9 per cent per year, or more than a quadrupling for the period. Yet because Russia's population grew at an average of 1.5 per cent per year, its growth of output per capita was below, or at best equal to, that of Japan.

The change in the nature of output provides one of the most striking instances of structural transformation. By 1940 manufacturing had become the leading sector in the Japanese economy, accounting for 53 per cent of the net product. Services and agriculture contributed far less. The contrast with the 1887 Meiji figures is obvious. Similar changes are observable in the structure of employment. The importance of agriculture in the economy, for example, declined sharply, though it remained the largest source of employment (and underemployment). In Russia, as in Japan, manufacturing had become the leading sector by 1940, accounting for 45 per cent of net output. Here, too, services and agriculture accounted for less. Similar comparisons hold for the structure of employment.

Thus, the general pattern of change exhibited by Russia in 1940 was similar to that of Japan. The share of manufacturing in output was larger than that of agriculture or services. The share of manufacturing was lower in Russia in 1940 than in Japan; whereas in 1900 (if those figures are to be trusted) the reverse had been true— indicating a faster expansion of manufacturing in Japan during these years. In both countries agriculture was still the largest employer in 1940, though it had dropped substantially from 1900. The shares of employment in agriculture and manufacturing in 1940 were closer in the two countries than were the shares of output accounted for by these two sectors. These percentages reflect the fact that the differences in sectoral productivities were greater in Japan —where the value of output per worker in manufacturing was almost five times that of the output value per worker in agriculture—than they were in Russia, where the ratio was three to one.

Another notable difference between the two nations is to be found in the time patterns of the changes in structure. Japan experienced a rather steady decrease in the relative importance of agriculture after the 1880's. In Russia, on the other hand, the decrease in the role of agriculture was very gradual until 1928, after which it changed radically downward to the levels indicated in Table 10.1. The speed with which Russia moved away from agriculture in the years between 1928 and 1940 is seen more graphically when comparisons are made with countries other than Japan. Japan in the Meiji years had experienced rapid structural change. But it took other industrialized nations thirty-five years or more to experience the proportionate changes in agricultural shares that Russia experienced in the twelve years after 1928.

Also of note is the ability of both Japan and Russia to raise their levels of investment. In 1937, as Table 10.1 shows, gross domestic capital formation in Japan was 24 per cent of gross national product. Compared with the Meiji era, it had nearly doubled. In Russia in 1937 gross investment was 26 per cent of gross national product—undoubtedly an appreciable increase over the prerevolutionary decades for which, unfortunately, we do not have figures. Though investment ratios above 20 per cent were not unknown in Western experience, no Western country, when at levels of national product per capita similar to those in Japan and the Soviet Union in 1937, devoted anywhere near that proportion of national product to capital investment.

A further factor pertaining to economic growth of the two countries involves foreign trade. Exports in Japan rose during the entire transformation period until they equaled about 20 per cent of GNP in the 1937–1940 period. This jump was one of the clearest contrasts with the past, because before Meiji the Japanese economy had been isolated from the outside world. The Russian experience was rather different. Foreign trade grew until World War I, but its importance decreased substantially after the Communists took power. Exports were more than 10 per cent of GNP in 1913; they fell to less than 1 per cent by the end of the 1930's.

The economic transformation achieved by Japan and Russia was also reflected in the development of modern transportation systems, financial mechanisms, and industrial organizations. Yet

despite these considerable achievements, it would be wrong to characterize the two economies in 1940 as "developed" or "mature."
These are vague terms to be sure, but they can be applied with relative justification to the economies of the United States and Western
Europe just before World War II. The Japanese economy was
divided into two sectors: a growing, modern high-income sector
using advanced, foreign technology, and a traditional lower-income
sector retaining a large share of employment in far less productive
occupations. Nearly one-half of the labor force remained engaged in
agriculture. Many of the services were within the "traditional"
sector, and even within manufacturing, small enterprises continued
to employ sizable numbers. Russia's economy, too, was a dual one,
with some modern industrial branches, but a large, quite backward
agricultural sector. Economic growth was pushed hard after 1928,
with great shifts in structure of output and inputs, and massive
additions to the industrial capital stock. But the level of efficiency
and quality was for the most part low. Modern methods had been
borrowed, but not yet mastered.

All these factors help account for the low per capita income position of both Japan and Russia in 1940. When compared with the
more uniformly developed economies of the West, they were still
behind.

Growth Phases

A brief and rather schematic chronology of modern economic
growth in Japan and Russia for the entire period might be useful
before taking up comparisons. In Russia by the 1860's there was
already considerable manufacturing; in Japan it was barely getting
under way. Between the 1880's and 1900, however, industrialization
in both countries accelerated. Thereafter their patterns of growth
diverged. Japan's economic development from 1900 to 1940 took
the form of long upward swings marked by troughs in 1900, 1931,
and 1940. In Russia the First World War and the Bolshevik Revolution marked a sharp break in growth, which was followed by a decade
of disorganization. A new phase of growth, however, was inaugurated in 1928 with the five-year plans, and it continued until the
Second World War. An overall view of the industrial growth of the
two countries in the transformation years is presented in Table 10.2.

Japan's industrialization began hesitantly during the Meiji years

TABLE 10.1. Comparative Economic Data
(*in percentages*)

	JAPAN		RUSSIA	
	1889–1902	*1902–1940*	*1860–1900*	*1900–1940*
1. Gross national product: Average annual rate of growth	2.8	3.4	2.5	2.7 or 3.9[1]
	1887	*1902*	*1940*	*1900*	*1940*
2. National product by sectors of origin:					
Agriculture	41	40	16	55	29
Manufacturing[2]	20	25	53	33	45
Services	39	35	31	12	26
	1887	*1902*	*1940*	*1900*	*1940*
3. Share of labor force:					
Agriculture	73	66	44	77	54
Manufacturing	13	17	31	12	28
Services	14	17	25	11	18
	1887	*1902*	*1937*		*1937*
4. National product by end uses:					
Consumption	80	77	65	NA[3]	63
Gross capital formation	13	13	24	NA	26
Government	7	10	11	NA	11

[1] See text for brief discussion of index number problems.

[2] Includes: manufacturing, mining, construction, transportation, communication, and public utilities.

[3] No data for national product by use are available for the prerevolutionary period.

SOURCES:

Japan: All data are calculated from K. Ohkawa and H. Rosovsky, *Japanese Economic Growth* (Stanford: Stanford University Press, 1973), pp. 10, 280, 286, 310.

Russia: 1. Rates of growth of GNP are calculated as follows: From 1860–1913: R. Goldsmith, "The Economic Growth of Tsarist Russia, 1860–1913," *Economic Development and Cultural Change*, IX (April 1961), p. 472 (with the assumption that the average rate 2.5 per cent applies equally to the pre- and post-1900 period); from 1913–1928: A. Maddison, *Economic Growth in Japan and the USSR* (New York: Norton Press, 1969), p. 155; from 1928–1940, R. Moorsteen and R. Powell, *The Soviet Capital Stock, 1928–1962* (Homewood, Ill.: Irwin, 1966), pp. 361–363 (with a downward adjustment of 10 per cent in 1940 for territorial changes).

2. National product by sector: For 1900, Prokopovich data as presented in A. Vainshtein, *Narodnyi dokhod Rossii i SSSR* [National Income of Russia and the USSR] (Moscow, 1969), pp. 62–63; for 1940, A. Bergson and S. Kuznets, eds., *Economic Trends in the Soviet Union* (Cambridge: Harvard University Press, 1963), p. 344.

3. Share of labor force: From G. Ofer, *The Service Sector in Soviet Economic Growth* (Cambridge: Harvard University Press, 1973), p. 187.

4. National product by end uses: A. Bergson, *The Real National Income of Soviet Russia since 1928* (Cambridge: Harvard University Press, 1961), p. 237.

between 1868 and the mid–1880's. There was little economic growth. Yet a series of notable institutional innovations in unification occurred during which aspects of feudal localism were suppressed. These helped prepare the stage for the surprising growth that was to follow.

T A B L E 1 0. 2.   **Average Annual Rate of
Growth of Industrial
Output, Selected Periods**
(*in percentages*)

JAPAN	RUSSIA
1887–1902: 5.5	1860–1885: 4.0
1902–1931: 6.1	1885–1900: 6.7
1931–1940: 8.9	1900–1913: 3.6
	1913–1928: 0.5
	1928–1940: 9.8 or 16.1[1]

[1] See text for brief discussion of index number problem.

SOURCES:

Japan: K. Ohkawa and H. Rosovsky, *Japanese Economic Growth* (Stanford: Stanford University Press, 1973), pp. 10, 284.

Russia: 1860–1913, R. Goldsmith, "The Economic Growth of Tsarist Russia, 1860–1913." *Economic Development and Cultural Change,* April 1961, p. 462–463, column 3; 1913–1928, A. Maddison, *Economic Growth in Japan and the USSR* (London: George Allen and Unwin, 1969), p. 164; 1928–1940, R. Powell, "Industrial Production," in A. Bergson and S. Kuznets, *Economic Trends in the Soviet Union* (Cambridge: Harvard University Press, 1963), p. 178, ("adjusted total" in 1937 and 1928 prices).

The first stage of modern economic growth in Japan began roughly in the mid–1880's and lasted until about 1900. Overall growth of output exhibited a quickened pace—averaging about 2.8 per cent as Table 10.1 shows. Though this was less than Japan's later rates of growth, it was quite respectable—equal to that of Germany's between 1870 and 1913 but below that of the United States's, which led the field with 4.3 per cent. Agriculture also increased, at an annual rate of about 1.7 per cent, and provided not only food for a growing urban labor force but also export crops of silk and tea. Industrial output went up at a rate of 5.5 per cent per year, among the highest in the world at the time. Most notable were the beginnings of the cotton textile industry, in which investment increased substantially. Gross domestic capital formation rose 3.9 per cent per year. However, because prices of investment goods were falling relative to other prices, the proportion of GNP devoted to investment remained at 13 per cent between 1887 and 1902 as measured in current prices. Japan's public sector was crucial in this investment spurt. These were the years in which the systems of transport, communication, and public utilities were greatly expanded and improved. These were also the years in which Japan appeared on the world trading scene. Japan's total trade—exports plus imports—grew at a rate of almost 9 per cent per year from 1887 to 1902.

In Russia, as in Japan, the period from the 1860's to the mid–1880's was more noteworthy for its institutional reforms than for its economic growth. The immediate effects on industrialization of the dominant institutional reform of the early 1860's—the abolition of serfdom—were rather negative. Industrial output did increase in the 1860–1870 decade, but only at the rate of 2 per cent per year. Because of the way the abolition was carried out, labor mobility continued to be restricted, agricultural technology was not stimulated, and the development of an effective internal market was not fostered. However, again as with Japan, the groundwork for future growth was laid in institutional reforms. There was also substantial construction of railroads. Russia's railroad network in 1860 totaled 1,000 miles; in 1885 it exceeded 16,000. Overall, it is estimated that the Russian national product grew at the rate of about 2 per cent per year from 1860 to 1885; agricultural output at about 1.5 per cent per year; and industrial output at 4 per cent per year.

From the mid-1880's to 1900 Russia experienced a burst of industrialization. Under the leadership of the Russian government, and with the very active participation of foreign capital from advanced Western nations, the Russian economy moved ahead quickly. The further development of the Russian railway network was of special importance. The 1885 track mileage more than doubled by 1900, and this expansion had a dramatic effect on the location of industry. It made possible, for example, the uniting of iron ore and coking coal sources in the southwest region of Russia, which then developed into the major metallurgical base for the country. Further, the extension of the railroad network was a key factor in the increasing role of the market in agriculture.

Estimates of Russia's national product for the period indicate that it grew at a rate of about 3 per cent per year. Agriculture rose about 2 per cent per year. Industry was up 6.7 per cent per year for the entire 1885–1900 period, and a robust 7 per cent per year for the decade of the 1890's. In this one decade, the output of cotton yarn and sugar doubled, coal and oil almost tripled, and iron and steel more than tripled.

The first four decades of the twentieth century marked a new phase in the growth of both economies. After 1940 differences in the growth patterns appear, but by the 1930's both Japan and Russia still exhibited rather similar levels of industrialization in terms of output per capita, structure of output and employment, and shares of total output used for consumption, capital formation, government administration, and defense.

Through the years between 1900 and 1940 the Japanese economy expanded at an increasing pace. This phenomenon, which became especially evident after 1950, can be called "trend acceleration." For Japan the years 1900 to 1931 constitute a second stage of growth. Throughout the entire three decades the growth rate of output was more rapid than at the end of the nineteenth century, but within these decades the great boom culminating at the time of World War I and the slowdown during most of the 1920's can be discerned. Many significant economic changes occurred during these years. One was the relative decline of the primary sectors and, in a broader sense, of the traditional economy. This decline led to the formation of the "differential structure," an economic situation in which a growing productivity and wage gap existed between the modern and the traditional sectors. Its social consequences were the division of Japan into two camps, one increasingly rich and progressive, and the other poor and falling further behind. Between 1902 and 1931 the GNP in Japan advanced at a rate of 2.7 per cent per year, agriculture at a very low 0.6 per cent per year, and industry at a very high 6.1 per cent per year. In exports Japan shifted more and more to textiles, particularly cotton; indeed, during the boom associated with World War I it succeeded in displacing a number of European producers in African and Asian markets. Economic relations with Japan's growing empire also became more important in these years. Korea and Taiwan became prime sources of rice and sugar imports as well as prime recipients of Japanese investment funds.

Japan's third stage of modern economic growth, encompassing the investment upswing of the 1930's, was aborted by the outbreak of World War II. In the decade of the thirties the Japanese economy expanded impressively. GNP grew at a rate of 5.6 per cent per year. The retardation of agriculture, however, became severe and the social and economic misery this slowdown engendered caused grave tensions. Closely related to these economic factors was the rise of militarism and fascism, which eventually plunged Japan into aggression and war. As Japan became increasingly cut off from Europe and America, trade and investment were directed more and more toward the empire.

In Russia the industrial expansion of the 1890's was halted by the general European recession that began in 1900. In the years of

1900 to 1905, years in which there was much peasant unrest as well as war, Russia experienced little industrial growth. From 1906 until the beginning of World War I, however, industry grew rapidly at 5.4 per cent. Significantly, this renewal was accomplished without the leadership of the Russian state—something new was occurring in the Russian economy. On the eve of World War I the economy seemed to have taken on a self-sustained character. Entrepreneurial activity in industry and finance had come of age. Russia, in one sense, was becoming for the first time part of the general European economy. Though its national product per capita was far below that of the leading industrial nations, its total industrial output was fifth in the world, and in the production of such industrial raw materials as oil and timber it was second only to that of the United States.

The Bolshevik Revolution of November 1917 was followed by counter-revolution and Civil War lasting from 1918 to 1921, during which the government instituted centralized controls. With the end of the Civil War these controls were eased, and in this atmosphere the Russian economy was able to rebuild itself to its prewar dimensions. Most of its human entrepreneurial and managerial capital, however, had been severely depleted in the interim. Yet by 1928 the Russian economy had reattained and somewhat surpassed its prewar levels. GNP was 13 per cent higher than in 1913, agricultural output 16 per cent higher, and industrial output 8 per cent higher. The average annual rates of growth implied by these figures were, of course, very low: 0.8, 1.0, and 0.5.

With the First Five Year Plan in 1928 the Soviet Union embarked on a program of stepped-up industrialization. Centralized planning and control were introduced and agriculture collectivized. In the twelve years of the pre-World War II plan era, the Russian economy was radically altered. Not only did output levels soar, but the structure of the economy changed with a speed that was without historical precedent. The flow of inputs into the modern sectors of the economy increased dramatically. Labor employment in nonagriculture, for instance, rose at a rate of about 6 per cent per year, five times the growth rate of population. To accomplish this transformation, more than twenty million people were moved from the rural areas to the cities—the rate of urbanization advancing from 18 per cent in 1928 to 32 per cent in 1940. Investment was pushed to the high level of 25 per cent, and the input flow of fixed capital to the economy climbed at a rate of from 9 to 11 per cent per year, 40 per cent of it going to industry in order primarily to increase the capacity of the producers goods sector. The share of producers goods in total industrial output went from 40 per cent in 1928 to 61 per cent in 1940. The productive capacity of such industries as iron, steel, and coal increased fourfold or more. Entire new industries, such as heavy chemicals and aluminum, and entire new regional complexes were formed. However, the last few years of the period, 1937–1940, witnessed a noticeable slowing down in Russia's economic growth, partly a result of the preparations for war (production of military equipment instead of capital equipment) and partly a result of the stultifying effect of the Stalinist purges.

As indicated earlier, the measurement of Russia's growth of output between 1928 and 1940 is complicated by the drastic structural transformation and the relative price changes that took place in consequence. Richard Moorsteen calculates that the Soviet ability to produce its 1937 mix of national product grew from 1928 to 1940 at the rate of 9.3 per cent per year. If the 1928 product mix is taken as a norm, however, the growth rate would be calculated at 5.1 per cent. The two rates are widely divergent, though both are high. Agriculture showed practically no growth during these years; increases in crop production were offset by decreases in livestock production as peasants slaughtered livestock during collectivization. But industrial output grew dramatically. Here, however, measurement is heavily affected by the weighting system used, being calculated at either 9.8 or 16.1 per cent per year.

Growth Mechanisms

It is difficult to present a coherent and succinct analysis of growth mechanisms at work in the economies of Japan and Russia during the years of transformation. The period is long—and composed of the three subperiods that have just been described—and growth mechanisms within each country changed. Moreover, the elements of the growth mechanisms resist easy compartmentalization. Five different elements of these growth mechanisms are discussed below, without adhering to a strictly chronological approach and without forgetting that their boundaries are fuzzy and often overlap.

DIRECT ROLE OF GOVERNMENT

During the entire transformation period the direct role of the state was more crucial in Russia than it was in Japan. In Japan and prerevolutionary Russia the powers of direct government control were limited. Government could act as entrepreneur, subsidize, grant concessions, supervise, favor, and discriminate, but it had to work by economic means within the context of the market. The state did not control the economy by direct decree, as became true during the plan era in Soviet Russia. Yet, the direct role of government in Japanese growth was by no means unimportant. Its direct contribution in the last third of the nineteenth century in fostering modern economic growth was great. Even so, in the twentieth century, except for the military controls of the 1930's, the government assumed an indirect posture more in keeping with a market economy.

In the years of early industrialization the Japanese government operated under a number of constraints that contributed in no small degree to the way in which it shaped its programs. One was time. As with Russia, problems of political power along with foreign-policy and military considerations were key factors in economic policies during the Meiji period. It was felt that a considerable increase in national power based on a modern economy was absolutely necessary in order to maintain Japan's independence. If this expansion in national power could not be accomplished fairly quickly, foreigners might decide that Japan, too, was ripe for colonial exploitation. Time was equally precious at home, for here also inaction might give the opposition, those negatively affected by the restoration, a chance to regroup. Only the speedy initiation of new programs could keep the Meiji government in power. A second constraint pertained to the limitations imposed by Japan's somewhat unusual status in the world community. Because its tariff autonomy had been taken away by the treaties with the Western powers, Japan was not able to aid its developing industries by protective duties. It had to act directly. Government planning, symbolized by the "Memorandum on Industries" of 1884, took account of these problems and projected a ten-year set of production goals.

Government action took the form of direct investment in the industrial sector. Until about World War I, these investments generally exceeded those of the private sector. At the beginning of the Meiji period, there was a limited supply of experienced entrepreneurs, and the government itself undertook the initiation of industrial enterprises in a number of fields. But before long the government began to leave to the private sectors those industrial areas in which Japan had comparative advantages (labor intensive industries, especially textiles) and in which private firms had a chance of surviving even in the face of foreign competition. Thereafter, the state con-

cerned itself mainly with developmental bottlenecks the private
sector could not manage. Government was also active in improving
the quantity and quality of social overheads and of course it took full
responsibility for raising Japan's military capability. Indeed, during
the Meiji era a large part of central government capital formation
can be accounted for by summing up expenditures on public works,
particularly railroads, and military investments. Construction—road
building, port improvements, government buildings—which required high capital output ratios—accounted for more than two-
thirds of public capital formation. If reconstruction expenditures
related to natural disasters such as earthquakes and typhoons are
added, it is possible to account for more than 70 per cent of government investment expenditures. Even in the private sector, investments were about equally divided between construction and durable
equipment until the time of World War 1, when equipment began
to assume new weight.

In Russia the direct role of the government loomed large throughout the entire transformation process, but especially in the decade
of the 1890's under the tsarist regime and in the plan years, 1928
to 1940, under the Communist regime. Both these time spans fit well
within the general pattern of state-led Russian growth referred to
earlier. In both periods, it is difficult to differentiate with complete
success direct government activity from indirect.

In the 1890's, under the vigorous leadership of the minister of
finance, Count Witte, the Russian government pursued a forceful
program of stimulating industrial development. One of the prime
elements in this program was the expansion of railroad construction.
In the early 1860's most of the railroad lines were constructed by
private companies, on the basis of government concessions. In the
1880's government policy changed to direct government construction
of new lines, the purchase of many private lines, and the strict
supervision of the remaining private lines. During the 1890's alone,
as was mentioned earlier, the total mileage of Russian railroads
almost doubled. Witte himself took a very active part in directing
this railroad construction, and he was largely responsible for the
building of the great Trans-Siberian line begun in 1892 and completed in 1904. The expansion of the railway system had, to use
Albert Hirschman's terminology, "forward linkages" and "backward
linkages." The forward linkages concern the industrial benefits
resulting from improvement of the transportation system; the backward linkages involve the demand for industrial goods induced by
the railroad construction.

The impact of the railroad program was strengthened by a number of other government programs. These included payment of top prices for domestically produced goods as a means of encouraging private industry; prepaid orders, which tended to act as direct government investment; and extremely high tariffs to protect domestic production, as exemplified by the tariff of 1891. The government also pursued policies to attract foreign investment. In this regard it moved toward currency convertibility and toward the gold standard—to a great extent through the forced exportation of grain (brought about by heavy governmental financial pressures on the peasantry) and through the maintenance of a surplus in the balance of payments.

After 1900 the direct role of the government decreased in importance as an element in the tsarist growth mechanism. Though the role of government increased again when the Communists took power in 1917, it did not reach the heights now associated with the Soviet economic model until the inauguration of the plan era in 1928. At that point the direct control of the government over the economy became, at least in a formal sense, total. In reality the central regime was not able to exercise its control in a totally effective manner. Nevertheless, the plan era can be characterized as one of direct, centralized administration, analogous to military administration; it was, in effect, a "command economy." The levels of output as well as of intermediary (from producer to producer) and input (capital and labor) flows to individual sectors were determined centrally on the basis of a formal set of economic plans and controlled by means of a centralized administrative bureaucracy, and agriculture was collectivized. The growth mechanism became one in which the state not only mobilized resources through enforced high rates of investment and saving but directed them—both material and human—into the high growth sectors. The growth mechanism was also affected by governmental attempts to improve the quality of material and human resources and their overall and specific employment in the production process.

INDIRECT ROLE OF GOVERNMENT

The central government could also exercise a good deal of indirect influence on the economy, especially in Japan where political leaders and businessmen were usually allies and occasionally associates in pursuit of common goals.

The dividing line between direct and indirect government activity—as between direct government investment and the granting of credit by the government—is frequently fuzzy. Yet some vital activities clearly fall in the indirect category. One of these is institution-building. A number of institutions were developed between the 1860's and the 1940's that facilitated the transformation of Japan and Russia to industrial life and that enhanced their capacity to absorb foreign technology and organizational patterns.

The institutional reforms of the early Meiji era, mentioned earlier, are examples. The government's abolition of the wasteful status restrictions of Tokugawa samurai society; its extension of freedom of occupation, residence, and tillage to all; and its abolition of restrictions on internal and external travel and communications were essential steps. Certificates of ownership made land transferable, and in place of the premodern and nonuniform Tokugawa land tax the government substituted a monetized tax based on land value. With this predictable income the government was able to minimize samurai discontent through pensions. It was also able to start costly modernization programs in communications and education. Parallel measures for conscription and education had a decided bearing on the future labor force. Currency and banking reforms also were a matter of high priority. The National Bank Act of 1872 marked the formal beginning of a modern banking system, and a unified currency system came into being in 1874. Eleven years later the Central Bank of Japan was founded. Because Japan lacked a capital market, the government provided medium- and long-term credit to industry through specialized banking institutions. Government inspection and quality control of exports was also established; applied to raw silk, it made it the largest of Japan's exports.

After the Meiji period, government institution-building was not extensive, although there was some activity during the depression years of the 1930's. At a time when economic conditions were precarious, government and business jointly attempted to curb competition through the control of output and prices and the allocation of markets and sales quotas. Such government sponsorship of cartels established the pattern of "administrative guidance" that proved to be so important in the post-World War II period.

In Russia, as in Japan, the period of the 1860's and 1870's was also one of great institutional reform. The abolition of serfdom, vital as it was for its eventual effect on the Russian growth mechanism, was not the only government reform with a telling effect on the economy. The establishment of the zemstvos (1864) represented a decentralization of government authority in certain activities, including education, medicine, roads, insurance, and food reserves. Although these local government bodies, which lacked sufficient tax and administrative powers, were at best junior partners of the central government, their establishment did loosen central control and created an environment conducive to greater economic activity. The zemstvo reform was followed by a municipal government reform (1870) that established for the cities many of the principles and practices that had been set up for the districts and provinces under the zemstvo reform. The reform allowed an electorate qualified through tax status to select town councils. As a consequence the influence of businessmen and industrialists expanded, thereby fostering economic development. A highly successful reform of the legal system (1864) created an independent judiciary and created a system wherein legal conflicts were handled in open court rather than in bureaucratic secrecy. The inauguration of reliable legal procedures was crucial for economic progress, especially within the private sector. Also of importance was the military reform (1874) that reduced the term of service from twenty-six to six years, spread the obligation to serve, and introduced elementary education for all recruits. This reform contributed to the growth in the quantity and quality of the industrial labor force. Finally, a series of specific economic and financial reforms was promulgated: the establishment of a single state treasury; publication of the annual budget; the creation in 1866 of the state bank to function as a central bank in matters of money, credit, and finance; and the creation of other banking and financing institutions for agriculture and industry.

After the Bolshevik Revolution, and especially after the beginning of the plan era, the emphasis was on direct, rather than indirect, government participation in economic matters. In the command economy, however, the government not only ordered compliance with its economic plans, which were legally binding upon the responsible economic agents, it also employed a wide array of indirect methods to bring about behavior it believed would contribute to the fulfillment—and overfulfillment—of the plan targets. An economic reward and penalty system for workers and managers was keyed to plan fulfillment. Material perquisites (apartments, special food supplies, and others) were attached to high administrative and managerial status in order to encourage and increase the supply of managerial personnel. Broadly based political campaigns enlisting popular support were mounted in pursuit of economic goals. Further, the quality of physical and human capital was improved through substantial increases in education and training and through programs for the advancement of science and technology.

NONGOVERNMENTAL INSTITUTIONS

There were also institutional reforms and developments in the private sector that had a considerable effect on the growth mechanisms of Japan and Russia. Market mechanisms became increasingly important in both countries from the mid-1880's until World War I, and remained so in Japan throughout its transformation.

In early Meiji the issue had been the initial establishment of a few modern industries; by the turn of the century, the task was the independent expansion of these industries. Gradually and increasingly, the economy responded to market signals, to the rate of return on capital, and to the profit motive. Private modern investment became the main dynamic source of growth as agriculture and the traditional economy faltered and government influence became more indirect. The pattern of growth between 1900 and 1945, with its "trend acceleration," can be most easily described by listing certain characteristics that together form a specific pattern. First there was the long upward swing in the rate of growth of GNP—3 per cent between 1901 and 1917 and 6 per cent between 1931 and 1937—and the downswing from 1917 to 1931 at the rate of 2.75 per cent. These long swings were more pronounced in the rate of growth of private investment than in aggregate output, and can be referred to as "investment spurts." Each investment spurt brought a rise in efficiency as a result of innovational investments, and each was also identified with particular industries: the first spurt (1901–1917) was connected with cotton textiles, particularly integrated spinning-weaving mills, and the second (1931–1937) with heavy and armament-related industries. Over the years these spurts drove the rate of investment to higher levels, from around 12 per cent to above 20 per cent of the GNP. As a nation, the Japanese were willing to save increasingly larger amounts.

A principal element in the Japanese growth mechanism in this century then, was the sudden burst in investment from time to time. Such spurts brought with them new industries, technological progress, and higher levels of efficiency. Successive innovational investments introduced ever more efficient borrowed technology, which in turn led to trend acceleration. Income per capita also rose, which in its turn resulted in faster development through enlarged markets. Rising income per capita also generated improvement in the quality of human capital (better schools, better diet) and raised the household savings ratio. The combination of institutional innovations and what might be termed "learning by doing" continually expanded the range of relevant stock of unexploited technology in the twentieth century. The responsiveness of Japanese workers to wage differentials made it easy for the modern industrial sector to draw labor from the traditional agricultural sector. Japan's labor supply was very flexible; as wages rose in the modern sector (the result of the productivity increases), labor flowed into it. In effect Japan had the advantage of what is usually called "cheap labor." In the traditional sector of the economy productivity and wages could not keep up because factor proportions there retarded technological progress.

In the twentieth century, two other nongovernmental institutions arose in Japan that were to have lasting significance: the *zaibatsu* and *permanent employment*. Though the most famous zaibatsu (Mitsui, Mitsubishi, Sumitomo, and Yasuda) took form in the Meiji era, these business combines reached their greatest power toward the end of the 1920's, and their power was based largely on the great advances made in industrialization in the first two decades of this century. At the risk of oversimplification, it can be said that in the nineteenth century commerce was the chief activity of the zaibatsu; that around World War I it was industry, with particular emphasis on coal mining, shipbuilding, engineering, and glass; and that in the 1920's it became finance. The zaibatsu were leaders in the development of technologically sophisticated industries. They were the major innovators and importers of Western technology. They provided low-income Japan with the possibility of exploiting economies of scale, and their diversification permitted what has been called "combined investment," that is, the simultaneous development of complementary industries. The zaibatsu also economized on what must have been a scarce factor: individuals capable of running modern businesses; and through the operation of their affiliated banks, they were most adept at mobilizing scarce capital resources. Given that the issue of that day was growth rather than economic democracy (as it is today), there developed in Japan a certain kind of "bigness" that was unacceptable elsewhere but quite suitable in its setting.

Permanent employment was another peculiarly Japanese invention that came into prominence between 1900 and 1920. It was out of keeping with the nineteenth-century industrial labor situation, in which piracy of workers was common and turnover rates were extremely high. But after the turn of the century, a growing number of workers, especially in large enterprises, was hired on a lifetime basis, and much attention was devoted to noncash benefits, such as housing, stores, and medical care. One immediate reason for the creation of this system was the desire of enterprises to undermine the powerful and troublesome regional labor recruiters, and the consequent division of labor markets was most convenient for the big producers. Another reason was that permanent employment gave the Japanese entrepreneur a labor force without incentives to oppose technological and organizational progress, including the labor-saving type. Lifetime employment also created the type of labor force in which the enterprise had a willingness to invest through, inter alia, on-the-job training. This system, however, was essentially confined to modern large-scale industry, and there were always temporary workers who could be and were laid off when business conditions deteriorated.

In Russia, before the Communists took power, the government exercised its influence over the market both directly and indirectly. From the great reforms of the 1860's to the First World War, private-sector institutions began to grow in numbers and strength. Even in the 1890's, when the direct role of the government was at its height, these institutions expanded. Between 1861 and 1873 more than 350 new companies were formed, but in the 1890's almost 700 were established. Active development of private institutions in the banking sector also occurred; by 1900 forty commercial banks with some two hundred branches were doing business. The credit generated domestically was substantially augmented by foreign credits. Initially, foreign credits were acquired primarily as a result of government loan guarantees. As confidence in the Russian economy grew, however—full gold-standard convertibility of the ruble was attained in 1897—unguaranteed, private-sector foreign investment in Russian industry increased in importance.

After 1900 several organizational changes took place in the private sector of the Russian economy. First, cartels developed to a marked degree. They rose primarily as a response to the recession crisis at the turn of the century, and their main function was to limit competition through the joint control of marketing. It has been argued that they tended to limit production rather than encourage it; it cannot be said, therefore, that they had the same positive effect upon economic growth that the zaibatsu, with their multipurpose activities, had in Japan. Second, the cartels found themselves more and more dependent on the banks after the direct role of the government in the economy diminished. Russian private banks were originally organized on English lines rather than German, that is, they were essentially deposit and short-term-credit banks rather than investment houses. But as the investment role of the government receded, Russian banks moved into the void. The Saint Petersburg banks were organized on the German investment-bank model, and at the beginning of the war, twelve joint-stock banks (nine of them in Saint Petersburg) held 80 per cent of the total bank capital. They dominated activity in the major industries and Russian financial relations with foreign countries. Third, entrepreneurship after the turn of the century became more and more russified. Between the mid-1880's and 1900 foreign capital and management was a moving force in Russian industry. But after 1900 investment in Russian industry was done increasingly through Russian banks, in which foreigners could invest but not control. Russian banks and syndicates even began to float the stock of purely Russian companies on West European exchanges, and Russian managers came to occupy more important positions within companies that had earlier been dominated by foreign managers.

After the Soviets assumed power and after the beginning of the plan period, nongovernmental forms of economic organizations became of little account. Strictly speaking, collective farms are nongovernmental organizations, though for this analysis it is better to consider them governmental. However, many of the growth-inducing aspects of the zaibatsu and permanent employment in Japan can also be found in Soviet economic institutions. Combined investment, bigness, the careful use of scarce managerial resources, and the encouragement of on-the-job training have also been elements of the Russian growth mechanism. Other elements—the successful fostering of domestic technological progress, for example—have not.

AGRICULTURE AND GROWTH

The agricultural sector played a pivotal role in Japanese growth during the Meiji years. In the absence of large capital imports, the initial establishment and subsequent development of the modern economy depended on the accelerated growth of the traditional economy, a growth the premodern economy was capable of producing. The expansion capabilities of the agricultural sector, however, were limited, and its growth rate began to taper off in the early twentieth century. After World War I its importance diminished abruptly. Thereafter, a new growth mechanism came into being.

Controversial as the data are, it is nonetheless clear that agricultural output increased rather significantly in the Meiji period. Agriculture was able to supply the economy with its principal exports of silk and tea in order to finance imports of foreign machinery and expertise; with the goods to take care of a growing population; with an expanding, nonagricultural labor force; and with a market for the early industrial products. Output grew faster than in the preceding Tokugawa era, less through the application of Western technology than through a more intensive and widespread application of the best traditional methods of cultivation. The government took an active part in spreading the best indigenous techniques. Veteran farmers were sent throughout the country, experimental stations were established, and modern scientific analysis was applied to traditional technology. The incentive mechanism was improved through the reforms in land registration and the institution of a predictable land tax. Eventually the entire country attained something very close to "best practice" levels. By the time that point was reached in the early twentieth century Japan had more than three million workers in manufacturing; textiles and similar manufactured products had made rapid progress, and alternative sources of surplus were being developed.

In Russian economic growth agriculture also made a substantial contribution, but less through increased output than through increased exports. Output rose somewhat above the growth of population (1.7 per cent compared with 1.5) and because a disproportionate part of this population gain was urban (10 per cent of the total in 1861; 15 per cent in 1897) the countryside was an important factor. Its principal contribution was in providing grain exports, which gave Russia a favorable balance of trade and helped attract foreign investment. Grain output in 1900 was about twice that of 1860, but the level of grain exports was five times greater. Food products had made up 40 per cent of exports in 1860, but they reached almost 70 per cent in 1900. These new levels of productivity were possible only under the unrelenting pressure of the tsarist government, which put exports first. An internal market was not created. Emancipation of the serfs in 1861 left the peasants with insufficient land allotments, burdensome redemption payments, and the substitution of the commune for the earlier political and fiscal power exercised by the serf-owners. The landholding nobility did little to improve its land, peasants were land hungry, and high redemption payments limited reinvestment in agriculture. The post-Emancipation strengthening of the commune also perpetuated backward technology and limited mobility.

Government policy toward the peasant commune changed after the turn of the century as a result of mounting peasant uprisings. The Stolypin reforms, introduced in 1906, encouraged the establishment of large, consolidated, private farms. In the brief span of time before the Russian Revolution, almost 25 per cent of the peasants left the communes to set up their own farms. The intention of the regime was to encourage the growth of a group of rich, productive farmers who would be politically supportive, who would market a large share of their output, and who would create an internal market for agricultural equipment and consumer goods. In their short existence, the Stolypin farms did make contributions in these directions.

The post-1928 years constituted the third period in which agriculture played a considerable role in Russian growth mechanisms. These were the years of central plans and collectivization. Agricultural output did not increase in the pre-World War II decade, but even so collectivization, in the overall context of the Soviet industrialization drive, was not a failure. Agricultural policy in the Soviet growth mechanism was in one sense similar to agricultural policy in Meiji Japan in that it was designed to provide the means of transferring population from the rural to the urban industrial areas; to provide the food to feed the growing urban population; to provide raw materials for industry; to provide exports that could finance the importation of industrial inputs; and if possible, to provide huge increases in productivity so as to permit all these other objectives to be accomplished without reducing the consumption levels of the population.

Clearly, the last objective was not accomplished. But the first was, and to a remarkable extent the others were also. These aims were realized in part because the organizational structure of the collective farm made it an effective device for the regime to collect a healthy share of agricultural output, even if the collective farm itself was not an effective instrument for increasing output. Thus, from 1928 to the end of the 1930's, the marketings of agricultural output rose 65 per cent and of food products 62 per cent, even though agricultural output did not grow. This increase in marketings was a vital contribution to the industrialization program. At the same time the urban population doubled between 1928 and 1938. Grain exports, however, especially in the early 1930's, jumped substantially with the result that the level of food consumption per capita in the cities dropped by more than 20 per cent. The human cost in the countryside was higher still. Finally, figures for the post-1928 era show that the marketings of nonfood products, such as cotton and other fiber crops, wool, and tobacco, rose somewhat more rapidly than those of food. This increase reflects the importance placed on supplying industry with agricultural raw materials.

FOREIGN TECHNOLOGY

The borrowing of advanced technology from the industrialized nations of the West was crucial to the economic growth of both Japan and Russia. In Japan the importation and diffusion of Western technology received marked attention from the beginning of the Meiji period. Training programs were set up, technicians were brought in from abroad, and Japanese were sent to study in foreign countries. Modern machinery, embodying advanced technology, was imported in the process of building new industries and overhead capital. Furthermore, throughout the twentieth century the spurts of autonomous investment—the key Japanese growth mechanism—introduced and extended successive waves of borrowed technology, embodied and disembodied, into the Japanese economy. The Japanese, it should be stressed, were not inventors of new technology, but they did become most proficient at adapting and even improving Western techniques for their own purposes. Improvement engineering or value engineering became a fine art in Japan.

Three aspects of this process of borrowing are important. First, Japan's success in assimilating foreign technology was aided by a number of institutions that sprang up in the course of the transformation period, particularly the zaibatsu, permanent employment, and administrative guidance. Each of these contributed to Japan's capacity to absorb advanced, foreign technology. Second, Japan faced the problem of adapting advanced technology that had been developed for economies in which capital was relatively abundant and labor relatively scarce to a situation of plentiful labor. Attention to factor proportions was essential to competition in international markets, but the Japanese needed to combine this with reliance on their chief resource, that of labor. The Japanese explored with creativity the paths mitigating the incongruity between required factor proportions and domestic factor supplies and prices. One method of lessening the difference was the selection of those modern industrial activities that were relatively the most suitable to domestic factor proportions—for example, textiles during the 1910's and 1920's. Another well-known method was fuller utilization of capital through the more intensive use of labor. Multishift systems were used throughout the period of modern economic growth in Japan. The partial substitution of capital by labor through subcontracting, even in some technologically advanced industries, was also practiced. As a result of these adaptations of borrowed technology, the absorptive capacity of manufacturing for labor was increased.

Third, Japan was unable to rely upon foreign capital until after the Chinese indemnity of 1895 and the New York and London loans for the Russian-Japanese War in 1904–1905. Before then, both the Japanese and the foreign lenders were wary about the safety and security of such investments.

Though both countries depended greatly on Western technology in their growth processes, Russian industrialization, especially in the nineteenth century, relied more on foreign entrepreneurs and foreign investment. As a result of the protective tariff of 1891, foreigners who wished to do business in Russia had to do it through direct foreign investment. The backwardness of the Russian economy and the tremendous opportunities for profit had a great appeal for the foreign investor. In the 1890's foreign capital accounted for almost one-half of all new capital invested in Russian industry. In 1900 foreigners owned more than 70 per cent of the capital in mining, metallurgy, and engineering. This foreign investment greatly expanded the capital stock of Russia. Foreign technology was brought into Russia in the advanced capital equipment itself—and in the form of human capital: the foreign technicians and experienced businessmen and managers who came to Russia. Steel mills built in southern Russia after the mid-1880's were of the same technological level and size as those being built in Western Europe. Moreover, with the participation of foreigners in management, those mills kept up with West European progress and remained in the mainstream of world steelmaking. Foreign firms in competition with Russian firms also forced the latter to be more efficient if they wanted to survive. Though the protectionist tariff did shield Russian firms from foreign competition, it could not shield them from competition of foreign firms in Russia. Indeed, in helping to bring foreign firms to Russia, the tariff enhanced domestic competition.

In the 1920's an attempt was made to enlist, and in many instances bring back, the participation of foreign managers to assist in the restoration and expansion of Soviet industry and its technological level. The program of foreign concessions accounted for only a minuscule proportion of industrial output; even so, its role should not be overlooked because it was more extensive than is generally realized. Almost all sectors of the economy were at least touched by it, and in some—coal mining, electrical equipment, communications, motor vehicles—the program appears to have had considerable impact.

Under the impetus of the five-year plans and the industrialization drive of the 1930's, the Soviets undertook a massive program of importing foreign technology. In addition to the importation of advanced technology, the Soviets imported skilled workers, technicians, and engineering consultants. The years of most intensive construction were 1930 through 1932. Almost 7,000 foreign specialists were reported to be at work in Soviet industry in 1932. One source claims that no plant of any size was built in these years without a Western technical or construction connection. And Stalin reportedly said in 1944 that during the 1930's two-thirds of all large industrial enterprises in the Soviet Union had been built with United States help or technical assistance.

In their drive to transform their economy as quickly as possible, the Soviets borrowed technology from the West on an evtraordinary scale. It would have been economically irrational to do otherwise. They went on to combine borrowing with heavy investment in their own science and technology research and training programs. Though the returns from this program were great, the Russians have not been as successful as the Japanese in mastering modern production technology. Their shortcomings here become even clearer in the contemporary period.

Agriculture

The role of agriculture as a growth mechanism has already been touched upon. But because agriculture remained important in both countries as a source of employment and as a supplier of labor long after the structure of output had shifted toward the industrial sector, it requires treatment as a sector of the economy.

The dimensions of agricultural growth in Japan from the 1860's to 1940's can be quickly summarized. Agricultural output expanded with increasing rapidity throughout the Meiji era and until World War I. From then on its growth declined precipitously; even in the 1930's, when other sectors of the economy rebounded, agriculture did not recover. In fact, the trend of decline was reversed only in the second half of the 1950's. Throughout this thirty-five-year period, rice remained the major crop, and the small peasant farm the major unit of production.

What was so noteworthy in Meiji Japan from the economic point of view was that agricultural productivity was raised without recourse to imported Western technology. Productivity increases were based on improvements in the old ways of doing things and on the spread of these superior ways from the advanced western part of Japan to the backward eastern part. The kind of technology perfected in Japan at that time—frequently referred to as Meiji technology—used land and labor intensively and was very sparing in its use of capital.

At the beginning of the twentieth century opportunities for traditional technological progress still existed, but the areas of possible improvement were becoming more limited. Most farmers were already using greater quantities of fertilizer; diffusion of better technology had already occurred in many sections of Japan; and seeds, especially in western Japan, had also reached much higher levels of quality. By the early 1920's further progress based on traditional technology became unlikely, however, and conventional inputs had reached their most refined level. From then on agriculture became the sick man of the Japanese economy. Output was unsatisfactory, and once again better ways of doing things were needed. However, better ways would have required a very different type of technology. The time had come for a more capital-intensive system of cultivation involving more machinery and greater investments. Many factors stood in the way: small units of production; and unfavorable man-land ratio; the large numbers of people still remaining on the land and excluded from the possibilities of industrial employment; the competition of cheap colonial production in Taiwan and Korea. All of these factors combined to create more than three decades of agricultural depression. And the history of these post-1920 years is replete with tenant unrest, cries of parasitic landlordism, and agrarian misery. What had worked so well in the nineteenth century had turned to ashes in the twentieth, and through the end of the 1930's no solution came into sight.

One rather startling aspect of Russian agricultural development in this eighty-year transformation period was the meager increase in the productivity of land. In very rough terms, gross agricultural output (crops and livestock products) in 1939 was only about two and a half times what it was in 1860 and the sown area just about twice as large; thus, output per acre for the entire eighty years was up only about 30 per cent. Output per acre grew at the same pace as sown area in the years until 1913, both then being up 56 per cent. But between 1913 and 1939, per acre output dropped 17 per cent while sown area increased 27 per cent.

In the 1860–1913 period Russian agriculture was dominated by small-scale operations in which the use of agricultural machinery, fertilizer, and scientific methods was rare. These aspects of advanced technology were limited mainly to some western regions and to industrial crops. Yields per acre and per man were both low by the then current standards—a circumstance caused primarily by the fact that the three-field system with multiple strips had been preserved. As the population increased, so did the importance of periodic repartition of the land by the communes. In fact, because the rural population grew fairly rapidly in the second half of the nineteenth century, the strips got smaller and smaller, at times becoming less than three feet wide. The Stolypin reform of 1906 was designed to encourage peasants to withdraw from the communes and consolidate their strips into farmsteads, and one quarter of the peasant households did take advantage of this program before it was interrupted by the war.

Soviet agriculture from 1928 to the end of the 1930's did not fare nearly so well as industry and most other sectors. Gross agricultural output on the average in the 1938–1940 years was only slightly above that of 1928. The output of crops was up 13.7 per cent, but the output of livestock products was down 13.9 per cent from 1928 as a result of the heavy destruction of livestock herds. The stock of cattle fell from 60.1 million head in 1928 to a low of 33.5 million head in 1933; it recovered to a level of 53.5 million in 1939, but then fell again to 47.8 million in 1940. Other livestock herds experienced similar patterns. In the decade after 1928 the population of the Soviet Union increased by about 14 per cent, which meant in effect that total agricultural output per capita was actually down by about 10 per cent.

With collectivization large-scale farm operations came to dominate Russia's rural scene. Agricultural machinery was introduced extensively, the use of fertilizers and irrigation began to increase, and attempts were made to improve production techniques. Nonetheless, there was a decided drop in land productivity. Mechanization and efforts to improve farm methods did, however, make possible a decline in the number of agricultural workers (but not the man-hours worked); they were also able to keep labor productivity from falling. By world standards, Russian agriculture in 1940 was very inefficient in all respects, including the level of farm management and peasant morale. Only in its ability to extract marketings from the peasantry was the Russian agricultural system reasonably successful.

Industry

The growth of industrial production in Japan and Russia in this period of transformation may be compared in terms of three groups of industries. These groups, fully described in Table 10.3, are as follows: Group 1 industries are dominated by food processing and kindred activities. These industries, which include wood and clay products, are forms of production whose traditional character remained pronounced, and whose techniques were generally of low capital intensity. Group 2 industries represent textile and leather products, and they occupied an intermediate position in terms of capital intensity. Group 3 production consists mostly of chemicals, metals, and machines; generally, these activities were of a "heavier," more modern character and representative of what might be called capital-intensive, "post textile" technology.

In Japan industrial output was dominated during the nineteenth century by the Group 1 industries. In the twentieth century two rather distinct changes occurred in the structure of output, however: the great relative gains of Group 2, especially around the time of World War I; and the even greater relative gains of Group 3 industries as Japan prepared for war in the 1930's. In 1919, for example, output was split as follows: Group 1, 20 per cent; Group 2, 51 per cent; and Group 3, 29 per cent. But as Table 10.3 shows, when the economy was already heavily influenced by the military, these percentages changed drastically.

The Group 1 food industries and Group 2 textile industries, especially cotton cloth, were relatively developed in Russia prior to 1860, but from 1860 to 1913 Group 3 industries—coal, ferrous metals, and oil—developed more rapidly. Some rough data indicate that in 1897, Group 1 accounted for 29 per cent of total employment, Group 2 for 32 per cent, and Group 3 for 39 per cent. Again as Table 10.3 shows, these proportions had all changed by 1940. It must be noted, however, that (1) the Russian data for 1897 and 1940 are from different sources and thus their comparability may be limited; (2) the employment and output data for 1940 are also from different sources, limiting their comparability; and (3) Group 1 includes lumber and wood products. In Russia this is a substantial industry (in 1940 it accounted for 17 per cent of employment and 22 per cent of output), and has certain aspects of Group 3 industries. If it were switched from Group 1 to Group 3, then Russia's employment and output structure in 1940 would look

T A B L E   1 0. 3.   **Shares of Output and Employment
by Industrial Groups**
(in percentages)

	GROUP 1[1]		GROUP 2[2]		GROUP 3[3]	
	Employ-ment	Output	Employ-ment	Output	Employ-ment	Output
Japan						
1909	24.8	29.6	62.8	50.7	12.4	19.7
1919	20.9	20.0	54.8	51.0	24.3	29.0
1940	18.8	19.0	24.4	18.4	56.8	62.6
Russia						
1897	29.4	37.2	31.6	34.8	39.0	28.1
1940	33.6	42.7	21.1	20.2	45.2	37.1

[1] Group 1: Food; lumber and wood products; ceramic, stone and clay products; printing, publishing, and allied industries.

[2] Group 2: Textiles; leather and leather products.

[3] Group 3: Chemicals, petroleum, coal; rubber and rubber products; iron and steel; non-ferrous metals and products; transportation equipment; machinery; electrical equipment; other tools and equipment.

SOURCES:

Japan: All data are from K. Ohkawa and H. Rosovsky, *Japanese Economic Growth* (Stanford: Stanford University Press, 1973), p. 83.

Russia: For 1897, from M. I. Tugan-Baranovsky, *The Russian Factory in the Nineteenth Century* (Homewood, Ill.: Irwin, 1970), p. 273; 1940, employment from *Promyshlennost' SSSR* [Industry of the USSR] (Moscow, 1957), p. 24; and output calculated on basis of data provided in N. Kaplan and R. Moorsteen, "An Index of Soviet Industrial Output," *American Economic Review* 50 (June, 1960), p. 296.

strikingly like that of Japan's. One remaining difference is that in Japan, the Group 3 employment share was lower than its output share, indicating an above-average labor productivity for these industries; in Russia the reverse was true. One possible explanation for this difference is the large measure of mining activities in Russia, an industry with low labor productivity.

Another comparison between the two countries' industrial sectors pertains to the scale of production. The differences in this regard between Japan and Russia are striking, as the data given in Table 10.4 reveal. Though both economies moved toward increasing large-scale production, Russia in 1910 already had more than half of its factory labor force in units employing more than 500 workers, whereas Japan in 1940 was still below that figure.

Finally, no comparison of Japanese and Russian industrialization should omit specific consideration of the labor supply. In very broad terms, and from the point of view of entrepreneurs, the labor situa-

T A B L E 1 0. 4.   **Proportion of Workers in Factories of Different Sizes**

(in percentages)

NUMBER OF EMPLOYEES	JAPAN		RUSSIA	
	1909	*1940*	*1910*	*1950*[1]
Less than 50	45.6	36.5	11.6	9.2[2]
50 to 499	33.6	27.2	35.0	21.2
More than 500	20.9	36.4	53.4	69.6

[1] 1950 figures for Russia should not be greatly different for the unavailable 1940 data.

[2] This figure is proportion of workers in factories of less than 100.

SOURCES:

Japan: Calculated from Table 4.5, 4.6, 4.7 in K. Ohkawa and H. Rosovsky, *Japanese Economic Growth* (Stanford: Stanford University Press, 1973), pp. 83, 86.

Russia: 1910 from P. A. Khromov, *Ekonomicheskoe razvitie Rossii v XIX–XX vekakh* [The Economic Development of Russia in the XIX–XX Centuries] (Moscow: Gospolitizdat, 1950), p. 301; 1950 from TsSU, *Promyshlennost' SSSR* [Industry USSR] (Moscow: Gostatizdat, 1957), p. 15.

tion in Japan was nearly always favorable. The relatively advanced levels of education assured the presence of qualified people. The desire to work was strong and levels of discipline were high. Most important, the entrepreneur was able to hire workers at very advantageous wage rates, which, in general, lagged behind increases in labor productivity. From the 1860's until at least World War II, Japanese business had the considerable competitive advantage of cheap, but good, labor.

In any comparison of the industrialization process in the two countries, it must also be kept in mind that Japanese wage-employment system in large, modern enterprises has had its widely known peculiarities, symbolized by the terms "seniority wage scale" and "lifetime commitment." In Japan the level and composition of wages were determined by individual enterprises rather than by an impersonal labor market. The Japanese wage-employment system also included these characteristics: wages were closely linked to personal factors such as level of education and specific schools, age, and length of service in an enterprise; widespread on-the-job training; the particular job and the individual's efficiency had less of an effect on the wage than the cost of living and the worker's status; a strong and reciprocal sense of commitment obtained between the worker and his firm—especially pronounced in large enterprises; the rate of labor turnover was very low for these firms, and there was little movement to smaller units or from smaller units. These characteristics, it must be repeated, bore on that minority of the total labor force fortunate enough to be attached to large and modern enterprises. Small-scale enterprises, in which wages were low, were however also likely to exhibit paternalism of a more personal nature. The movement between village and factory also operated, until World War II, to reduce and restrain sectoral and class consciousness. Industrial growth in Japan did not prevent, however, the usual consequence of crowded, squalid housing conditions for the workers.

Russian industrial workers in the years before the revolution were tied even more to the land than their Japanese counterparts. They often were members of village communes and returned to the communes for part of the year to help with the harvest. Even those who had broken all strong personal ties with the countryside did not shed overnight their peasant mentality. Russian workers generally lived in miserable conditions. They were poorly paid, terribly overcrowded, had little education; they were a destitute and exploited labor force. Even though their wages were low, however, it has been argued that from the standpoint of the entrepreneur they were an expensive factor because their productivity was also very low.

In the first decade after the revolution, the industrial situation in one sense worsened. Many of the most experienced and qualified people were no longer in industry or deprived of positions of responsibility for political reasons. Yet during the post-1928 plan period industrial output did improve as the result of the widespread government program of education and on-the-job training. One contrast with Japan is that though pay scales did vary with education and qualification, the amount of pay within the Russian scale was directly a function of how much the worker produced. Furthermore, in the hurly-burly of the industrialization drive of the thirties, labor mobility, especially within given geographic areas, was very high.

Foreign Trade

In no sphere are differences between Japanese and Russian patterns of development more clearly seen than in foreign trade. Japan's foreign trade grew rapidly throughout its transformation, whereas Russia's declined markedly in the twentieth century. Japan's exports consisted primarily of manufactured goods, which it traded for raw materials, whereas Russia exported grain and other raw materials to buy manufactured items.

Japan's foreign trade expanded twice as fast as the world trade rate from the 1880's to World War I, and ten times as fast in the interwar period. Throughout most of these years Japan was an exporter of manufactured products, with its chief customers located in Asia and North America. The principal products exported changed from silk in the nineteenth century to cotton textiles after World War I. Machinery exports gradually became more important in the 1930's. Before World War II, then, Japanese exports were dominated by the products of "light industry," among which textiles were the leading item. These industries engaged in exporting also showed a good deal of "export dependence," that is, they sent abroad a sizable proportion of their output.

The success of Japan as an exporter is to be explained primarily in terms of its ability to reduce costs and keep its products competitive on the international market. There were brief periods when an acceleration of growth was caused by a greater demand for Japanese products, such as during World War I, but in the long run it was the export industries, made more efficient by repeated injections of foreign technology, that managed to find willing customers abroad.

Despite such a good performance in foreign trade since joining the world economy, Japan, until very recently, encountered the external restraint of foreign payments deficits. These deficits acted as a ceiling, periodically blocking further growth near the peak of investment spurts. Japan's foreign reserve position was to a considerable extent determined by its trade balance, so that expansions of exports and imports were permanent factors in determining when the ceiling came into effect. On the import side the severest "supply restraint" was the importation of raw materials, fuels, and, in the twentieth century, food necessitated by the lack of land and natural resources. This restraint was always operative before World War II, despite successful substitution for imports other than raw materials and fuels. But import substitution could not possibly go far enough, and an adverse balance of payments repeatedly compelled yen devaluations during the 1920's and 1930's. The external constraints on modern economic growth in Japan undoubtedly had crucial psychological, political, and organizational consequences before 1945. Some of the most imaginative economic institutions were closely tied to resource needs—for example, the large trading companies. Its poverty in resources was also an ostensible reason for Japan's entry into World War II in the wake of the U.S. oil embargo. In general, this poor raw material base created a psychological atmosphere of poverty and uncertainty that no growth rate statistics could cure.

In Russia's case political constraints following the revolution were critical in reducing its level of trade and involvement in the world economy. Before 1913 the trade of tsarist Russia manifested all the characteristics typical of an underdeveloped economy. Russia exported raw materials and imported machinery and other industrial items. Its exports consisted chiefly of grain, lumber, and oil; indeed, before the turn of the century Russia was the second largest producer and the largest exporter of oil in the world. Its imports before 1913 consisted mainly of machinery and equipment and certain materials that it did not produce: rubber and nonferrous metals. Imports also included some items it did produce in increasing quantities but for which the domestic demand outstripped local capacities: rolled ferrous metals, copper, coal, and cotton.

Of critical importance were the imports of machinery and equipment. From the middle of the 1880's to the beginning of the First World War, these imports increased fivefold. In 1913 they constituted 75 per cent of domestic machinery and equipment production. Much of this machinery was introduced through foreign-owned firms, which figured so prominently in the Russian economy at this stage. As a result of foreign investments, Russia generally maintained a surplus of commodity exports over imports. After the turn of the century, the outflows from Russia of dividend and interest payments to foreigners became greater than the inflows of foreign investment, giving the illusion that Russia was a capital exporter.

Russian trade fell off dramatically after the war and the revolution. The share of exports in national income which was 10.4 per cent in 1913 dropped to 3.1 per cent in 1929. While the overall policy of the Soviet government in the five-year plans was to assure the rapid development and independence of the Soviet economy, foreign trade was designated as being a vital factor in the period of the First Five Year Plan. With the emphasis in the plan on industrial capital formation, imports of machinery and equipment again assumed a position of great importance. By 1932 they rose to a level of 55 per cent of total imports; imports of certain types of machines (turbines, generators, boilers, machine tools, and metal-cutting machines) rose to between 50 and 90 per cent of the increase in supply of these goods in the years of the first plan, 1928 to 1932. On the whole, imports of capital goods were 12 to 14 per cent of gross investment during the first plan. Furthermore, imports of certain basic industrial materials (lead, tin, nickel, zinc, aluminum, and rubber) accounted for 90 to 100 per cent of the amounts consumed in the Soviet economy during much of this period.

After the completion of the First Five Year Plan, Soviet involve-ment in trade decreased—largely a consequence of the policy of nondependence on capitalist nations. But certain financial devel-opments were at work also. Because of the depression that had grip-ped the market economies, world prices of agricultural goods and other raw materials fell relatively more than did prices of machinery items. Thus, it became more and more expensive for the Soviets to proceed with their trade. Furthermore, they found it difficult to acquire foreign credits they felt they could afford.

For reasons such as these, Soviet trade plummeted after 1932. The share of exports in national income, which had reached a high of 3.5 per cent, skidded to 0.5 per cent in 1937. Imports of capital goods fell to 2 per cent of gross investment in the Second Five Year Plan period, 1933 to 1937. The dependence on imports for key items decreased—for some, rather abruptly: the importation of tractors, for example, dropped from almost 60 per cent of the growth of the tractor stock in 1931 to 0.0 per cent in 1932. By 1937 imports of only copper, lead, tin, and nickel accounted for more than 20 per cent of total internal consumption of these materials. Under the First Five Year Plan, then, imports played a rather significant role in Russian economic growth. Clearly, if there had been no trade at all, Soviet industrialization would have been seriously retarded. Subsequently, however, foreign trade was much less of a strategic factor in Soviet growth, and with the construction of domestic production capacity the Soviet economy became increasingly self-sufficient.

In sum, the Japanese and Russian economies produced compar-able per capita production despite the background of different tradi-tions and policies. Japan's Meiji leaders entered international society at a time when the free-enterprise model was overwhelmingly the most prestigious, and this model conformed with their own prefer-ences and recollections regarding the inefficiency and injustice of late feudal struggles for freedom from baronial control. From the first these leaders tried to stimulate and activate; they chose, in 1881, to sell most of the government's investments to the builders of the future zaibatsu combines. Yet those builders were full partners with the politicians in state-building, and the heritage of the family firm, regulated like a feudal warrior house through founder's rules, car-ried its own stern injunctions against waste and frivolity. In a variety of ways the preferences, though not the institutions, of the past served the purposes of the present.

In Russia the tradition of central government intervention and foreign participation in industrialization, one that had developed

TABLE 10.5. International Comparisons

	JAPAN	RUSSIA	GERMANY	FRANCE	ITALY	SWEDEN	U.K.	U.S.A.
Average Annual Rates of Growth (in percentages)								
National Product								
1870–1913	2.7[1]	2.5	2.8	1.6	1.4	3.0	2.0	4.3
1913–1938	4.0	2.8 or 4.7[2]	1.6	0.9	1.7	1.8	1.1	2.0
National Product Per Capita								
1870–1913	1.7[1]	1.0	1.6	1.4	0.7	2.3	1.1	2.2
1913–1938	2.7	1.9 or 3.8[2]	1.1	0.8	1.0	1.3	0.7	0.8
Agricultural Output								
1870–1913	2.0[3]	1.7	1.5	0.7	NA	1.7	0.0	2.3
1913–1938	1.2	1.0	0.0	NA	NA	0.0	0.9	1.1
Industrial Output								
1870–1913	5.6[3]	5.2	4.4	2.6	3.7	5.9	2.0	5.0
1913–1938	7.1	4.0 or 6.8[2]	1.6	0.4	2.0	3.3	1.7	1.7
Population								
1870–1913	1.00	1.52	1.16	0.17	0.66	0.70	0.88	2.09
1913–1938	1.33	0.89	0.51	0.02	0.67	0.46	0.43	1.17

Absolute Levels

GNP in 1937 (in billions of 1964 dollars)	37	90–93	43	42	27	NA	NA	228
GNP per capita in 1940 (in 1964 dollars)	554	510–542	1,101[4]	1,017[5]	580[6]	NA	1,234[7]	1,886

SOURCES:

Rates of Growth: All data are from A. Maddison, *op. cit.*, pp. 154–155, 157, 159, 161, 164, except that for Russia, the period 1928–1938, for National Product and National Product per capita are constructed from R. Moorsteen and R. Powell, *op. cit.*, pp. 361–363, and for Industry from R. Powell, *op. cit.*, p. 178.

Absolute Levels: S. Cohn, *Economic Development in the Soviet Union* (Lexington: D. C. Heath, 1970), pp. 111, 112.

[1] 1879–1913.
[2] See text page 162.
[3] 1874–1913.
[4] 1937.
[5] 1931.
[6] 1941.
[7] 1937.

after Peter I, affected the development of early industrialization. The Great Reforms, however, proved less effective in removing rural barriers to agricultural development than did the Meiji reforms in the same years. Until the last decade of the empire, individual free-holding and a domestic market did not develop as a rural basis for rapid industrial progress. Only with collectivization did political discontinuity bring the total centralization attempted by the era of plans. Seen in this light Japan's extraordinary political continuity throughout the period under review—one of institutions, purposes, and elites—may well seem the single most favorable factor for that country's development.

International Comparisons

The economic growth of Japan and Russia during their trans-formation to modern societies may be compared with that of selected Western European countries for which certain strategically important information is available. The countries used in this comparison are Germany, France, Italy, Sweden, the United Kingdom, and the United States, and the data—ranging from agricultural output to national product per capita—are presented in Table 10.5.

In terms of the growth rate of gross national product in the pre-1913 period, both Japan (2.7 per cent) and Russia (2.5 per cent), who were just getting started, compare well with the other countries. They grew faster than Italy, France, and the United Kingdom, and just a little bit slower than Germany and Sweden. Only the United States grew appreciably faster.

With regard to GNP per capita in this period, Japan (1.7 per cent) was still relatively high, surpassed only by the United States and Sweden. Russia's performance (1.0 per cent) was not as impressive, being excelled by all except Italy.

In the 1913 to 1938 period Japan and Russia led all the other nations in both GNP and GNP per capita growth. To a great extent their lead was the result of the Great Depression in the Western nations, the effects of which were avoided by Japan and Russia.

In agricultural output in these two time spans, Japan and Russia were at or near the top of the list—as they were in industrial output too. Their growth rates are quite impressive, especially that of Japan's, though if the 1928–1940 period had been listed separately, the Soviet Union would have shown the greatest increase. Russia's population growth was high in the pre-1913 period, Japan's average; in the post-1913 period Japan's population growth was the highest, Russia's about average.

By 1937 the Soviet Union's gross national product was second only to that of the United States at a level about 40 per cent of America's. Japan's GNP in 1937, however, was lower than everyone's except Italy's. Yet in terms of GNP per capita, by 1940 Japan and Russia were almost identical. Theirs was about on a par with that of Italy, half those of France and Germany, a little less than half that of the United Kingdom, and about 30 per cent that of the United States.

Chapter Eleven

SOCIAL INTERDEPENDENCE

FOR BOTH JAPAN AND RUSSIA the 1860's ushered in three-quarters of a century of relentless and frequently tumultuous change. Remnants of the old societies succumbed through far-reaching government programs and through the indirect but equally fundamental consequences of rapid modernization. The most thoroughgoing social planning, instituted after changes of direction in leadership, occurred at the beginning of this transformation period in Japan. In Russia it came shortly after the revolution, with the most dramatic transformations sweeping through Soviet society in the 1930's. Yet hardly a single decade in these years between 1860 and 1940 passed without accelerating the momentum of social change. Despite unparalleled rates of change, however, important continuities survived.

Similarities between Japan and Russia again offer a starting point for our comparative analysis. The steady growth in their population, for example, resulted in an average increase for each of between 10 to 13 per cent per decade. For both, the number of workers and service personnel increased much faster. Differentials in educational achievement between generations, between sexes, between regions, and between settlements of different sizes became critical in determining qualifications for entry into a narrow, but growing, spectrum of prestigious and well-paid occupations. At least at the beginning and at the end of this transformation period, rural control was realized in large part through strong village and intervillage organizations responsive to directions from central authorities. Unequaled rates of urbanization propelled both countries away from previous land-based techniques of mobilizing resources. Family solidarity was maintained despite new pressures to expand rural production as individuals were sent out to provide urban labor and to receive an education. A dual society emerged in both nations. At one extreme were the bureaucrats, the intellectuals, and the many employees of large firms, sharing the scarce claims to job security. At the other extreme were ordinary peasants, lacking more than a minimal education, and often unable to find more than a temporary and tenuous position in urban society. Widespread upward mobility supplied the critical link between the diverging segments of these dual societies.

These were some of the similarities; a survey of differences between Japan and Russia, however, often causes these numerous similarities to be ignored. And there were, of course, differences. Soviet society was shaped by revolution and civil war and by a decade of vacillation and experimentation that culminated in a massive peacetime mobilization labeled "the building of socialism." When the nineteenth century reform movements in the two countries are compared, the reforms in Russia prove less conclusive. Literacy spread more slowly than in Japan, urbanization lagged until a decade after the revolution, and the growth of ownership of land developed haltingly until the eve of the revolution, only to be canceled out in the collectivization campaign. In Japan, on the other hand, family unity, village solidarity, and urban order supplied a more lasting foundation for steady change. In Russia continued reforms tentatively propped up tottering organizational forms until new patterns were laid down in the 1930's, powered by deliberate efforts to recast social classes and to remold personal relationships. Similar forces of modernization were unfolding in Japan and Russia, but the twists and turns intended to keep each country moving forward involved far greater compulsion and cost in Russia.

Human Resources

The demographic transitions in Japan and Russia followed similar paths. From an initial state of holding somewhat less than 3 per cent and roughly 6 per cent of the world's population respectively, Japan and Russia grew through higher birth rates than death rates and, to a much lesser extent, through an expansion of empire (albeit short-lived for Japan) to more than 4 per cent and 8 per cent respectively of the enlarged 1940 world total. The rate of natural increase in each country normally fluctuated mildly, with birth rates generally exceeding death rates by 10/1,000 to 20/1,000. The rate of natural increase was commonly somewhat higher in Russia, but several brief jumps in death rates, especially during wartime, narrowed the long-run gap between the two countries.

Japan and Russia experienced unusually rapid transitions from high birth rates and death rates to more moderate rates. Japan moved a decade or more ahead of Russia in the steady decline of these rates, but Russia practically caught up in the 1930's. Although it is difficult to identify patterns during the chaotic decade of the 1930's in the Soviet Union, death rates were clearly falling faster than in Japan and, if legal abortions had not been suddenly discontinued, birth rates would also have approached Japanese levels. In both countries these swiftly declining rates signified a quick transition to few births per mother and to long life expectancies, a transition that was not to be completed until well after World War II.

As much larger populations became available for production and became claimants for housing, consumer goods, and services, qualifications for access to the growing wealth of each country underwent frequent change. During the first decades after the reforms of the 1860's former samurai and former serf-owners abounded in elite positions. Compensated with state bonds for the loss of their hereditary stipends or serfs, and taking advantage of their high levels of literacy and expectation, members of both groups began the struggle to establish themselves in new elite positions with an advantage. Many former serf-owners experienced little abrupt change, however. They continued to be hereditary nobles and to own estates, relying on the labor of peasants whose small allotments of land failed to provide a sufficient income for both family support and redemption payments. In contrast, former samurai, almost all without land, were cast adrift to scramble for administrative, military, police, and teaching positions. Seeking to begin afresh in new careers, many vacated castle towns for villages or left Tokyo (formerly Edo, renamed with the transfer here of the imperial seat) to return to native areas. The liquidation of the samurai stratum occurred with remarkable ease and at relatively modest cost after the rebellions of the 1870's. The old elite was more quickly converted to new tasks and moved to new locations in Japan.

By the 1930's a different kind of elite had consolidated its grip on the newly erected factories and government buildings of Russia and Japan. Whether they were industrialists, financiers, or, landowners or—in opposition to terms that smacked of the bourgeoisie and the kulaks—state managers, administrators, or collective farm directors, these individuals demonstrated similar leadership capabilities in relying on educated and skilled subordinates and on government or party authorities in order to improve the position of their organizations in a highly competitive environment. In Russia the entrepreneurs of the earlier decades had yielded to the loyal bureaucrats who applied party directives; in Japan the merchant groups had produced zaibatsu as well as myriads of small businessmen. After the revolution Russia's elite, unlike that of the 1860's, was more fully mobilized in the direct service of goals determined by the Communist Party or its representatives; Japan's elite had long professed, and usually proven responsive to, goals phrased in terms of service to the country.

By the 1930's class position corresponded closely to educational achievement. The fraction of 1 per cent of the population that had obtained higher education gravitated to upper administrative posts and to the professions. Recipients of a full middle-school education, who included as many as 10 per cent of their age group in the Soviet Union by the 1930's, found various white-collar posts, which increased in number in the 1920's and 1930's. Others with middle schooling and, perhaps, some technical education competed for skilled factory jobs. Most factory workers performed manual labor requiring little specialized training. Until the 1920's the majority of the Japanese industrial labor force was made up of young, unmarried females supporting themselves and assisting their families by several years of debilitating labor. Most males who failed to complete more than six years of schooling in Japan or more than three years in Russia continued as farmers. (It is possible that the additional time required for language study in Japan reduced this imbalance somewhat.) The ladder of education, difficult and costly as it was to climb, determined the range of occupational alternatives for the vast majority of Japanese and Russians.

With educational achievement often making a rise in social class possible, it is understandable that access to education became critical. Three contrasts in this regard stood out: (1) men had more access than women; (2) city residents had more access than villagers; and (3) youths were at an advantage because each decade tended to bring an increase in the average number years of schooling. In the late 1920's urban males in Russia were 48 times more likely than rural females to receive higher education. By the 1930's men were losing their priority in the Soviet Union, however, and parental wealth remained a more decisive factor in Japan.

Primary education spread more quickly in Japan. Two decades before World War I Japan was approaching universal schooling, whereas Russia barely exceeded 50 per cent in primary schools. Yet secondary enrollments, and especially university enrollments, were higher in Russia. Japanese rates in secondary and university registrants advanced gradually after World War I, but great strides in the 1930's thrust the Soviet Union far ahead in these categories. In short, the Japanese population approached universal literacy earlier and had a higher proportion with primary-school training throughout the transformation period; the Russians, gaining rapidly at the end of the period in primary education, had made higher levels of education available to more people throughout its transformation.

As individuals of all classes became better educated, the quality of their lives changed in many respects. Newspapers and, by the 1930's, radios and loudspeakers offered information, indoctrination, and, at times, contending points of view. Standards of living rose, particularly for the urban, educated sector of society. Social welfare measures, especially in the Soviet Union, reached large numbers of people. Mass transportation and electrification were rapidly developed, in Japan in particular. For most of these years levels of consumption were climbing. Yet during the final decade or two, in neither country were generous portions of the quickly growing national product distributed to satisfy mass needs. A more varied diet for a steadily growing population, separate apartments for an urbanizing population, diverse consumer goods for those whose aspirations had been lifted, all were to a remarkable extent sacrificed to the other priorities of the new Japanese and Russian leaders. These shortages were all exacerbated during the war years.

A brief comparison between Japanese and Russian village youths of the 1870's, 1900's, and 1930's concludes this summary of human resources. The customary ways in the village of the 1870's remained virtually unaffected by the recent reforms. Most who went to school became at best minimally literate and had relatively little chance of successfully escaping their villages. In both Japan and Russia the generation entering school shortly after 1900 encountered a somewhat changed situation. Youths had the opportunity to outdistance their parents by acquiring skills needed in the village or by gaining access to urban occupations. These opportunities were probably more easily seized by Japanese peasants who had already been freed from legal barriers to mobility and migration in the 1870's. In Russia, by contrast, the strengthening of village-wide redistribution of land and control over migration preserved certain constraints on freedom of movement until 1905, some until 1917. The slow pace of change in Russian villages is apparent from data on individuals born as late as 1906, which reveal that 60 per cent of all who survived to maturity never received more than three years of schooling, and that only 7 per cent completed middle school. Nonetheless, even this degree of schooling represented a remarkable improvement over the opportunities available to previous generations. As a dual society emerged in both countries, rural children found it easier to move temporarily to cities, but still had little chance of securing a place in the small modern urban sector.

By the 1930's, however, the distribution in social classes was radically altered. Unskilled urban workers multiplied through an influx of peasant children. Skilled workers and employees in many service occupations increased even more quickly. At the end of the period the proportion of the labor force in farming had fallen below 50 per cent in both countries. A vastly expanded, much better educated Japanese and Russian population had, to a large extent, shifted into new occupations. Youths in the 1930's were fated to be called to war, but they began with many more options than their predecessors had ever known. In Russia the upheaval of many in high positions during revolution and civil war, collectivization, and purges, together with the lowering of tuition and the encouragement of new uses of female labor, provided options that suddenly blossomed into millions of success stories. War continued and indeed expanded the opportunities. The first years of fighting in Japan witnessed an acceleration in the learning of skills through subcontracting in industry and military training. Both Japan and Russia survived the wartime devastation with reserves of skilled manpower, though Japan was fortunate to emerge with fewer mortalities.

Patterns of Settlement

In one important respect settlement patterns in Japan and Russia were considerably different during the transformation period. Urban population totals between the 1870's and the 1920's rose from 5 million to 20 million in Japan and from 7 million to 25 million in Russia. The number of peasant households remained nearly constant at 5.5 million in Japan; however, whereas in Russia the rural population doubled to approximately 120 million, reaching roughly 25 million households. Japan, unlike Russia, had accomplished its early transformation without any notable growth in its rural population.

Between the 1860's and 1940's, demands on villagers mounted

without corresponding increases in benefits. Initial modernization, the development of a sharp duality between town and village, and the commercialization of agriculture might have threatened to undermine village solidarity. Yet in Japan and Russia village controls were successfully preserved during the difficult first decades of reorientation—decades in which newly granted freedoms enabled rich peasants to buy more land and land distribution, as a result, became more and more unequal. In Japan village controls continued to be quite smoothly maintained despite some disorder in the 1920's; the rise of rich landlords had not come at the expense of the old elite or of pre-existing village bonds, but rather as a part of a continuing process that was facilitated by the early reforms and the growing commercialization of agriculture. In contrast, village solidarity in Russia was maintained through the old practices of collective redistribution of redemption payments and, to some extent, of lands. It was also maintained through village-wide constraints on peasant migration. When these practices were subjected to intense criticism, new reforms were enacted that made it easier for peasants to leave the village and to accumulate their own land.

The middle decades of this period were a time when kulaks gained prominence, but they were also a time when Russian village controls became especially inadequate. Kulaks, who acquired the lands of the old nobility and threatened village-wide bonds based on obligations owed in common, had little time to establish themselves, and by the 1920's they operated in an atmosphere of loosely harnessed and government-aroused hostility. Reversing the pattern of unequal land distribution may have been necessary for the restoration of village controls in the Soviet Union, but it was accompanied by great violence. The liquidation of the kulaks, unlike that of the samurai, was carried out with widespread killings and deportations to labor camps. Following the collectivization of agriculture, requisitions at fixed prices replaced the market mechanism.

The process of consolidating groups of villages proceeded smoothly in Japan, but lagged in Russia until collectivization. Replacing periodic markets and fairs with both local centers of government and commerce has been essential for each modernizing society. In Japan the hamlet had already been absorbed into larger units, and during transformation it quickly became a subdivision of newly designated mura. As commerce in stores spread, local cities absorbed the trade previously centered in periodic markets. In Russia the integration of clusters of villages through a unit called the *volost* proved abortive, as fairs and periodic markets retained their importance longer and the gap between village and town widened at an alarming pace. Both the mura and the volost date from before the nineteenth century, but they were strengthened as administrative units as part of the reform process.

New burdens were placed on rural society in the 1930's. Female farm labor was called upon to fill the gaps resulting from the departure of males to cities and, especially near Japanese cities, the shift of males to part-time or full-time nonagricultural employment. Collective farms reduced costs in wages and urban produced goods while using female labor at an ever increasing rate. Reliance on female farm labor improved the capacity of both countries to mobilize for rapid industrialization and war.

Japan remained more urbanized than Russia from the 1860's to the 1930's. Each country in these seventy years experienced one decade of stagnation in city population, decades, however, in which herculean efforts vital to retooling cities for subsequent development took place. During the ten years after the Meiji Restoration and after the Russian Revolution cities were markedly altered through changes in land use and in the distribution of social classes. Urban growth generally moved ahead quickly in the remaining decades. While there were only 2.5 million people in Japanese cities of more than 50,000 inhabitants in the 1870's, the total had risen to 10 million by 1920 and to 25 million by 1940. Russian cities grew more slowly. Only 12 per cent of the population resided in cities of 20,000 or more people as late as the 1920's (Table 11.1). After the 1920's a great spurt occurred, bringing this total to about 25 per cent in 1940, just 13 points behind Japan's percentage. Whereas Japan of 1930 and more populous Russia of 1926 were even with 31 cities each of 100,000 or more people, Russia pulled ahead by 1940 with 82 cities at this level. Japan had maintained an extraordinary pace of urbanization from 1890 to 1910 and again from 1920 to 1940, achieving the swiftest urban transformation in the world during the course of this half century. Yet Russia had accomplished in barely one decade more than half of the urban growth that had required fifty years in Japan.

The Japanese were not only more urbanized in this period, they also were more concentrated in large cities. The Soviet Union, with well over twice the population of Japan in 1930, was roughly 30 per cent ahead in the absolute number (as distinct from percentage) of people residing in cities of more than 20,000 and about even in residents of cities with 100,000 or more. Yet it had only half as many residents in cities of 500,000 or more and less than one-third as many in great cities with more than 2.5 million people. Furthermore, Jap-

T A B L E 1 1. 1   **The Urbanization of Japan and Russia**

		Percentage of Population in Cities			
SIZE OF CITIES		1867–1878	1897–1898	1920–1926	1939–1940
(in thousands)					
Japan:	10+	11	19	32	44–48
	20+	9	14–15	24	38
	100+	6	8	18	30
Russia:	10+	9	12	13–14	26–27
	20+	5	9–10	12	24–25
	100+	2	4	6–7	16

anese cities were increasingly clustered in four major industrial regions, which by 1940 included 75 per cent of the urban population. Huge metropolises and even megalopolises developed in Japan.

Another contrast between the urbanization of Japan and of Russia was the greater continuity of cities in Japan. Only seven of the twenty largest cities in Russia in 1811 remained in the top twenty in 1940, whereas in Japan as large castle towns were being converted into provincial administrative centers, the only major change in the ranking of cities occurred with the rise of prominent seaports like Yokohama and Kobe during the nineteenth century.

In addition to these differences in the process of urbanization, Russia experienced far more disorder, culminating in revolution in its cities. Because the old samurai elite in Japan had always ruled from cities, the country lacked strong rural interest groups, and for this reason it may have been easier for Japan to sacrifice rural concerns for urban growth—in other words, to spur urbanization and the development of a dual society. Channels of communication between cities and villages were also well developed in Japan, permitting information and reforms to reach the rural masses quickly. Not until the 1930's did the Soviets devise new forms of urban-rural relations, which allowed them to sacrifice rural interests without compunction while fostering urbanization.

In short, as the population of Japan and Russia increased, it was redistributed to cities. This process proceeded more quickly and more smoothly in Japan, without sizable jumps in rural population and without prolonged urban disorder. The emergence of a new rural elite was not accompanied by mounting hostility. Diminished control over villagers and particularly over the flow of goods from villages to cities never undermined the continued growth of the modern sector of Japan's dual society. Russia's villages were finally merged into larger units, and its cities too grew at unparalleled rates. In the early 1870's only 14 million of the 100 million inhabitants of the two countries resided in cities, but in 1940 nearly 100 million of their 265 million inhabitants were urban.

Organizational Contexts

Organizational frameworks changed drastically in Japan and Russia between 1870 and 1940. Families were successively altered in size and age composition through changing birth rates and death rates, and they declined as units of production. Expanded opportunities for women to secure nonagricultural labor, to receive an education, and to live in nuclear families away from domineering mothers-in-law certainly improved the position of women. As specialized organizations for education and production spread, individuals spent increasing amounts of time outside of the family context. The assertion of individual rights gradually weakened the authority of household heads. Yet the extent of these changes during the first decades of this period should not be overestimated. Arranged marriages persisted, wives continued to be responsible for the care of their husbands' parents, and most families stayed together as units of farming production. In Japan the civil code of 1898, which embodied many of the characteristics of traditional families, remained in force until after World War II.

Prior to the Russian Revolution, Russian families were already beginning to diverge from these old ways. Individualist and even antifamily views, many of which were also expressed in European countries, gained spokesmen among disaffected Russian intellectuals. After the revolution, advocates of altering and displacing the family succeeded in efforts to enact new legislation liberating women, easing divorce, and giving to individuals other rights that weakened family control. Although many of these policies were reversed during the 1930's—when divorces became more difficult to obtain and when the family again came to be regarded as the foundation for social control—the legacy of the revolution undoubtedly eased the realization of a new husband-wife relationship, one that served as the core of a remodeled urban family in keeping with changes in employment opportunities and education.

An interesting similarity between the Japanese and Russian

family systems of the 1930's is that both were proudly proclaimed at home as models vastly superior to Western individualism and to other family systems throughout the rest of the world. In Japan filial piety was portrayed as the foundation for obedience to the emperor. In the Soviet Union the equality of husband and wife was viewed as the proper soil for the growth of a new socialist personality. Yet these different ideals concealed many similarities in the processes of family change that corresponded to similarities in demographic transition and urbanization. Strengthening family controls was a goal shared by leaders in both nations.

Though the family might be legally strengthened in an urban environment, however, it could not remain essentially an all-inclusive, self-sufficient unit. The place of employment became a supplementary point of identification critical to integrating urban residents in their new surroundings. In Russia a large industrial labor force appeared earlier than in Japan, but for a long time serf labor predominated. After serfdom was abolished many workers continued to be responsible to the village community when temporarily away from home. With his serf-labor heritage and his enduring identification with the village, the prerevolutionary Russian factory laborer was never joined by effective ties to the factory organization. The swift expansion of the Russian industrial labor force between 1890 and 1914, centering around large factories, contributed to the creation of a concentrated and often disruptive fraction of the urban population. Japanese factories developed more slowly and relied more heavily on female labor until after World War I. Meanwhile, small Japanese firms employing traditional methods proved capable of integrating the urban working force.

New forms of factory organization evolved in both countries during the twenties and thirties. Regularized methods of hiring, training, promoting, and paying were devised. Educational achievement was relied on to assess the potential of recruits. By the 1930's large enterprises could assure workers of their long-run need for them. The system in Japan of basing wages primarily on seniority and of stressing employee benefits helped establish a program of permanent employment in the large enterprises. In the Soviet Union new forms of worker participation in decision-making under the leadership of Communist Party members were accompanied by piecework methods of pay. Both systems countered problems of high turnover and a chaotic labor market. The Japanese system elicited a strong commitment to the firm, making possible the orderly growth of the large firm which in turn became the apex of a pyramid of small subcontracting companies. The Soviet system with the factory under state management also insured orderliness, enabling the industrial force to grow at an extremely fast rate after private firms had been eliminated.

The factory organization that was created in each country was bound together not only by contractual relationships, but also by an orientation toward the individual employee's personal welfare. The paternal style of management in Japan and management on behalf of the state in the Soviet Union made housing facilities available and provided special benefits that eased the lot of the recent migrant. Enterprise unions operated within narrow limits without the right to strike, but they did contribute to the worker's security in the organization.

Administrative and party bureaucracies were also part of this picture of organizational frameworks. With the disbandment of samurai administrations throughout Japan, a civilian bureaucracy was formed, roughly one-tenth as large as the total number of former samurai household heads. For the most part drawn initially from the samurai class, and enjoying high status as the loyal representatives of the emperor, rather than of the shogun or daimyo as before, these bureaucrats acquired some of the aura previously reserved for samurai. Passing through nearly identical educational and career experiences, these officials were molded into an exceptional corps of committed and able men whose extensive influence penetrated to local levels. This civilian bureaucracy grew steadily to more than 200,000 men by the end of the 1940's, overwhelmingly concentrated in Tokyo. A large military bureaucracy was, of course, also exerting an increasing impact on Japanese society during its transformation.

The imperial bureaucracy in Russia was much larger than Japan's fledgling counterpart, but it grew more slowly after the 1860's. There were many channels of entry, including the opportunity for continued service by the nobility. Yet many Russians decided not to serve, preferring other professions. The bureaucracy was not as unifying a force in Russia and was probably more unwieldy because of its low morale and greater diversity.

After the revolution the civilian bureaucracy expanded quickly, absorbing activities previously carried out by the private sector. In addition, party members not in the bureaucracy assisted through their leadership and watchfulness. More so than in post-1920 Japan, the Soviets fostered a new elite ethic, reminiscent of that of Japan's samurai past, sharply focused upon the importance of service to the state. The new Russian state and party apparatus permeated

Russian society as a vast organizational network, and permitted subordinate, but not independent, organizations with the exception of the newly reinforced family structure. Other organizations such as unions of professionals could operate only under tight party supervision. One distinctive base for the organization of work was the labor camp, to which millions of Soviet citizens were sent as prisoners during the 1930's.

The organizational transition, then, was easier in Japan. Though personal loyalty to lords was redirected to the emperor, family solidarity remained relatively unaffected. Loyalty and commitment continued to characterize the relationship of an individual to his family, to his firm, and to his bureaucracy. All of these organizations were changing, but without threatening the basic values or allegiance of their members. In Russia the development of new organizational forms proved more difficult. Village organizations that had supplemented and then supplanted serf controls were undermined, but the family and the firm were unsuccessful in filling the vacuum. In the end new administrative and party organizations, involving more supervision of private actions and more coercion, created orderly conditions that elicited the kind of commitment evident in Japan even in the absence of families and firms. In the 1930's new directions of national leadership in both countries brought existing patterns of loyalty into question, but new leaders succeeded in imposing their authority.

Redistributive Processes

The redistributive processes of mobility and migration between the 1860's and the 1940's reached record proportions in Japan and Russia. Most of the movement was in one direction: individuals born in rural farming households established themselves as urban workers and as white-collar employees. Indeed, during the fifteen years prior to the Second World War, the net flow of individuals into cities in the two countries combined totaled more than 40 million out of a total population that was slightly more than 240 million in 1940. In the Soviet Union the rural-urban flow represented one of the largest movements of people within such a short time span in world history.

As has been noted, the urban organizations that received these upwardly mobile migrants had acquired new forms by the 1930's, improving their capacity for readily absorbing large numbers. For most of this period, however, the orderly movement of individuals depended primarily on relationships within the village of departure. The contrast between primogeniture in Japan and allocation of village lands according to the number of sons in Russia (a form of multiple inheritance) became of heightened significance as death rates fell, enabling more sons than previously to survive to maturity. Japanese migration went smoothly. There the head of the household normally designated younger sons, who were expected to leave the household in any case by the age of twenty, to go to the city, and he made use of village contacts to help place these sons. There was no expectation that a son would return except for brief visits and to choose a wife, and yet, the migrant was not completely independent of his relatives, who had assured his successful start in the new environment. The essential ingredient in this formula for smooth migration seems to have been the structure of the family system, which required children to leave home when they were not inheriting.

Russian males between the ages of sixteen and thirty also provided the majority of migrants to cities. In the last decades of the nineteenth century village lands were distributed to a household according to the number of sons. The result was that families were reluctant to permit sons to depart for long. Village practices hindered the full separation of individuals who moved to the city. Those who did escape permanently to the city, especially after the revolution, managed to sever their rural ties quickly, unlike the Japanese.

Two avenues of mobility merit special attention. By the 1930's, and even earlier in Japan, entry into higher levels of education in both countries required success on highly competitive entrance examinations. To the extent that one was successful in gaining admission to certain schools, one was virtually assured of prestigious and lucrative employment. A second route, more accessible to rural youth, was through the armed forces. Conscription had long been used in Russia and was introduced in Japan in 1873. Thus, peasants in both Japan and Russia throughout this period were regularly conscripted, trained, and then discharged by armed forces organizations. For many of those who were not Great Russians, this experience introduced customs of the majority of Russian people, and promoted their upward mobility in the predominantly Russian environment. During the Civil War in Russia service in the Red Army became a distinct advantage in qualifying for later rewards. Particularly in the 1930's, the army in Japan became a primary vehicle for socialization as well as for technical training that helped men qualify for higher income and prestige. In both countries the armed forces assisted in the early introduction of modern techniques into rural areas and later were crucial in diminishing the gap between the levels of the dual society.

The consequences of the Russian Revolution for social mobility were widely observable. Inequalities in the distribution of land were reduced. Great differentials in wages were leveled, although in the thirties they again widened considerably. Private wealth could no longer be accumulated. The employment of others became illegal and even self-employment became increasingly difficult. The only reliable sources of income that endured were farming tiny plots of land and supplying one's labor to the state or to a collective.

The enormous downward mobility, departure and forced deprivation among the people with the most wealth and the establishment of new criteria for advancement came at an opportune time, when the needs of the modern sector were quickly changing. Even in Japan it was not until the 1920's that the standards for entry into and promotion within the modern sector became formalized. The proportion of Japanese outside of agriculture who were self-employed was also falling. Educated salaried employees of large firms were becoming more numerous, and, unlike the situation in Russia, the number of employees of small firms was increasing even faster. Moreover, family ownership of land, of factories, and of other forms of property continued to give advantages to young Japanese in their pursuit of the new opportunities of the 1930's.

Personal Relationships

Throughout this discussion of social interdependence the contrast between evolution and revolution has been observed. The greater continuity of Japanese society during this three-quarters of a century is more obvious in aspects of personal relationships. Both societies, of course, had turned to merit criteria and highly specific work relationships by the 1930's. More and more the individual was being judged, not by his parents, but for what he could do to further the goals of specialized organizations. The essential difference between Japan and the Soviet Union in this regard lay in how often and for what was one to be judged—and by whom. In Japan the individual was relatively secure, knowing that performance on designated examinations and the selection procedures of a company, albeit with properly cultivated personal contacts never ignored, were well-spaced hurdles en route to advancement by seniority. Those who failed to clear the first hurdles still breathed in the only slightly diluted atmosphere of intense group solidarities.

The individual in the Soviet Union was less secure in his job, his neighborhood, and his home. The unconditional loyalties owed in Japan were to symbols of the past and to the stable group settings of the present. The loyalties demanded in Russia, however, were apt to be to symbols of an uncertain future and to its not always predictable or distinguishable representatives. Agitation and terror threatened personal trust. In speech the Japanese clung to honorific forms of address as the Russians ventured into the new language of comradeship. Yet despite these startlingly different experiences, Japan and Russia emerged in the 1930's with exceptionally unusual and similar populations, both submissive in the throes of rapid change and remarkably quick to respond to the acceleration of that change.

International Comparisons

Transitional societies vary enormously in rural-urban migration. Some, like Japan and Russia in 1870, preserve most of the social attributes of societies whose populations are still unacquainted with the industrial revolution. Others, like Japan and Russia in 1905, are inextricably caught in the throes of modernization, in which the rural sector or the small urban sector reliant on unskilled labor continues to predominate. Exceptional cases, like Japan and the Soviet Union in 1940, achieve recognition as latecomers in the modernization process, although most indicators of high modernization are still at least a decade away from realization. Great differentials in such indicators as demographic rates, educational achievements, levels of urbanization, and occupational distributions characterize the diversity of societies in this transitional category.

There are, of course, other measures for gauging the rate of transitional change in modernizing societies. And each measure carries with it the built-in question of how long the transition takes as the society passes various landmarks on the path of modernization. With regard to human resources, declining birth rates and death rates are measures, as well as the long-run growth in the proportion of the labor force in industrial, clerical, and technical and service positions. Examination of settlement patterns in modernizing societies can reveal sharply varying rates of urbanization. A century of transition in some societies has produced relatively minor shifts away from agriculture and only a 10 or 15 per cent increase in the percentage of the population in cities; elsewhere the figures are more dramatic. The changing distribution of occupants, however, indicates substantial visible or disguised urban employment, together with what are uninvitingly called "parasitic cities," corresponding to the level of development of productive forces. After an initial change in these indicators, in fact, many societies have witnessed a slowdown in urbanization while remaining as primary producers.

The rate of growth and transformation of the urban population is another basis for categorizing transitional societies. Whereas in a small number of countries high levels of geographic mobility have been primarily responsible for the rise within half a century from 10 to 30 percent of the population in cities of at least 20,000 people, in Japan and Russia this rise was accompanied by an unusual degree of upward mobility. Geographic mobility into cities was remarkably coordinated in both countries with opportunities for social mobility within the cities. Similarly, the explosive growth of large cities in Japan and Russia was sustained by the expansion and filling in of other levels of the urban hierarchy. Above all, it must be recognized that massive, rural-to-urban migration is primarily a phenomenon of this transitional phase and that societies differ in the speed and smoothness with which it is accomplished.

Japan and Russia had exceptional rates of urbanization, the former with relatively steady growth from 1895 to 1940, and the latter with a spectacular spurt from 1926 to 1940. During the periods of greatest movement into cities, Japan and Russia were noted for their remarkable organizational patterns which gave direction to solving some of the problems of coordinating the migration. Facilitating the selection of suitable migrants in both countries was a substantial rise in rural educational programs, with nearly universal literacy among youth realized in Japan by about 1900 and in the Soviet Union by the late 1920's. The spread of literacy in rural Japan and of small-scale industries in rural Russia prior to the 1860's had provided favorable conditions. Also dealing with the problems at the source of movement was the tremendous control exerted by the Japanese family on the selection of migrants. In Russia for the first half of this period the village collective retained control over redemption payments and simultaneously over migration. Later, when most migration to cities took place, the inauguration of collective farms together with the revival of the internal passport system permitted migration to be carefully regulated. Unlike many countries where village controls have been subverted in an early stage of the transitional process, Japan and Russia seemed to have preserved and reinforced techniques for regulating the flow of migrants out of the village.

At the other end of the flow were various methods for integrating the migrants into the urban environment. One factor in urban stability during the final decades of this period was the recently evolved system of permanent employment with large firms in Japanese cities. Similarly, in the Soviet Union many of the benefits of urban life were distributed according to employment-related criteria. Both the Soviet Union, with its tight party and police supervision of urban employment and residence, and prewar Japan, with its noted system of neighborhood or ward associations, found ways for newcomers to identify and to be identified in cities.

A mixture of tradition and innovation thus characterized the controls on urban migration that evolved in Japan and the Soviet Union. Both inherited traditions of elite geographic mobility as well as of widespread movement of young males into cities, and both utilized traditional forms of family, community, and administrative regulation. As the volume of migration expanded, both devised new means, particularly of urban reception. Relying less on family and community, the Soviet massive migration involved enticing rural residents with significantly superior urban conditions and opportunities while at the same time punishing deviance with an unprecedented administrative apparatus of observation and terror.

China before 1949 is representative of those transitional societies that remained no more than about 10 per cent urban. The rise of treaty ports attuned to foreign trade, and in some cases nuclei of an embryo industry, did not foster a corresponding development of provincial and local cities. The movement into cities of some absentee landowners and hired laborers was accompanied by a breakdown in certain traditional bonds of urban association without the creation of new patterns comparable to those in Japan and Russia. Only after the revolution in 1949 did rural-urban migration increase rapidly. This migration was accompanied by such tight controls that when it was eventually determined that the urban population was excessive, waves of *urban-rural* migrants were produced after the Great Leap Forward (and again after the Cultural Revolution). Whereas the Soviet Union had demonstrated the potential of planned accelerated urbanization, China was the first society to engineer a reverse flow to the villages. After more than a century of transition, the Chinese could achieve fast and rapid controlled migration, but they were still groping for a strategy that would permit the effective distribution of nonagricultural manpower among settlements of various sizes.

Other latecomers to modernization have experienced clusters of squatters' settlements and massive unemployment in urban areas. Superior facilities in urban areas and rising expectations lure rural residents away from the disguised unemployment in their villages, where the able-bodied population exceeds the number of those who can be fully utilized under existing conditions. In Asia, Africa, and Latin America burgeoning population rates and the rush to the city have created pressures for diverting resources to the needs of migrants. Japan and Russia were unusual among latecomers in not having to face the spiraling costs of this kind of migration.

Both Japan and Russia seem to have achieved rapid urbanization without much premature urbanization and with efficient methods of selecting and utilizing migrants to urban areas. The interplay of migration and the expansion of job opportunities in cities is subject to some coordination by central planners, but it is also responsive to the different forces that alternately hold and release rural residents and attract or repel them in cities. Presumably, the traditional methods of control and association in Japan and Russia served to accelerate and reduce this flow of manpower in a relatively effective manner for the course of modernization.

Chapter Twelve

KNOWLEDGE AND EDUCATION

BOTH COUNTRIES ENTERED the modern period with formidable advantages in the realm of knowledge and education. Japan had had long training in the values of East Asian civilization, with its respect for learning as a guide to morality and the basis for governance, and began with a very high level of popular literacy that eased the government's needs to communicate its intentions. Russia began with a high level of advanced education, but its popular training was hampered by social and physical distance between groups. Japan's sweeping changes in the 1860's disestablished the privileged military class and forced its members to take up roles in the new society; Russia's disestablishment of serfdom presented the government with problems of extending its communication and concern to a far greater number than ever before. Japan's educational changes worked to rationalize and centralize the networks of schools that had existed; in Russia such networks had to be brought into existence to a much greater extent. With a larger intellectual elite and one far more isolated from its rural contemporaries, Russia was more concerned over dangers of diffusing education and participation; Japan, however, saw such diffusion and participation as a learning device for activating previously unresponsive areas and groups. In Russia secularization began earlier and was completed after the revolution. Modern Japan endowed its polity with semireligious overtones. By the twentieth century, when virtually all of the age cohort was receiving indoctrination from standard textbooks, the home and army barrack operated to reinforce the lessons that the schools taught, and the instruments of modernization spread a newly articulated belief in imperial divinity.

217

In both countries trends of urbanization, industrialization, and mobilization put great emphasis on the printed word. Japan's internal communications were tighter by virtue of its compact structure, but the impressive railroad network that Russia developed also served to bind the country together. Japan's advantages of scale and access to water power speeded the process of rural electrification that supplemented the rail network. In both nations impressive publishing industries poured out a stream of translations and newspapers, magazines, pamphlets, and books.

Throughout the period, and especially after the revolution, levels of coercion and control were substantially higher in Russia than in Japan. In explanation, Russia's problems of scale, of centralization, and of participation were far greater. The tsarist autocracy modernized with consistent protest from below, and the revolutionary government felt itself at war with entire classes. In Japan the early political upheaval and the government's resolve to institute a constitution brought a quick solution to problems that vexed Russia until the revolution, and the Japanese commitment to peer groups as the new society took shape tended to minimize the more abrasive forms of discontent. The Japanese government seldom trusted, but neither did it greatly fear, its people.

Institutional Setting

Japan and Russia share a basic similarity in the period of transformation in their successes at preserving certain important traditional value orientations while building an extensive and effective system of educational institutions designed to impart to the mass of citizens those skills and other attitudes necessary for rapid modernization. Much of the success of both countries in this endeavor lies in the effectiveness with which the state assumed leadership in the diffusion of education. Even before the 1860's the government in both nations had taken broad initiatives in this area, but thereafter, and particularly in Russia after 1917, the pervasive urge of both Japan and Russia to "catch up" with the West imparted a new urgency to the need for education as a tool both to instill in the nation a uniform spirit of dedication and to arm the people with the skills necessary to achieve wealth and power.

Efforts were made by both governments to discourage private initiative which might challenge state dominance over all formal education. In Russia the basis, however modest, for a centralized, official school system covering all levels had been set in the eighteenth century. The system remained in many ways unfulfilled, however, throughout the nineteenth century, particularly at the primary level, where church schools continued to perform a major function. Though the church schools, as mentioned earlier, were financed by the state and posed no particular threat to it, they were never considered to be a substitute for the ideal of a uniform system of public primary education. This was particularly true after 1917, when the militantly atheistic educational policy of the new regime demanded the abolition of all educational functions of the church and the total centralization of all education in the state. By 1900 the public and church institutions were supplemented by a number of nonstate schools and academies established through private bequests, but these too were closely regulated before 1917 and absorbed into the state educational system thereafter.

In Japan education had been largely secularized during the Tokugawa centuries of Confucian influence, and although missionary sponsorship of education was welcomed during the early years of the Meiji era, its religious thrust was always limited. As the modern structure became perfected in the last decade of the nineteenth century, the new state ideology of imperial divinity imposed further constraints on sectarian training. Thereafter, central direction and uniformity characterized Japanese education for the masses. Private academies and colleges mushroomed in twentieth-century Japan, but the principal path of prestige lay with the better funded and more favored national institutions. The multiple hierarchies that existed in twentieth-century Japan made it possible for some of the principal private secular universities to articulate with political and economic establishments of their own.

Private universities in Japan constituted roughly half of the total, a clear contrast with the exclusively state-run system in Russia. The great bulk of students at private universities, however, were at secular institutions that provided little or no ideological threat to the state. Some of the secular universities (particularly Waseda) were founded, it is true, in a spirit of opposition to the Meiji oligarchs, but such opposition was wholly accepting of the state itself. And by the 1920's, economic weakness and political pressures had assured that the private universities were little more than variants on the theme of state-controlled higher education.

In addition to the limitation of and control over private education, a persistent tendency existed in both Japan and Russia throughout the years of transformation to assert central bureaucratic control over local initiative in education. Both nations went through similar periods—Japan in the 1870's and Russia in the 1920's—when the sheer political and economic survival of a new regime necessitated leaving considerable educational control to the local level. Nevertheless, the ultimate tendency was to centralize all direction of educational policy in the national government. Both nations had very powerful ministries of education throughout their transformation that not only administered the apparatus of schools but also undertook broad functions of cultural control. The ministry of education in Japan by the 1930's was sponsoring research into the national heritage and devising a variety of new techniques for spreading nationalistic culture. The Russian ministry of enlightenment (later commissariat, then ministry once more), as the name suggests, undertook educational functions that went considerably beyond simple schooling, actively endeavoring to formulate and propagate a sense of a national culture based before 1917 on the old principles of "official nationalism" and after the revolution on socialism.

Compulsory Education and Mass Literacy

By the end of the period of transformation, programs of compulsory primary education in both Japan and the U.S.S.R. had produced populations that were wholly literate (with minor exceptions among certain Soviet minorities) and responsive to standardized communications from the central government. The timing of this achievement in the two countries, however, is in striking contrast, with Japan well ahead of Russia both in the initial commitment to compulsory education and in the pace with which it was effected.

Japan had an impressive amount of commoner schooling already in effect by the 1860's, estimated at 40 per cent for the total male population as compared with a negligible percentage for Russia. One critical factor in this earlier accomplishment had been the unusually positive attitude of the Japanese elite toward commoner education, an attitude that was in turn reflected in Japan's early commitment to compulsory primary education. The first national law of education was decreed in 1872, only four years after the Meiji Restoration, establishing four years of compulsory education for both sexes. This minimum was increased to six years in 1907, by which time more than 97 per cent of school-age children were attending public primary school. Starting with a far better base and hampered by less resistance either from the elite or commoners than Russia, Japan never even attempted to measure national "literacy" and was able to achieve effective mass literacy by the end of the nineteenth century.

Russia's achievements, on the other hand, were significantly less in the earlier period, and were handicapped by the persistence of negative attitudes on the part of both state and the populace in regard to mass education. The tsarist regime throughout the nineteenth century doubted its own ability to control the content of printed communication and hence tended to regard mass literacy as a potential political threat. The state accordingly concentrated most of its educational energies on the higher levels, particularly specialized institutes and universities; the Russian peasantry itself was not free of suspicion of learning, and at times responded with hostility to state educational initiatives when they did occur. Only when education became clearly linked in the public mind with social betterment did it meet with public acceptance and support. It was only after the Revolution of 1905 that the tsarist state made a clear commitment to the creation of mass literacy—a full generation later than Japan did. By then, however, 90 per cent of all males under thirty-five in major cities had achieved functional literacy (often through their own efforts). So, too, had some 70 per cent of young urban females. The main task, then, was to spread literacy to the countryside. After 1905 Russia made great strides in accomplishing this task, and especially when the new Soviet regime gave its full commitment to universal primary education. Russia's national minorities, particularly the Muslim groups where literacy remained low, were a special problem. Only under the Soviet regime was serious attention given to the spread of literacy among all such minorities.

Although formal schooling came in both nations to be the major source of education and literacy by the 1940's, training in the military and in the factory helped considerably in the spread of education by expanding both literacy and technical skills, particularly in the early stages of transformation. Both army and factory proved highly effective channels of education, and for that reason were consciously supervised by the state. In neither case did such education prove subversive of political order, with perhaps the exception of army officer training in Japan, which was in many ways responsible for the civilian-military tensions in the Japanese polity in the 1930's.

One aspect of the achievement of compulsory education was the expansion of educational opportunity for women, who in both countries were mobilized as a critical segment of the industrial labor force.

In Japan, however, despite the provision of primary education for women from the very start, further opportunities were severely limited. Japanese women before 1945 were, with few exceptions, excluded from the prestigious state universities and relegated to a separate track of women's colleges that provided domestic skills rather than professional training. This lack of educational opportunity is reflected in the small percentage of women during these transitional years who were prominent in Japanese cultural life.

In Russia, however, where women had long played a conspicuous role in higher culture, the opportunities for professional training through the educational system were substantially greater than in Japan. By 1897, for example, more than six thousand women in Russia had received a university education. And after 1917 opportunity for Russian women was increased even more dramatically, making them by the end of the period far more conspicuous in positions of responsibility than in Japan.

Communications

Both Japan and Russia in the second half of the nineteenth century transformed their systems for public and private communications by the application of new technology. Each of the two states was fully aware of the necessity of an effective national communications network, and gave high priority to the establishment and spread of modern postal and telegraph systems. Russia had instituted such systems well before the 1860's and was quick to adopt telegraphy, but Japan caught up quickly, passing Russia, for example, in per capita mail volume in 1880, doubling it within another decade, and remaining at much higher rates for the rest of the period. In per capita telegram volume, however, Russia, partly because of an earlier start and partly because of geography, remained well ahead of Japan until 1914, when war and revolution caused a serious disruption of communications.

State sponsorship of communications networks in the nineteenth century was paralleled by the emergence of a national "communications market" in both countries. An important part of this phenomenon was the creation of a class of "professional communicators": journalists, popular writers, and later radio broadcasters. Perhaps the most important vehicle of mass communication in the first stage was the daily press, which grew rapidly in both nations in the late nineteenth century. By 1900 both Japan and Russia had a thriving daily press, consisting of several large, economically viable newspapers with national distribution and circulation figures in the hundreds of thousands.

With the continued growth of the communications market in both nations, there evolved a far more diversified and cosmopolitan popular culture in the twentieth century than before, in many ways of a level comparable with Western Europe if not the United States. This change is apparent in the spread of popular magazines, of a great variety of specialized journals, and in the tremendous success of motion pictures in both nations. Besides importing thousands of films from abroad in the late 1920's, Japan and the Soviet Union were producing more than 200 feature films a year, which placed them in the top ranks of the film-producing nations of the world.

The balance of public and private roles in the national communications market of both countries was a source of considerable tension throughout the period, and the solutions reached by the two nations differed in important respects. In general, the private sector of national communications was both larger and less restrained in Japan than in Russia. In the first half of this transitional period, for example, the daily press in Japan was not only an exclusively private endeavor but was in many instances overtly critical of the government. The Japanese government instituted censorship measures from an early date in the development of the press, but these were never wholly effective. In the twentieth century, the press itself became increasingly apolitical and more of a profit-oriented enterprise, so that tension with the government was automatically reduced. In the 1920's and especially the 1930's, government control of the press in Japan, and particularly of small political journals, was substantially increased yet never became uniformly effective. Despite rigorous efforts to silence the press by Japanese authorities, a real if slender degree of freedom survived even into the war years.

In Russia the situation was quite different. Under the empire, to begin with, the state played a much greater role in the development of the press than it did in Japan. The various ministries of the government, for example, published their own newspapers, which threatened to preempt the role of private journalism. Most of the largest newspapers of late imperial Russia were privately owned, however, and at times assumed a boldly independent stance in spite of close government censorship. Then with the establishment of the Soviet state, the balance was radically tipped in favor of state control and the entire communications market was in effect nationalized for the ends of the state. The drastic decrease in private communicating at all levels is reflected in an acute drop in the volume of mail, which regained pre-1914 levels only in the 1950's. At the same time varied and intensive development of public communication for political uses took place in the 1920's. The graphic arts, film, and theater were successfully mobilized, and the more conventional media exploited, for propaganda purposes.

Scientific Knowledge and Technical Education

The Japanese and the Soviet governments held highly utilitarian views on the uses of advanced modern knowledge, which they saw primarily as a means of creating the practical skills necessary for catching up with the West rather than as an end in itself. Both countries pursued a systematic policy of fostering the natural sciences over the humanistic and social sciences, and of stressing the practical application of all research. In Russia this policy was a tradition that had been initiated by Peter I and vastly expanded under the ministry of Count Witte in the 1890's. Neither in Russia nor, to a lesser extent, in Japan did this emphasis exclude fundamental research. Both before and after 1917 Russia supported basic scientific inquiry to a far greater degree than any but the most advanced European nations, a policy that was never abandoned even amidst the strongest pressure to concentrate on "useful" knowledge.

As noted earlier, the Japanese, because of their isolation from Western knowledge during the Tokugawa period, were faced with a greater challenge of gaining equality in modern learning. Building on the important foundations laid by scholars of "Dutch Learning," however, and heavily encouraged by state policy, the Japanese managed in the space of three decades after the Meiji Restoration to construct an entire native establishment for acquiring and disseminating modern knowledge. The techniques were similar to those used earlier by the Russians, namely, the import of foreign experts and the dispatch of native students for study abroad in an effort to create a self-sustaining national scientific community. This process took roughly one century for the Russians; it took only about one-third of a century for the Japanese. By 1900 Japan had an establishment of universities, museums, research centers, and libraries comparable in most respects to those of Western Europe.

It was not until the twentieth century, however, that the Japanese were able to produce scholars and scientists who were capable of contributing to the advancement of knowledge at a world level of the sort which Russians had been producing since the early nineteenth century. But by the 1920's, a number of Japanese researchers, notably in such areas as medicine and theoretical physics, had achieved international recognition. Cultural and linguistic differences continued to isolate the Japanese scientific community to a degree never experienced by the Russians, and as a consequence it was not until after the Second World War that Japan was fully accepted as a ranking member of the world community of knowledge.

As in so many other areas, the state in both countries assumed principal responsibility in all phases of the importation and advancement of modern knowledge. The sophisticated Neo-Confucian academic tradition of Tokugawa Japan was easily converted into a new state-sponsored establishment of modern learning which perpetuated the Confucian emphasis on the concern for knowledge and education as a major function of the ruler. In Russia the Academy of Sciences, which had been the major vehicle for promotion of advanced learning in the eighteenth century, continued throughout the period of transformation to serve a central role as the official agency for the regulation and advancement of modern knowledge.

In neither Japan nor Russia did such attention to advancement of the higher levels of knowledge lead to a neglect of the training of the middle levels of technical experts necessary to man an industrializing state. The best indication of their success in this respect is that neither ever suffered a major shortage of engineers and other technical personnel. By the late nineteenth century both nations were equipped with a complete infrastructure of modern professions, all of whose members were organized into national societies with regular internal communication. Within the system of formal education the two countries devoted close attention to a network of technical and vocational schools. In Japan, this program was consummated in the last decade of the nineteenth century, whereas in Russia certain advances in the creation of these schools under the empire were greatly expanded by the heavily utilitarian educational policies of the Soviet regime.

The Political Uses of Education

Both Japan and Russia were quick to appreciate the possibilities of controlled political socialization presented by accelerating enrollments in the state primary schools, although in Japan, as opposed to the U.S.S.R. with its state nurseries, all socialization in the critical years before age six remained under traditional family control. It was through the use of overt political indoctrination in education that both Japan and Russia strove to counter the erosion of parochial national identity brought about by the massive introduction of universalistic modern knowledge from abroad. This elusive balance of the universal and the particular in the content of education is a critical problem faced by all latecomers to modernization.

Meiji Japan's system of formal education was in many ways free of overt political content in its early development. A reaction set in, however, in the 1880's following an intensive debate among intellectuals and policy-makers over Japan's cultural identity. The debate prompted the gradual formulation between 1890 and 1910 of an official state ideology, which was in many ways a reformulation of a variety of older conservative traditions. This "emperor system" ideology was incorporated into the uniform national primary school textbooks from 1905, and it placed heavy stress on devotion to the emperor, obedience to parents and superiors, and general submission to the collectivity. Successive revisions of the textbooks through the 1930's heightened the militaristic and nationalistic aspects of elementary education.

In Russia the tsarist regime was scarcely insensitive to the political uses of education, Russia having been unique in the pervasiveness of its official ideology as early as the 1830's. Nonetheless, it was only with the Soviet regime that the most thorough and systematic exploitation of education for state ends was instituted. While there is a certain parallel here with the politicalization of Japanese education around the turn of the century, the contrasts are important. The ideology of the Soviet regime was far more than a mere redefinition of existing nationalist strains, as it was in the Japanese case. Rather, Soviet ideology sought to create new parochial loyalties in the name of a universal cause. Under Stalin a more particular Russian emphasis was reasserted, involving a cult of the nation's glorious past, which was not unlike the emphasis being made in Japan at the same period. Nevertheless, the Marxism-Leninism of the Soviet regime was clearly of a revolutionary stamp when compared with the Japanese "emperor system."

This contrast may to a degree be explained by the special need under the new Soviet state to break down old loyalties and create new ones. It was an effort the Japanese had been spared, at least at the level of conscious policy, by the automatic elimination of the samurai elite through economic inflation. The samurai class having disappeared for all effective purposes by the 1890's, the Japanese state was free to convert the values of that class to the uses of the nation as a whole. In the Russian state, however, the survival of the gentry as a class into the early twentieth century encouraged the development of a wholly new, revolutionary ideology to counter it, a process that would later be repeated by China.

A further contrast between Japan and Russia was that in the Soviet Union the politicization of education extended even to the highest level, whereas in Japan it was largely confined to the primary and secondary levels. Russian universities maintained compulsory courses, for example, on the history of the Communist Party as a continuation of a constant process of indoctrination during the education of the citizenry. In Japan the universities—and in particular the most prestigious imperial universities—upheld even into the war years a proud tradition of academic freedom and in a number of celebrated incidents challenged efforts of the state to impose any sort of political control over them. Though in most such confrontations the state proved the victor, the overall content of university education remained mildly hostile to it, as demonstrated by the consistent popularity of Marxism on Japanese campuses from the 1920's.

The Role of Intellectuals

Intellectuals—in the broad sense of those receiving an advanced modern education—present an acute problem to any modernizing state. They are at once essential to the nation for their expertise and a threat to the polity because of their leadership potential and because of their easy tendency to be alienated if not properly recognized and rewarded. In neither Japan nor Russia during their period of transformation did any more than a small percentage of the educated elite ever become sufficiently alienated from the state to pose an open political threat—in short, to become an "intelligentsia." Yet in both, however small the absolute numbers, the intelligentsia played an important political role.

In Japan and Russia there was a strikingly similar pattern in the evolution of intellectual protest. In both, a tradition of intellectual radicalism was laid in the nineteenth century by disaffected members of the old elite in response to their gradual loss of power. This style of radicalism was in both nations of a backward-looking, populist cast, seeking strength in older rural traditions against the pressures of modern urban change. In Russia this gentry intelligentsia emerged as a clearly rebellious force in the first half of the nineteenth century, and reached a peak of strength in the *narodnik* (populist) movement of the 1860's and 1870's. In Japan there had been many examples of disaffected samurai before 1868, and in fact this disaffection was the prime force behind the Meiji Restoration. With the success of that political revolution, however, there remained important segments of the samurai class which did not share the forward-looking attitudes of the Meiji leaders and which broke into open rebellion in the 1870's. The most important single figure in this rebellion was Saigō Takamori, leader of the 1877 Satsuma rebellion, whose populist radicalism and stress on introspective self-cultivation bore a broad similarity with alienated Russian intellectuals of the same period.

This initial style of intellectual radicalism in both Japan and Russia was in many ways the protest of a group that had become the *victim* of modernization. By contrast, the new style of radicalism manifested in the early twentieth century was rooted in a social stratum that was the *product* of modernization, the new elite produced by the modern system of state education. In general terms, this group owed its status less to birth than to achievement in the educational system, although all in it were not of purely commoner origin. They were distinguished from the older intelligentsia by a far more Western and forward-looking posture, though they had also absorbed, if often unconsciously, the entire nineteenth-century tradition of radical protest.

The most dramatic contrast between Japan and Russia in respect to these new intelligentsia lay less in their ideologies than in their success. In Russia it was the intelligentsia that guided the revolutions of February and October 1917. In Japan such truly modern intellectual protest was small in scale and clearly unsuccessful. For the most part it was in fact strongly inspired by the Russian Revolution, emerging on a clearly organized scale only after the First World War and taking the form in the 1920's of a vigorous student movement, through which Marxist modes of thought gradually premeated the Japanese intellectual world. But despite its early strength, this protest was effectively stifled in the 1930's by heavy state repression which resulted in the arrest of thousands of young Japanese intellectuals.

In the long run, of course, this seeming victory of the intellectuals in Russia and defeat in Japan is deceptive. On the one hand, the gradual political establishment of the Soviet regime led to controls on intellectual protest that were very similar to those in Japan in the middle and late 1930's. In Japan, on the other hand, the defeat of the nation in 1945 and the discrediting of the old regime led to a broad revival of left-wing intellectual protest that has continued to the present day and has accorded radical intellectuals a degree of freedom never recovered in the Soviet Union.

International Comparisons

Both Japan and Russia can on the whole be said to have caught up with the first modernizers by the outbreak of the Second World War. In levels of education, networks of national communication, and the production of advanced modern knowledge, they were on a par. Indeed, hindsight suggests that both were in fact moving *past* some Western European nations in significant respects by the 1940's. The war, of course, was to disrupt this pattern for at least a decade. Yet the accomplishments of the two nations in the third period, that of high modernization, encourage a positive evaluation of developments in Japan and Russia in the 1920's and 1930's. In those decades the only nation in the world clearly far ahead of both Japan and Russia was the United States; by the same yardstick, however, Japan and Russia were to be the only nations in the following period that were to reach a level comparable with the United States.

In mass education Japan was able to convert an extremely strong premodern base with minimal trauma and to achieve the effective institution of compulsory primary education for both sexes a full generation in advance of Russia. In this respect, the experience of Russia may be more typical of a latecomer, with the development of a sophisticated apparatus of higher education *prior to* the expansion of primary education. On the whole, Russia was able to avoid the disrupting problems of surplus education at the top level, problems common to many late-latecomers in the contemporary period and which create in such nations as India and the Philippines a university-educated elite for which no jobs are available. The ability of both Japan and Russia to devote sufficient attention to the middle levels of technical and vocational education is a strength not always common among latecomers.

As the world's first conscious modernizers, operating in a setting without foreign-aid programs, both Japan and Russia had to invest impressive fractions of government and private income in the drive to develop education networks. The early Meiji determination to "seek wisdom throughout the world" had been preceded by Russian students who studied at Western universities earlier. Once the systems were complete in the twentieth century, however, foreign study could be restricted to special reward for the few instead of the anticipated path for the many, and great savings were possible in consequence.

Two interesting comparisons can be found in Japan's near neighbors. In Korea social disorganization hampered effective measures for education until the Japanese annexation of 1910. Thereafter the Japanese worked cautiously to build a primary school network and even more slowly to provide higher education. By the 1940's only 40 per cent of school-age children were receiving education, whereas higher schools and the imperial university found Japanese nationals heavily overrepresented. Higher education was in Japanese, and at the last even lower education was also. Thus, in a setting in which popular nationalism represented the threat of antigovernment activity, the same Japanese educational administrators showed a very different attitude toward the steps to be followed. Publications and communications of all sorts were carefully restricted as well.

In China traditional literacy profited from all of the cultural factors that obtained in Japan and benefited further from the stimulus of open and competitive civil-service examinations. Economic and social problems of the late eighteenth and nineteenth century operated to produce a decline in effectiveness of traditional institutions, however, and Japan's literacy rates were almost certainly considerably higher than China's by the 1860's.

Japan's success in resisting Western imperialist pressures and in defeating the Russians in 1905 helped cause the abandonment of the traditional civil-service examinations in China and triggered a rush of Chinese students to Japan. In 1906 alone between eight thousand and thirteen thousand Chinese students, to cite the extreme estimates, were to be found in Tokyo. This was the beginning, and not the end, of a larger movement abroad to centers of modern education. Political disorganization in twentieth-century China and ambitious plans to build a modern educational system produced a disproportionately top-heavy structure of foreign-trained intellectuals and underschooled commoners. Just at the time when Japan was reducing its rewards for foreign study and limiting itself to the products of Japanese institutions, official and unofficial China was building in rewards for foreign education. What resulted was an impressive intellectual elite of world citizens often out of touch with many of their countrymen, while the world saw top Japanese educators as more narrow, inarticulate, and restricted. The Japanese, however, were the products of and securely grounded in their own society and system.

Both Japan and Russia shared one special advantage in educational and research development, the lack of any institutions to challenge the initiative of the state. This advantage was one that not all of the first modernizers had and may not have needed: England, France, and the United States all developed strong traditions of private and parochial education which were perhaps a stimulus more than a hindrance (although the problems of parochial schools in France, for example, were certainly more divisive than stimulating). For Japan and Russia, as latecomers, state initiative in such matters was a strength, whereas in many ways it might have been a stultifying influence in firstcomers.

Both nations, as noted, were sensitive to the political uses of education, and developed clearly articulated educational ideologies. All latecomers have a special need to find ways of asserting a parochial national spirit in the face of the internationalizing tendencies of universalistic modern knowledge. Yet this necessity was certainly acute for the first modernizers as well, most notably in the period between the two world wars when national rivalries were intense. The content of education in both Japan and Russia during the 1930's was extremely parochial, though in this respect it was probably not very different from that in the Western European nations (certainly not in Germany). The balance of the parochial and the universal in education seems to be a problem that may indeed become more acute in the process of modernization.

In comparison with nations coming to the process of modernization later than themselves, the experience of Japan and Russia regarding the role of the state in building systems of education and research has a general relevance. This relevance may be fairly empty, however, because in very few latecomers do any strong private institutions exist capable of efforts comparable with those of the state. The point is best restated negatively: neither Japan nor Russia was burdened with strong private institutions (for example, an independent church) that might hinder the development of modern education and knowledge. In many latecomers, however, religious institutions and antimodern traditions of learning pose a clear threat to state initiatives in educational modernization.

Yet it may be that those nations that began the process of modernization a generation or two later than Japan and Russia have certain special advantages. At the very least, they have faced a profoundly different situation. In communications, for example, nations modernizing after the 1940's have had available the two powerful tools of radio and television. These modern tools help create a situation profoundly different from that in Japan and Russia in the nineteenth century, where the telegraph and the printed word were the only available technologies of communication. These new technologies may, of course, be as dangerous as they are useful to late modernizers: they enhance the options of forces hostile to the nation as much as those of the state itself.

In more general terms, nations that began modernization after the Second World War were faced with an array of modern knowledge that simply cannot be assimilated in a generation, as Japan was able to do in the late nineteenth century. Furthermore, their expectations are higher because of instantaneous international communication. Nor can the techniques of the importation of modern knowledge used by Japan and Russia be safely repeated by those coming to modernization later. To give one common example, the dispatch of students abroad in search of modern knowledge, which was a productive technique for nineteenth-century Japan and Russia, has often resulted in a highly destructive "brain drain" for twentieth-century modernizers.

In terms of the political uses of education, both Japan and Russia suggest that twentieth-century modernizers will need to give similar attention to the inculcation of a national identity through education. Their example is probably not a very difficult one to follow, though the tendency of most nations is to overemphasize the political aspects of education and hence impair the spirit of free and objective inquiry so necessary to the advancement of modern knowledge. Japan and Russia in the 1930's both demonstrated the dangerous extremes which the parochial element in education may reach in times of general political stress, and suggest that the greatest challenge in maintaining the balance of national and universal emphases in knowledge and education may lie with protecting the latter.

Chapter Thirteen

CONCLUSIONS: TRANSFORMATION

THE CRITICAL UNIFORMITY of Japan and Russia during this period of transformation was the ability of government leadership to mobilize people and resources for very considerable efforts. It is true that in Russia this ability broke down, but the events that constituted that collapse—the revolutions in 1917—also constituted the first step in the reestablishment of this very characteristic on an unprecedented scale. The greatest variance between the two countries lies above all in the differences in the amount of coercion involved. The imperial regime in Russia from 1860 to 1917, and especially the Communist regime thereafter, employed far more coercion than did the government of Japan. The remarkable thing about the Japanese development was the high level of coordination and control obtained with relatively low levels of coercion. None of the many fundamentalist reactions against modernization in Japan surfaced into major social obstructionism.

It is important not to underestimate the problems involved in converting Japanese and Russian premodern circumstances, which were in some respects conducive to subsequent modernization, to the requirements of political, economic, and social transformation. A history of borrowing without endangering the national identity had to be tested by imports on an unprecedented scale. Likewise, the preservation of imperial systems was placed under stress by many new factors, including the replacement of the old elite strata with new bureaucrats and managers. Indeed, the reluctance of tsars to accept new forms of representation and the glorification of emperors proved in differing ways to be eventual sources of instability.

What loomed ahead as one of the most serious problems to be

faced at the onset of the transitional period was the need to rechannel
the agricultural surplus from the elite consumers of samurai and
serf-owners without at the same time causing a great rise in local
consumption or a decline in production, and without resulting in
extensive violence or costly long-term payments that would threaten
the cooperation of skilled and experienced persons in the modernization effort and in the accumulation of funds for investment. The
principal task in Japan was to eliminate samurai stipends and to end
the prerogatives of this closed class. The chief barriers to Russian
modernization were attitudes and habits of the peasant population
that had been created or at least perpetuated by serfdom. Owners
had to be dispossessed of their serfs as a first step. The solution to this
problem turned out to be remarkably easy and quick in Japan, but
in Russia, though serfs were emancipated, there were extended delays
concerning redemption payments and political participation.

The extent to which Japan and Russia were able to modernize
their societies after the 1860's may be explained on the basis of their
capacity to meet what may be called the requirements of transformation for latecomers. These requirements include: first, the ability
to borrow extensively from abroad without losing the sense of national identity and the capacity to adapt foreign institutions to
domestic ends; second, the conversion of premodern patterns of
coordination and control from their original purpose of preserving
a predominantly rural and agrarian society to that of fostering rapid
political, economic, and social change; third, the adoption of policies
designed to accelerate the growth of the traditional economy as a
basis for modern economic growth; fourth, the facilitation of rural-
urban migration at a rate commensurate with the development of
political and economic capacities; and fifth, the rapid spread of primary education, and the provision of technical and advanced education directly related to the pace of change.

International Context

Borrowing from abroad is an obvious necessity for latecomers
to a process under way elsewhere, yet heavy borrowing can serve
to undermine the potential for converting existing institutions. The
proper blend of preservation and replacement may be difficult to
determine. Experience with foreign models in the premodern era

may have eased some of the problems for Japan and Russia in making the necessary determinations. Selective borrowing that neither threatens national identity nor leads to the large-scale diversion of funds from the priorities of modernization presumably need not be preceded by the long history of adopting foreign models, a history characteristic of premodern Japan and Russia. Yet in an era of advanced international communications it is difficult to establish conditions of relative isolation, positive national identity, and a careful selectivity in choosing what to borrow from abroad. The extreme isolation of Japan before the 1860's, and the special forms of isolation of Russia before the eighteenth century and after 1917, especially under Stalin, seem in some perverse way to have been intimately linked with a subsequent thirst for selective imports. More than any other country contemporary China appears to be repeating this scenario of calculated isolation, insistence on the vitality and superiority of strategies developed internally, and selective borrowing.

While the international context of modernization was similar in Japan and Russia in that both succeeded in preserving their national sovereignty as they sought to transform their societies along the lines pioneered by the West, in other respects Japan was better able to maintain a continuity of policy. Despite the hazards of war, Japan was more prudent in its participation in world politics, and until 1941 succeeded in avoiding foreign commitments that would risk major defeats. The Russian governments were less successful in this regard, and became involved in wars for which they were not prepared and which profoundly interrupted programs of domestic development. Japan was better able in the period from the 1860's to the Second World War to borrow from the West without incurring the cost of serious military defeats.

Political Development

High on the list of requirements for rapid modernization is the presence of strong government at the national, intermediate, and local levels. Russia and Japan both possessed this requirement before their transformation began, although Japan was exceptional in the degree to which its elite provided effective authority at all levels. With the expansion of the Communist Party of the Soviet Union the basis for an administrative elite comparable in effectiveness with that

of Meiji Japan's was created, and during the first two five-year plans
its authority was extended to the countryside.

The composition of the elites of both countries underwent
drastic, even revolutionary, changes over the eighty years of transformation. In retrospect, however, it can be said that the fact that
their societies had possessed extensive old elites—as well as the institutions to train and employ them—was of far more help than hindrance in the process of development. Even so, neither the existence of
strong governmental organs nor a large and disciplined bureaucracy
is alone sufficient to bring about the transformation of societies.
Powerful central governments may well sacrifice policies designed to
bring about development to more short-range objectives, and the
most extensive networks of skilled administrators are as likely to serve
the cause of the status quo as of creative change. What distinguishes
Japan and Russia from many other nations aspiring to develop is
not only that the human and institutional requirements were present
but that they were accompanied by the resolve to direct them toward
the goals of transformation.

Economic Growth

The relatively fast per capita rate of growth achieved by Japan
and Russia between the 1860's and the 1940's—surpassed before 1914
among major countries only by that of the United States, Sweden,
and Germany; and unsurpassed in the 1930's—was achieved by converting existing institutions and by borrowing from the more developed countries.

The changing role of the two governments in their economies is
probably the clearest instance of converting premodern institutions
to new tasks. The considerable capacities of both governments before
the 1860's in the economic sphere, devoted primarily to maintaining
the existing agrarian economy, were soon turned to the encouragement of modern economic growth. To a greater extent than in the
Western countries, the Japanese and Russian governments were able
to influence the economies of their nations both directly and indirectly—directly through investment and through expenditures aimed
at providing the necessary infrastructure of highways, railways, ports,
and other public works; and indirectly by creating the institutional
framework of land reform, local government, currency, taxation, and

banking required for industrial growth. The role of the two governments up to 1914 represented little more than an intensification and
redirection of their earlier functions, with the Russian government
usually more directly involved than the Japanese. After 1917, of
course, the role of the Soviet government became, at least in theory,
total, whereas that of the Japanese did not increase substantially until
the influence of the military grew in the 1930's.

A more pronounced conversion took place among those with
entrepreneurial talent, represented by the pre-1880 merchant. They
were transformed in Japan at a faster pace than in Russia into a class
of manufacturers and financiers. The Russian entrepreneurs, unlike
their Japanese counterparts, depended more on foreign participation
and government regulation, although in the decade before 1914 a
substantial number of relatively independent cartels were being
formed in Japan. Except for a brief period under the New Economic
Policy, independent enterprise was not a factor in Russia after 1917,
whereas in Japan it grew in importance during the postwar years.

In the relationship of agriculture to manufacturing, there was
also a marked conversion from the earlier period. The agricultural
sector provided vital savings in the two countries—both of which had
unusual agricultural conditions during their premodern era—which
in turn provided surpluses that gave them important advantages after
the 1860's.

In the realm of technology and specialized institutions, Japan and
Russia relied extensively on the more modern West. Russia had more
recent experience with organized and centralized borrowing, but
nonetheless there were many similarities between them in the
scope and forms of this process. No other latecomers to modernization in these years, and perhaps few in later periods, devoted so much
attention to the incorporation of foreign technologies and institutions into their existing frameworks. There were also, of course,
differences between the two countries in the borrowing process.
Russia relied to a great degree on foreign capital and entrepreneurs,
so much so that in some branches of the economy, more than one-half
the capital was in foreign hands until the twentieth century. Under
the Soviets, however, technological transfers and participation of foreign specialists was intensive only during the First Five Year Plan.
In Japan this process was carried out without substantial foreign
management, except in a limited and controlled form during the
early years; in the years after 1905 foreign capital and technology
became more important as the industrial plant matured.

Social Interdependence

Much can be learned about the common features of social integration in these two societies by considering what was avoided during this period of transformation. First, they avoided extreme rates of natural increase. Death rates fell slowly, and they were soon followed by declining birth rates. Second, they avoided cutting off the avenues of upward mobility. In the rapid shift from being societies of essentially closed classes, both allowed the route of social mobility to open. Third, except for the period immediately before and after the Russian Revolution, they avoided a breakdown of rural controls. Strong rural organizations were reasserted and migration out of the village took place in an orderly and initially gradual fashion. Two of the most obvious differences between the many countries that are still relatively nonmodernized and Japan and Russia in the late nineteenth century are the quick sudden drop in death rates in today's modernizers and their higher levels of urbanization.

Japan and Russia were distinguished as premodern societies by their relatively high percentages of city populations, but even these figures became modest when compared with those shown by many modernizing societies. Yet in both Japan and Russia the pace of further urbanization remained slow until the transitional period was well along. Although it would appear to be impossible to reverse the flow of migrants into cities in any of today's modernizing societies, the lesson of Japan and Russia suggests that tight controls on movement, high degrees of organization associated with places of urban employment, and the coordinated development of a pyramid of cities would help accelerate the modernization process. Smaller societies may not be capable of developing complete urban networks like those in Japan and the Soviet Union, but China is a large country that still exhibits a low level of urbanization and may now be applying the lessons of carefully controlled urban growth and coordinated expansion of cities at various levels of the pyramid.

What is particularly impressive is the extent to which premodern levels of social interdependence were convertible to the requirements of modernization. As relatively urbanized societies before the 1860's, Japan and Russia were more readily convertible to modern requirements than most latecomers have been. Because borrowing is much more difficult in matters relating to social relationships than it is in others, the ease with which a society is able to achieve a moderate birth rate, open opportunities for social mobility, and control the gradual migration from the countryside to the cities must depend primarily on pre-existing conditions.

In both nations these pre-existing conditions were more readily convertible than they are in most societies, but there were, nevertheless important differences between them also. In Japan the changes associated with rural-urban migration proceeded at a brisk but fairly even pace throughout its transformation, moving ahead somewhat faster in the 1930's. In Russia almost all aspects of this urban-rural migration lagged in the latter half of the nineteenth century, gaining momentum only in the first decade and a half of the twentieth. War and revolution abruptly interrupted the process, but when it resumed under government sponsorship in the late 1920's it proceeded at a pace unprecedented in any other society.

Knowledge and Education

The expansion of education and communications in relation to economic and political development goes far toward defining the character and even the success of the transformation of a society. Unlike eighteenth-century Italy, which had to export some of its most highly trained persons, or twentieth-century India, with its unemployment among skilled cadres, or Turkey, unable to find domestic employment for thousands of people qualified for semi-skilled industrial posts, Japan and Russia were relatively successful in training and deploying both skilled and semi-skilled personnel.

The difficulties that each did experience are nevertheless instructive. Japan began with great advantages of scale. Its economy and polity had undergone extensive centripetal influences, so that developments at the central port cities were quickly felt in even remote parts of the country. Its population was concentrated along a coastal strip in such a way as to maximize advantages from development of modern transportation. Its premodern heritage of literacy and respect for the written word encouraged the coordination and rationalization of educational facilities. Even so, Japan's concentration on the practical aspects of modern learning slowed the development of a higher-level scientific establishment. Fortunately, its access to the technology and goods of the Western trading states prevented what could have been impediments to rapid economic growth. Russia, in contrast, experienced problems of scale and distance in communications, and lacked the broad social base for literacy that existed in Japan. Its experience of Western orientation in higher culture had produced a small but active elite fully conversant with modern science, however, with the result that its developments were strong at the top and weak a the base level where Japan's were strong. The cost of this discrepancy was that the intellectual elite were also in good measure alienated, and was a central factor in nearly all manifestations of urban and political discontent down to and throughout the revolution. In the interwar decades and particularly in the 1930's, however, political pressures and greater distance and relative isolation from scientific trends in the modern advanced countries characterized both Japan and Russia.

That the otherwise impressive performances of these countries included such obvious shortcomings suggests that for later modernizing countries, where pressure for transformation will be, if anything, more acute, problems of phasing will be the rule rather than the exception. Given the fact that increasingly problems are the result of political decisions and economic resources and not of the workings of chance, an essential factor in mobilization will be the capacity of the political system to identify and respond to them as they arise.

Both Japan and Russia shared two crucial characteristics in their experience with transformation: their capacity to coordinate and control human and natural resources and their capacity to borrow institutions, technologies, and capital from more developed countries without any essential sacrifice of national sovereignty. By converting these capacities to new uses, they were able to achieve the comparatively rapid transformation in the early decades after the 1860's. In this period, the capacity for social coordination and control that had served in Russia in the seventeenth and eighteenth centuries to mobilize the country in the face of foreign enemies, and in Japan to create an integrated and almost self-sufficient society, were employed with equal vigor to transforming their countries. The capacity to borrow that had led them to adopt Byzantine and Chinese models in earlier centuries, and had led the Russians to a partial and defensive adaptation of Western institutions in the eighteenth century, prepared them for the very extensive reliance on Western models and assistance in the nineteenth and twentieth.

It is nonetheless significant that the conversion of premodern institutions, particularly in the critical realm of politics, played a larger role on the whole than borrowing. Technologies, legal assistance, and even constitutions can be borrowed. What cannot be borrowed is a chain of relationships extending from a generally accepted overall authority to local functionaries, and linked by officials with adequate training to administer the system. Peasants and local authorities, and others at intermediate levels, cannot be expected to contribute a sizable share of their incomes to the central government unless there is considerable agreement on the common welfare these resources are designed to support and on the legitimacy of the government that sets the priorities. A workable system of political coordination and control existed to guide Japan and Russia through the difficult tasks of transforming an agrarian and rural society into an industrial and urban society because a well-developed political system had existed for two or three centuries before the 1860's. This transition from pre-modern to modernizing political leaders in Japan and Russia was much less traumatic than in any Western country, with the possible exception of England, and the great reforms of the 1860's and 1870's were initiated by leaders with experience within the old societies and not as a result of a general overturn of political and social structures.

The shared characteristics of Japan and Russia during their years of transformation should not, of course, obscure marked differences between them. Certainly the Meiji Restoration, although not a revolution, was a more crucial change in political relationships than the relatively minor reorientation of the bureaucracy that took place in Russia in the 1860's. Again, during all phases of the transformation thereafter, in the later nineteenth century, in the first two decades of the twentieth, and in the 1930's, the level of coercion employed by political leaders against each other and by the government against opposition groups and the population was much greater in Russia than it was in Japan.

Japanese political leadership was more stable and consistent in guiding political, economic, and social change throughout the period of transformation. In Russia it proceeded more fitfully, with advances in the 1860's and the 1890's, between 1906 and 1913, and after 1928. Indeed, the revolution in 1917 was in some respects the most radical the world has known, and it is customary (by analogy with the French Revolution) to regard the empire as "old regime" and the Soviet state as something quite new and different. Yet in terms of a political system with strong links from the center to local communities, without serious challenge by other established institutions, and with the capacity to mobilize the human and natural resources of the country, the similarities before and after 1917 are probably more notable than the differences.

The ability to convert a premodern system of coordination and control to new uses, as Japan and Russia exemplified, raises the question of whether other latecomers that do not have a similar institutional heritage can manage societal transformations. Most of the later developing countries of Africa and Asia, for example, have only a limited experience with independent government that is national in scope. The capacity to borrow ideas, institutions, and technologies from abroad depends to a considerable degree on the existence of an adequate system of domestic coordination and control. The decision to borrow, the ability to select and adapt, and the process of grafting foreign institutions onto the local body politic, requires stability and skill. This capacity is of greater necessity when the receiving country is engaged in creating a national state out of formerly independent or autonomous territories and defending itself against competing states. Both Japan and Russia sought to engage in imperial expansion during their transformation, but both had established states with well-defined frontiers recognized by the community of nations long before the 1860's.

The transformation experience of Japan and Russia also raises the question of whether an adequate resource base is not also a requirement of transformation. One key element in economic growth is the capacity to produce a surplus from the premodern economy to invest in modern economic growth. Here again, coordination and control are vital. Japan is a poor country by most standards, lacking in most resources and its rich soil burdened by a dense population. Russia, by contrast, has within its borders almost all the resources required by an industrial society. The ability of Japan to equal and at times surpass Russia in per capita productivity may be accounted for by the intensive methods with which the existing resources were developed, by the nurturing of skills necessary for development, and by the importation of resources lacking at home. By contrast, Russia's tendency has been to use extensive methods, relying on its wealth in land, resources and manpower with a relative neglect of skills and technology. As this applies to other latecomers, the lesson would seem to be that—so long as the country is not as barren as a Saudi Arabia or a Kuwait without petroleum—what counts in the ability to undertake societal transformation is less the amount of wealth in resources than the experience and political capacity of the leadership to mobilize the nation for an intensive use of the resources that are available.

There is one respect in which the experience of the Japanese during this period is likely to be a far better guide for other latecomers than is that of the Russians. Russia constituted probably the last example of a great continental power with quite low levels of population density. China is also a great continental power, but it starts the process of modernization with very high population densities indeed. In the modernization effort, especially in agriculture, Russia has been able to operate by extensive rather than by intensive development. Japan could not adopt such a method. From the very first the Japanese were forced to seek their prosperity in a careful increase of productivity along the lines of comparative advantages in international trade. For them these comparative advantages lay overwhelmingly in light industries, for which raw materials could be imported and a very considerable amount of the value of the finished product added in manufacture that utilized large amounts of labor. For other latecomers it may very well not be in the light industries that their comparative advantages lie. It may be in services or in modernized agriculture. No other latecomers, however, are likely to succeed without concentrating primarily on their comparative advantages in international trade rather than on their comparative internal advantages.

Part III

The Contemporary Era

STUDENTS OF MODERNIZATION have at their disposal many examples of the transformation of societies to modern values and institutions. Almost all countries have undergone or are undergoing this process. No more than a dozen, however, are now highly modernized, and their experience with the problems of this level of development is limited to only a few decades. Despite the brevity of their experience, it is fairly clear that highly modernized societies differ substantially in structure and scale from those in the process of transformation. The characteristics of high modernization vary sufficiently from those of transformation to call for a different set of requirements. Policies that may be successful or even essential to meeting the requirements of transformation may be marginal or even counterproductive to sustaining high modernization. The pragmatism of the pioneers of modernization is frequently turned into dogmatism by their successors, and such dogmatism stands in the way of the continuing pragmatism necessary to overcome the ever-changing challenges of transformation and high modernization.

In the international context, a much greater interdependence exists now than it did in earlier periods, not only among highly modernized societies but also between them and the less developed nations with which they exchange essential resources. As manufacturing becomes more sophisticated and diversified, the intense nationalism characteristic of transformation is invariably modified by a recognition of increased reliance on foreign suppliers; investments and finance also reveal similar tentacles of interdependence. In international politics nuclear weapons make the security of each country far more contingent than before on the actions of others, including those at great distance. In these various ways, national policies become correlated to the international environment. The achievement and maintenance of a high level of modernization comes to depend on participation in the international marketplace of politics, commerce, and finance, and countries unable to compete in this larger arena are likely to be limited to lower levels of development.

The domestic political issues that arouse most concern in highly modernized societies tend to be less those that pit one social stratum against another—as they did in the earlier processes of modernization—than those of common concern to all strata, such as inflation, the administration of social programs, and patterns of urban and suburban settlement, problems, in other words, that involve the allocation of large amounts of resources among many public needs. The earlier ideologies concerned with the allocation of resources among employers, workers, and farmers tend to decline in importance; instead, new ideologies, such as those advocating fair treatment for women and minority groups, now press for acceptance. As the administration of public goods assumes greater importance, issues of policy are resolved increasingly in debates within bureaucracies and through participation of nongovernmental organizations representing the special interests of diverse groups. Electoral participation remains important in societies with a heritage of civil rights, in representing other, less organized regions and groups.

Economic development in advanced societies depends more and more on science-based technology in both agriculture and industry, with the latter concentrating on the production of a great diversity of consumer goods. This new economic orientation contrasts with the simpler technology and the greater emphasis on producer goods in earlier stages of industrialization. The size and interdependence of the productive facilities of highly modernized countries permit unprecedented economies in the scale and level of productivity. At the same time, extensive production may tend to exhaust currently available resources and pollute the environment. Consideration of these trends, combined with population growth, has led some to predict an end to the rates of economic growth that typified the era of transformation. A more widely held view, however, maintains that as new technologies are developed under the pressure of necessity, new sources of energy and of raw material will become available. The costs of these new technologies cannot yet be foreseen, however, and may require a reordering of values and institutions as profound as that accompanying transformation. The level of production now permits greater emphasis on the needs of the consumer than of the producer, and the managers of the economy have the capacity to favor welfare over profits as the main goal of production. Societies achieve the capacity to provide the necessities of life to all.

The degree of social interdependence in highly modernized societies can be readily observed and quantified, making possible projections to conditions that are rapidly being approached. Well over 90 per cent of the population lives (or will soon live) in urban areas. Some 5 per cent of the diverse and specialized labor force is employed in agriculture, 30 to 40 per cent or more is in industry, and 50 per cent or more is in services; this is a remarkable alteration in percentages when more than 80 per cent of the labor force in premodern societies was in agriculture and less than 10 per cent each was in crafts and services. Today life expectancy at birth is aproaching 75 years or more, as compared with 25 years or less before the modern era. Though some forms of illness tend to become more common, from indulgence due to abundance and from the stresses of modern life, the diseases that caused widespread death in the past have been brought under control. Through birth control, fertility is reduced and brought into rough balance with low mortality, thereby restoring the low but fluctuating rates of population growth that were also characteristic of societies before their transformation.

The marked rise in opportunities is generally accompanied by a growing isolation of individuals and of families. A half or more of the citizenry may change residence after birth, and the concurrent weakening of the church and other social organizations helps induce greater alienation and loneliness. Alienation and anomie seem to increase with modernization. The restraining influences of family and culture appear to survive through the period of transformation, but in highly modernized societies many individuals are socialized with no firmer guidelines than personal experience and peer-group influence. The willingness to delay gratification—to save for investment rather than to consume—is essential to the process of transformation; yet this willingness often gives way to a tendency toward immediate gratification, which is characteristic also of premodern societies. This apparent decline in widely accepted modes of behavior is accompanied by a more rational and cosmopolitan outlook, and a capacity to empathize with diverse attitudes and cultures and to tolerate ambiguity.

Knowledge and education grow in importance as societies become more highly modernized, and the ability to maintain and develop advanced technologies comes to be widely regarded as more important than capital and resources. It has been estimated that advanced societies devote as much as one quarter of the gross national product to the production and distribution of knowledge in all of its forms, and some 3 per cent to basic and applied research. As many as 2,000 students per 100,000 population may be enrolled in institutions of higher education, as compared with less than 100 in undeveloped countries. Advanced technical skills are also required for a wide range of positions. Above 90 per cent of the population complete primary education, and secondary education is almost as widespread. Highly modernized societies all reach the point where individuals without formal education can find employment only with great difficulty. Research and education further universally valid knowledge, and thus contribute to the convergence of highly modernized societies. Even so, because many of a nation's idiosyncratic values and institutions that are not obstacles to modernization continue to function—indeed, are essential to sustaining its capacity for effective action—an educational program must encompass one basic aim: it must encourage values essential to the expansion of science and technology without ignoring those values that support the peculiar institutions central to each society's pursuit of common objectives.

There is a tendency in popular social science literature to regard the process of modernization as completed in highly modernized societies. Catchwords like "postindustrial," "postmodern," and "posthistorical" reflect this view. Moreover, it does seem clear that many of the trends characteristic of the process of transformation do come to a natural conclusion. When 90 per cent of a population is literate, has completed primary and even secondary education, lives in cities, and is employed in industry and services, the transformation appears to be achieved. The completion of the demographic transition, an economic growth approaching the limits of available resources, and of the earth's capacity to sustain pollution, the equal availability of public goods, even to groups previously subject to discrimination, all appear to mark the end of certain kinds of change.

Other kinds of change, however, are not completed. Most importantly, the growth of knowledge represented by the scientific and technological revolution shows no signs of abating. Research on many subjects vital to human welfare continues at an increasing rate, and this augmentation cannot fail in turn to affect political, economic, and social development in ways that cannot yet be foreseen. The integration of society within national boundaries that was characteristic of transformation also continues in the form of international interdependence, thereby opening up the prospect that the levels of development achieved by the highly modernized societies may eventually encompass the globe. It seems likely that this will occur not through parallel developments in each society, but rather through increasing international integration resulting from the expansion of transnational public and private values, institutions, and processes. The scope of change in the contemporary era for highly modernized societies is thus as great as in the period of transformation, although not as well understood.

The characteristics of societies that have achieved and can sustain high levels of modernization may be said to include the capacity to accomplish five tasks successfully. These tasks may be delineated as follows: (1) to participate competitively in a political economy that includes markets and suppliers in many countries—in contrast with simply borrowing selectively as during transformation; (2) to administer a complex society with diverse activities that must be performed with adequate autonomy to be able to draw efficiently on special interests and expertise and coordination to be able to function effectively in an integrated society—in contrast with the earlier tasks of converting premodern capabilities to modern uses; (3) to bring a high level of technical knowledge to bear on production and on the development of new raw materials—in contrast with the mechanization of agriculture and the development of producer capacity, which were the primary tasks of transformation; (4) to devise patterns of social interdependence suited to a highly specialized and mobile population—in contrast with earlier problems of adapting a rural population to urban pursuits; and (5) to organize research and education that are central to sustaining a high modernization—in contrast with an earlier period when advanced research was not a primary necessity and mass education was concerned chiefly with providing an uneducated population with elementary skills.

Chapter Fourteen

INTERNATIONAL CONTEXT

WHAT ARE THE WAYS in which the international environment created by the Second World War and the subsequent development of world politics have affected Japanese and Russian efforts to catch up with the West?

For more than a decade after the close of the war Japan, defeated and occupied, was not a principal actor on the international stage. The Soviet Union, victorious and enjoying enhanced international prestige, was likewise excluded from the councils of the Western nations. Success in war confirmed the prestige of the Soviet leadership, whereas defeat and reform discredited many of the generation of Japanese leaders who had given foreign expansion priority over domestic development. The Soviet Union, having overcome the threats that German militarism had posed to its security, now struggled for freedom from the constraints imposed by American-led containment. Japan, in ironic contrast, saw its war goals substantially achieved: the resources of areas once denied to it were made available by the collapse of colonialism in Asia, an era of free trade permitted dramatic growth of exports, and its inclusion in the zone of American guaranty permitted vast economies in defense expenditures. As a result, the development of a consumer-oriented economy was fostered in Japan, and the long-emphasized priority of heavy industry and defense predominated in the U.S.S.R.

War and Aftermath

The war was a time of isolation for Japan and the U.S.S.R. Both participated in it as part of larger alliances, but neither fully trusted or communicated with its allies, and both fought alone. The Soviet Union never encouraged close coordination of effort with its allies, from whom it received massive infusions of matériel, and Japan kept its German and Italian allies ignorant of its plans to enter the war. Until late in the war the Soviet-Japanese Treaty of Neutrality seemed one of the more successful of the pacts of the period, but when the Japanese experimented with a Russian channel to capitulation in August 1945 the Russians responded with a declaration of war.

After 1941 Stalinist fears of subversion from abroad combined with military reverses to push the regime back to interior lines. Foreign contacts were sharply limited despite the rhetoric of alliance and common anti-Fascist effort. As reverses gave way to victories in 1943 and 1944 Russian power moved into Eastern Europe, but the continued fear of subversion brought determined and successful attempts to fix submissive and pro-Soviet regimes on the countries occupied.

Japan's announcement of an anti-imperialist "New Order in East Asia" in 1938 strengthened expansionist trends, and the initial victories of the Pacific War seemed to bring the promise of a regional hegemony. The victories were short-lived, however, and Japan soon found itself cut off from its empire. Shortages of resources, especially oil, made it impossible to exploit the raw materials of Southeast Asia, and the inability to replace lost air cover doomed the Japanese Navy in its battles in Philippine waters in 1944. American bombing then disrupted communication lines with Korea and Manchuria and even within Japan itself. Japan gave up all its foreign posts and representation, and American Occupation personnel screened all Japanese contact with the outside world. The foreign office, left without a function, provided the personnel for the liaison office that mediated between the Japanese government and the Occupation forces. Despite foreign occupation, Japan was more cut off from the outside world than it had been since the Tokugawa seclusion.

The war also wrought vast destruction in both countries. German military operations on Soviet territory destroyed approximately 70 per cent of Russian industry, 60 per cent of the transportation facilities, and vast amounts of housing in the occupied areas. Russian loss of life directly attributable to the war has been estimated at more than seven million soldiers and as many civilians. The peak of physical destruction came during the early stages of the German attack, so that it was almost half a decade before unimpeded reconstruction attempts could begin.

Japan's early victories were won with minimal cost in life and property, and it was not until after the war had turned decisively against it in 1944 and 1945 that those costs became great. American naval, and particularly submarine, tactics destroyed all but a fraction of Japan's modern shipping, and by war's end stocks of desperately needed raw materials were virtually gone. In the last years of the war, American bombing destroyed almost all of Japan's urban networks with enormous loss of life and housing, while casualties among army and navy forces cut off in the distant points of empire became heavy. Approximately 1,850,000 Japanese lost their lives during the war, more than one-third of them civilians who were trapped by walls of flame in the fire raids that destroyed more than 40 per cent of the total urban area. The end of hostilities brought the repatriation of 6.5 million Japanese from abroad. Another three-quarter million, in Russian hands, were repatriated slowly and hesitantly, with the result that many failed to survive their labor in Siberia. Thus the two countries suffered comparable destruction and damage to their industrial and urban centers. The damage in Japan, however, came late and was followed quickly by reconstruction assistance; in Russia the destruction came early and war and isolation brought less assistance in reconstruction.

If the wartime destruction they suffered was comparable, the political consequences of the war for Japan and Russia were not. In Russia the military setbacks of the early war years were followed by defections in German-occupied territories. These were soon overshadowed, however, by a wave of patriotism stimulated by German atrocities and by the regime's successful invocation of the traditions of national unity against foreign foes that traced back to Ivan IV, Peter I, and Alexander I. A relaxation of party controls also abetted the patriotic fervor. Russia's ultimate success in the war confirmed the support of the many who had benefited under the five-year plans, and served to justify and legitimize the policies that had been developed under the leadership of Stalin. Yet the end of the war did not lead to a further relaxation of party controls; rather, the regime used domestic hardship and international insecurity as justification for a return to the harsh standards of political discipline that had been established in the 1930's.

Japan's startling victories in the early years of the Pacific War brought euphoric belief in the national mission and political leadership. Later, the exhausting and increasingly unsuccessful effort to exploit the new lands and defend the new communication lines generated a growing sense of disaster and a declining feeling of identification with the regime. In the war's final years a deeply divided elite struggled to end it while commoners struggled to maintain their lives in a grim setting of food shortage and insecurity of personal life. The surrender of 1945 found much of the industrial economy destroyed and the exhausted masses totally disabused of their faith in Japan's leadership. Japan's defeat served to reduce potential opposition to the fundamental changes in Japanese society and government that followed. Reforms initiated by American Occupation forces encountered little opposition and, indeed, much enthusiasm: conservative Japanese were accustomed to submit to authority, and less conservative Japanese responded with hearty approval. A new generation soon arose that marked a break with Japan's earlier leadership in its desires for innovation and near-revolutionary change.

The postwar international relations of the two countries also present comparable contrasts. The Soviet leadership's suspicious view of its allies was reflected in the assurances it requested and received at Yalta and at Potsdam. As Russian armies occupied additional territory in Eastern Europe and Northeast Asia, the regime asserted increasing local political control. By the time it decided in 1947 against participating in the Marshall Plan, a clear decision for autarky and unimpeded leadership of Eastern Europe had been made. Unsuccessful efforts to assert further Russian hegemony in Azerbaijan, Greece, Berlin, and finally Korea brought the Soviet Union into confrontation with the United States. These policies required the maintenance of many aspects of the wartime garrison state, and it was not until the death of Stalin and the gradual emergence of a new generation of Soviet leaders that political institutions and practices began to change. The Russian perception of postwar international relations in terms of a juxtaposition of Communist "democracies" opposed by "imperialists," which included its wartime allies along with West Germany and Japan, shaped its priorities in economic and political programs.

The Western powers, under the leadership of the United States, demobilized rapidly. The American Marshall Plan made it possible for the European powers to rebuild their shattered economies. England maintained its economic priorities by divesting itself of empire, while France and the Netherlands sought to maintain international stature through gradualist and piecemeal decolonization in North Africa and Southeast Asia that brought them into conflict with nationalist forces. American support for these policies, at first denied, was eventually forthcoming because of rising concern over the Soviet ability to take advantage of political instability in the underdeveloped world. The victory of the Chinese Communists in 1949, followed by their intervention in the Korean War a year later, seemed to confirm fears of a bipolar world conflict. These concerns lived on through the 1950's, although the death of Stalin, the Korean truce, and the Geneva agreements on Indochina brought some relaxation of the tension.

Japan was almost entirely without international concerns before the Korean War. With the restoration of sovereignty following the peace treaty in 1951, it gradually returned to international participation under the sponsorship and protection of the United States. Its international setting was thus economically favorable and politically relatively relaxed. It no longer had any "enemies" and was surrounded by satisfied powers, one of which occupied it. It was thus spared the necessity of real decisions until it had to choose in 1952 between the Chinese governments in Taipei and Peking—which was not in any case a free choice. It was therefore at liberty to concentrate upon domestic development.

Under the leadership of the American Occupation a series of institutional reforms were promulgated dedicated to the abolition of the military and the encouragement of political pluralism in place of the defeated leadership. The 1947 constitution, with its renunciation of war and of military force, came to serve as the symbol and guarantee of these ideals. As in the Meiji era, when abolition of the unequal treaties was contingent upon institutional change, Japan was again obliged to reform as a condition for the resumption of its sovereignty. Unlike the Meiji era, however, when Japan emerged into a world rapidly being divided by imperialist powers and an Asia in which only China and Korea seemed to offer it opportunity for developing its interest, postwar Japan returned to international affairs to find China and Korea under firmly nationalistic governments and South and Southeast Asia newly independent. Mainland markets formerly vital to Japanese exports were closed, though raw materials from other areas which had been denied earlier were soon available. The opportunity and instability of international affairs in South, Southeast, and Eastern Asia no longer operated to disorient politics within Japan. Provisions for racial equality adopted by the United Nations and the United States removed conditions offensive to Japanese pride in prewar days. The People's Republic of China was barred from the United Nations and Western international activities and blacklisted for its participation in the Korean War. Japan's stability and recovery became central to the United Nations presence in Korea and to United States policy in Asia. The United States-Japan Security Treaty signed in 1951 provided American support against external threat and internal dangers externally inspired. In many respects

Japan had won the war while losing it, and profited from an international climate that imposed staggering burdens on the Russian economy.

Balance Sheet of Confrontation

The Korean War confirmed the United States and the Soviet Union in their posture of confrontation, and the ensuing hostility created an environment that favored rapid growth in Japan while imposing heavy burdens on Russia's development.

Russia emerged from the war as the political and ideological leader of the Communist countries. Through the Warsaw Pact it assumed military leadership of its bloc in order to offset the efforts of the NATO powers to rebuild military strength in Western Europe. It maintained almost full mobilization and military occupation of areas it had come to control late in the war, and on occasion it intervened militarily in these areas, as in Hungary in 1956 and Czechoslovakia in 1968. Though it felt free to call upon its Eastern European allies for substantial economic contributions, the U.S.S.R. also gave considerable support to China. The arms race required Soviet expenditures equivalent to approximately 10 per cent of its GNP throughout the postwar period. Soviet development of nuclear weaponry required a complex technology and the investment of enormous resources; and its initial leadership in the exploration of outer space, symbolized by the success of the sputnik satellite in 1957, constituted impressive evidence of the maturity of its science and technology. Russia was limited to its resources in these efforts, however, for its own allies were less developed and the confrontation with the West placed sharp limits on Soviet ability to import advanced equipment and technology. Trade with the United States remained below the prewar level until the economic agreements of 1972. The export of advanced technology from the United States and many European governments was restricted by fears that it would benefit the Soviet military establishment.

In the Pacific and East Asia, Soviet policy centered on close cooperation with the new People's Republic of China until the late 1950's. The decade opened with a Soviet-Chinese alliance directed against a supposedly still dangerous Japan and its allies, to which the American-Japanese Security Pact of 1951 was a response. That Pact provided American guarantees in return for the right to maintain military bases in Japan to protect the country from attack and also to suppress, at the request of the Japanese government, domestic disturbances provoked by a foreign power. The treaty was revised and renewed for a second ten-year period in 1960, with the language about internal subversion removed, and it continued in force after 1970 with the understanding that either country could terminate it with one year's notice. For several years the Soviet Union tried to resume its pre-1905 rights in Manchurian transportation and development, and until 1953 it maintained joint stock companies in China similar to those formed in Eastern Europe for the exploitation of mineral resources; in addition it offered loans for economic development, and sponsored massive exchanges of trainees and instructors to study and teach the Soviet model of modernization. The chief beneficiary of this movement was probably the People's Liberation Army, which was completely re-equipped and provided with a modern jet air force. China's confidence in its own power and in the technological superiority of its Soviet ally was reflected in vigorous border tactics in Tibet, in a series of threats to Quemoy and Taiwan, and finally to India in 1962. Politically and ideologically, however, the replacement of Stalin by Khrushchev diminished Russian claims to dominance, and by the end of the 1950's the closeness of the Moscow tie had been fundamentally weakened by economic and ideological disagreements. The perception of Sino-Soviet cooperation survived its reality, however, and contributed importantly to Japan's ability to attract American and Western assistance.

The San Francisco Treaty of Peace of 1951 restored Japanese sovereignty, and the Security Pact negotiated at the same time recognized Japan's "right of individual or collective self-defense," thus legitimizing the Police Reserve that had been established with the withdrawal of American troops to Korea in 1950. Renamed the Self-Defense Force, the new military, which came to number 250,000 air, sea, and land forces by 1970, provided a limited defense establishment that was supplemental to the protection American guarantees provided against outside aggressors. Japan quickly resumed the forms of international activity and responsibility. The treaty left in limbo Japan's rights to Okinawa, which remained under American rule until 1972 when its return to Japanese sovereignty was widely heralded as signifying the end of the postwar era. At American insistence Japan agreed to recognize the Republic of China (Taiwan) rather than the People's Republic of China, although it developed a lively trade with Mainland China as well. Subsequent to the improved relations between America and Communist China in 1972, Japan switched its recognition to Peking, without, however, sacrificing its leading position in trade with Taiwan.

In the early 1950's treaties of peace were worked out with the newly independent nations of Southeast Asia. Reparations in goods and services, negotiated in connection with these treaties, brought Japanese traders and manufacturers back into the area. In 1956 Japan ended the state of war with the Soviet Union, and in December of that year, with the Russians no longer invoking their veto over Japanese entry into the United Nations, Japan became a member. It also became a contributing member to the Colombo group of nations working for economic development in South and Southeast Asia, the General Agreement on Tariffs and Trade (GATT), and the Organization for Economic Cooperation and Development (OECD). It hosted the Olympic Games in 1964, sponsored the creation of the Asian Development Bank in 1966, and held an international exposition in 1970. Thus the period of near-isolation for China and vigilant containment for Russia coincided with one of re-engagement for Japan.

The economic recovery of Japan and Russia in the 1950's and 1960's showed certain similarities that derived from parallel experiences. Both countries came out of the war with industrial plants substantially destroyed, but their productive skills had been sharpened during the long struggle with the world's most advanced industrial powers. The plants had to be rebuilt, and they were naturally reconstructued along the lines of the most recent and advanced technology that was available. Russia, however, had to give first priority to security and international responsibilities, and was not sufficiently developed to support rapid growth in both consumer and defense production. Russian defense costs held steady at about 10 per cent of GNP; Japan, through inclination and from necessity, had very modest defense costs that remained below 1 per cent of GNP.

While the U.S.S.R. was cut off from foreign technological help, the Japanese were its chief beneficiaries. Japan's access to imported technology, most of it American, was vital. Between 1950 and 1968 approximately 10,000 separate agreements—through purchase, contract, or cooperation—on the import of technology were concluded at a total cost of close to $1.5 billion. Japanese industry was rebuilt on the most advanced levels available, at a fraction of the cost and time that would have been required for developing it without outside assistance.

United States assistance was also important to Japanese economic recovery through the role that the American market came to assume for Japanese industry. Further, American sponsorship introduced Japan to all important international organizations and friendly markets and greatly eased Japan's access to raw materials. Japan's exports grew approximately 15 per cent a year in the fifties, more than double the world rate. Its trade with the United States came to make up approximately one-third of its total balance, and Japan became (after Canada) America's second largest trading partner. Japan's recovery, therefore, began with badly needed payments for goods and services provided during the Korean War in 1950, and its achievement by 1970 was symbolized by large and growing trade surpluses with its industrial trading partners until rising energy costs brought an end to this in 1973. Even so, the international setting was not sufficient to account for Japan's new industrial development, though it was essential to it.

The Challenge of Interdependence

The early 1970's brought an end to the postwar era of confrontation. On both sides there was an easing of ties in consequence of the recovery and development of the participating states. This process was hastened by the evidence from Vietnam of the impossibility of controlling nationalist or "people's liberation" movements without recourse to means of total destruction that were no longer practical because their employment would threaten the user.

By the late 1960's the Sino-Soviet alliance of the previous decade had changed to bitter hostility. Soviet enmity and border activity had become a source of deep concern to China, resonating as it did with instability within the Chinese leadership during and after the Cultural Revolution. Both sides struggled for a leading role in supporting Vietnamese insurgency, but both became concerned about gaining the support of former enemies in the event of possible hostilities. The themes and rhetoric of the ideological confrontation of the 1950's declined in relevance.

The metamorphosis of Japan into the third most productive economy in the world brought strains to the American-Japanese alliance. Japanese trade imbalances with the United States changed to impressive surpluses, and for a United States struggling with inflation and war in Vietnam the sudden prosperity of its former protégé offered tempting identification of it as a scapegoat. Japan proved slow in responding to complaints from Americans anxious for trade and capital liberalization. Trade restrictions that had been instituted to protect a weak economy were still in force long after they had served their purpose. Japanese economic recovery, so long heralded as a triumph, was beginning to be spoken of as a problem for American policy.

In the summer of 1971 the American government announced a startling 180-degree change in its policy toward China, and followed this declaration of rapprochement with steps to force resolution of the international monetary crisis. President Nixon's visit to China, where he worked out a form of de facto recognition of the mainland regime while maintaining formal relations with Taiwan, was quickly followed by a trip by Japanese Prime Minister Tanaka, who reversed these priorities by establishing formal relations with Peking while maintaining de facto recognition and trade with Taiwan. Nixon also traveled to the Soviet Union, and then welcomed Secretary Brezhnev to the United States. Japan in turn moved quickly to improve its relations with the U.S.S.R. Japanese-Soviet trade had been growing rapidly since the 1950's, and by 1970 Japan was Russia's largest trading partner among the industrialized states (as it was Mainland China's, after Hong Kong). It was characteristic of the structure of the new Japanese economy that its imports from the Soviet Union (as from the United States) consisted chiefly of raw materials, while Japan exported manufactured goods, technology, and even fully equipped plants. Japan also undertook to contract for a modern seaport to be constructed in the Bay of Wrangel off northern Siberia. Japan continued to insist upon Russian return of the southernmost Kuriles as a condition for a formal treaty of peace with the Soviet Union, but the Russians refused to discuss the issue—apparently from fear of setting a precedent for demands for rectification of their borders with the People's Republic of China. Similarly, Japanese hesitated to assist Siberian fuel development from fear of antagonizing China, whose border problems would be increased if Russian access to energy supplies were improved.

The 1970's thus saw the priorities and assumptions of the 1950's and 1960's become obsolete. Japan's resumption of full independence called for a stronger posture and commitments, and the new complexity of East Asian relationships seemed likely to offer wider oportunities for contacts and choices. The Soviet Union likewise adopted a more flexible outlook that reflected greater self-confidence at home and appreciation of the advantages of international interdependence.

International Comparisons

The role of the international environment after the 1940's in the transition of Japan and Russia from transformation to high modernization may be compared with the experience of other countries in terms of discontinuities in leadership, participation in and obligations to alliance systems, access to and extension of foreign aid, and the degree of internationalization.

Discontinuities in leadership were naturally far greater within the defeated countries than among the victors. The break with past political leadership as a result of the war was even more complete in the countries where Communist parties gained control. In most of the countries of Eastern Europe—Albania, Bulgaria, Czechoslovakia, Hungary, Poland, and Romania—as in North Korea, Communist control was achieved subsequent to Soviet military occupation. In other countries in Europe and Asia where native revolutionary movements, often led by men of considerable political experience, gained control—Yugoslavia, North Vietnam, and China—wartime movements of guerrilla leaders achieved national domination. Political discontinuity was probably greatest in the former colonial countries. More than seventy countries in Asia and Africa gained their independence as a result of the war.

Both Japan and Russia contributed importantly to these changes; the Japanese by helping to destroy colonial governments in Southeast Asia and in particular the Nationalist government of the Republic of China, and the Russians by sponsoring Communist regimes in areas they occupied. Within Japan defeat and occupation had the effect of freeing the country from a generation of leaders that had given foreign expansion priority as a requirement of national development, and of creating an environment for the inauguration of policies that would affect domestic economic growth. In Russia military victory solidified prewar domestic pragmatism into postwar dogmatism; policies toward development that had been flexible and imaginative on the problems of transformation in the 1930's had, by the 1950's, hardened into rigid and unyielding positions on postwar problems.

The postwar years saw all the developed countries involved in the confrontation of the Cold War, but Japan's international position was nevertheless unique. Unlike Germany or Italy, Japan was not threatened by division of its home territories, a nearby Soviet land border, or a strong and experienced domestic Communist party. As the only developed power in Asia, it was able to profit from its supply role in the Korean conflict; thereafter its provision of bases for American forces, and services for those forces, accounted for steady surpluses of foreign currency. Until the 1960's most Japanese felt themselves involuntary actors in the international politics in which their country participated. Their full autonomy in the sixties, however, found them uniquely free of expensive constraints. Their constitution and the American guarantee supplied built-in protection against heavy defense expenditures; their security pact with the United States did not commit them to specific participation as NATO did the Atlantic powers; a nearby Chinese military colossus, not perceived as a threat, offered further restraint on the development of conventional forces; and the requirements of a "low posture" stance in Southeast Asia reinforced domestic psychological and political disinclination toward rearmament. Thus Japan came closer than any other developed state to having a free choice in the degree of international involvement while experimenting with abstention from offensive weaponry or forces.

Japan's position with reference to access to foreign aid was also far more advantageous than that of Russia and comparable to that of America's allies in Western Europe. The United States made loans and grants for economic development and military assistance between 1945 and 1969 totaling some $138 billion. Japan's share was more than $4 billion, chiefly in the period to 1961. American aid provided 38 per cent of Japan's imports during the Occupation years, a time when export earnings were particularly slim. On a per capita basis American economic aid for Japan was $27, as compared with $77 for Western Germany, $51 for Italy, and $122 for the United Kingdom. America's other allies received proportionately more, but the relation of costs to productivity in Japan produced a multiplier effect of special importance. The subsequent and nongovernmental transfer of American technology was more important still. The Soviet Union and its Warsaw allies received virtually no U.S. assistance. Some of the East European countries contributed to the reconstruction of the U.S.S.R. through reparations, joint stock companies, and favorable terms of trade. After the mid-1950's, however, the Soviet Union extended loans and grants to the countries in its orbit (including Cuba and China) totaling an estimated $8 billion to $10 billion. Russia also administered a program of grants to other countries, principally India, Iraq, and Egypt, that amounted to some $1.5 billion. By the end of the decade Soviet aid to China had ceased, and China had instituted a small aid program of its own. In 1964, after its entry in OECD, Japan also pledged itself to work toward the allocation of 1 per cent of its GNP to foreign aid, and utilized by choice multilateral agencies in giving this assistance.

Despite the confrontations of the Cold War and the tensions of an era of revolution and disorder, the postwar world was also characterized by unprecedented internationalization. It is possible to distinguish a scale ranging from the wealthiest and most developed countries, in which international contacts were only in part sponsored or controlled by government, to the newly independent and developing countries with limited reserves of foreign exchange, in which international contacts were predominantly governmental. Russia, for reasons of political control and economic stringency, was closer to the latter, with a minimum of unrestricted and private contact across its borders. Japan until the mid-1960's, when it entered the circle of OECD "developed" countries, was somewhere in between. Its international contacts were limited first by Occupation controls and then by self-imposed fiscal controls. Legislation sponsored by the Occupation authorities, designed to protect Japanese industries from take-over and competition by better financed outside interests, helped to preserve the Japanese market for Japanese producers well into the sixties. The Occupation years and those that followed were also, however, Japan's first big experience with non-Japanese, for millions of Americans passed through Japan's cities and bases. The late 1960's and 1970's saw Japan more fully internationalized; restraints on foreign capital and goods diminished in response to the fiscal and trade policies of the United States, and Japanese capital went abroad in search of investment in ever larger amounts. Significantly, the number of Japanese who traveled abroad increased dramatically, reaching 1,392,000 in 1972, a jump of 45 per cent over 1971 and 400 per cent over 1968. Foreigners who visited Japan in 1972 numbered 724,000, a rise of 10 per cent over 1971.

In the postwar years competitive economic assistance, the decline of colonialism, and internationalization were all factors that contributed to an environment favorable to economic development. The postwar economic benefits were unevenly distributed, however, and political considerations and population growth diluted the gains for many. Japan, more than any other country, profited from this enviroment. Its capacities permitted it to take full advantage of its position as nonparticipant in the international struggle for power, and it outstripped all other countries in its rate of development. Russia did not benefit in any comparable way. With heavy defense and political expenditures, it could take only limited advantage of the opportunities offered by the postwar international environment.

Chapter Fifteen

POLITICAL STRUCTURE

IN THE AFTERMATH of the Second World War, a defeated Japan and a victorious Russia followed paths of political development that in certain respects were more acutely divergent than ever in the past. Success confirmed the autocratic policies of Stalin in Soviet Russia, whereas in Japan the democratizing and decentralizing reforms of the American Occupation served to revive parliamentary democracy. Though developments in the 1950's—de-Stalinization in the U.S.S.R. and the reversal of a number of Occupation reforms in Japan—modified this early postwar divergence, the contrast between the formal political systems of the two nations has remained clear-cut into the 1970's. Japanese political life today is based on open competition of legally constituted representative bodies and interest groups; Soviet political life is based exclusively on the Communist Party, which serves as a unitary clearinghouse for legitimate political power. Despite certain liberalizing tendencies in the Soviet Union in recent years, there continues to be far more overt political coercion than in Japan, where political dissenters enjoy freedom of expression and crucial issues are discussed in a broad public forum.

In some respects, however, Japan's ideally pluralistic political structure has in actual practice operated at levels of political consensus and uniformity which are as high as in the Soviet Union. In both nations, for example, a similar unified consensus (only recently challenged in Japan) has prevailed on the national priority of rapid economic growth. In both nations, the government assumes a far-reaching role in the planning of the national economy, although Japan, of course, still remains a market economy. One marked contrast in national priorities is in the realm of defense, with the Soviet Union maintaining a proportionately far larger military force, which in turn creates political tensions from which Japan has been on the whole free.

In the actual operation of the Japanese party system there has similarly been more uniformity than the pluralistic structure would suggest, inasmuch as a single party has been in firm control for all but three months of the last thirty years. Opposition parties have been highly vocal in Japan, but their numbers have remained small. The shifts of power in the national government have been conducted largely through clique maneuvering within the ruling party. In the Soviet Union, on the other hand, there has been increasing accommodation of diverse political interests despite the formal monopolistic role of the Communist Party.

In leadership as well, the two countries are similar in that both polities are staffed by a highly homogeneous and generally respected official elite, sharing similar educational experience and political assumptions. While this homogeneity in the Soviet Union is achieved through the Communist Party, it is maintained in Japan through patterns of recruitment and promotion that are essentially the same for all large organizations, public or private. The lower levels of conscious manipulation in achieving such homogeneity in Japan are to some degree facilitated by near-total ethnic homogeneity. In the Soviet Union constant attention must be paid to the problems of assimilating the ethnic minorities into the political system.

Apart from contrasting political structures and similar levels of political stability, Japan and the U.S.S.R. share a basic overall similarity: as they have become more highly modernized both have found it necessary to eliminate, or at least modify, the most overtly coercive and one-dimensional policies of the period of transformation. The achievement of advanced industrial status has decreased the sense of urgency to catch up with the West and in turn created a diminished ability on the part of political leaders and the political systems as a whole to demand sacrifices for national goals. Yet spiraling levels of societal complexity and interdependence have created new demands for flexibility and differential treatment in the political system. Thus, whatever the specific contrasts in the operations of the respective polities, Japan and the U.S.S.R. have in this period seen a basically similar tendency toward increasing accommodation and sensitivity to diverse interests within the political systems, and their leaders have become less inclined to make radical changes through governmental programs.

National Priorities and Legitimation

The end of the Second World War had predictably contrasting impacts on national priorities in Japan and the U.S.S.R. The victory for the Soviet Union—enormous as the cost was in lives and material resources—served to confirm and even to strengthen the political regime of Stalin. In Japan the effect was precisely the opposite. Total defeat thoroughly discredited the old political system and resulted in seven and one-half years of forced occupation by the United States, during which time a new constitutional structure was established. This "democratization" of the Japanese political system may have been less thorough than the Occupation reformers had hoped, but it nevertheless broke many old habits and created a regime clearly distinct from that in the Soviet Union, which continued to rely on the decisions of one man and his close advisers.

Not only did the outcome of the war confirm an obvious divergence between the political systems of the two nations, but it also altered their respective national policies. Granted that for both nations the paramount political aim throughout the postwar era has been to achieve as fast a pace of economic development as possible, the pursuit of this objective has been shaped by their widely differing international contexts. For Japan, stripped by the armistice of a military role in world affairs, economic development could be promoted as an end in itself. For the U.S.S.R., deeply engaged in the Cold War and eager under any circumstances to realize its new "big power" status, economic development became a prominent factor in insuring the nation's political security and well-being. The achievement of strategic nuclear capabilities in the 1950's marked the success of this Soviet effort and the beginning of the transition to a period in which political leaders could view economic development as an end to be pursued for a host of interconnected reasons, among which diplomatic objectives were but one. Similarly, the end of the Occupation in 1952 and the more recent emergence of Japan as a world economic power marked the beginning of a transition to a situation in which economic and diplomatic objectives could no longer be considered in isolation from each other.

Any consideration of the means by which the governments of the two countries regained legitimacy in the eyes of their constituents must go beyond the simple contrast between compulsion in the

U.S.S.R. versus free institutions in Japan. Although certain strongly repressive features of Soviet political life remain, their importance for the legitimization of the government has been substantially reduced, especially in connection with the impact of the successes scored in economic and social development and on the international stage. Indeed, the success of the Soviet and Japanese governments in the postwar era has more than anything else endowed them with legitimacy and earned them public support. Such acceptance and backing are reinforced in turn by the family and the community, where values that promote political loyalty are for the most part successfully inculcated in the rising generation.

Policy-making and Personnel

The first postwar decade saw the final achievement of institutional stability in both nations after many decades of stress and uncertainty. The Japanese inaugurated a new constitutional system in 1947 which, despite some initial threats against it by left-wing political forces, has proved remarkably stable, with cabinets surviving longer than any have since the 1890's. In the Soviet Union the death of Stalin in 1953 created a brief period of considerable uncertainty, but in the end a successful reversion from personal to party rule was effected, first under the hegemony of Nikita Khrushchev and then more systematically under Leonid Brezhnev. In many respects, of course, this stabilization of the political institutions in the two nations has been fostered by the absence of any major wars on convulsive international crises. But whatever the influence of the international environment, Japan and the U.S.S.R. passed through the postwar years with political systems far more stable than those of the previous half century.

In comparing the political structures of contemporary Japan and the Soviet Union, consideration must be given to the conventional contrast between a "Communist" and "capitalist" form of government. Two preliminary qualifications in such a comparison are in order: first, the focus here is on the internal political configuration of the respective countries and not on whatever implications the terms may have for foreign policy and the international order; second, such labels as "communism," contrasted with "capitalism," "pluralism," and "democracy" all too often denote ideal patterns that may be but dimly reflected in the actual functioning of political systems.

Given these qualifications, some extremely important contrasts still exist between the systems of Japan and the Soviet Union. The Communist Party's monopoly of all political power in the U.S.S.R., formalized in law, has no parallel in the more pluralistic Japanese state with its diversity of legally constituted and openly competing parties and groups. There is also a great deal more overt coercion exercised within the Soviet system than within the Japanese, although a careful study of the more subtle means of coercion might reveal the Japanese to be more restrictive than commonly thought. It is also obvious that all major economic activity continues to be administered through the state in the Soviet Union, where governmental organs manage directly a far larger portion of the GNP than they do in Japan.

Though these contrasts are important, in certain other broad respects Japan and the Soviet Union seem quite similar. Their high levels of economic development, for example, require large national institutions, whether public or private, to make critical planning decisions affecting diverse areas of life in both nations. While private ownership may give Japanese industrial managers a higher degree of formal autonomy than those in the Soviet Union, their success or failure depends increasingly on their ability to undertake long-range planning and to coordinate the degree of planning required by highly modernized societies with that of the state itself. Some form of national planning institutions are more necessary in more tightly organized advanced industrial societies than they are in premodern or transitional societies, and truly autonomous economic activity of individual enterprises or sectors is simply no longer possible in either Japan or Russia.

Some serious qualifications to the term "pluralism" as applied to contemporary Japanese polity might also be added. The heavy stress upon the interests of the national collectivity as opposed to those of individuals and groups has characterized all modern activity in Japan since the Meiji Restoration, thanks to the persistent impulse to catch up with the West, and in the 1970's it continues to mute the distinction between public policy and private interests. A further factor working to moderate the pluralism of the Japanese polity is the sustained unity of the elite, a unity that helps to link together all separate areas of administrative activity, whether business, politics, or the state bureaucracy. These factors work to give the Japanese polity what is in relative terms a far more "monolithic" cast than is suggested by the ideal of a pluralistic system, so cherished by the re-formers during the occupation.

The Soviet polity, on the other hand, appears to be far less unitary or "monolithic" than that term would suggest. Soviet industry is not organized along the lines of the banks and trading companies that so effectively coordinate the private sector of Japanese economic life. Lacking such effective coordinating bodies, the state fre-quently—and tacitly—has to permit individual and local deviations from general and often unrealistic norms set down by central plan-ning organs. Since Stalin's death the Soviet political system has also shown itself to be quite responsive at times to interests within the state and party bureaucracies and the public at large, interests that compete on the basis of political strength for the limited resources available. The definition of needs is made as much despite as because of the organizational form of the various interests, and "democratic centralism" continues to set the bounds of internal discourse. None-theless, the day-to-day workings of the Soviet political system reveal an increased reliance upon pluralistic competition and careful pow-er bargaining.

A comparison of the elites that staff the upper levels of the policy-making structure in the two countries also reveals similarities whose roots reach deep into the period of transformation. Both continue to have the benefit of an elite class whose common experience, edu-cation, and values serve to temper and moderate the elaborate process of bargaining and compromise that gives stability to the respective polities. One of the best indicators of elite homogeneity in both the U.S.S.R. and Japan is the frequency of "elite interpene-tration," by which members of one segment of the administrative leadership transfer to another with little difficulty, thereby creating overlaps that further enhance the system's ability to respond to con-flicts of interest.

However great the postwar changes in the social composition of the Japanese elite may be, it continues the Meiji pattern of drawing on a fixed hierarchy of educational institutions for the top leader-ship. In addition, the system of promotion by seniority (but with adequate allowance for merit)—a system common to virtually *all* Japanese organizations in the modern sector—assures that those in key positions of power at any one time will be of the identical generation. Thus, whether a man is a business executive, a section chief in the bureaucracy, or a member of the national Diet, the chances are that he will have attended a prestige university, that he will be of a predictable age, and that he will share very much the same values and style of life. This rather than social origins accounts for the "monolithic" impression that the Japanese social order creates on outsiders.

The uniformity of the Soviet elite is both more recent and more carefully controlled than Japan's, but the end result is similar. The unique institution of the Communist Party plays a large role in enforcing this uniformity in a way that is not necessary in Japan. Only since World War II has there appeared a generation of leaders raised and educated wholly within the Soviet system. The Stalinist purges in the 1930's hastened this process by eliminating many of the more diverse elements in the early Soviet leadership, and the final demise of Stalin himself opened the way to a standard pattern of elite recruitment. The decline in the rate of economic expansion during the 1960's further strengthened homogeneity at the top levels, both by reducing the need to bring in large numbers of "outsiders" and also by keeping intact working groups that had coalesced during the previous decades of the most rapid growth. Naturally, this homogeneity has a strongly negative side, in that higher echelons of leadership have been increasingly static and now consist of men conspicuously older than their counterparts in Japan, and who often preserve the outlook and methods of the 1930's and 1940's. Within Japanese politics and business, however, the occasional maverick and self-made man serves to emphasize the possibilities for rapid mobility that were created by the discontinuities within the elite structure in wartime and immediate postwar years.

As it has throughout its history, the Soviet Union must still deal with the consequences of a national heterogeneity which has no parallel in Japan. Inequalities of national representation persist in the Communist Party, and Great Russians continue to dominate the leadership of all-union agencies. Yet at the elite level, at least many of the worst inequities appear for the time being to have been resolved through party recruitment policies and through advanced training establishments run by party, academic, and military organizations. To be sure, important cleavages remain, but these are of another sort; existing bureaucratic "chains" or "groupings" are defined by their engagement with special functions within the state more than by the social or economic backgrounds of their members.

Special Interests

The political systems of the Soviet Union and Japan, apart from the markedly different roles of political parties, are both dominated by central "regimes" consisting of the Communist Party and the state bureaucracy in the U.S.S.R. and of nationally elected office-holders, top civil servants, and major industrialists in Japan. Associated with these regimes, however, are numerous particularistic interests, which, with varying degrees of effectiveness, make their needs felt at the center. It is in relation to the political participation of these groups that some of the most important contrasts between the two nations can be noted.

Foremost among potentially distinct interests is the military, but in both countries it has for the most part been effectively neutralized as an independent political force. The Japanese prewar military establishment was totally dismantled during the Occupation, and the political power it had come to hold by the end of the previous period was eliminated by the new constitution. The civil control of the military was in many ways the most critical and durable of all the Occupation reforms, because it eliminated the one segment of the prewar Japanese elite that possessed its own distinct system of education and was guided by its own peculiar values. Since 1950, Japan has gradually built up a new military establishment, known euphemistically as the "Self-Defense Force," to circumvent the constitutional ban in Article 9 on the maintenance of a war potential. By 1970 the SDF's manpower stood at about a quarter million well-trained and well-equipped men. The memory of the prewar political power of the military, however, has served to hold the SDF in check so that it scrupulously maintains an attitude of strict professionalism and is accorded very little influence within the political system.

The Russian military machine is more than tenfold that of Japan. Its claims on national resources are enormous, and its role in Soviet foreign policy has yet to be fully appreciated. From the very beginning, however, Communist Party leaders have devoted extraordinary attention to assuring that the military is fully integrated within the total polity and that it possess only minimal independent political power. This control is achieved through a variety of mechanisms such as extensive party surveillance over the military and its training institutes as well as over the educational programs carried on for its recruits. Far more important than these mechanisms, perhaps, are the memories engendered by the heroic joint efforts of the army and the regime during the Second World War, memories that are still carefully preserved by active propaganda. The tradition of military subordination to political authority, then, which dates back to the tsarist regime, has been maintained, and this basic relationship shows no prospect of being violated in the foreseeable future. More conspicuous than tension between military and civil authorities in the U.S.S.R. has been competition among various services of the military for funds, which has become an important aspect of all national debates on the allocation of resources.

A second special interest group within the two polities, and one which looms far larger in the Soviet Union than in Japan, is that of the national minorities. The Japanese have only one such group of any size, the Koreans, who at 600,000 account for less than 1 per cent of the total population. But while discrimination against Koreans persists and provides radical parties with an obvious rallying point, their minuscule size assures that they will never be more than a squeak in the political system as a whole.

In the Soviet Union the issue of national minorities is entirely different. Those who are not Great Russian account for about half the total population and are rapidly increasing in numbers—and in levels of education and social development. Soviet leaders have responded to these changes with a wide variety of measures, ranging from efforts to stimulate group feelings within each of the individual Turkic peoples as a counterweight to pan-Turkic consciousness, to efforts at russifying minorities through large-scale settlement of their territories by Great Russians. Since the mid-1960's, however, several areas have witnessed organized agitation and violence—notably the Baltic, the Caucasus, and the Ukraine. On the whole, though, the elaborate mechanisms that have been devised to deal with the potential political threat of the nationalities have been successful, and the force of central policies has far outweighed separatist pressures. The harsh treatment dealt all independent public manifestations by religious groups in the Soviet Union is justified on similar grounds. Because some organized religions—notably Judaism and Catholicism—have been closely associated with particularist national aspirations, they have aroused the same fears as other centrifugal forces in the state.

Japan has adopted policies calling for total separation of church and state, and the official manipulation of both Buddhism and Shinto for nationalist purposes, widespread before the war, has largely ceased. For their own part, the religious sects have sustained the long tradition of submission to political authority. The one exception, and an important one, is the militant Buddhist Sōka Gakkai movement, which since 1964 has been active in national politics through its political arm, the Kōmeitō (Clean Government Party), and has achieved some dramatic successes in national elections. The Kōmeitō has shown no signs of posing any threats to the political order, however, and has generally behaved with considerable moderation and propriety.

Labor as a special-interest group has never achieved the same degree of political authority in the U.S.S.R. and Japan that it has wielded in Western nations. This tendency still obtains today. The Japanese labor-union movement expanded greatly under encouragement from the American Occupation and came to be a major source of support for the Socialist Party. This party, however, has yet to gain real political power in the "one and a half party system" that has characterized postwar Japan. Furthermore, most Japanese unions are organized on an enterprise rather than a trade basis, and tend to be well integrated into Japan's paternalistic system of industrial management. Only rarely does labor resort to open confrontation, though in years of unprecedented growth it has seen little need to do so. Soviet trade unions wield much less political power than do those in Japan, despite efforts after the death of Stalin to assign more responsibility to these organizations. The Soviet trade unions remain closely guided "from above" by the Communist Party, their principal area of participation being in low- and middle-level decisions relating to such matters as work quotas and bonus systems. They are still denied the right to strike, and they are prohibited from participating in vital decisions such as those on resource allocation and wage levels. The growing numbers and prestige of middle-class office workers and technical personnel has tended further to diminish the authority of labor in both nations.

The agricultural population in both Japan and the U.S.S.R. has dropped radically with urbanization, and today rarely adopts militant political attitudes. As for national political power, however, Japanese farmers have during much of the postwar period served as an important (though diminishing) source of support for the ruling conservative party, in return for which they have demanded and gained a generous system of price supports for agricultural products. In the Soviet Union, the agricultural sector is the object of considerable solicitude on the part of national leaders, who are aware that production failures on the farm helped considerably to weaken the power of Khrushchev. Yet this does not translate into political power for agriculture as a whole, and particularly for the large number of poor peasants who remain all but ignored by the urban-based, industry-minded regime.

The ability of the Japanese and Soviet polities to win the support of new groups and to incorporate them into their day-to-day functioning is demonstrated by the assimilation of persons with a higher education—those in the white-collar or professional stratum. The rapid growth in white-collar positions has been a prominent feature of the social evolution of both nations since the Second World War, particularly in the years of greatest economic advancement. Even so, all but a small number of these people have been readily absorbed by the political structure. In Japan such new professionals have come to exercise no great political authority; in the U.S.S.R., however, though they have only recently reached the upper ranks of the party, they have long formed the largest single group of its membership. The only educated groups that have not been so successfully assimilated have been Japanese students and certain intellectuals there and in the Soviet Union. The student movement has been an important political force in postwar Japan; in the mammoth demonstrations staged during the crisis over the 1960 security treaty, students and intellectuals joined with other left-wing groups and succeeded in toppling the Kishi government. The conservative party, nonetheless, remained firmly in control and the political system continued to function effectively. In the Soviet Union a small but vocal dissident movement made up of professional people and members of the intellectual elite caused some repercussions in the 1960's, but is declining in the face of concerted police action combined with a policy of sending prominent critics into forced exile abroad. To the extent that such dissidents have been individuals who suffered severely under Stalin, it is questionable whether this particular type of political opposition will continue into a second generation. By and large Soviet students and older professionals have shown themselves to be politically passive, preoccupied with their own careers and with national economic and social development, which they see as congruent objectives.

Increasing prosperity in Japan and in the Soviet Union has caused the consumer as a special-interest group to assume increasing weight in policy-making, although only Japan can be said to have an organized consumer movement. In the Soviet Union, nevertheless, the demand that resources be shifted from capital investments to consumer goods and services has made itself felt in every quarter. Under pressure from this inchoate "movement," certain Soviet periodical publications have assumed responsibility for voicing consumer views and have endeavored systematically to sample public opinion on matters of concern to the consumer.

The top strata of the ruling elite in both Japan and the Soviet Union are virtually all male. Beneath that level, however, the Soviet Union is conspicuously in advance of Japan in the extent to which women have, as a group, gained access to the political process. While Japan can boast of only 3 per cent of its women being part of the national political machinery, women constitute 20 per cent of the membership of the ruling Communist Party of the Soviet Union, and are numerous in both middle-level, decision-making posts and in the professions. They enjoy extensive juridical rights and are tightly organized, especially for participation in international organizations. Yet in neither nation do women constitute a strong and independent political force, the recent organization of consumer protests in Japan perhaps being a partial exception to this general pattern.

Finally, it should, of course, be recalled that in Japan all of the special interests considered above participate politically through a multiparty system, whereas in the U.S.S.R they are articulated through the single apparatus of the Communist Party. The groups thus formed in both countries, whether independently constituted political organizations or informal "factions" within a single party, take on the character of interest groups with identities transcending the specific issue that brought its members together. An interesting addition to the process of political action in Japan is the formation of "citizens groups" to protest specific threats to the environment. These have assumed considerable importance in many areas, but they have not as yet been translated into larger-scale and enduring patterns. The existence of such diverse groupings provides both societies with "safety valves" through which many pressures and dissatisfactions can find a normal outlet within the fabric of the political system. Such safety valves and their continued ability to function provide a gauge of the success of these two political systems in adapting to the demands of high modernization.

Conflict and Its Resolutions

Since the early 1950's the combination of institutional stability and continuing economic and social development has served in both nations to keep political conflict far less violent than it was in the preceding period. The postwar years have on the whole been peaceful for both nations, with the result that the diminished conflict has been external as well as internal.

The decline in political violence has been accompanied by a considerable diminution in the use of overt coercion by the state. In Japan the governmental machinery for police surveillance and thought control was entirely dismantled under the Occupation, and in the U.S.S.R. the death of Stalin led to the abolition of most of the forced labor camps and a general reduction in police surveillance.

Measurable levels of political violence are higher in Japan than in the Soviet Union, where all forms of political activity—and even communication—outside of the Communist Party are strictly forbidden. Because extraparliamentary politics are legal in Japan, however, the government is obliged to accept strikes and demonstrations as normal, seeking only to keep them nonviolent. To this end it has created a specially trained force of riot police (*kidōtai*). Notwithstanding the many instances of political violence that have occurred over the years, extraparliamentary politics has itself become routinized, ritualized, and even compartmentalized to such an extent that it does not present a threat to the normal institutional life of Japan.

In contrast, the Soviet Union, with less political violence, continues to employ far more state coercion of all sorts to prevent its occurrence. As in earlier years, opposition to secondary effects of economic development is still a principal source of political violence, though in the 1960's some violence was generated by those who felt public policy was lagging behind the country's needs. Related to both sources of violence is the great effort constantly expended in the Soviet Union to propagandize the public with national symbols, ideals, and goals.

Consistent with their earlier notions of law, both Japan and the U.S.S.R. remain nations in which prescribed legal norms are substantially tempered by frequent resort to personalistic means of conflict resolution. At the same time, over the past two decades both have moved increasingly toward an order based upon legal norms. The American Occupation resulted in a far-reaching reform of the Japanese legal system along Anglo-American lines, though it was subsequently revised somewhat to accord with Japanese custom. In the U.S.S.R. both official and dissident critics of Stalinism have based their case on provisions of the Soviet constitution of 1936. Notwithstanding these developments, it is not a common occurrence for citizens of either nation to resort to the police or courts as a means of settling private disputes. Law, in short, continues to be predominantly a prerogative of the state rather than an instrument of the public, with the resolution of most conflict occurring through conciliation, third-party mediation, and personal bargaining.

International Comparisons

In highly modernized societies political structures and procedures must be adapted to conditions created by contemporary technology. They must respond positively to the needs of new groups brought to the fore by the transformation, preserve internal stability amidst continuing rapid change, and facilitate participation in international agencies. For the early modernizers these tasks, while by no means easy, were simplified by the fact that during their period of transformation they had little need to press the pace of change or to resort to severe measures for mobilizing the population. Because their transformation had been achieved under less strained circumstances, Great Britain, France, and the United States had few extreme measures that had to be rescinded once a high level of development had been attained. The primary contrast between the recent political experience of Japan and the U.S.S.R. on the one hand and the earlier developers on the other is that the former have had to devote relatively more attention to modifying policies and institutions of centralized control that had been created in the years of transformation. In Japan this occurred suddenly under the impact of the Occupation; in the U.S.S.R. the process of modification has extended over a generation and is still under way. In both of these successful latecomers it has constituted the principal postwar political concern, as compared with the early developers.

Because Japan and Russia are among very few late developing nations that are becoming highly modernized, it is impossible to prove that other latecomers will eventually share their political concerns. However, it appears likely that those late developers that have instituted tight and centralized political controls in order to guide the process of transformation will eventually face the same need to modify them once high levels of development are attained.

How late developers will maintain internal security as they assume the characteristics of highly modernized societies is also suggested by the experiences of both Japan and the U.S.S.R. From the limited evidence available—which to be sure does not include the Soviet secret police—it appears that the sizes of the police forces required to keep order in Japan and the U.S.S.R. in proportion to the population are roughly comparable with those of the United Kingdom and the Federal Republic of Germany, somewhat smaller than those of France and Italy, and less than half the size of those of the German Democratic Republic. Even if the Soviet figures are distorted by the exclusion of those military personnel whose function is primarily domestic, the fact that both Japan and Russia have smaller police forces than other countries with comparable political systems is of significance.

The relative stability of the polities of Japan and the Soviet Union can be appreciated in terms of their capacity to effect smooth transfers of executive authority. Not only does this contrast with their own history over the immediately preceding generations, but it is sharply distinct from the experience of many other late developing countries where transfers of power set off a general and often violent debate over the type of system through which the new authority should be exercised. An indicator of paralysis in parliamentary systems is the constant turnover of cabinets and ministries, just as the entrenchment of one group of leaders for life is generally indicative of paralysis in Communist systems. By this measure, too, Japan and the U.S.S.R. appear relatively stable. Japan has not been subject to the parliamentary ping pong that incapacitates Italy, and Russia has freed itself from the long-term control of an unchanging faction such as that which continues to dominate the life of the German Democratic Republic.

Further evidence on the relative stability of the two governments comes from the incidence of protest demonstrations. These are, to be sure, almost entirely suppressed in the U.S.S.R. and a common occurrence in Japan. But it is well to note that the number of protest demonstrations in Japan between 1948 and 1967 was below the figure for France and the Federal German Republic, and that the number of deaths resulting from such demonstrations was extremely low in Japan as compared with these same countries. Though several hundred deaths from political violence are reported to have occurred in the Soviet Union in these same years, even that figure is relatively low in proportion to population and by comparison with most other countries, especially those undergoing rapid change. A fully satisfactory measure of political stability does not yet exist, though the fate of political opponents of the government is clearly much harsher in the U.S.S.R. than in most other countries.

If violence has ceased to be a feature of the political life of Japan, and has been substantially curtailed in Russia, it is in large measure because economic development has kept pace with public expectations. Even among the early developers this achievement is far from universal, as the experience of Great Britain and Italy attests, nor is it common in later developing countries, as the cases of Yugoslavia and Czechoslovakia indicate. Reinforcing the positive influence of economic development is the effectiveness of political socialization in Japan and Russia. Studies of Soviet and Japanese children indicate that the two countries are relatively successful in communicating their dominant ideals to the young. The substantial amount both countries spend on education and the high percentage of the population in school, together with the unusually great amount of radio and television time devoted to news and special features, suggest both societies have ample channels for reinforcing the initial socialization.

Satisfactory measures of the openness of Japan and Russia to innovation do not exist, and the ad hoc impressions of observers present a mixed and even contradictory picture. It would appear safe to conclude, however, that in the political sphere both countries now seem relatively disinclined to tinker with functioning institutions or to create new ones unless a strong need to do so is acknowledged. Neither Russia nor Japan, for example, moved with the speed of Great Britain or even the United States in recognizing and acting upon the need for strong national organs to manage environmental issues. Japan lags behind even such less prosperous societies as Hungary and Poland in the development of welfare institutions. The U.S.S.R. has been conspicuously slower than West European and North American countries in applying computers (not to mention office machines) to public administration. On the other hand, the fact that both rank higher than such early developers as France and Great Britain in the training of scientists and engineers indicates their continuing commitment to those forms of innovation and change which new knowledge brings.

Available indicators on the integration of Japan and the U.S.S.R. into international life are incomplete and those available are not without contradictions. Nonetheless, they point to degrees of transnational engagement that are in general comparable to those of the early developing nations, although the specific forms in each case are different. The U.S.S.R. deploys more government personnel in posts abroad than any other country except the United States and holds the same position with respect to foreign aid. Even so, it appears to be far less thoroughly integrated into world communications and travel than many less developed nations, and ranks below all other early developers with respect to its participation in international organizations. Japan, by contrast, is on a par with the major nations of Western Europe and North America in regard to membership in international organizations. Yet at the same time the volume of travel to and from Japan is lower than that of Ireland, Mexico, and Argentina, and Japan's direct involvement in formal international trading communities and regional federations is quite minor compared with the far less developed member nations of COMECON, or of the several other regional associations in Europe, Asia, and Latin America.

Chapter Sixteen

ECONOMIC STRUCTURE AND GROWTH

SINCE THE SECOND WORLD WAR the Japanese and Russian economies have been approaching the structure and production levels of the most highly modernized societies in the world. By the 1970's, reflecting both their output growth and their large population, Russia and Japan produced respectively the second and third largest gross national products in the world (behind the United States). Their estimated GNP per capita in 1973, though lower than that of many advanced economies, was also high: Japan, $3,822; Russia, $2,450 (the United States, $6,127).

Japan's economic growth was a good deal faster than that of the Soviet Union in the postwar years. As Table 16.1 shows, from 1950 to 1973 Japan's GNP climbed at a rate of 9.9 per cent per year compared with Russia's 5.5 per cent. Its GNP per capita increased more than twice as fast as Russia's. Indeed, Japan's rate of growth in these years was the highest in the world. Moreover, it rose in the decade of the sixties compared with the fifties. Russia's rate of growth on the other hand, though relatively high over the whole period, fell after the 1950's.

Japan and Russia have also been approaching the sectoral structure of the most highly modernized societies. These societies, by the early 1970's, were usually allocating 40 per cent or more of their labor force to services, 40 to 50 per cent to manufacturing, and 15 to 20 per cent or less to agriculture. As can be seen in Table 16.1, Japan in 1970 had achieved this allocation of the labor force, and in fact by 1972 the share of its labor force in agriculture had fallen to under 15 per cent. Russia, however, was further from

T A B L E   1 6 . 1 .   Comparative Economic Data
(*in percentages*)

	JAPAN		RUSSIA	
Average Annual Rates of Growth:	*1950–1973*		*1950–1973*	
Gross National Product	9.9		5.5	
GNP Per Capita	8.7		4.0	
National Product by Sectors				
· of Origin:	*1940*	*1970*	*1940*	*1970*
Agriculture	16	6	29	24
Manufacturing	53	50	45	47
Services	31	44	26	29
Share of Labor Force Employed in:				
Agriculture	44	19	54	27
Manufacturing	31	41	28	45
Services	25	40	18	28
National Product by End Uses:				
Consumption	65	52	63	58
Gross capital formation	24	40	26	30
Government	11	8	11	12

SOURCES:

Japan: On average annual growth rates: U.S. Department of State, *The Planetary Product in 1973*, INR RS–32 (Oct. 30, 1974), Appendix Table 1; K. Ohkawa and H. Rosovsky, *Japanese Economic Growth: Trend Acceleration in the Twentieth Century*, (Stanford, Calif.: Stanford University Press 1973), p. 311; on national product sectors: Ohkawa and Rosovsky, *ibid.*, p. 283; on labor force shares: Ohkawa and Rosovsky, *ibid.*, p. 311; and on national product: Ohkawa and Rosovsky, *ibid.*, p. 287.

Russia: On average annual growth: U.S. Department of State, *The Planetary Product in 1973*, INR RS–32 (Oct. 30, 1974), Appendix Table 2: TsSU SSSR *Narodnoe Khoziaistvo SSSR v 1972* [The national economy of the USSR in 1972] (Moscow: Statistika 1973), p. 7; on national product sectors: U.S. Congress, Joint Economic Committee, *Soviet Economic Prospects for the Seventies* (hereafter *SEPS*), p. ix; on labor force shares: Gur Ofer, *The Service Sector in Soviet Economic Growth* (Cambridge: Harvard University Press 1973), p. 187, and *Narkhoz 72,* p. 501; on national product end use: U.S. Congress, *SEPS*, p. 160.

the highly modernized structure. Its labor share in agriculture, though half of what it was in 1940, was still large, and its services share was relatively small.

Japanese and Russian progress toward high modernization has required, and continues to require, crucial changes in the mechanisms and institutions of growth that proved so successful in the eighty years of transformation. It has called for a shift from a relatively small group of managers and workers concentrating on a limited number of important tasks—steel, coal, textiles, railroads, highways, central cities—to a much larger and more complex enterprise involving a large number of technical specialists and new relationships within management and between management and labor. The means used to mobilize skills and resources during transformation were not well suited to these new tasks in Russia. Japan also has had its difficulties, though it has been better able than Russia to adapt to the requirements of highly modernized societies.

Some of the reasons Japan's economy developed more quickly seem clearly to reflect its heritage of values and institutions; other factors may be attributed to the characteristics of the postwar era. Japan entered the modern era in the 1860's with greater urbanization, better communications, and a larger reservoir of administrative skills than did Russia; these capabilities were refined further in the course of its participation in the world market during the transformation period. With time, however, the Japanese economy became rigid, especially insofar as new enterprise was concerned. New ventures and ideas came to be judged not only on the basis of their intrinsic merit, but also in terms of who made the suggestion, what his connections were, and where he had been to school. Its defeat in 1945 was unquestionably a disaster for Japan in many ways, but it also had the effect of wiping away these economic rigidities. New leaders arose in business and government and they proved to be dynamic, pragmatic, and adaptable to the economic challenges of the postwar era.

Russian political and economic leaders have thus far not been as flexible. Though there has been much discussion of economic reform since the death of Stalin in 1953, and attempts at reform have been undertaken, effective change has not been brought about. The Soviet economy is, to a considerable extent, still guided by the economic doctrines developed in the 1930's. A new generation, educated and trained in the postwar period, is coming to positions of power and may be more successful in effecting the changes that are necessary to cope with the problems faced by highly modernized societies.

The difference in the amount both countries spend on defense has also influenced their relative growth. The full impact of substantial defense expenditures on growth in a fully employed economy is a matter of debate, but few deny that the effect is significant. Military expenditures draw away investment and skilled personnel from growth areas. Japan's low defense burden—less than

1 per cent of its GNP as compared with Russia's close to 10 per cent—has given it a decided advantage in its pursuit of high economic growth.

Management of a Complex Economy

One of the more notable contrasts between the processes of economic growth in Japan and the Soviet Union has been in planning and administration, with the U.S.S.R. maintaining the extremely centralized forms of each that it developed in the 1930's. The difference between the two countries in this regard has been lessened, however, by the unusual degree of cooperation between public and private institutions in Japan's free-enterprise economy. This blending of public and private does not negate the distinctions between capitalism and socialism, but it does modify them.

The continuance of highly centralized economic management in the U.S.S.R. was a part of the general extension of Stalinist administrative methods into the 1950's. This policy was strengthened by the objective of attaining military parity with the West, an aim largely achieved by the end of the fifties. The military achievement of the Soviets coincided with the rise to power of a new generation of leaders who welcomed the opportunity to consider broad economic reforms.

Starting in the 1930's, the Soviet economy was divided for administrative purposes into industrial branch ministries. Political leaders and planners communicated directly with these ministers, and the reward system was tied to the performance of the enterprises within each ministry. This division had its positive effects, but it also created internal empires and institutional barriers between these empires. To correct this situation, a regional form of economic administration was introduced in 1957. The entire economy was organized into roughly 100 regions, with all of the industrial enterprises in a region administered by an economic council of that region. The various regional economic councils in a given republic were administered through a council of ministers for that republic, and the various republics in turn by the council of ministers of the U.S.S.R. in Moscow.

The regional form of organization had certain advantages—it increased the efficiency of local resources thereby reducing some of the wastes of departmental duplication—but it also had many weaknesses. Overall coordination and control proved to be extremely difficult, and the industrial supply system for key materials became almost totally confused. Equally important, the ability of the center to encourage the introduction of new technology was hampered because research and development organizations were no longer tied to central ministries that could press for fresh ideas and techniques. Moreover, one organizational reform followed another so quickly that regional managers did not know from one day to the next just who would be giving the commands—all of which generated an environment hardly conducive to an efficient economic operation. Not surprisingly, the regional form of economic administration was abandoned in 1965 after the removal of Khrushchev, and the branch ministerial form was reestablished.

Discussion of economic reforms picked up in intensity in the early 1960's. Both plan construction and plan implementation were viewed as needing an overhaul. The methods used to formulate economic plans had not changed for thirty years. They relied heavily on labor-intensive and data-intensive methods of plan calculation. The growth and development of the economy compounded the difficulty of planning and control from the center. As the number of firms and the number of specialized products expanded, the number of interrelationships among firms and among different products expanded enormously. The greater sophistication of new products required highly specific inputs, thus narrowing the range of tolerable quality variations and acceptable substitutability of input products. Economic growth and development had both an extensive and intensive effect on centralized planning, increasing the required size of the planning force and also demanding much more precision. One Soviet economist predicted that if the methods for plan construction were not made more efficient, by 1980 the entire Soviet labor force would be required for planning and administrative work.

The deficiencies in plan implementation were even more manifest. They were largely the consequence of the incentive mechanism which paid substantial monetary rewards for the successful fulfillment and overfulfillment of assigned targets by economic units at various levels in the economy. One defect of this system was that rewards were for relative rather than absolute performance, that is, for performance relative to targets. The enterprise manager would therefore strive for high performance but low targets, and attempt to limit overfulfillment so as not to give the planners a pretext for excessive raising of future targets. This situation also entailed a reluctance to innovate, for the rewards of innovation were too short-lived to cover the risk of innovation failure. It led as well to the intentional understatement of production potential, information sorely needed by the central planners for the purposes of effective plan construction.

Another problem inherent in the Soviet planning system was the dominance of quantity as a reward criterion. Soviet firms tended to be interested only in their own production rather than in the needs of those who purchased and used their products. Under the pressures of a system that rewarded the quantity of output, quality was cut, assortment and delivery agreements were violated, the supply system became unreliable, and little thought was given to improving products to make them more useful to the purchaser. Indeed, when innovation was successfully forced on a firm it was usually innovation in productive processes rather than in the product itself. Finally, great wastes derived from using inappropriate physical measurements as production targets: with tons as the unit of measure, enterprises preferred to produce heavy rather than light machinery.

These planning defects were magnified by the growth and development of the economy. Also, the deficiencies of centralized planning were less tolerable than they had been previously because they were no longer as strongly counterbalanced by equivalent strengths. These strengths, which included the ability to enforce the preferences of the political leaders on the economy to accomplish gross movements of resources and to restructure the composition and use of output, were by the early 1960's no longer so important.

The original goals of the Soviet leaders when they embarked on the industrialization drive and first employed centralized planning had been by this time more or less achieved. An industrialized economy had been created. The task was no longer further massive changes, but growth within the given (or slowly changing) structure. This could be accomplished only through more efficient use of resources. The priorities in terms of particular commodities were no longer as simple and clear as they had been previously. Without a few obvious, high-priority sectors on which to concentrate, and low-priority sectors to absorb the shock of errors, Soviet centralized planning was in difficulty. In an environment where the need was for micro efficiency, where myriad choices had to be made, the strengths of centralized planning were blunted and its weaknesses highlighted. The seriousness of the situation was dramatically brought to the

attention of the Soviet leaders by the decreases in the rates of growth
of output and factor productivity after 1958. Of particular importance was the decrease in the productivity of capital. The growth-
producing power of a forced high rate of investment had been the
core of the Soviet growth mechanism under centralized planning.
Soviet leaders viewed its erosion with alarm.

A number of developments followed. One was the flowering of
mathematical methods and computer techniques in economics.
Though they have not had a direct effect on the ways in which
Soviet plans are constructed, they have revolutionized economic
thinking and economic science in the Soviet Union. A second development concerned the Soviet consumer. In an attempt to increase
labor productivity through the increase in consumer welfare, and
the latter as end in itself, more attention has been paid to the volume and the composition of Soviet consumer goods. Consumers are
being given more of a say in determining the composition of output
of consumer goods. And finally, a whole set of institutional reforms
was introduced beginning in 1965. The number of targets sent to
a Soviet enterprise were reduced, and the main success criteria were
changed from output to volume of sales and profit. The hope was
that with an increase in decentralized decision-making and with
more use of value and profit criteria, the micro efficiency in the
Soviet economy would improve, thus raising the factor productivity
and leading to a return to higher levels of economic growth. But
it would appear that the economic reforms of 1965 have not been
successful and more and more talk is turning to other types of institutional changes, for example, the development of large production
associations. These would combine a number of enterprises and
bring the advantages of economies of scale and diversification. It
has also been hoped that, through their research and development
departments, such associations would encourage a greater willingness to innovate and to increase the pace of technological change
in the Soviet economy.

The principal economic aim of the Japanese government, between the end of the Occupation and the "Nixon shocks" that
forced revaluation of the yen in 1971, may be described as that of
maximizing the rate of growth of output. In recent years this policy
has sometimes been referred to as "growth at any cost"—not an un-
fair label—and has consisted of three closely related approaches: a
taxation policy that minimized the public draft on resources; encouragement to industrial, largely private, investment; and promotion of exports.

Through its taxation policy, the Japanese government assisted firms and industries that were investing and expanding swiftly. Capital gains taxes, for example, were low or nonexistent; interest income was taxed at lower rates than wages and salaries; and accelerated depreciation allowances were most generous. Surpluses thus remained in the hands of the most progressive (for purposes of economic growth) elements in the private sector, available for private investment. The public draft on resources was negligible.

The government also pursued an energetic export-promotion policy until the late 1960's. Financial advantages were available to leading exporters; Japanese goods were actively pushed by government agencies; help in marketing was supplied; and promising technological opportunities were called to the attention of producers. The government did a great deal to upgrade the reputation of Japanese goods.

In practice, government objectives have resulted in the targeting of specific growth industries. Initially, the selections were steel, shipbuilding, coal, power, and fertilizers. In the 1960's, attention shifted to automobiles, electronics, petrochemicals and computers. Targeted industries were always the beneficiaries of extensive protection, on the theory that it would take some time for them to achieve internal viability and external comparative advantage. Although this policy can be criticized from many vantage points, and was not always successful, it is certainly true that many lusty infants were protected well into maturity. The great virtue of Japan's industrial policy has been to provide help for the most promising areas of growth.

Japan's governmental economic policy has not been an innovation of the postwar period, but an effective continuation of directions taken as early as the nineteenth century. Most recently, the talented bureaucrats of the Ministry of International Trade and Industry (MITI) have been among the chief architects of the policy, and they have consistently emphasized working through the market. Central planning in Japan, such as it is, can at best be called indicative. Success has depended on a broad consensus between business leaders and government officials.

In some ways, this harmony was achieved at the expense of the consumer and the public. Growth, exports, and investment were the favorite children; social overheads, welfare, and low-priced consumer goods were treated as stepchildren. This is the view of critics, but proponents of the government's policy could also make a strong case. First, they consider Japan's postwar policy a national investment effort, with the payoff for the majority of the population

coming in the 1970's or 1980's. Second, they assert that Japanese industrial policy gave the country the advantages of capitalism and
socialism at the same time. Capitalism's main advantage is efficiency,
which was assured by allowing competition and market forces to
play their role; simultaneously, close and harmonious government
and business connections, together with rational and integrated
policies, permitted considerable political control over the growth
process. Third, they argue that the capitalist-socialist approach has
resulted in relatively logical, clear, and consistent industrial policies—and is one of the best examples of "catch-up economics." Industries were selected and helped in orderly sequence, based on the
proven historical pattern in Western countries; the consequence was
the evolution of an ever more mature and sophisticated Japanese
economy in record time.

By the early 1970's certain adverse side effects of rapid growth in
a complex economy, such as environmental pollution and urban congestion, were becoming matters of concern in both Japan and Russia.
These problems are, however, much more intense in Japan. For its
area, Japan has the largest gross national product in the world;
more economic activity takes place per unit of land than in any
other country. The consequences in terms of noise, water and air
pollution, and urban congestion are severe. Moreover, though government policy in both countries has stressed the maximization of
the rate of growth of aggregate output, there has been a particular
shortage of resources devoted to social (as opposed to personal) consumption in Japan.

Growth and Productivity

AGRICULTURE

The overall pattern of a growing share of the national product
in manufacturing and services as opposed to agriculture was visible
in Japan and the U.S.S.R. For each of these sectors the elements of
growth require separate examination.

On the eve of the Second World War, agriculture was in a state
of decline in both Japan and the Soviet Union. An outdated technology and imports of cheap colonial rice combined to squeeze the
Japanese farmer, while in the Soviet Union there was no growth per
capita in agricultural output from the beginning of collectivization
in 1928 to the death of Stalin in 1953. In the years since the war,

there have been considerable changes in the agricultural sector, partly due to the greater use of modern, science-based technology, and partly due to the determination of both governments to increase agriculture productivity.

The proportion of the Japanese labor force engaged in the primary industries of farming, fishing, and forestry declined from 48 per cent in 1950 to 19 per cent in 1970. This sector now produces about 6 per cent of the GNP, a relative productivity well below the national average. Both sets of statistics, however, are slightly misleading. Although the proportion of agricultural employment is still relatively high—it is about 5 per cent in the United States and less than 10 per cent in West Germany—many Japanese farmers today work only part-time and much of the labor is supplied by women, not infrequently older women.

In Russia the proportion of the labor force engaged in agriculture, including forestry but excluding fishing, remains higher than in Japan. Even so, it has declined from 48 per cent in 1950 to about 27 per cent in 1970. Agriculture in the Soviet Union, according to recent Western calculations, still accounts for almost 25 per cent of the gross national product, and therefore fluctuations in agricultural output have a strong effect on the GNP. The slowdown in agricultural growth since 1958, compared with the forward spurt between 1953 and 1958, has played an important part in the overall slackening of the rate of growth of the Soviet economy.

The most obvious change in postwar agriculture in Japan has been the accelerated growth rate. In the interwar years, Japanese farmers were barely able to push production ahead at 0.5 per cent per year. Now agricultural output is expanding at more than 3 per cent per year, faster than at any time in the last 100 years. The government has made a point of ensuring that domestic agriculture is profitable by protecting the farmer against competition from cheap Korean and Taiwan foodstuffs and by maintaining high domestic prices.

The Japanese farmer has also benefited from comparatively low input prices. Rapid progress in fertilizers, tools, vinyl sheets, and other products of a highly advanced economy have been available to farmers at favorable prices. Industry lent support in the form of mechanical and engineering improvements designed for conditions prevailing on small farms, such as power tillers. One of the consequences of these improvements has been that economies of scale are making their first appearance in Japanese agriculture. To be sure, their payoff is still constrained by the size limitations on farms stipulated in the American-sponsored land reform (three hectares, except for twelve hectares on Hokkaido) but these cannot remain valid for long.

The leaders of both countries have made determined efforts to increase productivity in agriculture. In Japan, because the farmers easily took advantage of the new agricultural technology, little has been necessary beyond policies of protection. Unlike Russia, agricultural self-sufficiency is not a possibility in Japan, and under current conditions Japan has no real comparative advantages in agriculture. It would be more logical, from a strictly economic perspective, for Japan to be far more reliant on cheaper food imports. However, agriculture continues to be a vital source of political support for the ruling Liberal Democratic Party, and it is also a significant source of employment. Furthermore, there is a reluctance in Japan to be dependent on foreign sources of food. The protection of this sector therefore has remained a matter of government policy.

The improvement in Russian agricultural output came somewhat later, and has fluctuated in response to rather erratic changes in policy. In the first post-Stalin years, 1953 to 1958, output grew at a rate of 6.8 per cent per year, or about 40 per cent for the five-year period. Total man-days worked in agriculture (collective farms, state farms, and private plots) rose slightly, but labor productivity shot up quickly. The doubling of the real wages of collective farmers—a greater increase than that received by urban wage earners—was in large measure responsible for the improved output.

The capital stock in agriculture, contrary to what is frequently believed, grew substantially faster than output, resulting in a sizable drop in capital productivity. Sown acreage went up during the five years by more than 20 per cent due to the "new lands" program so strongly pushed by Khrushchev. Yields per acre also rose, mainly as a result of the increase in capital, fertilizers, changed crop mixes (the "corn program"), and, perhaps, better farming.

From 1958 to 1964, the year of Khrushchev's fall from power, the growth rate of output became dependent upon the growth rate of inputs, which was reduced by more than half. The result was a fall in the growth rate of output from 6.8 per cent per year between 1953 and 1958 to 1.7 per cent per year in the 1958–1964 period. Furthermore, in one year of disastrous weather, 1963, grain production was so low that the Soviet Union had to import 10 million tons of grain from the West simply to maintain a minimally acceptable level of food supply.

Real wages of collective farmers also grew by less than 15 per cent in the five-year period after 1958, which had a disincentive effect on the effort put forth. It also had a quantitative effect: farmers, especially the young, able-bodied ones, were discouraged from staying in agriculture.

The growth rate of agricultural capital stock fell slightly after 1958, though it still remained quite high, but capital productivity declined. The abolition of the machine-tractor stations in 1958, which showed promise of helping to improve the efficiency in Soviet agriculture by eradicating dual management of the farm, may have contributed to this slide in productivity. With the abolition of the stations, effective tractor repair facilities were markedly reduced. Disabled tractors, coupled with a chronic shortage of spare parts, brought a stockpile of nonoperating machines.

The "new lands" program more or less came to an end by 1958, thereby removing a source of growth. The situation was made worse because in response to pressure exerted by Khrushchev for greater output, the new lands were cropped continuously with grain. After a while their yields began to drop. To compensate, Khrushchev in 1962 embarked on his "plow up" campaign, in which millions of acres of grassland were to be plowed and planted with more intensive crops like beans, peas, and sugar beets.

Khrushchev felt that the key to agricultural productivity lay in better managers and improved administrative methods. He continuously altered organizational arrangements, seeking to bring forth local initiative while maintaining central control. After 1958 these organizational changes tended to raise the power of party officials over government officials, with the net effect of reducing the quality of management. His successors, more influenced by agricultural interest groups within the bureaucracy, instituted some agricultural policy changes of their own: annual grain procurement targets for the individual years of the Eighth Five-Year Plan (1966–1970) were set at a constant level not much above that of the previous five years; prices were raised, with higher price incentives established for overplan deliveries; investment in agriculture was enlarged from 10 per cent of total state investment between 1961 and 1965 to 26 per cent through 1969. Output growth picked up in 1970, but the following year output remained fixed, and in 1972 (another disastrous winter) it fell off sharply, again necessitating massive Soviet grain imports from the West amounting to almost 30 million tons.

A comparison of Russia's collectivized agriculture with Japan's small-farmer structure underscores some of the problems confronting the Soviet system. Though centralized planning makes possible rapid improvement in the rural wage structure, large increases in the area under cultivation, and sweeping changes in the pattern of crops, it also has involved frequent and drastic changes in policy that are disruptive to agricultural production. In Japan the government intervenes primarily to protect the small farmers in their confrontation with urban change and foreign competition, but decisions regarding capital investment and crops are made primarily by individual farmers. This contrast in national policies is modified to some degree by the fact that a significant proportion of the meat, poultry, and vegetables marketed in the U.S.S.R. are produced on the private plots of collective farmers, which are essentially outside the structure of central planning.

INDUSTRY

Japan and the Soviet Union have both sought to promote a high rate of growth in industrial output in the postwar years—and they have succeeded better than any other advanced economy. Between the two, Japanese industrial growth was faster. Industrial output in Japan in the period 1953–1972 grew at the robust rate of 13.1 per cent per year, compared with a rate of 7.7 per cent per year for the Soviet Union. Japanese industrial expansion was primarily based on large private productive investments and the importation and modification of superior foreign technology.

Industrial production in a consumer economy requires a sophisticated technology that must be continually refreshed by infusions of new knowledge from other advanced societies. A certain level of industrial technique can be achieved without such an exchange of information and technology, but as both Japan and Russia demonstrated during their periods of isolation, the more developed an industrial structure is the less likely it is to thrive solely on its own.

Importation of technology had a vital impact on Japanese industrial growth. The postwar economy, unlike that before the war, possessed the considerable benefit of spillover from Japan's own military inventiveness. In a sense Japan was compelled to rely more on its own potential during the 1930's and 1940's and this prepared the way for a swords into plowshares path of progress after the war. The gap between the best international practices and the average technological level within Japan was very much widened by the disruption of normal international relations beginning in the 1930's and ending in the early 1950's with the restoration of Japnaese sovereignty. During these fifteen years or so of isolation, Japan's relative technological level declined because progress in this sphere was more rapid among the few countries pushing back the frontiers of technology. The very size of the gap meant that many old and established Japanese industries had slipped backward, and also that the nation was behind in an entire range of new economic activities that originated beyond its frontiers. After the 1950's, Japan was able simultaneously to improve the way of doing familiar things while doing entirely new things. It was able to do so for a variety of reasons, among which trained manpower may have been the most important.

The long-range effects of spillover are often neglected because the effect of this phenomenon is considered to be only of short-term importance, which is not necessarily true. The Japanese machinery industry in 1930, for example, was very small; it constituted only 19.7 per cent of total value-added in manufacturing. From 1930 to 1940 the value-added by the machinery industry rose to an astonishing 48 per cent, and the reasons are clear. At that time, the mass production of machinery was strongly pushed by the government because it was related to the production of munitions and armaments. In many senses this was artificial growth and at the expense of more peaceful activities. Nevertheless, the machinery industry did concentrate heavily on the production of arms and similar items, and in doing so it did receive the opportunity to engage in mass production, to develop know-how, and to raise manpower skills. That this effort was directed toward war may have been crucial in stimulating native inventiveness and skills. International cooperation became harder to obtain, and from the late 1930's on the Japanese had to stand entirely on their own feet. From the technical point of view, they managed quite well. Japanese ordnance, warships, and planes were generally of acceptable and competitive quality. After the war, the value-added by machinery dropped sharply to a level of 20.8 per cent in 1955; even in 1961, it was only 32.3 per cent.

But the important point here, which regards spillover, is that much of what was learned and invented before and during the war could be transferred to useful postwar activities. Aircraft manufacturers switched to the production of motor scooters and automobiles. Some munitions manufacturers started to make sewing machines. The optics industry, relying extensively on what it had learned during the war in making gunsights, bomb sights, and other optical equipment, developed outstanding lines of cameras. Scattered throughout Japanese growth industries there are now men at the helm who had earlier held positions of responsibility in the armed forces.

Japan's postwar reliance on Western technology may be measured by royalty payments, which shot up quickly after 1950 to reach an average annual rate of growth of 33 per cent between 1955 and 1961; the rate then declined to 7.5 per cent until 1966. As the technological gap closed, the rates of growth in acquisitions started to taper off. This technology was infused simultaneously into both old and new industries. As previously noted, postwar Japan found itself behind world leaders in a range of older and well-established techniques. These were the industrial activities in which a prewar base had existed—such as branches of engineering, iron and steel, and chemicals—but owing to isolation and war the quality of the base had deteriorated. Japan was lagging even further behind in the "new" activities that were born in the countries between the late 1930's and early 1950's. Television, many synthetics, and most other science-originated technologies lacked a prewar base altogether. One important indication of Japan's economic strength was that it was able to attack both kinds of backwardness simultaneously.

It is difficult to quantify assertions of this type, although there are some Japanese attempts to do so. In 1956, according to calculations of the government's Science and Technology Agency, simultaneous infusion was in full swing. About half of the imported technology was brought in to improve activities originated before the war; the other half was purchased to engage in entirely new lines of production. By 1966 the situation had been fundamentally altered. Prewar activities had caught up, and imports concentrated overwhelmingly on continuing to bring in what was new.

The progress of Japanese industry has naturally been concentrated in those areas where technological progress and export opportunities have been most promising. As a result, the postwar output has been dominated more and more by such industries as chemicals, machinery, and electrical equipment, while the older textile manufactures have declined in relative importance. The achievements in iron and steel, consumer electronics, shipbuilding, automobiles, and most recently, computers are generally associated with large enterprises, many of which had former zaibatsu connections. Yet the mixed scale structure of Japanese industry has not disappeared. Medium and small establishments continue to be—even at present—sizable sources of employment. Large-scale establishments (more than 500 workers) dominate the industries that have stood in the limelight, but employment in food processing, and even in textiles, continues to be predominately in units using fewer than 50 workers.

This mixed scale structure has been an enduring feature of Japanese economic development. It is undoubtedly related to the continued—though declining—availability of surplus labor, because small-scale industry required low wages in order to survive. Japanese industry seems also to have done especially well in maintaining close integration between firms of various size. Subcontracting and credit by big producers is extensive, although the presumption is that these arrangements generally favor the larger partner. Nevertheless, the close links have undoubtedly helped smaller units to become more progressive.

By contrast with Japan's growth record, Soviet postwar industrial growth, while high, fell from a rate of 10 per cent per year between 1950 and 1960, to less than 7 per cent in the period from 1960 to 1972. An annual rate of growth of industrial production of almost 7 per cent is still quite high, but the decrease in industrial growth since the mid-fifties has been a matter of concern for Soviet leaders.

The causes of this decline can be seen in the data on the growth of combined labor and capital inputs and combined input productivity. Though the rate of growth of inputs into industry fell only from 6.1 per cent per year from 1950 to 1960 to 5.7 per cent per year between 1960 and 1972, input productivity growth dropped from 3.5 per cent per year in the former period to under 1 per cent per year in the latter. Thus, the causes of the decline in the growth of industrial production in the 1960's and early 1970's involve not so much the decline in the growth of inputs into industry as they do the decline in the growth of their productivity—a set of circumstances unlike the Japanese experience.

Among the causes of this drop in the growth of factor productivity has been the Soviet military and space program. Since 1958, Soviet expansion of its military program has taken the path of sophisticated weaponry rather than manpower. Indeed, the size of the armed forces has decreased. The heavy emphasis on new and advanced weapons contributed to the decrease in the growth of investment. Of even more importance was the fact the military drew off a large share of the best scientists and engineers, and the best and latest machines and materials. This drainage had a debilitating effect on the entire civilian industrial sector, but especially on those industries that were undergoing a revision of their technologies, that is, a transition to more advanced techniques and more sophisticated goods. These industries were hindered in their ability to obtain the best trained personnel and the new types of equipment they needed. Furthermore, in Russia it does not appear that technological spillover from military to civilian production has counted for much. Factor productivity also suffered from the ways in which the industrial labor force was made to increase quickly, as it did despite the small cohorts reaching the age for finding a job. This growth in the supply of labor to industry was made possible by reductions in the armed forces, in the agricultural labor force, in the numbers of non-workers (especially women and youth) and in the potential number of students. Overall these sources of supply had the effect of reducing the quality of the industrial labor force.

Both Japan and Russia have borrowed technology in recent years from other highly modernized countries. Japan has borrowed in order to become competitive internationally, which it has done with astounding success, and Russia has borrowed less, and less effectively, in order to meet internal needs. Furthermore, much of the Soviet native capacity for technological innovation has been absorbed by the defense industries.

Just as Japan and Russia had entered the modern era with a reservoir of skilled and literate workers, so also they entered the postwar era with trained and competent labor forces and with an elastic labor supply for modern industry. Moderate rates of population growth made labor available from the agricultural sector, and increasing agricultural productivity kept labor costs relatively low.

The Japanese economy between 1950 and 1970 was still in some ways a dual economy: an advanced industrial sector coexisted with a traditional sector of small-scale industries and services, and agriculture. Despite high wartime mortality, the traditional sector provided a large labor pool, to which were added not only the large numbers returning to the homeland from what had been the Japanese Empire, but also the potential recruits born during the postwar baby boom. Though wage increases were considerable at times, in general labor productivity rose more than wages; in those industries that took the greatest advantage of imported technology, the cost of labor input per unit of output declined.

In the Soviet Union the supply of labor to the industrial economy was less bountiful. Wartime mortality had been even higher in Russia, and wartime birth rates low; the cohorts entering the labor force by the late 1950's were unusually small.

In Japan labor organization along the lines of enterprise unions has been weak and institutional arrangements favored management. Still many Japanese industrial workers, as noted previously, have the status of "permanent employees," which gives them a form of job security. It also reduces labor mobility and the businessman's need to bargain with his workers This peculiarly Japanese system of labor relations has frequently been described as "paternalistic." While this may be true, it should be recognized that both sides received considerable economic benefits.

The institutional organization of labor in the Soviet Union also favors management, that is the government. Labor unions in Soviet Russia are not independent organizations representing the interests of their members in conflicts with management. Rather, they are instruments of the state to mobilize labor in the pursuit of state policy, namely, high economic growth. Labor unions, for example, attempt to stimulate increased output through the organizing of "socialist competition" among enterprises, and within enterprises, among workshops and individuals. In recent years, in order to maintain their credibility to workers, and thus maintain their usefulness to the government, Soviet labor unions have given more attention to the protection of workers' rights in conflicts over skill classifications, bonuses, demotions, dismissals, and related matters.

SERVICES

It is a commonly held view that the relative role of services—commerce, finance, public administration, health, education, entertainment, and personal, domestic, and business occupations—grows as economic development progresses. Data on development confirm this view as do the data for Japan and Russia presented above in Table 16.1. However, the higher service share in Japan and the contrasts between Japan and Russia in regard to services warrant attention. A careful study of data from the early 1960's shows that the labor share in the service sector in Japan is greater than would be expected in a country at its level of development, and that the share in the Soviet Union is substantially lower than would be expected. How is this to be explained?

The relative growth of services in a nation's economic development is a consequence of both demand and supply factors. On the demand side, as consumers' incomes rise, the amounts they spend on services increase relatively rapidly, compared with the added amount they spend on agricultural and manufactured goods. Second, as an economy develops, it tends to become more specialized, the number of links within it increases, and the demand for services, especially commercial and financial services, likewise goes up. Third, there is a tendency for government expenditures on public administration and public services—health, education, and welfare—to rise in response to the needs created by industrialization and urbanization. On the supply side, as a result of the relatively lower level of labor productivity in services, relatively more labor is drawn into this sector than into manufacturing. Finally, urbanization itself is both a demand and supply factor. Urban dwellers want many services—banks, stores, real-estate offices, restaurants—and they themselves add to the supply of potential service workers.

An extensive analysis of how these factors have operated in Japan and Russia is beyond the scope of this study, but some references to them in the course of a brief comparison of the Japanese and Russian service sectors can be made. The positive deviation of the service share in Japan from the norm associated with its level of development (measured by income per capita, urbanization rate, and labor participation rate), and the negative deviation in Russia take on some interesting and unexpected shades when the service sector is disaggregated first into commerce and finance on the one hand, and into other services on the other, and then when each category is further disaggregated. The labor force share in commerce and finance in Japan is far above the norm, but in other services it is just about at the norm for its level of development. For Russia, the picture is similar, but reversed. Furthermore, when the labor force shares in commerce and finance for the two countries are compared directly, Japan's labor share is seen to be more than three times that of Russia's (17 per cent versus 5 per cent).

The reasons for this difference relate to both the role of private enterprise and the organizational structure of industry. Japan's private enterprise offers many small-scale commercial services, which are not in evidence in the Soviet Union. In a market economy, moreover, the financial sector is involved in acquiring funds from individual savers, distributing them among investors, and transferring the investment proceeds back to the savers. In the Soviet economy the first and third of these activities is almost entirely avoided, and the second is handled in a centralized way, generally in accord with an established plan, thus circumventing major search-and-decision activity. Further, the wholesale supply system in the Soviet economy is relatively smaller than in Japan because under the Soviet planning and control system, the organs of public administration take over many of the functions of wholesale trade. And perhaps even more important, because of the great uncertainties of interfirm relationships in Soviet industry, firms in Russia are generally larger and more self-sufficient than they are in Japan and other countries, and thus there are fewer links for the supply system to connect.

As a consequence of these factors in Russia, it is commonly held that the labor force share in public administration is larger in the Soviet Union than in Japan and other market economies. This is not, however, true. This share is about 2.5 per cent in the Soviet Union, 4 per cent in Japan, and 5 per cent in the United States. Furthermore, it is also not true that excess Soviet administrators are "hiding" in industry. The percentages of administrators in Soviet industry are below those in Japan and other advanced economies (though in regard to engineers and technicians alone they are substantially higher in the Soviet Union). Despite widespread views to the contrary, then, views held both inside the U.S.S.R. and outside, the Soviet Union is a relatively underadministered economy, which may account for its poor administrative performance.

One factor contributing to the relatively low level of services in the Soviet Union is Marxist ideology. Marx viewed services generally as being unproductive and attacked tradespeople as speculators. In the Soviet Union Marx's disparagement has been translated into little esteem and slim wages for workers in commerce and in most other service activities. In Japan attitudes are quite different. The Japanese have a long tradition of quality service, a keen sense of taste in matters of art and culture and related aspects of the service sector. Japanese service workers, therefore, are accorded more esteem and better wages than their Soviet counterparts.

In one service sector, however, the U.S.S.R. surpasses Japan: public health, education, and welfare services. The Soviet Union has a very high labor force share in education and science, more than twice that of Japan's and greater even than that of the United States. Its labor share in health and welfare also exceeds Japan's, though this is primarily because the Japanese government's commitment to health and welfare is relatively weak.

The higher Soviet labor force share in public services is an indication that the Soviet government quite early recognized that these services are also economically productive. They are investments in human capital that contribute to the goal of economic growth.

Relations with the World Economy

Probably the most acute contrast between the Japanese and Soviet economic systems is in their relations with the world economy. The differences include disparities in their international economic presence, attitudes toward foreign trade, the administration of trade, and the relation of trade to domestic economic development.

In the past twenty years Japan's exports have grown rapidly—even more rapidly than output and world trade—so that its share of world commerce has also increased. A noticeable change has also occurred in the quality of products entering international trade. Before the Second World War, "Made in Japan" was a definition of poor quality; more recently, "Made in Japan" has come to mean excellence in design and workmanship at competitive prices. The postwar situation also brought into prominence products of high consumer visibility: cars, cameras, calculators, and so forth. In very recent years, yet another change of considerable importance for the world economy has evolved. From the 1880's to the late 1960's Japan had always displayed a tendency toward chronic balance-of-payments deficits. From 1968 through 1972, Japan assumed the position of a surplus country. The oil crisis in 1973 and the growing shortages of other raw materials, however, have threatened Japan's ability to maintain a payments balance.

The international economic presence of Japan seems larger than ever at present, but in actuality Japanese historical trends point toward a more domestically oriented economy. The export share in aggregate demand, for example, climbed steadily from 5.5 per cent in 1907 to 17.0 per cent in 1937, but by 1955 it had fallen to 9.4 per cent and in 1965 it was still only 12.6 per cent. Similarly, the incremental contribution of exports to incremental aggregate demand is well below prewar levels: 27 per cent in the 1930's as compared with 15 per cent in the 1960's. But this lesser dependence on the foreign sector is not strange when the nature of Japanese exports and imports is taken into consideration. The Japanese economy after the Second World War combined several characteristics that gave it a historically unique character: a large country (population more than 100 million); a rich country, without raw materials (import dependency ratios in excess of 90 per cent for many vital natural resources); and an economy expanding much faster than that of most other countries (at least twice as rapidly and frequently three times as rapidly). This unusual combination has resulted from a concentration on raw material imports and manufactured exports. It has been accompanied by a protective trade policy, so that by 1971 approximately 90 per cent of exports were manufactures and a similar proportion of imports were foodstuffs and raw materials.

Roughly twenty years of this type of development have created a variety of problems. Japan has been a successful exporter of increasingly sophisticated products because modern industries grew rapidly with the help of large domestic markets, protective government policies, easily available foreign technology, and favorable savings-investment conditions. Further, export prices in postwar years remained steady while most other prices rose, an indication of the role of cost-reducing technology in exports. Yet after World War II the Japanese market was never particularly hospitable to the manufactures of other countries. This situation was due to the pursuit of infant-industry policies, which carried over well into adulthood for many manufactures, and to the increasing excellence of Japanese products with which it was difficult to compete. No doubt an undervalued yen also provided further assistance. Not surprisingly, these elements have gradually led to growing international resistance in the face of chronic Japanese surpluses. This resistance has been exhibited in upward revaluations by other nations, protectionist threats among importing countries, and an insistence on greater access to the Japanese market.

Export problems have been accompanied by import problems as well. Resource consumption growth rates have accelerated to the point where import dependency is 100 per cent for many necessities, and above 75 per cent for many others. The extraordinary growth of the Japanese economy has meant that its appetite for world resources has become truly gargantuan. In 1969 Japan consumed 9 per cent of the "free world's" petroleum, 16 per cent of its iron ore, 16 per cent of its zinc, and 19 per cent of its nickel. Further growth at the current rate of 10 per cent would obviously create more economic and political problems. In the early 1970's there was already great nervousness in many parts of the world concerning Japan's needs for raw materials, and the energy crisis in the winter of 1973–1974 revealed its precarious position in this respect.

By contrast, Soviet policy toward foreign trade until recently was not to encourage its growth but to reduce it so as to lessen the dependency of the Russian economy on other economies, especially those of the advanced capitalist nations. This policy is not precisely the same as that of "autarky," as is often contended, for when in the short run imports were necessary to fulfill a plan, such imports were secured. In this approach, exports were viewed solely as necessary evils required to finance the desired imports. The long-term policy was to avoid dependency on the West by developing an internal capacity to produce the inputs normally required to fulfill the production plan. The expected result of such a policy, especially for a continent-spanning country like the Soviet Union with a diverse resource base and a large population, was to be relatively low levels

of foreign trade. And as has been noted, Soviet trade did fall to extremely low levels in the 1930's after implementation of the First
Five Year Plan.

Since the 1950's this essentially political aversion toward trade
has been modified: first with regard to the nations within the socialist bloc because of the proclaimed friendly atmosphere prevailing
among them; and then, in more recent times, with regard to the
advanced industrial nations because of the growing feeling of
military security and the reduction of hostility between the Soviet
Union and the West. The volume of Soviet foreign trade began to
pick up after the war. By 1950 the value of trade turnover was three
times the 1930 level, and in the ensuing ten years it doubled again.
The ratio of Soviet exports to national product, however, has remained low, considerably below that of Japan's, even though it rose
from the 0.5 per cent of 1938 to about 2.5 per cent at the end of the
1950's and roughly 3 per cent at the end of the 1960's.

In the early postwar years Soviet trade was predominantly with
other Communist countries. Trade with Communist nations in 1955
constituted almost 80 per cent of the total, whereas only 5 per cent
was with the industrial West. Trade with non-communist nations
then began to increase proportionally faster, and by the end of the
1960's Soviet trade with Communist countries was 65 per cent of
the total, with the less developed countries about 13 per cent, and
with the advanced industrial nations about 22 per cent.

The commodity composition of Soviet trade during the 1960's
was strikingly different from that of Japan's. Soviet imports consisted
mainly of machinery and equipment (about 35 per cent) and consumer goods (about 30 per cent). Almost 75 per cent of the machinery and equipment was imported from Eastern Europe, the remainder from the industrially advanced nations (40 per cent of
imports from the industrial nations consist of machinery and equipment). Approximately half of the consumer goods imports was food,
a percentage that varied with agricultural output in the Soviet
Union. (In normal years Russia is a net exporter of grain, most of
it exported to Eastern Europe.) Manufactured consumer goods increased in importance, most of them originating in Eastern Europe,
but toward the end of the 1960's more and more came from the
industrial West.

Soviet exports in the 1960's consisted primarily of fuels, raw
materials, and semifinished materials. These items made up 75 to
80 per cent of the Soviet's total exports to the industrial West. They
were also dominant in Soviet trade with Eastern Europe, though

they dropped during the decade from about 70 per cent of total Soviet exports to the bloc to about 55 per cent. At the same time, Soviet machinery and equipment exports to Eastern Europe increased from 13 per cent of total exports to 22 per cent. The bulk of Soviet exports of machinery and equipment have gone to Eastern Europe, with the remainder shipped to the less developed countries. Exports of oil during the 1960's doubled, largely on the basis of increased exports to the advanced industrial nations. By the beginning of the 1970's, Russia was exporting about 20 per cent of its total output of crude oil, with almost 45 per cent of its exports of petroleum and petroleum products going to the industrial countries.

Foreign trade, as we have seen, has been a critical element in the postwar economic growth of Japan, both in terms of the importation of advanced foreign technology and in terms of the development of export industries. This process has not been nearly so evident in the Soviet Union. Soviet trade has been inhibited both by the policy of nondependence, noted above, and by restrictions imposed by the industrialized Western countries. In addition, however, the benefits from trade have been limited by certain features of the Soviet system of centralized planning. The centralization of foreign-trade decisions, coupled with an overriding political objective of the fastest possible economic expansion, has led to a focus on imports to the detriment of exports, and to the view of imports and exports as interdependent. Such a policy considers trade as barter, which in turn encourages bilateral exchanges. These developments have received further emphasis by the chaotic nature of internal prices in the Soviet's centrally planned economy. Soviet production planning methods depend to a great extent on physical, engineered, input-output relationships. Such an approach cannot be taken, however, when deciding what exports should be used as "inputs," to "produce" certain desired imports (the "outputs"). Decisions regarding choice and levels of exports require a much different method from the engineering approach of Soviet production planners. For such a decision system, national prices (or what is the same thing, the information provided by prices) are needed, as is a methodology for using them. The Soviets are beginning to explore these issues, but up to now they have relied heavily on bilateral barter arrangements with both traditional exports and exports of some industrial items they produce on a large scale.

Another hindrance to the effective operation of Soviet trade relates to the difficulties faced by Soviet planners in constructing internally consistent plans embodying, even at a high level of aggregation, more than a thousand products. Alterations in foreign-trade plans or activities upset the balancing process, and thus planners may themselves be disposed to downgrade the importance of trade. Foreigners are not permitted to buy Soviet goods at will because plans will thereby be disrupted; furthermore, Soviet planners are not willing to sell goods at their irrational internal prices. This "commodity inconvertibility" has been one of the factors resulting in currency inconvertibility, which in turn has contributed to the low level of multilateralism in Soviet trade, and to reduced benefits from trade.

More directly, the importation of advanced foreign technology has been hampered by the administrative organization of the Soviet economy and the managerial incentive system that has been employed. The primary operational units in Soviet foreign trade are the foreign trade organizations, which are juridical, independent budget organizations having monopoly rights over the export and import of a defined group of products. Currently they number about fifty, more than half of them concerned with machinery, equipment, and instrument products. They conduct all the trade negotiations with foreign firms for the Soviet enterprises involved in the importation of foreign goods. Further, the managerial incentive system, as discussed above, encourages Soviet managers to avoid innovations. Consequently, the difficulties confronting ministers in getting managers to adopt new technology is compounded with respect to foreign technology by the interposition of an independent organization, the foreign trade organization. In addition to the cumbersomeness of this arrangement, the foreign trade organization has its own incentive criteria, separate from those of its Soviet clients. Understandably, the behavior that results from such a situation is not always conducive to efficient selection, pursuit, and implementation of advanced foreign technology.

Russia is generally not competitive in those world markets dominated by advanced technology, one reason being the lack of competitive pressure on Soviet firms to sell in world markets. Rather, as has been noted, the producing firms were judged by their ability to meet production targets established by the planning authorities (in the more recent period, to meet domestic sales and profit targets). Moreover, under the Soviet planning system, the stress has been on output; firms have operated under conditions of constant, usually excessive demand. Sales of output were assured. Under such conditions, the quality of output has suffered, undermining the development of exports in fields where quality is a factor.

Furthermore, the centralized direction of the economy devoted to the objective of rapid growth contributed to the inward-looking nature of Soviet economy, that is, the needs of the internal planned economy were paramount. Under such conditions, when foreign technology was imported it was used in industries serving the needs of the internal economy rather than for the development of export industries that could compete on world markets.

One essential difference in the relation of Japan and the Soviet Union to the world economy stood out clearly in the petroleum crisis of 1973, which was a dramatic example of a more general crisis involving the scarcity of raw materials, one that highly modernized countries have only gradually come to recognize as a crucial challenge to their continued growth. For Japan the Arab oil embargo loomed as an economic disaster of unprecedented proportions.

By the early 1970's Japan's dependence on the outside world for energy, metallurgical raw materials and food had become extraordinarily great and threatened to become greater. Japan responded politically by reducing rates of resource consumption, by expanding its capacity for nuclear energy, and by acquiring contracts for the construction of petrochemical and other large-scale enterprises in the Middle East as a means of earning back its petroleum expenditures. The principal effect of this crisis on the Soviet economy, self-sufficient in petroleum and most other raw materials, on the other hand, was to raise the prices of both its imports (due to inflation in its trading partners) and its exports (oil and gold). It almost certainly benefited from these developments.

International Comparisons

The comparative postwar performance of the Japanese and Russian economies in relation to several of the highly developed economies of the world are illustrated by the data in Table 16.2 below. Their comparative levels in 1972 are also presented. What is clearly apparent from the data is that the growth rate of the Japanese economy since 1950 has been remarkable. In gross national product it was 9.9 per cent per year and 8.7 per cent per year in per capita terms—substantially greater than the growth rates achieved by other advanced economies. The growth rate of per capita output that Japan maintained implies a doubling of per capita output in less than eight and a half years. Growth rates achieved by the Soviet

TABLE 16.2. International Comparisons, 1950–1972

	JAPAN	RUSSIA	WEST GERMANY	FRANCE	ITALY	U.K.	U.S.A.
Rates of Growth, 1950–1972 (in percentages per year)							
Gross national product	9.9	5.4	6.0	5.2	5.2	2.5	3.8
GNP per capita	8.7	3.9	5.0	4.2	4.6	2.1	2.3
Comparative Levels							
GNP in 1972 (in billions of dollars)	341.0	548.7	292.0	220.8	118.4	152.3	1155.0
GNP per capita in 1972 (in dollars)	3218	2217	4736	4269	2179	2731	5532
Investment share in GNP, in 1972 (in percentages)	36.5	32.4	26.5	27.4	20.2	19.0	18.6
Distribution of labor force in 1972 (in percentages)							
Agriculture	15	26	8	13	18	2	5
Manufacturing	43	45	56	46	49	51	36
Services	42	29	36	41	33	47	59

SOURCES:

Japan: On growth rates: U.S. Department of State, *The Planetary Product in 1972*, RESS–46 (Dec. 14, 1973), Appendix Table 1; K. Ohkawa and H. Rosovsky, *Japanese Economic Growth: Trend Acceleration in the Twentieth Century* (Stanford, Calif.: Stanford University Press 1973), p. 311; on comparative levels: Department of State, *Planetary Product*, Appendix Table 3; on investment share: Patrick and Rosovsky, *Asia's New Giant: How the Japanese Economy Works* (Washington: Brookings Institution Press 1975 or 1976), Table 1.1; on distribution of labor force: International Labor Organization, *Yearbook of Labour Statistics, 1973* (Geneva: ILO 1973), pp. 318–336.

Russia: On growth rates: Department of State, *Planetary Product*, Appendix Table 2; on comparative levels: ibid., Appendix Table 3; on investment share: Table 16.1 revised to 1972 by U.S. Government data; on distribution of labor force: TsSU SSSR, *Narodnoe Khoziaistvo SSSR v 1972* [the national economy of the USSR in 1972] (Moscow: Statistika 1973), p. 501.

Others: United Nations, *Statistical Yearbooks, 1964 and 1973*; Patrick and Rosovsky, *Asia's New Giant: How the Japanese Economy Works* (Washington: Brookings Institution Press 1975 or 1976), Table 1.1; and ILO, *Yearbook, 1973*, pp. 318–336.

economy, although half that of the Japanese rates, were by world standards not unimpressive. They were on a level with France and Italy, below those of West Germany, but above those of the U.S.A. and the U.K. One reason for the high rates of growth of the Japanese and Russian economies can be observed in their high rates of investment.

Finally, the data on GNP and GNP per capita, and on the sectoral distribution of the labor force in the recent period, demonstrate that the economies of both Japan and Russia in the 1970's are on a par with those of advanced countries. In gross output, Russia is second in the world only to the United States and Japan is third. In terms of the other indicators of economic development, product per capita and distribution of the labor force, Japan is clearly at the level of the highly modernized economies, and the Soviet Union is approaching it.

Chapter Seventeen

SOCIAL INTERDEPENDENCE

THE PAST THREE DECADES can be divided into roughly equivalent periods of social change in Japan and the Soviet Union. First came the nearly unlimited mobilization for war, pursued through extreme efforts that probably demanded more daily sacrifices than measures undertaken by any of the other belligerents in that exhausting conflict. This period was followed by years of intensive reconstruction, which reached fruition somewhat more quickly in the victorious nation. Families after the 1950's, as they grew accustomed to fatter paychecks, turned their attention to new patterns of consumption and leisure typical of highly modernized societies. Even more anxiously than before, they sought to place their children at the desired step on the educational ladder. They were no longer confronted by substantial rates of population increase, dualistic occupational patterns, the breakneck pace of urbanization, or the backward conditions of village life. These factors began to fade or even to disappear completely as major considerations. Rising concern now centered on improving job satisfaction, enjoying the urban environment, and acquiring modern amenities.

A review of the postwar social differences between Japan and Russia must begin with the impact of defeat and occupation on such varied Japanese institutions as land ownership, education, and family practices, including inheritance and marriage. Japanese social practices, in other words, were substantially overhauled during the late 1940's, and following these changes occurred the swift decline in both birth rates and farm population, which dropped first to one-third and then to only one-fifth of the work force. In short, Japan was acquiring the attributes of a highly modernized society.

By the end of the 1960's the consumer society had taken hold in Japan far more visibly than in the U.S.S.R.

Victory reaffirmed Soviet methods initiated during the 1930's, but with the death of Stalin many extreme practices were discontinued. Reforms came gradually from within and, even more than in Japan, reversions to previous practices were feared by many. Indeed, there was no basic change in many of the restrictions on travel abroad, on publication, on freedom of assembly. The Soviet formula accommodated more fragile personal ties, as evidenced by higher rates of divorce and labor turnover, through greater state obligations including day-care centers, state pensions, and inexpensive or free higher education and health care. Nevertheless, the rural population continued to be relatively numerous and poor; during the 1960's the monolithic methods popularized in the spirit of building communism continued to elicit remarkable compliance. In Japan, on the contrary, college youth openly rebelled in an uncertain interlude away from families, but their open resentment toward society would not long outlast the acceptance of a job that would promise thirty years of employment with a single company.

Human Resources

A final glance at population attributes reveals many signs of convergence. After a brief postwar rise in birth rates, the rate of natural increase in each country fell from about twenty per thousand to less than ten per thousand. Accounting to some extent for the swift decline in Japanese birth rates were the earlier legalization of abortion and the increased average age of marriage. Although the drop in birth rates was slower in the Soviet Union, the decline continued longer until the two nations were almost even, despite the fact that many non-Slavic peoples in the U.S.S.R. maintained high birth rates. It was above all the growing urban component of the population in both Japan and Russia that was deciding to have fewer children. With death rates falling sharply in the Soviet Union, the natural increase in population during the twenty years after 1950 was substantially greater than in Japan. Even with gains in population through annexations, the Soviet Union's total population, decimated by the war, had dropped to just 2.2 times the 83 million in Japan in 1950. By 1970, however, the earlier margin had almost been regained as the Soviet Union nudged over 240 million whereas

Japan had only recently surpassed 100 million. Their somewhat similar experiences with the ravages of war and their strikingly similar long-run demographic transition have caused Japan and the Soviet Union to resemble each other in the abnormally high number of single elderly women, in the decline in average family size, in the disturbing reduction of entrants into the labor force (except in years when postwar babies have come of age), and in the low average age of the population.

As their combined population was slipping below 10 per cent of the world total, the quality of that population as measured by years of education and training and by occupational distribution was steadily improving. For instance, in 1939 only 8 per cent of Russian workers had received at least seven years of education; thirty years later the figure had risen to more than 50 per cent. The average education received by both peasants and clerical workers was steadily rising. Most who dropped out during middle school, including many of the 1 per cent of Japanese who were still unofficially handicapped as remnants of the Tokugawa outcast groups and members of certain ethnic minorities in the U.S.S.R., lacked skills for advancement. But for those who stayed in school, the competition to demonstrate superior capabilities through examination was becoming more and more heated.

Following the war the relative importance of social classes in Japan was affected by purges of some in high positions, by the dissolution of the zaibatsu, and by the virtual confiscation of lands owned by large or absentee landlords. Some of these changes brought Japanese patterns closer to those of Russia, though the persistence of small-landowners and of small-businessmen as well as the revival of large corporations signify obvious differences. Japan kept well ahead in the decline in the agricultural population; in fact, since 1940 agricultural labor as a percentage of the total Japanese working force has been reduced by more than half. The main pull has been into tertiary industries, not secondary industries as in the U.S.S.R. Villages have witnessed a large increase in part-time farming families, often with women and the elderly doing most of the farming. However, in Japanese urban areas female labor has been much less utilized than in Russia.

Reforms in both countries have diminished the differences in wages, with more deliberate and concerted reductions in the Soviet Union, though nonwage differentials, such as the opportunity to shop at special stores, still distinguish the Soviet elite from the rest of the population. One factor contributing to less disparity in wages was the discarding of Soviet piece-work systems of remuneration for time-wage payments. Russia has also introduced and extended minimum wages. Similarities between the two countries can be found in the continued growth in the number of white-collar employees, mainly in large firms, and in greater opportunities for internal migration, facilitated in Japan by the withdrawal of legal support for primogeniture, by the reduction of inequalities in rural income, and in both countries by growing labor shortages serving to benefit the newly employed. Though migration is unrestricted in Japan, various restrictions still apply on movement in the Soviet Union, affecting departures from collective farms and settlement in certain large cities such as Moscow.

Two consecutive decades of steady increases in wages and other benefits have given rise to a pervasive consumer orientation and to an acute awareness of shortcomings in state decisions affecting welfare provisions and private opportunities. In the postwar period Japan has introduced modern social-welfare policies, although these are still not very substantial in spite of pressures from greatly strengthened labor unions. Individuals continue to rely to a large extent on financial assistance from family members and from enterprise funds in times of need. Retirement for men in Japan is normally at age 55, some five years earlier than the normal age in the Soviet Union. With these relatively early ages of retirement, both countries now face the critical necessity of reemploying pensioners in the short-handed labor force. The growth of free or heavily subsidized public services has proceeded at a faster pace in Russia to the point where the social wage (benefits not doled out in private wages) is now about one-third of earnings, mostly spent for pensions and education. The social wage provides public services to Soviet citizens in large part required of the private sector in Japan. In both countries much of the social wage including pensions is distributed according to employment-related criteria.

In a consumer age what is important is not only how much the consumer has to spend but also on what he or she may be able to spend it. In the U.S.S.R. housing and transportation costs to individuals are remarkably low, whereas food expenditures absorb a large proportion of the family budget. In recent years, however, cooperative housing projects have been built, enabling individuals impatient with long waiting lists for scarce and cramped quarters to use their own funds for construction. The housing shortage, together with the high cost and unavailability of automobiles, has especially limited the independence of youths and the elderly. Bonuses of late have declined as a form of payment in Russia, but Japanese workers rely on sizable biannual bonuses to save large sums for retirement, for their children's college education, and for big expenditures such as initial payments for apartments, for automobiles, and for modern appliances. Japanese consumers have a much wider assortment of quality goods from which to choose. However, high rents in large cities do not permit the majority of them to enjoy apartments much superior to those in Russia. With wages based to an unusual degree on seniority, many older Japanese employees are favored by large salaries, while older Soviet workers, also educationally handicapped in relation to recently trained youth, are not accorded such deference. No doubt Japanese wage earners nearing retirement are better able to keep some hold over family members, even those residing away from home, by virtue of these differentials favoring experience.

In short, these two countries have achieved significant attributes of high modernization: low rates of population growth, an occupational distribution weighted in favor of the secondary and tertiary sectors, nearly universal secondary education, and high rates of attendance in colleges and institutes. They have emerged as nearly full-fledged consumer and welfare societies. In the process of finally realizing these gains Japan has moved more quickly in providing a variety of modern conveniences to large numbers of households, but the U.S.S.R. has realized some of its promise by making partially available an unusual array of inexpensive public services, especially to its urban population. Despite similarities, they present contrasting and not wholly accurate images today of rampant consumerism and unequaled welfarism, neither of which is deeply satisfying for its neglect of the other.

Patterns of Settlement

Before World War II a persistent and widening gap developed between urban and rural life-styles. Following the postwar realization of high levels of urban mass consumption, the consequences of this dichotomy stirred public attention as never before. In Japan rising government subsidies of rice prices as well as improved access of villagers to remunerative nonagricultural work began to cause a narrowing in the gap between urban and rural living standards. More and more rural residents became commuters, leaving the daily farm chores to their less employable relatives. Separated by vast distances from the principal cities, Soviet farmers have been slower to find rewarding alternative employment. The retarded development of modern farming techniques has also prevented the release of their labor. Nonetheless, minimum wages have been established for collective farmers. Further, state farms, superior in the educational preparation of their residents as well as in the regular wages paid to them, have grown at the expense of collective farms. Today the 40 per cent of the Soviet population not living in cities is divided quite evenly between these two forms of farming complexes.

In both countries the place of the village in the emerging society has not been fully resolved. The autonomous village has clearly disappeared. The Soviets were first to sound its death knell with collectivization in the 1930's, but the Japanese have moved rapidly since the postwar land reform as common interest associations based on geographic units larger than the village have spread, providing joint ownership and direction of many factors of production. The fact that even oldest sons now leave in pursuit of higher wages in Japanese cities points to the irreversible process under way. In Japan the commonly recognized problem, however, is the institutionalization of small plots, which stymie the efficient concentration of land for modern farming technology. In the U.S.S.R. the task of improving agricultural productivity is much more troublesome, with private plots still embarrassingly essential and overdue programs for large-scale investment in agriculture still showing uncertain success. The difficulty of motivating educated youth to return to the village to apply their skills to rural problems remains particularly serious in the Soviet Union.

Since World War II urbanization has been accompanied by abrupt drops in rural population. The number of urban residents in Japan and Russia has climbed steadily, after brief declines at the end of the war, more than doubling in a quarter of a century. Japan's city growth has continued to be ahead, reaching 70 million in cities of just over 100 million people and one-half of the total population in cities of 100,000 or more inhabitants. The densely populated urbanized area extending from Tokyo to Osaka has 45 per cent of the nation's inhabitants and an even higher proportion of youths in advanced levels of education and newly found employment. The larger the city, the faster has been the growth in its metropolitan area. Japan has truly become the society of the megalopolis.

The pace of urbanization, as the rate of natural increase, has lagged about one decade behind in the U.S.S.R. Only at the end of the 1960's did urban growth in the Soviet Union drop to roughly 2 per cent annually. By this time the Soviet urban population had risen by almost 80 million in thirty years. Whereas there had been only 82 Soviet cities with 100,000 people in 1939, by 1970 the total had reached 221, far more than the 135 now present in Japan. Of course, even with twice as many urban dwellers as in Japan, the Soviet Union still requires at least another decade to sustain 70 per cent of its population in cities.

The addition of a combined total of well over 110 million city residents has produced an explosion of urban problems for both countries. Nearly all city dwellers now live in rows of apartments, although in newly mushrooming satellite suburbs, especially in Japan, less densely settled quarters are available. The proliferation of pollution, the scarcity of recreation facilities, and the crowded state of mass transportation head the long list of urban troubles, which despite the existence of enviable mass transportation facilities and relatively low crime rates, appear as serious concerns, particularly in Japan, for the near future.

Japan has had an obvious advantage in accelerating urbanization which may already appear as a disadvantage at a time of mounting urban problems. Compact and populous, it has proceeded with unusual haste in integrating rural and urban areas. Efforts are nearly complete to have nearly everyone no more than a few hours by rapid train from the several great cities of the land. In the Soviet Union, meanwhile, regional differences persist within its vast expanse, with some areas still experiencing high rates of natural increase and even continued growth in rural population. If the Soviets can somehow find a convincing answer to the unassailable argument that the larger the city the greater the productivity, they will seemingly be in a better position for effectively turning their immense planning resources to new planned cities and planned networks of cities.

Organizational Contexts

Postwar trends toward the democratization of Japanese organizations and the de-Stalinization of Soviet organizations are reflected in changes within the family structure, economic enterprises, and administrative bodies.

During the American occupation of Japan provisions of the legal code as it affects the family were rewritten. The legal powers and responsibilities of the family head were removed; and primogeniture gave way to equal division of inheritance. All children, not just the firstborn, now have responsibility for their aging parents, and women are assured various forms of equality with men. Though the new laws have not resulted in high divorce rates, which have increasingly appeared in the Soviet Union, they have made it possible for women to take the initiative in filing for divorce and they have strengthened the independent nuclear family, making it easier for a young couple to move away from the father-in-law's home and weakening the hierarchical bond between main and branch families. At the same time many traditional family roles have persisted. Husbands spend leisure hours away from home, arranged marriages continue to be widespread with few chances for the partners to meet before the ceremony, and attitudes, especially in rural areas, are still relatively traditional.

The obstacles in the way of female emancipation are of a different order in the two societies. In many respects women in the Soviet Union have been emancipated. The wife of a Soviet white-collar employee is frequently employed in responsible, if not usually well paid, positions such as in medicine or education. Yet her problem remains to convince her husband to share in household chores and child-rearing so that both can find time for leisure. A Japanese wife, however, is limited by a much lower earning power. In effect, she is given exceptional control over home and children in return for not pressing for equal jobs and opportunities to enjoy leisure. An obvious difference is that the two-income family has become a reality in the Soviet Union but not in Japan. A less obvious similarity in comparison with other modernized societies is that Russian and Japanese couples lead unusually separate lives—in one country because each has a meaningful job; in the other because the husband stays away from home.

Success in both countries has been measured since the 1950's primarily in terms of salaries. A Japanese aspires to a position as a "salaryman," where he can receive ample and rising wages, secure employment, and assistance in activities outside of the job. Paternalism remains more important in small firms, but the expectation of lifetime employment with a single large enterprise elicits strong loyalty from the salaryman too. The youthful job seeker in the Soviet Union also is very much concerned about his salary, but lacks the same long-run attachment to a particular firm. If he has received a specialized education, then he must first fulfill a two-year obligation to work wherever the state assigns him, a way of meeting the labor needs of areas lacking in appeal. Afterward, he may be temporarily attracted by high wages in Siberia or the North; however, unappealing living conditions contribute to high turnover rates there. In Japan as in the Soviet Union labor needs have consistently outpaced labor supplies, long-term unemployment has not been a problem, and this has been an age of decline in unskilled labor and of further gravitation toward salaried employment in large bureaucracies.

De-Stalinization has been most visible in the reduced use of prison labor, in the reduced penalties for absenteeism, and in the introduction of a myriad of improved material incentives. There has been no basic change, however, in the multitude of state controls over the crucial decisions of an individual's lifetime. Wielding potentially unchecked power, the party and state machinery have recourse to various devices for keeping the individual in line. They can deny a person promotion or not allow him to practice the job for which he is trained; they can fail to authorize him to live in the city of his choice; they can make it difficult for the spouse or other family members to keep their jobs or pursue their education. Failure to give uncritical, ritualistic support to party decisions remains a serious offense, especially for those in vulnerable positions such as government, education, and the arts, and also for those still in school, whose access to further education can easily be blocked. Opportunities to publish, to maintain contacts with foreigners, and to travel abroad are all viewed as privileges in this highly regulated society. Recent efforts to restrict the advancement of Jews give vivid evidence of how this panoply of controls can be applied.

In both Japan and the U.S.S.R. the organizational man has been offered a bond to counteract the anonymity of urban sprawl. In return for paternalistic protection from their firms, Japanese are expected to provide unstinting labor. So far the widespread sentiment of identification with one's place of employment has been maintained in spite of postwar criticism that has stirred opposition to the worthiness of private enterprise goals. Symbolic of the ideal work relationship in the Soviet Union are the "Communist Saturdays," when everybody works without pay in demonstration of a nationwide unanimity of purpose. Although for many these occasional days of donated labor are regarded as a burden, even more than in Japan the success of the collective at work and of the nation are praised as worthy goals along with individual reward following the socialist principle of "to each according to his work." Meanwhile, of course, the goal of "building communism" is used to justify intolerance of deviance, incessant indoctrination, and occasional ruthless punishment.

Redistributive Processes

In both Japan and Russia in recent decades migration and mobility have persisted at high rates, although some of the nationalities in the U.S.S.R. have remained fairly immobile. The single most thoroughgoing change was the postwar land reform in Japan, which in just a few inflationary years resulted in the virtual elimination of tenant households without the onus of prolonged repayments, without bloodshed, and without ill feelings—conditions that accompanied earlier Russian transformations of agrarian relationships. Apart from the reforms of the late 1940's in Japan, neither society has undergone any pronounced effort to modify interclass relationships.

Today there are three moments of decision in both societies that are critical for social and geographic mobility: the passage of school entrance examinations; the choice of first employment; and the selection of a marriage partner. All of these decisions are normally made within a five- or ten-year span. The elite in each society has various ways of enhancing the prospects of its children on the entrance examinations and in securing desirable employment. Relatively wealthy Soviets and Japanese place their children in the right schools at early ages and give them special tutoring for the most difficult entrance exams. In Japan the examinations are written, but in Russia they are oral. Each institution of higher learning gives a separate exam.

Alumni of costly private schools in Japan have a particular advantage in some areas, although the best universities are public. In the Soviet Union as in Japan, personal contacts, including the cultivation of a protector in a high place, can be especially useful in findnig favorable employment. In both countries informal groups of patrons and their followers exist in the academic field, in places of employment and elsewhere. Frequently in the U.S.S.R. such vertical relationships are important in guaranteeing political reliability.

Marriage is too often ignored as a factor in mobility. Through the deliberate choice of a mate (often by means of a modified form of arranged marriage in Japan) lifetime prospects can be enhanced or threatened. Considerable calculation of the qualities of a desirable spouse is likely to be present in these countries where newlyweds commonly must first live with their parents if they wish, as apparently almost all do, to remain in certain large metropolises. Marriage acquires special significance also for aspirants to positions for which essential personal contacts may best be cultivated through family relationships. All of these decisions affecting mobility take on added urgency in these competitive societies where aspirations are constantly being disappointed.

Personal Relationships

The ideals of Soviet society are so constantly reiterated that many Soviets as well as outsiders believe they are being practiced more than they are. Carefully regulated knowledge about the outside world, as well as about the past of their own society, reinforces the confidence of many of the Soviet people that they have been steadily outdistancing other peoples in realizing desirable goals. It would be a mistake to conclude that because a gap exists between what is proclaimed to be true and what is actually true the ideals of Soviet society are meaningless in influencing personal relationships. Even though the focus here is primarily on prevalent behavior, the potential positive influence of Communist ideals on unselfish, unstinting relationships with others should not be overlooked.

The disparity between the ideal and the actual in the Soviet Union is nowhere better observed than in the contrast between the treatment of customers in Japan and Russia. The most frequent form of contact in a modern society is the fleeting exchange between sales personnel and customers. In Japan there is a feeling that a certain standard of service is owed the customer; in return for a possible payment there is an obligation. Soviet sales personnel, however, are more frequently rude to their customers. Many of the inefficiencies that make daily living in the Soviet Union exhausting and frustrating exist not only because of the low priority given consumer interests, but also because of widespread disregard for the convenience of others.

In the contemporary era, the Japanese, probably even more than the Soviets, have fostered a commitment to collectivities. An individual belongs to long-enduring vertically structured groups that penetrate to a considerable extent into the private lives of their members and emphasize procedures for maintaining and restoring harmony. The discontented in the Soviet Union must remain isolated for fear of exposure through group supervision. But not the discontented in Japan where new collectivities are being developed with a certain regularity. The postwar search for a single overriding group solidarity, for instance, has spurred a religious revival among less educated and mobile persons, a notable example being the sect known as the Sōka Gakkai (Value Creating Association).

In both countries the stress on group bonds persists. Many forms of attitudes and behavior, acceptable elsewhere, are discouraged. Yet as people have become accustomed to prosperity, they have developed a fascination with foreign goods, closely following new styles in music and fashion. Fads may not be a sign of individualism, but they do raise the possibility of generational clashes and new differences between social strata. To counter the influx of new ideas, the Soviet authorities have been more assiduous than ever in glorifying the motherland and the military and in magnifying the cult of Lenin, but the Japanese response remains ambivalent. Unquestionably, as the goals of material plenty are approached in the next two decades, the Soviets will face the challenge of specifying more precisely the meaning of Communist personal relationships and the Japanese will succumb to the necessity of reintegrating traditional values into a more coherent set of modern ideals.

Japan and the Soviet Union, trailing by a decade, have both achieved high levels of development within this short span of three decades, as indicated by the stabilization of their population growth at a low rate of increase and by the slowdown in urbanization to the point where cities no longer grow faster than the increase in total population. The achievement of advanced modernization has been accompanied by a relaxation of demands for conformity: the tentative steps in the Soviet Union to de-Stalinize socialism and the imposed reforms during the American occupation of Japan to democratize the imperial system of control. As a result, the rights of individuals in both countries are more broadly conceived than during the 1930's.

Restrictions still continue, however, on individual rights, carryovers from the more disciplined attitudes of the past. In Japan an unusual conformity survives in community behavior and in the acceptance of family authority. Moreover, the small share of national wealth spent on social welfare places a severe burden on those with below-average wages. In short, there is a high level of conformity with a low level of coercion and few welfare benefits. In the U.S.S.R. many rights are severely restricted. Few are able to emigrate, to travel abroad freely, to receive foreign publications, to maintain unobserved contacts with foreigners inside their country, or to express publicly critical opinions on a wide range of issues. While family and peer group pressures are less restrictive with regard to such decisions as marriage and divorce, government decisions affect many aspects of the individual's personal life, including the availability of contraceptives and the variety of films. Conscious efforts by the Soviet leadership narrowly limit freedom of choice. To an unusual extent, direct limitations on freedom are still used in the Soviet Union to mobilize resources, whereas in Japan the cumulative decisions of individuals with few legal restrictions result in the furtherance of modernization.

International Comparisons

The compressed course of modernization for the few latecomers successful in threading their way quickly through the transitional phase leaves a trail of problems to be resolved in the following phase of high modernization. Relatively sudden shifts in policy are required when migration into cities slacks off, when the number of entrants into the labor force declines, and when competition for jobs with the greatest income, prestige, and power intensifies. Increasingly, the competition of urban educated youths for scarce jobs takes place in the context of a society with substantial emphasis on mass consumption. The development of a new mixture of benefits and rewards for large numbers of people becomes a critical factor in sustaining widespread participation in the pursuit of upward mobility and in exacting occupational performances necessary for continued rapid modernization.

The emergence of a mass consumption society is a useful focus of comparison. The concept of mass consumption has taken on universal significance in relatively modernized societies with the greater availability of automobiles, television sets, and other consumer durable goods. It was only in the 1950's that the early modernizing societies, with the United States in the vanguard, stepped resolutely into this age of consumerism; yet the allure of the mass products in these societies has quickly raised expectations in countries at various stages of transition. As latecomers to modernization that by the late 1950's had the potential to make available to large numbers of their people some of these new products, Japan and the Soviet Union serve to highlight some of the possible responses to the mounting pressures of consumerism.

Both have faced the problem of lingering discrepancies between urban and rural living conditions. One hypothesis that we tentatively propose is that as urban migration—which has already created a society that is at least 50 per cent urban—slows down, the gap in living conditions, in wages, between town and country must be substantially closed if rapid modernization is to continue. Still burdened by a relatively large rural sector, the Soviet Union has been tardy in closing this gap. In contrast, Japan was well ahead in the postwar period in narrowing the differences between rural and urban incomes. Items for mass consumption have been more accessible to Japan's rural population than Russia's. Yet after some initial efforts in the 1950's to provide rural incentives, Soviet leaders in the past decade have brought about a marked improvement in the well-being of the rural population, including the introduction of a minimum wage, pensions, and other benefits heretofore unavailable to collective farmers. Even certain urban consumer benefits are now filtering into the villages. The acute rural-urban dualism that characterized the transitional period is still far from being overcome in either country, but the many steps already taken to alleviate some of these disparities are causing them to resemble other advanced modernized societies more closely.

A second duality in living standards has also shown signs of breaking down within Japan and the Soviet Union. The cleavage in wages and benefits within cities has been reduced in favor of the unskilled or semi-skilled often not employed by large firms. In this respect the Soviet Union, with its more abundant social-welfare measures that constitute a sizable part of the benefits available to the urban poor, has proceeded with more alacrity than Japan. As the shortage of labor has become severe in cities, wage differentials have been cut. Not only state subsidies, but also the conversion from piece work to hourly wages and the concerted effort to boost blue-collar wages have typified Soviet policies. In Japan employment has been shifting to large firms that continue to offer higher wages, better working conditions, more job security, and increased benefits. Meanwhile, labor shortages have forced the small firms to offer similar inducements. A Soviet worker in light industry or a Japanese worker employed by a small firm must still cope with inferior conditions, but these intersectoral differences have been considerably lessened. All these factors are indicative of a greater integration of the urban labor force. Further study is needed to determine whether we are correct in arguing that the leveling of these differences in comparison with the transitional period is important for continued rapid modernization.

Consumption of appliances and other durables probably has become the greatest single force for motivating labor. Reduced disparities in wages and benefits and a rise in the availability of consumer goods have promoted the prevalent attitude toward work as a necessary source of income for "the good life." The successive popularity of new varieties of consumer durable goods, the growing interest in the use of leisure time, and the faddishness of aspects of life associated with the West all motivate individuals to seek more remunerative jobs. In lengthening the period of compulsory education, and in expanding the number of entrants into higher education, Japan and Russia have linked life's best rewards to educational performance in a very competitive environment of heightened aspirations.

The common elements of the Japanese and Soviet experiences are suggestive about what is necessary to maintain rapid development in already highly modernized societies. It must be noted, however, that it was precisely when the old sources of mobilization were becoming less relevant in the late 1950's and early 1960's that a clear discrepancy can be observed between accelerated Japanese development and reduced Soviet development. One part of the common experience was a decline in wage differentials after a long record of extensive and ever widening urban-rural cleavages. Another common element still present in the two countries is the borrowing of items of mass consumption from the most modernized societies and making them increasingly available. This diffusion has involved changes in diet and clothing along with an array of modern conveniences, including the automobile.

The Soviet Union, which has been slower to make available consumer goods, has not fared as well in raising productivity. It is not unlikely that some time in the middle of this contemporary period the key motivational factors in the choice of careers and in the application of skills were undergoing change, and that patterns of wage distribution and consumption in Japanese society adjusted more quickly to the new demands of the advanced modernized society. Yet the adjustments made in the Soviet Union on the distribution of wages and benefits were essentially similar to those made in Japan and may have also permitted relative success in sustaining rapid modernization.

Chapter Eighteen

KNOWLEDGE AND EDUCATION

IN KNOWLEDGE AND EDUCATION Japan and the Soviet Union have come to assume in recent decades the general characteristics of the most modernized nations: large and growing institutions of higher education, strong commitments to advanced research and development, expanding networks of modern electronic communication. Regarding both of these elements of society, of course, important contrasts remain, reflecting distinctive features in their political and cultural systems. The level and content of their higher education are comparable, but the Soviet Union considerably outstrips Japan in expenditures on research and development (primarily because of a far more extensive military establishment), and Japan considerably outdistances Russia in modern communications (primarily because of a far more compact and homogeneous society). Perhaps the most compelling similarity between the two nations is that their respective emphases on knowledge and education had not by the early 1970's made any conspicuous difference in their national purpose and social stability, both prime objectives during their years of transformation.

The Growth of Mass Higher Education

In the fifties and sixties both Japan and Russia gradually shifted the focus of their efforts in education from the attainment of universal primary education to the achievement of mass higher education. The Soviet Union had by the early 1950's completed the task of extending functional literacy to the entire population and of making provisions for six (and later eight) years of compulsory education, thereby correcting the dangerous topheaviness of the educational system inherited from the tsarist regime. The more recent extension of compulsory schooling to nine years in Japan and ten in the U.S.S.R. has caused the virtual disappearance of secondary education as a distinctive stage, and a fresh wave of interest in the nature and quality of advanced training.

The ways in which the two nations have developed their systems of higher education are thoroughly comparable. Both acknowledge higher education to be a factor critical to the economic growth that is a central policy objective of their national policies. As of the early 1970's, the two societies had achieved a level of participation in advanced study that was competitive with, and in some respects in advance of, West European and North American nations. About 31 per cent of the Japanese and 34 per cent of the Russian college-age cohorts were receiving some form of higher education. Japan has taken steps to rectify its earlier backwardness in educating women by permitting them to obtain a higher education; the proportion of females in higher education has risen from about 2 per cent at the end of the war to nearly 33 per cent in 1970. Meanwhile, the Soviet Union has opened up new opportunities for advanced training of its minority nationalities.

In both Japan and Russia the dramatic rise in enrollments in higher education has been accomplished through a broad variety of institutions offering different programs of varying quality. Both systems are dominated by a few prestigious universities and specialized schools offering a first-rate education to a small elite; these same institutions lead in the production of new knowledge. The vast majority of students in both countries, however, are enrolled in facilities of far lesser quality and prestige, in which education is often conducted on a mass scale. In the U.S.S.R., these schools of higher education are usually decentralized, and cater to the specific training needs of the particular locality. Japan has a similar system of state universities in each prefecture, but most of nonprestige higher education continues to be carried out by private schools that are heavily concentrated in the great urban centers of Tokyo and Kyoto-Osaka.

The most renowned institutions in both nations are supported by the state and are either free, as in Russia, or charge a modest tuition fee, as in Japan. By contrast, the more numerous private universities in Japan must demand a relatively high tuition fee. In the

U.S.S.R. grants for student aid vary widely within and among most schools in accordance with the priority assigned the training in a particular facility or discipline. A noteworthy aspect of the U.S.S.R.'s program is the extent to which it employs financial aid as an instrument for channeling personnel into specific areas of study.

Young Russians and Japanese recognize the critical role played by education in their own social and economic advancement and therefore make great efforts to obtain it, notwithstanding the strain imposed by the severely competitive situation. Both countries favor examinations that test achievement rather than aptitude, with heavy stress put on memorization and on technical skills; composition, for example, is largely neglected in favor of mathematics (in the teaching of which Japan and Russia have gained international recognition), natural sciences, and modern languages.

The similarities extend also to the content of the university curriculum, which in both nations is oriented toward professional training. The attempts during the American occupation to force the Japanese university system into the American mold, with its emphasis on broad, liberal education, met with scant success. A distinction may be drawn between curricular priorities, for the Japanese give special attention to training in law and economics—the professional skills needed for business and government administration—whereas Soviet universities still favor the natural sciences and engineering. In the technical and professional cast of the curriculum, however, there is little difference. The universities are dedicated to producing not a broadly educated elite but rather the experts needed to manage a modern industrial society.

Control over educational policy remains centralized and even in Japan rests to a significant degree with the state. Centralization has brought many practical benefits in connection with standards and manpower planning, but it has also contributed to the formalism that has already generated calls for university reforms. A growing segment of Japanese higher education (although almost no elementary and secondary training) is in private hands, but even here the ministry of education exercises extensive controls that are the more effective because of the great financial pressures on nonstate schools.

For all the problems faced by Japan and the Soviet Union regarding the maldistribution of quality education and the weight of bureaucratism in their systems of higher education, both have met with striking success in their efforts to produce large numbers of highly motivated and well-trained experts. Dissatisfaction with the quality of higher education is more noticeable in Japan than in the

Soviet Union, but even Japanese students are for the most part quiescent and on the whole satisfied with their educational experience The bulk of students in the two nations are quite apolitical, professionally oriented, and concerned primarily with the challenges and security that the economic prosperity of their country promises them.

The Production of Modern Knowledge

Japan and the U.S.S.R. have seen a general shift in recent years from the absorption of useful foreign knowledge to a concern with the production of new knowledge. Defeat in World War II broke Japan's partial isolation from contemporary scientific and technological innovations and again launched her on a period of catching up with Western knowledge. In the course of the postwar decades, Japan has closed this gap in most areas and become a full-fledged member of the international scientific community. The Soviet Union has similarly emerged from the partial isolation of the Stalinist era and has established increasingly close ties with producers of scientific knowledge throughout the world. It has consistently devoted substantially greater attention to science and technology than Japan; in 1970, the proportion of GNP allotted to research and development was 4.2 per cent for the U.S.S.R. versus 1.8 per cent for Japan. This difference in part reflects the far larger military budget of Russia, but Japan, notwithstanding its smaller military establishment, has been steadily adding to its investment in research and development, having "caught up" with Western knowledge in the 1960's.

The evolution of Japan and Russia as leading participants in the world community of knowledge has been far more apparent in the natural sciences (in which the Japanese have won two Nobel prizes, the Russians four) than in the social sciences, where political constraints have slowed progress. In the U.S.S.R. the constraints were in the form of pressure to conform to strict interpretations of Marxism-Leninism; in Japan the newfound prestige of a rigidly applied Marxism in the wake of the collapse of the militarist state in 1945 resulted initially in a generally dogmatic approach to the social sciences. In the past twenty years, however, pressures to conform have diminished in both nations, which have recognized the importance of social science research to the understanding and management of institutional development. Work in the social sciences still remains to an extent in the "catching-up" stage through which work in the natural sciences had earlier passed, and both countries tend to look to American research methods.

Modern Mass Communications

Modern, well-developed systems of mass communication are enjoyed by both the Russians and the Japanese. Japan is considerably more advanced in this respect, having the advantages of a more homogeneous population, a compact national territory, and exceptional expertise in electronics. The sale of television sets—an important socializing force—has boomed, faster in Japan, though, than in Russia. In 1960, the U.S.S.R. had less than one-third the number of sets per capita than Japan, although the proportion had risen to two-thirds by 1970. Per capita radio rates show an initial advantage for the Soviets (205 per 1,000 population in 1960 versus 133 for Japan), which has been quickly overcome (in 1970: Japan, 551; Russia, 390). Japan also has far more telephones than Russia—twice as many per capita in 1952 and six times as many in 1970. Only in cinema attendance is the U.S.S.R. far ahead of Japan, with 1970 rates of 19 per capita per year versus 2.0 for Japan.

One rather obvious difference between the communications systems of the two nations today is that Japan's is monolingual and Russia's is based on the numerous languages of the Soviet peoples. Slightly more than half of all books published in the U.S.S.R. are in languages other than Russian, most of them designated for regional consumption. Many are translated from Russian or are closely similar to Russian models, but they nonetheless perpetuate the ethnic pluralism that has always been a feature of Russian and Soviet life. The strongly contrasting ethnic homogeneity of the Japanese naturally obviates such expenditures on minority communication, though the complexity of the Japanese writing system continues to demand outlays of money and energy for printed communication far greater than any other nation except perhaps China. Thus, to give one example, use of the typewriter is far less widespread in Japan than in the Soviet Union, which itself lags far behind Western Europe in this respect.

Among urban middle-class youths throughout the U.S.S.R., ethnic diversity is offset to a considerable extent by another factor common to both nations: a large, self-sustaining "youth culture."

Members of this culture seek to participate fully in the cosmopolitan life of their country. If the formal communications media in both nations (and especially in the U.S.S.R.) stress the dominant values of the respective societies, the youth cultures tend to express private values. Both youth cultures are sustained by a prodigious communications network of their own, one that is informal and based on recorded music, publications, and firsthand travel experiences, which now extend to foreign travel for Japanese. In the U.S.S.R. these channels and the ideals they propagate have often been the object of official scrutiny.

The Survival of Inherited Values

In spite of the inroads made by the so-called youth cultures, the values of austerity, hard work, and group loyalty are still stressed in contemporary Japan and Russia. Partly traceable in Japan to the Tokugawa samurai tradition, these values have pervaded most classes of society throughout the modern century. The Soviet regime has also sought vigorously to inculcate these values both within Great Russia and the national regions, a task made easier by the fact that among Russian peasants group loyalty has always been highly valued.

An interesting example of the parallelism of these efforts may be found in the resemblance of child-rearing techniques in Japan and the U.S.S.R. Children in both countries, until they are about six or seven, are given a great deal of loving attention in a way that encourages strong feelings of dependency. The main form of discipline thus becomes the withholding of approval or affection. When the child reaches school age, however, parental attitudes become sterner as the child begins to be carefully trained in school in attitudes of obedience to the group. The weakening of older family bonds in both societies has increased the importance of the schools in imparting values. This pattern of training in Japan produces personalities that prefer loyal service to the organization in which they function to unstructured individual competition for worldly success, a pattern reflected, for instance, in the Japanese practice of "lifetime employment" in a given organization. Soviet training tends rather toward developing a sense of engagement in an effort that is national in scope, as evidenced in persistent efforts to link labor in every field to nationally established objectives. The less developed sense of loyalty to intermediate organizations and institutions in the U.S.S.R.

may be both a cause and effect of the chronic problem of motivation in the Soviet labor force.

Beyond this concern for developing particularistic loyalties, a pervasive and powerful sense of nationalism can be found in both countries. The conviction persists that each nation is still engaged in a special mission to match the most developed societies, even in fields where equity has already been achieved. This feeling is fed by an acute sense of the long historical past, a consciousness carefully nurtured by the educational system. In the Soviet Union the added effort is exerted to link the historical experience of Russian and non-Russian nationalities. Religious faith and practice survive in both nations as carriers of national identity, but they are powerless to exert any direct molding influence on social and political values. One important exception to the general status of religion in the two nations is the Sōka Gakkai in Japan, a Buddhist movement that has grown to claim about 10 per cent of the population and which has become a powerful political force through its related party, the Kōmeitō. Other than this, the most vital religious life in both nations is probably that of the several evangelical sects, often with millenarian tendencies, but even these have exerted no discernible influence on national values.

The survival from earlier times of a consensus of values in both Japan and Russia over the past several decades in no way guarantees a stability of values in the future. In fact, the strains upon such a consensus appear to be mounting in both nations. Economic prosperity threatens to undermine the incentive to equal the West, an incentive that has done so much to sustain national values, and such specific modern developments as the spread of the automobile and the resultant demand for individual privacy pose serious threats to older collective loyalties. The future holds the possibility that a disintegration of inherited values may provoke a reassertion of strict state control over the formation of values. And there is ample precedent in the earlier experiences of both countries for that possibility.

International Comparisons

The increasing availability of uniform international statistics permits comparisons of Japan and Russia in the contemporary international context which were not possible for the period of transformation. Both are compared below with some thirty other nations that are, or are fast becoming, highly modernized.

By the 1970's the proportion of children—roughly six through eighteen—receiving primary *and* secondary education was more than 90 per cent in *all* of the advanced nations, confirming that a critical variable in the phase of high modernization is higher education. UNESCO statistics for the percentage of the twenty-to-twenty-four-age group enrolled in educational institutions in 1969 shows the U.S.S.R. to be second in the world with 27 per cent, well ahead of Japan (16) but also substantially behind the United States (48). In the European context, Japan appears to be about average: slightly under Sweden (18) and Denmark (18); about on a par with France (16) and Yugoslavia (15); and above West Germany (12), Austria (11), and the United Kingdom (10). Of the non-European nations, Israel (20) and the Phillipines (20) are both considerably above Japan, and clearly anomalies. The case of the Phillipines is particularly striking as one in which an excessive gap between rates of expansion in higher education and economic development has resulted in acute tension deriving from frustrated expectations.

These educational figures suggest the inordinately heavy emphasis the Soviet Union has placed on higher education in comparison not only with Japan but with most other nations in the world. Japan's continuing growth in higher education since 1969, however, has been more rapid than in most other nations, suggesting that it, like the Soviet Union, has adopted an American rather than a European model of higher education for the masses; since 1969 the gap between it and Russia in higher education has continued to contract.

It is difficult to find reliable measurements of advanced knowledge, particularly in the social sciences, for the purpose of making world comparisons. One indicator in the natural sciences, of course, is the number of postwar Nobel Prize winners, by which the Soviet Union (four) ranks fifth, after the United States (forty-six), Great Britain (twenty-two); Germany (nine), and Sweden (five); Japan with two prizes is tied for seventh place with Argentina, Australia, Italy, and Switzerland. Other indicators are those measuring research and development efforts. In terms of scientists and engineers engaged in research and development per 10,000 population, the U.S.S.R. in 1969 was highest in the world (38.2), followed by Japan (27.7) and the United States (26.2). It is not unlikely that some of the East European nations, such as Hungary and Czechoslovakia, for which this figure is not available, are comparable with these three leaders, but no Western European nation comes within range, the leading ones being the Netherlands (15.3), France (11.7), and West Germany (13.0). Many advanced nations have even smaller proportions, such as Canada (10.0), Sweden (6.6), and the United Kingdom (7.9).

These estimates of manpower devoted to research and development must be balanced with those of financial expenditures. In this perspective, Japan predictably falls below a number of leading European nations. In percentage of GNP devoted to research and development in 1969, the Soviet Union (4.2) is followed by Czechoslovakia (3.6) and the United States (2.8). In the range below the United States and above Japan (1.8) are the United Kingdom (2.4), Canada (2.4), Poland (2.3), the Netherlands (2.2), and France (2.0). Below Japan but above 1 per cent are Belgium, Austria, Israel, Sweden, Norway, and Yugoslavia. The most general conclusion to be drawn from these statistics is that Japan is unique in the high proportion of manpower and in the moderate proportion of GNP devoted to this effort, whereas Russia is unique in the very high proportion of both manpower *and* capital.

In mass communications Japan's consumer-oriented policies place it ahead of the Soviet Union and in the ranks of the most advanced nations. Japan's rate of 510 in daily newspaper circulation per 1,000 population is surpassed only by Sweden (534). The U.S.S.R. (347) falls below the United Kingdom (463), East Germany (445), Norway (396), and Denmark (368), but above Australia (321), West Germany (319), the United States (301), and France (238). In telephones Japan's relative ranking is far higher than Russia's. With 28.2 telephones per 100 population, it is less than that of the United States (60.4), Sweden (55.7), and Canada (46.8), roughly equivalent to that of Norway (30.7) and the United Kingdom (28.9), and well above the European average of 18.8. The Soviet Union, by contrast, with only 4.9 telephones per 100 population, ranks far below any European nation and is about on a level with Argentina (4.2) and Chile (4.0).

In radio use, however, the Soviet Union compensates for the low rates of telephone ownership, suggesting a strong bias for public over private communication. In fact, the rates of radio sets per 1,000 population in 1971 for both Japan (573) and the U.S.S.R. (408), while below the United States (1,623) and Canada (773), are ahead of all European nations (for example, Sweden, 370; the United Kingdom, 330; France, 313; Austria, 290; Italy, 214). In the more advanced medium of television, Japan (222 sets per 1,000 population) can match the West European nations, having fewer than Sweden (323) and the United Kingdom (298), but about as many as France (227) and Norway (229). None, of course, approach the level of the United States (449) and Canada (349). The Soviet Union's rate of 160 places it between Italy (191) and Spain (132).

One anomaly in the realm of mass communications is the surprising popularity of films in the Soviet Union even as late as 1970, by which time television had already dealt a severe blow to the cinema in all other advanced nations. The average of nineteen annual trips to the movies per capita in the U.S.S.R. was comparable with that of only a few nations at similar or lower stages of development (Italy, 11; Spain, 10; Bulgaria, 13). By contrast, the most economically advanced nations now have modest rates of cinema attendance: Japan, 2; the United States, 5; Canada, 4; Sweden, 3; France, 3.5; the United Kingdom, 3.2; and Australia, 2.6. Clearly, the cinema has been mobilized as an instrument of mass communication in the Soviet Union to an extent unique among the highly modernized societies, sustaining a precedent set in the prewar era and offering one explanation for the relatively few owners of television sets in the Soviet Union.

Chapter Nineteen

CONCLUSIONS: THE CONTEMPORARY ERA

OUR GENERAL CONCLUSIONS regarding the process of modernization in Japan and Russia in the contemporary era are that both have moved substantially toward the levels of development achieved by the highly modernized Western societies, but that Japan has moved further in this direction than the U.S.S.R. The faster social change in Japan may be attributed both to its easier transition from the policies of transformation to those required for sustaining highly modernized societies and to its greater experience with intensive development as a premodern society.

The Japanese and Soviet developments that have prompted these conclusions provide the basis, in terms of the five categories of comparison employed in this study, for a consideration of the problems faced by latecomers in making the transition from policies fostering rapid transformation to those that meet the needs of highly modernized societies. We also wish to consider in more general terms the patterns formed by this transition as they reflect the earlier experiences of the two countries.

International Context

One is impressed by the resiliency of relatively modernized societies such as Japan and Russia in the 1940's under the impact of the extensive destruction that resulted from the Second World War. One of the best indications that modernization does not consist primarily in factories and railroads but rather in human resources is the quick recovery made by Japan and the Soviet Union, as well as by Germany and other countries, despite great material losses.

Though the talents and abilities needed for a speedy recovery from the destructiveness of twentieth-century warfare may be available to any modernized country, the qualities necessary for further rapid modernization are less readily acquired. In this regard the capacity of the Japanese and Russians for renewed development has been notable. In neither country was the adjustment toward the requirements of high modernization accomplished with great ease. The Japanese scenario repeated the drama of the early Meiji period: an abrupt change in leadership and an official rejection of the past in favor of foreign models, both of which introduced a new stable setting for rapid modernization. After the end of the American occupation, momentum was maintained without further abrupt transformations. The corresponding evolution in the U.S.S.R. also produced a change in personnel following the death of Stalin in 1953, but with more vacillation regarding the style of leadership and the international environment.

The development of international relations since the 1940's has had a telling effect on the capacity of these two countries both for borrowing and for generating new technology in an era in which sophisticated technology has become a critical factor for maintaining the levels of manufacturing and services. In this respect there has been a marked contrast between Japan's development and the slower adjustment of the Soviet Union. In addition to systemic differences in institutional heritage, an important contributing factor has been the cold war. This time of tension resulted in an annual investment of some 10 per cent of Soviet resources in defense, proportionally ten times more than Japan's allocation for this purpose. It was also accompanied by a limited but substantial boycott in the technological realm by the more advanced Western countries. For Japan it was a period of rapid assimilation of Western technology. A related but essentially independent factor is represented by the xenophobic cast of postwar Soviet ideology. At critical points Soviet leaders have tended to regard foreign ideas as subversive, and during the initial postwar decade they isolated Russian intellectuals to a considerable extent from developments in the West.

The relative but nevertheless significant decline in Soviet rates of growth in the 1960's, accompanying the achievement of strategic parity with the United States, appears to have been one of the principal factors leading to the détente registered in the Soviet-American agreement of May 1972. Highly modernized societies seem to require the type of extensive involvement with other countries that Japan has enjoyed since the Second World War. Thanks to its more competitive technological skills, Japan has been better prepared than the Soviet Union for the challenges of interdependence. The fact that Japan is extensively dependent on other countries for raw materials as well as markets has made it very vulnerable during the energy crisis in the 1970's, and it is undertaking a flexible adjustment by diversifying its sources of supply and developing alternative types of energy. For the Soviet Union the costs of many years of hostile relations with highly modernized societies have been great, with the result that it has been slower to take advantage of the opportunities offered by détente than many expected.

Political Structure

An important similarity between Japan and the U.S.S.R. is the decrease in overt coercion by the state by contrast with the prewar period. The techniques of mobilizing support and political participation and of dealing with opposition have come to be based more upon legal guarantees and positive responses to major interest groups. If the glorification of the Japanese emperors and of the party chief Stalin is considered, along with the intolerance of diversity during the 1930's, these changes represent remarkable accomplishments.

Yet in this realm also the Soviet development has been much slower than the Japanese. The highly centralized direction that proved so effective in mobilizing Soviet society during the early five-year plans, and that carried the U.S.S.R. to victory in the Second World War, became an obstacle to adaptation when a greater complexity of society called for more flexibility and experimentation. The political leaders have had some success since the war in mobilizing Russia's extensive natural resources and in developing the skills of its peoples. But measures looking toward decentralization in the interest of efficient management are still perceived as a threat to the Communist Party's monopoly of power, and long-term change continues to depend on the gradual rise to positions of authority of younger officials with a less doctrinaire training and outlook. In Japan, by contrast, defeat served to weaken the influence of an older generation devoted to existing practices and brought a younger generation that was more pragmatic. These instances serve to underscore the fundamental importance of political systems, and the difficulties of changing them to meet the demands of high modernization.

Economic Structure and Growth

The search for new growth mechanisms to sustain and to accelerate economic development has involved greater reliance on acquiring and utilizing technological innovations. To attain growth in advanced industrial societies, the decision-making process and the incentive system must be modified from the prevailing practices of the transformation period. In the command economy of the U.S.S.R., the noncompetitiveness and centralized nature of the bureaucracy has inhibited this innovational process. The economic reforms that occurred in the twenty years after the death of Stalin were only partially successful in altering the methods of mobilization that had served their purpose in the early five-year plans. The Japanese economy, on the other hand, shows what can be achieved by much more extensive reliance on technological innovation. Favored both by the accession to influence of a new generation of pragmatic leaders and by a promising international environment, the Japanese drew on their heritage of competition in the international market to good effect.

In the 1970's Japan has surpassed Russia by a considerable margin in its rates of both savings and growth, and in the restructuring of its economic institutions along the lines called for by technology-intensive production for a consumer market. At the same time, Japan's economy is deeply dependent upon other nations for its raw materials, and is therefore more vulnerable to changing conditions of the international market. The widespread adoption and management of foreign technology has been much slower in the U.S.S.R., primarily for administrative and political reasons. Lacking the challenge of economic interdependence that has stimulated Japan's productivity, the Soviet Union has nevertheless been much freer from the vagaries of foreign trade.

Social Interdependence

Mutual cooperation and involvement acquire new meaning in the contemporary highly urbanized setting. The small family still practicing forms of ancestor commemoration and marriage arrangement, and the large corporation offering a paternalistic security and incremental salary based largely on seniority, preserve and cement critical bonds of solidarity in Japan. Ritualized support for the

Communist Party and the frequent exhortations to serve the collective operate in a less awesome way than in the years of Stalinism in favor of conformity in Russia. Intense group pressure on the individual to succeed now reaches a peak in both countries with the crucial entrance examinations to higher education. After graduation, more subtle pressures prevail with respect to the important task of labor motivation.

Mass demand for heavy consumer goods permeates modernized societies. New expectations convert the international environment into a bountiful, though not necessarily readily accessible, source of conveniences and fashions. Consumer motivations make possible new forms of control and coordination, while old forms based on more modest standards of living become outmoded. Both Japan and Russia have made numerous adjustments to the new age of consumption. In the U.S.S.R. these adjustments have been partial, as light industrial production remains a low priority and numerous goods continue to be in short supply. New channels for the enjoyment of leisure have been opening, however, including a vacation cult centering on such resort areas as the coast of the Black Sea. Japanese consumers since the 1960's have had much more unrestricted access to goods and services, while the frustrations have been those of space and crowding. Sought-after items appear in large supply and in a wide assortment. Indicative of the greater emphasis given to consumer tastes is the larger proportion of the Japanese labor force in the service sector.

Again the comparison of these two countries reveals a speedier and more complete adjustment to the conditions of high modernization in Japan. Conditions of Soviet life have not improved as quickly nor has labor motivation been equal to the tasks set forth in recent state plans. With plentiful jobs in both countries capable of supporting a minimal standard of living, the problem of motivation to encourage educational success and labor productivity has become centered in the availability of a new array of goods and services. The switch from Spartan conditions to more luxurious living may not necessarily lead to greater happiness, social consciousness, or environmental preservation, but it does seem to provide motivation for a higher rate of further modernization.

Knowledge and Education

It is in this period of high modernization that secondary and university education becomes available to a large portion of the population. Whereas the preconditions for modernization involve a considerable development of a primary education and specialized training for a select few, and the transitional process requires the development of universal primary education and tremendous growth in secondary education, it is only during high modernization that higher education comes to serve the average or better than average student. In both Japan and Russia aspirations for higher education have been at the center of individual expectations and ambitions; they have been encouraged by the governments' own policies and by economic realities. Hence the ability of governments to meet this new demand without impairing further economic development becomes a prime test of their overall effectiveness at the stage of high modernization.

With this summary of our findings regarding the five categories we have employed in this study, let us now consider how the patterns that they form relate to those of the premodern and transformation stages. We are particularly impressed, as our analysis of the modernization process in Japan and Russia indicates, with the extent to which the policies required by latecomers for achieving and sustaining high modernization differ from those of transformation, and also with the political problems faced by leaders in making this transition.

The experience of Japan and Russia points to the conclusion that latecomers to modernization require greater political control and coordination than early modernizers during their transformation if they are to achieve similar levels of development. Not only must they create networks of transportation, develop natural resources, construct manufacturing plants, and resettle a substantial proportion of the population from rural to urban environments (with all that this entails in the provision of food, education, and housing) more rapidly than early modernizers, but they must achieve these results while also engaged in the various tasks of nation-building: defending and consolidating national territories, formulating more effective systems of national administration, and adapting practices of political participation to changing interest groups and new expectations on the part of the public. All these prerequisites were achieved more gradually by the early modernizers, within a generally more stable domestic and international political environment.

The requirements of highly modernized societies are substantially different from those in the earlier process of transformation.

The domestic upheavals involved in changing from rural to urban settlement, from illiteracy to education, from handicrafts to manufacturing, and from local and regional autonomy to centralized government have been surmounted. The new emphasis is on degrees of specialization leading to greater international interdependence, political coordination and aggregation of a wider range of interest groups, the creation of services that engage a larger share of the labor force than manufacturing, greater social mobilization of a slowly growing population densely concentrated in urban centers, and universal secondary and extensive higher education to meet the needs of a science- and technology-intensive society.

The early modernizers were able to gain experience with the inexorable requirements of high modernization with much the same process of experimentation as that through which they met those of transformation, although they were not all equally successful in adapting their values and institutions to the new exigencies. Latecomers to modernization, by contrast, must anticipate significantly greater difficulty in making this transition. Their problem arises from the relatively greater adjustment called for in modifying the extremely centralized practices of transformation, which tend over the years to become dogmatically entrenched, and the relatively greater pragmatism that is essential in highly modernized societies.

It is in this context that the effects of the Second World War on Japan and Russia assume particular importance. In Japan that disaster broke the influence of the policies of transition that had become dogmatic articles of faith, whereas in Russia it tended to reinforce them. More generally, the record would seem to indicate that it takes a major change of leadership to destroy the authority of those wedded to the policies that become accepted wisdom during the era of transformation, and to bring to power those prepared to make the changes in priorities and institutions called for by high modernization.

The defeat of Japan in 1945 was such a national disaster, and the change in leadership was sufficiently profound, despite the survival of many prewar bureaucrats, to permit a fresh and pragmatic approach to the problems of the contemporary era. The depression that started in 1929 marked a comparable break in continuity in the United States, although a much lesser one to be sure, and the basic changes in the relationship of the public and private sectors introduced by the New Deal have become the characteristic American pattern of high modernization. Similarly, the political and economic transformations that have taken place in Germany and Italy since 1945, and less dramatically France since the national crisis produced by the Algerian war in the 1950's, have been the result of a new leadership that would have gained influence only much more gradually, if at all, without the challenge of defeat.

No doubt a country can make both the initial transition from premodern to transformational policies, and the later one from policies of transformation to those of high modernization, through the gradual process of adaptation brought about by generational changes in attitudes, but various interest groups become so entrenched that fundamental, essential changes in policy become difficult in the absence of crisis. The ability of political leaders to make the transition from transformation to high modernization in the contemporary era is profoundly affected by the extent to which strongly established policies are weakened or broken by a national crisis.

In this respect the Soviet Union represents a contrast with Japan in that victory in the Second World War had the effect of strengthening the accepted practices of the past generation and therefore of delaying the accession to influence of policymakers anxious to adapt Soviet values and institutions to new challenges. Most foreign observers associate "Stalinism" with repressive measures against political opponents, yet within Russia this term refers primarily to excessive administrative centralization. While monolithic decision-making may have been necessary when the main task was to industrialize a predominantly peasant society, in the contemporary era it can become an obstacle to the types of flexibility and experimentation called for by a consumer economy and by consumer-related institutions and political and social values. Stalin's death did not result in any meaningful, long-term change in bureaucratic centralization, and only the slow processes of the generational replacement of personnel have brought a gradual transformation in outlook. The Soviet political system, one with a radical ideology, has been relatively slow in adapting to the continuing challenge of technological change. To a considerable degree, this inflexibility has been inherent in the system, but adaptability was even further inhibited by victory in the war and by the insecurity of the postwar international environment.

In seeking to understand the high rates of change achieved by Japan and the Soviet Union in the contemporary era, it is also important to consider the longer term values and institutions that derived from their premodern experiences. We conclude that Japan's pattern of premodern values and institutions—which we have described as an "intensive" approach to economic and social policy in contrast with the "extensive" Russian approach—has been of particular significance in the contemporary era. Though Japan shared with Russia the greater difficulty of latecomers, as compared with early modernizers, in making the transition from the requirements of transformation to those of highly modernized societies, it was better prepared than the U.S.S.R. for the characteristic tasks of the contemporary era. The accelerating effect of defeat and occupation would have had less influence on Japanese development if it had not been prepared by long experience to meet the technological demands of the late twentieth century.

It has already been noted that the "intensive" Japanese approach before the modern era was reflected, as of approximately 1800, in higher urbanization and literacy and in the larger administrative elite in proportion to the population at a time when Russia was well in advance in its knowledge and use of modern techniques of manufacturing and communications. More generally, Japan increased output by a greater input of skills as Russia sought to achieve the same results by a greater input of material resources and manpower. This greater experience with technology-intensive methods stood Japan in good stead when it had to compete in international trade during the period of transformation without the benefit of protective tariffs. In the contemporary era, with ever greater effectiveness, Japan's intensive employment of skills has led to unprecedented economic growth. In Russia backwardness in advanced technology is acknowledged as a painful shortcoming.

Chapter Twenty

IMPLICATIONS FOR MODERNIZATION

BEFORE CONSIDERING the implications of this study for a more general understanding of modernization, it would be well to recall a few important similarities and differences between the factors which account for the rapid pace of modernization in Japan and Russia. The most striking and previously overlooked similarities existed in the premodern period. These two countries stood out—among societies prior to initial modernization—for coordination, control and mobilization of resources on an exceptional scale. These unusual capabilities which they possessed were well suited for adaptation to modern uses.

Similarly persistent differences between the two countries can be traced back to contrasting orientations in the use of resources before the 1860's. In the premodern period, Japan had much higher rates of urbanization and literacy, and this reflected the more highly organized character of its society. Russia, for its part, was in close touch with the West and was much better acquainted with modern thought and technology before its societal transformation accelerated in the 1860's. It was also much more richly endowed with natural resources (including sparsely settled arable land) and employed them lavishly, while densely settled Japan developed a greater capacity for organizing what would prove to be a relatively poor base of natural resources for modernization. This difference in resource utilization we have characterized as an "intensive" approach to social organization and change on the part of Japan, as compared with an "extensive" approach on the part of Russia.

This study identifies similarities not only in the presence of preconditions, but also in the speedy realization of requirements for transformation and for high modernization. Japan and Russia were able to transmute their earlier capabilities after the 1860's through reforms, and later in the Russian case through revolution as well, into policies that took advantage of the opportunities offered by the scientific and technological revolution. Remarkable parallels in the decade-by-decade transformation of the two societies over more than a century emerge in each area examined. Japan's more integrated society and, perhaps, its more marginal involvement in World War I, contributed to its survival during the period of transformation without a revolutionary upheaval. Following World War II, Japan has evidenced a greater capacity for adapting to the technology-intensive methods of high modernization, an adaptation aided by the accession to power of a new generation of leaders. Soviet administrative methods have proved to be more rigid, and the highly centralized approach of the earlier period has been slow to change.

Yet, for each of the three periods we assign more importance to the similarities than to the differences. Already in the premodern period, Japan and Russia seem to stand apart from much of the world. Whereas one rightly looks to the history of England and France for the roots of modernization, one might also, and with more relevance for the vast majority of societies, look to Japan and Russia for an understanding of the preconditions of rapid modernization for latecomers. As societies in transformation, they both experienced increased coordination and control while doing things more rapidly and on a much larger scale than the early modernizers had. And in the contemporary era they have continued to exhibit significant similarities in rapidly acquiring the characteristics of highly modernized societies. Being among the few latecomers to have approached the level of modernization attained by the firstcomers to this process, they provide records deserving careful analysis by those concerned with the problems of societal transformation.

Japan, Russia, and the Problem of Models for Modernization

At the conclusion of this study it is appropriate to ask whether either Japan or Russia, or the two nations together, constitute a distinctive model for modernization, and if so, whether any specific aspects of that model are of relevance to the several score of less developed latecomers. Such questions, after all, have underlain much of the literature on development and have frequently been raised with regard to the two nations studied here.

The early modernizing societies of Western Europe and the New World have often been taken by some as the primary models. They have been seen as an inexhaustible source of specific techniques and institutions to be borrowed or adapted by societies seeking to achieve more advanced forms of economic and social development. Many have challenged such a conception, however, basing their views on their analysis of various latecomers to modernization, such as Japan and Russia among others. To be sure, both the Japanese and the Soviets have borrowed extensively throughout their history, and in the recent period have relied heavily on "Western" prototypes. But the evidence presented in this book indicates that their borrowing has been highly selective, with numerous and major institutions of the prototype nation being all but ignored even as others were carefully studied and assimilated.

It is significant that many of the characteristics shared by Japan and Russia, which we have labeled the preconditions of rapid modernization, and the requirements of transformation and of high modernization, are similar to those of the early modernizing societies of Western Europe and the New World. To this extent Japan and Russia, and a few other late modernizing societies that have achieved a similar level of development, may be regarded as forming, together with the early modernizing societies, a common pattern of premodern and modernizing characteristics that we are inclined to regard as generally valid. As already noted, these common characteristics include capacities for centralized political control and coordination, for the management of resources in support of economic growth, for the encouragement of social interdependence, and for the production and distribution of knowledge through research and education. Essentially, these characteristics represent the ability of leaders, through public and private institutions, to mobilize the resources of a society for the purposes of modernization.

Japan and Russia—and a limited number of later modernizers—share these basic characteristics with the early modernizing societies. But as latecomers they also possess a distinctive characteristic: the capacity, within their political institutions, to withstand the much greater stresses that accompany the simultaneous pressures of transforming a society and of preserving its integrity in an environment of advanced societies, societies that are both an example and a threat.

One major conclusion of this study is that the kind of borrowing of institutions and techniques in which Japan and Russia both engaged so successfully is possible only under quite unusual circumstances. It is possible, in other words, when the borrower nation is capable of maintaining a concert of coordination and control between governmental leaders and a variety of domestic interest groups in a period of rapid institutional changes and of rising public expectations of political participation. Any claim that detailed aspects of the strategy of development used by either Japan or Russia might serve as prototypes on which other latecomers could pattern themselves would have to be grounded in an assessment of the particular borrower nation involved. If the process of borrowing of Western models by Japan and Russia is any indication, there is every reason to believe that features borrowed successfully in turn from Japan and Russia will have unanticipated consequences. After all, these features will also change contexts for the borrower, which are in turn foreign to Japan and Russia. If the borrower is incapable of modifying the new prototype to the extent necessary to fit its own circumstances without a loss of efficacy for modernization, no aura of "modernity" acquired from Japan or Russia as prototypes will of its own accord be conferred on the borrower.

The record to date makes it appear still less likely that Japanese or Russian institutions and techniques will provide easily borrowable patterns for other nations. With the partial exception of the period of its imperial adventures in the second quarter of this century, Japan has been notably reluctant to advance its own system as a prototype for others. Late-developing nations have not generally found Japanese practices to be readily transferable to their own conditions even when they would like to borrow them, although the study of Taiwan and Korea from this point of view might be useful. Soviet institutions and practices have served as patterns in the East European states reorganized under Russian influence after the Second World War, and, to some extent, in Cuba, Yugoslavia, and China. Though it may well be convenient to analyze the forms of institutional life in these countries under some general rubric of "Communist states," it is increasingly apparent that the differences among them reflect the considerable range of human and institutional resources of each society on the eve of its reorganization.

Stated differently, the Japanese and Soviet institutions and practices which could serve as prototypes are the product not only of the recent history of both countries, but of a constant interaction over the past century of new practices with a multitude of preconditions possessed by these countries even before the process of transformation began. The unlikelihood that latecomers will possess all the preconditions present in Japan and Russia a century ago, the extensive changes in the international environment of all nations

during the contemporary era, and the already considerable experience with modernization in most societies today, militate against
the successful application of either the Japanese or Russian prototype. Only further comparative study of late-developing nations will
make it possible to clarify the extent to which they will be able to
utilize specific patterns developed by Japan or Russia.

This is not to say that the Japanese and Russian experience has
no greater relevance to late-developing countries than does the experience of the early developers. On the contrary, this study points
to the conclusion that these two countries have a singular importance
to latecomers in that they have been remarkably effective in facing
the problems inherent to modernization. But assuming they do have
relevance, how is one to identify what is really crucial in their experience? Surely capitalist Japan and socialist Russia present abstract
principles of development as different from each other as the specific
institutions in which Japan's capitalism and Russia's socialism are
embodied.

Although this study has emphasized what we believe to be the
underlying similarities that exist between Japan and Russia, an effort
has also been made to appreciate the differences. At one level of
generalization it is fair to say that these differences are as sharp as
any that can be found between two nations at comparable stages of
development. Capitalism and communism are crucial elements in
this contrast and, of course, must be given due stress when speaking
of the most recent era. But because they affect only the last half
century, they scarcely constitute the basic juxtaposition running
through the entire histories of the two countries. The persistent difference between Japan and Russia, as noted at various points in this
study, is their contrasting pattern in the use of resources, namely in
Japan's "intensive" utilization of resources as opposed to Russia's
"extensive" use. This contrast would have been as valid in 1700 as it
is today, and it has left a stamp on their respective practice of
capitalism and communism that is so strong as to set each off from
other nations living under one or the other same general system.
With regard to the form of the overall development of the two
countries, the intensive-extensive distinction would appear to be
more basic in nature than the ideological distinctions that have
loomed so large in most treatments of this subject.

Notwithstanding this difference and certain other contrasts, at
higher levels of generalization there exist similarities between the
development of Japan and of Russia that are so fundamental as to
justify their being taken as the basis for a distinctive analytic model

of modernization. These similarities, we believe, lie not so much in any policies that either state has pursued during the past generation (although in many respects they are comparable) as in the preconditions present in both countries over a century ago. These preconditions, considered in detail in Chapter 7, include, in addition to those noted below, a degree of political integration, an economy capable of producing a surplus for investment, the foundations of an educational system, and relatively advanced urban and commercial development. They provide a basis for identifying a single pattern to which Japanese and Russian modernization conforms.

A cursory glance at this list of factors critical to the development of two successful latecomers suggests the extent of the difference between Japan and Russia, on the one hand, and most early developers on the other. To be sure, the preconditions for England, France, and the United States, for example, would include most of these elements. But for Japan and Russia the capacity of their successive governments to coordinate and control social energies, to mobilize resources, and to borrow selectively from abroad assume particular importance. Of earlier developing nations, perhaps only for Germany did these three characteristics figure so centrally in the process of modernization, probably because in many respects Germany was also the first successful latecomer. As early as the 1920's Thorstein Veblen called attention to similarities in the development of Germany and Japan, and a half century earlier both Russia and Japan had been drawn to German antecedents.

Such broad contrasts between the development of the Western countries and of these two successful latecomers underscore the truth that modernization is not a static or unitary process, and not a Western one either. The requirements of a country that began to modernize in the eighteenth century, when there were no precedents, were different from the requirements of a country entering the process a century later. To describe the process as a whole, all the changed local and international circumstances of late-developing nations must be taken into account. The pattern of development established by the Western nations that developed early is neither right nor wrong today. It is, however, ill-suited to describing a process that has changed in important respects and hence should be replaced by a pattern more relevant to latecomers.

Few today would deny that an analysis of the experience of Japan and Russia can substantially revise one's view of the Western pattern of development. What is not so clear is the extent to which the lessons drawn from Japanese and Russian experience will also have to

be revised before they can serve as a model to the process of modernization in the majority of other late-developing nations, especially
in those that lack the preconditions possessed by Japan and Russia
when they began the process of transformation. Such a question
cannot be answered on the basis of material covered in this study. Yet
because it is clearly of great moment, the relevance of the Japanese
and Russian experience deserves due consideration.

The Process of Modernization for Other Latecomers

The study of the process of modernization for latecomers should
begin with the realization of the vital distinction between the commonalities of all latecomers and their variances from one another
on the eve of contacts with the early modernizing societies. All latecomers face common problems in adapting to the patterns of modernization. Nevertheless, they vary greatly in their capacity for
institutional innovation through conversion and borrowing. The
first objective of research on latecomers should therefore be to determine what capacities were provided by their pre-existing social structure for taking advantage of the opportunities offered by the scientific and technological revolution.

For the most part, studies of premodern societies have not been
comparative; and, at least until recently, little has been known about
relative levels of development. The conclusion in this volume that
Japan and Russia by 1800 had reached advanced premodern development in comparison with other societies that were to become latecomers is based on recent reevaluations of the Tokugawa period by
specialists on Japan, on the extensively documented studies by Soviet
historians on the "seeds of capitalism" present in seventeenth- and
eighteenth-century Russia, on Western and Soviet study of Russian
political institutions, and on comparative studies using the urban-
networks approach. Systematic study of other premodern societies is
needed to determine their developmental progress. Such comparative study should also test the alternative hypothesis that the capability of societies for modernization, which we have discussed in this
volume in terms of preconditions, is not necessarily a direct function
of a stage of premodern development. Petroleum-exporting states in
the 1970's and 1980's, for example, although lacking most of the
preconditions characteristic of Japan and Russia, may be able to
achieve an overnight transformation by the interim use of unprecedented rates of per capita investment.

In considering the relevance of the Japanese and Russian experience to the problems of later modernizing societies, the critical differences in their premodern experiences must be analyzed. Only a few such societies resemble Japan and Russia in having experienced a continuity of territory and enduring central political institutions before the modern era. These include China, Korea, the Ottoman-Turkish empire, Persia-Iran, Abyssinia-Ethiopia, Siam-Thailand, and Afghanistan. The last two, and perhaps also Persia-Iran, preserved their political integrity less from internal strength than because they were able to maintain a precarious balance among conflicting great-power pressures. All of these countries were forced to grant varying degrees of privilege to the interests of more advanced countries, but none succumbed to colonialism for more than brief periods.

Other later modernizing societies, such as those of Latin America and the Caribbean, were formed as colonial outposts of European states. Even after gaining political independence they continued to reflect colonial characteristics in their exploitation of native majorities and former African slaves by minorities of European origin, and in their cultural and economic dependence on Europe and later on North America. Modernizing leaders in some of these countries—in contrast with those in the United States, Canada, Australia, and New Zealand—failed to gain dominant political influence until the second half of the twentieth century.

The one hundred or more societies of Asia, Africa, and Oceania that now form independent states have had little or no premodern experience with political integration. They constitute groups of peoples with diverse ethnic and political loyalties brought together under national governments for the first time. Most European governments faced similar problems of nation-building in the eighteenth and nineteenth centuries, but they were sufficiently advanced in economic development and social interdependence to be able to transform their societies despite the handicaps of disunity. The European wars and compromises of the nineteenth and twentieth centuries represent a part of the price paid in this process of reorganization and consolidation of peoples. In Europe this process has produced considerable stability under the conditions of the 1970's. In Asia, Africa, and Oceania, however, which are starting in the twentieth century from much lower levels of political integration, economic development, and social interdependence, it seems more likely than not that the process of reorganizing and consolidating peoples will be at least as prolonged and agonized as it was in Europe.

Japan and Russia were unusual in having structures readily convertible to radically increased needs for coordination and control. Most other societies, it appears, lack these capabilities. One objective of further research might be to specify how Japan and Russia varied prior to contacts with modernization in terms of the vulnerability of their principal structures of control and in the extent to which a foundation existed for activating new controls during the initial period of transformation. One implication for other latecomers would seem to be that they must first go through a series of conversions of political structures until patterns of control and coordination are established that are centrally oriented and relatively invulnerable to local and family influences. This process has taken place or is taking place in China now.

From the evidence presented on Japan and Russia we have concluded that successful latecomers to modernization all have certain important similarities and that the ability to achieve rapid modernization is a predictable consequence of identifiable conditions in the premodern period. Further research should test this conclusion and study the continuum of eighteenth-, nineteenth-, and twentieth-century societies varying in the extent to which they possessed conditions conducive to achieving modernization as latecomers. As the tools for comparing premodern societies become more refined, the objectives of this research might be to: (1) specify the preconditions of successful latecomers (based on a wider study than the comparison of two countries undertaken here); (2) compare the preconditions of latecomers to those of the early modernizing societies (attempted only briefly and tentatively in this study); and (3) arrange premodern societies along a continuum with respect to both the stage of development reached and the convertibility of existing patterns of control and coordination. In all this research, of course, the starting point for the further study of modernization should be a comparison of premodern societies.

Other societies have encountered a more burdensome task than Japan and Russia in meeting the requirements of modernization. Some have found that as old forms of control and coordination were undermined and new technologies, cities, and organizational forms were grafted onto pre-existing conditions, they had to search for alternative paths to modernization. Whether immediately or only after repeated setbacks, leaders in every case began to grope to find suitable strategies to accelerate the course of modernization. In this process of search for and application of new methods of modernization there is no reason to doubt that a country poorly endowed at the start with capabilities for modernization could actually meet with greater success than one inheriting a superior starting position. What would be required of these countries would be policies making maximal use of those assets available from their past together with efforts to seek and apply constructive alternatives as quickly as possible for those preconditions that are absent. The process of seeking alternatives is not used here in the sense of "borrowing," for substitutes must also have relevance to a nation's past. In light of the changing international environment, the methods for realizing the advantages of legacies from the past and, in the process, of borrowing from abroad to make up for internal deficiencies and to strengthen internal assets must continually be informed by the most recent worldwide conditions.

Similarities between Japan and Russia have proven instructive in determining what the requirements of successful latecomers are. On the basis of these similarities, we believe that other latecomers must fulfill the same requirements, taking care to do so in a balanced way because steps toward meeting one requirement produce ramifications for others. Regrettably, a comparison of two countries, both of which experienced their major modernizing transformations at a time when the international environment was different in important respects from that of today and tomorrow, does not permit going beyond an initial statement of possible requirements for latecomers and an introduction to the relationship of alternatives to certain germane preconditions. The opportunities for further research along these lines, however, appear especially promising. Such research should take into account the following set of priorities: (1) specifying the requirements of successful latecomers; (2) identifying the requirements for which countries with various missing preconditions had to find substitutions; (3) determining the ways in which changes in the international environment have altered the task of finding substitutions; and (4) arranging latecomers in a continuum with respect to the degree to which they have developed alternatives to the missing preconditions. The lessons of the rapid modernization achieved by Japan and Russia do not provide a single model to be followed, but they do focus attention on certain universal requirements for modernization and on the blend of past and present necessary for meeting them.

At this point, it is appropriate to consider the special relevance of comparisons between Japan and Russia for the modernization of China. Similar to Japan and Russia, China is a large-scale society, reflecting a continuity of territory and population going back many centuries. No more than in Russia did revolution signify that the past was irrelevant to the future. Beginning the modernization experience painfully slowly, China has recently accelerated its pace of change and today evokes great interest owing to the emergence of what in many respects appears to be a new model for meeting the requirements of modernization.

As a premodern society China represents an intermediate case between Japan and Russia, both of which had a great capacity for change at the start of the modern era, and numerous other societies, which seem to have had less capacity. In many respects China had reached an advanced stage of development by the sixteenth century, but clearly had been outdistanced by Japan and Russia by the nineteenth. China, too, had the advantages of a long tradition of unified, centralized government at the national level, yet had considerable difficulty in converting to new patterns of control and coordination at local levels.

Since 1949 the Chinese seem to have accomplished what few other peoples have done. They have gone from a basis of coordination and control highly decentralized and family-oriented to one capable of a much greater degree of coordination and one oriented to some conception of the Chinese entity as a whole. Among latecomers generally, it is exactly this extension of the mechanisms of control from the central to the local levels that remains problematic. Instability and disorder plague the attempts to reestablish social control on a new foundation. Careful study of the history of modernization in China in the light of this comparison of Japan and Russia should provide a firmer basis for generalizing about the relation between preconditions and alternatives.

While the interests of some of the authors and, perhaps, of the readers as well will turn from Japan to Russia to China for further consideration of the implications of this study, we anticipate that the comparisons carried out here have relevance also to many other countries involved in the modernizing transformation. The argument that these conclusions have relevance for China rests on the existence of general similarities between it and Japan and Russia in the stage they reached of premodern development, in the scale of the three countries, and in the extent of their isolation, at least during the early phases of modernization. Moreover, China explicitly adopted the Soviet model of modernization for a time. The same kinds of considerations may serve to distinguish between other countries to which the findings of the Japanese and Russian comparisons are applied. Special attention should be given to the variables of scale, isolation, models followed, and stage in the transformation already reached.

Just as conditions present in premodern societies facilitate or complicate the transformation to modernized societies, programs selected to realize rapid modernization have consequences for the subsequent phase of sustaining high rates of modernization. We have concluded that the adjustment to advanced modernization was earlier in Japan than in the Soviet Union. To a considerable extent this difference was inherent in earlier strategies. Stalinist methods are likely to produce similar complications elsewhere. Although we anticipate that few leaders would be deterred by the prospects of long-range problems when short-term results appear promising, nonetheless they should be aware of the implications of policies chosen during the period of transformation for the next stage of modernization. Japan's recent advantage over the U.S.S.R. in the rate of modernization suggests that it is desirable to avoid a highly authoritarian approach to the problem of transformation despite the undeniable need for strict control and coordination.

Further research on this phase of modernization can also be anticipated, though it must necessarily be limited in scope owing to the small number of countries that have proceeded this far. Among the priorities for further research we envision: (1) specifying the special requirements for sustaining rapid modernization in the phase of high modernization of latecomers (based again on a wider study than the tentative conclusions advanced here); (2) comparing these special requirements with those of the early modernizing societies to see if they have become identical to the functional requirements of the period of transformation; and (3) arranging advanced modernized societies in a continuum according to the degree in which they meet these requirements.

In conclusion we would like to suggest some general guidelines for further study of modernization. We recommend as the form for such studies direct and systematic comparisons among societies and among different stages of societal development. Numerous individual studies already exist on separate countries, but the kind of direct comparison that we have attempted to carry out of the major structural aspects of two large-scale societies is still rare. Such comparisons should be repeated and improved upon. We likewise favor a longitudinal approach to social change. In the conclusions of this study particular attention has been given to the relationship between premodern societies and the requirements of modernization, and between the methods of successful transformation and the adjustments for high modernization. It is desirable that other studies should also bridge these periods. We also believe that processes as multidimensional as modernization should be studied collaboratively by historians and representatives of other social science disciplines. Close collaboration that is not simply confined to an exchange of papers and joint publication should be a prime objective in future studies of modernization. Finally, for scholarship to be cumulative, a single study must be designed to open the horizons for a series of additional studies. We offer this comparison of Japan and Russia in the hope that it will inspire further research on the problems of modernization.

BIBLIOGRAPHY

The sources on which the authors of this study have drawn derive from their research and writing over the years. Most of the important work on the development of Japan and Russia is in the languages of these two countries.

This relatively brief bibliography is designed not for specialists in Japanese and Russian studies, but for those primarily interested in the comparative study of modernization who wish to pursue further the topics treated in this volume.

Modernization

APTER, DAVID, *The Politics of Modernization* (Chicago: University of Chicago Press 1965).

BANKS, ARTHUR S., *Cross-Polity Time-Series Data* (Cambridge: MIT Press 1971).

BANKS, ARTHUR S., AND ROBERT TEXTOR, *A Cross-Polity Survey* (Cambridge: MIT Press 1964).

BASTER, NANCY, ed., *Measuring Development: The Role and Adequacy of Development Indicators* (London: Cass 1972).

BELL, DANIEL, *The Coming of the Post-Industrial Society* (New York: Basic Books 1973).

BINDER, LEONARD, JAMES S. COLEMAN, JOSEPH LaPALOMBARA, LUCIAN W. PYE, SIDNEY VERBA, AND MYRON WEINER, *Crises and Sequences in Political Development* (Princeton: Princeton University Press 1971).

BLACK, CYRIL E., ed., *Comparative Modernizaton: A Reader* (New York: Free Press 1976).

BLACK, CYRIL E., *The Dynamics of Modernization: A Study in Comparative History* (New York: Harper & Row 1966).

BRODE, J., *The Process of Modernization: An Annotated Bibliography on the Socio-Cultural Aspects of Modernization* (Cambridge: Harvard University Press 1969).

DESAI, A. R., ed., *Essays on Modernization of Underdeveloped Societies,* 2 vols. (New York: Humanities Press 1971).

DEUTSCH, KARL W., *The Nerves of Government: Models of Political Communication and Control* (New York: Free Press 1963).

EISENSTADT, S. N., *Modernization: Protest and Change* (Englewood Cliffs, N.J.: Prentice-Hall 1966).

EISENSTADT, S. N., *The Political System of Empires: The Rise and Fall of Hstorical Bureaucratic Societies* (New York: Free Press 1963).

FLORA, PETER, *Modernisierungsforschung: Zur empirischen Analyse der gesellschaftlichen Entwicklung* [Modernization research: toward empirical analysis of societal development] (Opladen: Westdeutscher Verlag 1974).

FREY, F. W., ed., *Survey Research on Comparative Social Change: A Bibliography* (Cambridge: MIT Press 1968).

GEERTZ, CLIFFORD, ed., *Old Societies and New States: The Quest for Modernity in Asia and Africa* (New York: Free Press 1963).

GEIGER, H. KENT, *National Development, 1776–1966: A Selective and Annotated Guide to the Most Important Articles in English* (Metuchen, N.J.: Scarecrow Press 1969).

HOSELITZ, BERT F., AND WILBERT E. MOORE, eds., *Industrialization and Society* (The Hague: Mouton 1963).

HOROWITZ, I. L., *Three Worlds of Development: The Theory and Practice of International Stratification* (New York: Oxford University Press 1966).

HUNTINGTON, SAMUEL P., *Political Order in Changing Societies* (New Haven: Yale University Press 1964).

INKELES, ALEX, AND DAVID H. SMITH, *Becoming Modern: Individual Change in Six Developing Countries* (Cambridge: Harvard University Press 1974).

KAUTSKY, JOHN H., *The Political Consequences of Modernization* (New York: Wiley 1972).

KUUSINEN, O. V. et al., *Fundamentals of Marxism-Leninism,* 2nd rev. ed., trans. Clemens Dutt (Moscow: Foreign Languages Publishing House 1963).

LAGOS MATOS, GUSTAVO, *International Stratification and Underdeveloped Countries* (Chapel Hill: University of North Carolina Press 1963).

LEVY, MARION J., JR., *Modernization: Latecomers and Survivors* (New York: Basic Books 1972).

LEVY, MARION J., JR., *Modernization and the Structure of Society: A Setting for International Affairs,* 2 vols. (Princeton: Princeton University Press 1966).

MERRITT, R. L., AND S. ROKKAN, eds., *Comparing Nations: The Use of Quantitative Data in Cross-National Research* (New Haven: Yale University Press 1966).

MOORE, BARRINGTON, JR., *Social Origins of Dictatorship and Democracy: Lord and Peasant in the Making of the Modern World* (Boston: Beacon Press 1966).

POGGIE, JOHN J., JR., AND ROBERT N. LYNCH, eds., *Rethinking Modernization: Anthropological Perspectives* (Westport, Conn.: Greenwood Press 1974).

RICHTA, RODOVAN et al., *Civilization at the Crossroads: Social and Human Implications of the Scientific and Technological Revolution,* trans. Marian Slingova (New York: International Arts and Sciences Press 1968).

RUSSETT, BRUCE M., ed., *World Handbook of Political and Social Indicators* (New Haven: Yale University Press 1964).

RUSTOW, D. A., *A World of Nations: Problems of Political Modernization* (Washington: Brookings Institution Press 1967).

SINAI, I. ROBERT, *In Search of the Modern World* (New York: New American Library 1967).

SINAI, I. ROBERT, *The Challenge of Modernization: The West's Impact on the Non-Western World* (New York: Norton 1964).

SPITZ, ALLAN A., *Developmental Change: An Annotated Bibliography* (Lexington, Ky.: University of Kentucky Press 1969).

TAYLOR, CHARLES L., AND MICHAEL C. HUDSON, *World Handbook of Political and Social Indicators,* 2nd ed. (New Haven: Yale University Press 1972).

TOURAINE, ALAIN, *The Post-Industrial Society. Tomorrow's Social History: Classes, Conflict, and Culture in the Programmed Society* (New York: Random House 1971).

WEHLER, HANS-ULRICH, *Modernisierungstheorie und Geschichte* [Modernization theory and history] (Göttingen: Vandenhoeck & Ruprecht 1975).

WIENER, M., ed., *Modernization: The Dynamics of Growth* (New York: Basic Books 1966).

General and Comparative

ASIATIC RESEARCH CENTER, *International Conference on the Problems of Modernization in Asia* (Seoul: Korea University Press 1965).

BARGHOORN, FREDERICK C., "Soviet Russia: Orthodoxy and Adaptiveness," in *Political Culture and Political Development,* ed. Lucian W. Pye and Sidney Verba (Princeton: Princeton University Press 1965), 450–511.

BECKMANN, GEORGE M., *The Modernization of China and Japan* (New York: Harper & Row 1962).

BLACK, CYRIL E., ed., *The Transformation of Russian Society: Aspects of Social Change Since 1861* (Cambridge: Harvard University Press 1960).

BLOCK, HERBERT, *Political Arithmetic of the World Economies* (Beverly Hills: Sage 1974).

BRZEZINSKI, ZBIGNIEW, AND SAMUEL P. HUNTINGTON, *Political Power: USA/ USSR* (New York: Viking Press 1964).

CARRÈRE D'ENCAUSSE, HÉLÈNE, *L'Union soviétique de Lénine à Staline, 1917–1953* (Paris: Richelieu 1972).

COLE, ALLAN B., "Contrasting Modernization in China and Japan," *Chung Chi Journal* 4 (May 1965), 99–138.

COULBORN, RUSHTON, ed., *Feudalism in History* (Princeton: Princeton University Press 1956).

DOWSE, ROBERT E., *Modernization in Ghana and the USSR: A Comparative Study* (New York: Macmillan 1953).

EISENSTADT, S. N., AND STEIN ROKKAN, eds. *Building States and Nations,* 2 vols. (Beverly Hills: Sage Publications 1973).

FLORINSKY, MICHAEL T., *Russia: A History and an Interpretation,* 2 vols. (New York: Macmillan 1953).

GILISON, JEROME M., *British and Soviet Politics: Legitimacy and Convergence* (Baltimore: Johns Hopkins University Press 1972).

HALL, JOHN W., AND MARIUS B. JANSEN, eds., *Studies in the Institutional History of Early Modern Japan* (Princeton: Princeton University Press 1968).

HOLLANDER, PAUL, *Soviet and American Society: A Comparison* (New York: Oxford University Press 1973).

JANSEN, MARIUS B., ed., *Changing Japanese Attitudes Toward Modernization* (Princeton: Princeton University Press 1965).

KAHN, HERMAN, *The Emerging Japanese Superstate: Challenge and Response* (Englewood Cliffs, N.J.: Prentice-Hall 1970).

KASSOF, ALLEN, ed., *Prospects for Soviet Society* (New York: Praeger 1968).

KATSUDA, KICHITARO, "An Analysis of the Modernization of Russia," *Review: A Journal of the Study of Communism and Communist Countries* 29 (April 1971), 1–88.

KUYAMA, YASUSHI, AND NOBUO KOBAYASHI, eds., *Modernization and Tradi-*

tion in Japan (Nishinomiya: International Institute for Japan Studies 1969).

LARAN, MICHEL, *Russie–URSS: 1870–1970* (Paris: Masson 1973) .

LEVY, MARION J., JR., "Some Structural Problems of Modernization and 'High Modernization': China and Japan," *Proceedings of the Symposium on Economic and Social Problems of the Far East* (1962) , 445–458.

REISCHAUER, EDWIN O., *Japan: The Story of a Nation* (New York: Knopf 1970).

SANSOM, GEORGE B., *A History of Japan,* 3 vols. (Stanford: Stanford University Press 1958–1963).

SZALAI, ALEXANDER, ed., *The Use of Time: Daily Activities of Urban and Suburban Populations in Twelve Countries* (The Hague: Mouton 1972) .

TOBATA, SEIICHI, ed., *The Modernization of Japan* (Tokyo: Institute of Asian Economic Affairs 1966).

TREADGOLD, DONALD W., *The West in Russia and China: Religious and Secular Thought in Modern Times,* 2 vols. (Cambridge, Eng.: University Press 1973).

TREADGOLD, DONALD W., ed., *Soviet and Chinese Communism: Similarities and Differences* (Seattle: University of Washington Press 1969).

USSR ACADEMY OF SCIENCES, *A Short History of the USSR,* 2 vols. (Moscow 1965).

International Context

BRZEZINSKI, ZBIGNIEW, *The Fragile Blossom: Crisis and Change in Japan* (New York: Harper & Row 1972) .

CROWLEY, JAMES B., *Japan's Quest for Autonomy: National Security and Foreign Policy, 1930–1938* (Princeton: Princeton University Press 1966).

DVORNIK, FRANCIS, *The Slavs in European History* (New Brunswick: Rutgers University Press 1962).

EMMERSON, JOHN K., *Arms, Yen and Power: The Japanese Dilemma* (New York: Dunellen 1971).

GALTUNG, JOHAN, "Japan and Future World Politics," *Journal of Peace Research* 10:4 (1973), 355–385.

HELLMAN, DONALD C., *Japanese Foreign Policy and Domestic Politics: The Peace Agreement with the Soviet Union* (Berkeley and Los Angeles: University of California Press 1969).

HELLMAN, DONALD C., *Japan and East Asia: The New International Order* (New York: Praeger 1972).

KAJIMA, MORINOSUKE, *The Emergence of Japan as a World Power, 1895–1925* (Rutland, Vt.: Tuttle 1968).

KIRCHNER, WALTHER, *Commercial Relations between Russia and Europe, 1400 to 1800* (Bloomington: Indiana University Press 1966).

KOJIMA, KIYOSHI, *Japan and the Pacific Free Trade Area* (Berkeley and Los Angeles: University of California Press 1971).

KUTAKOV, LEONID N., *Japanese Foreign Policy on the Eve of the Pacific War: A Soviet View,* ed. G. A. Lensen (Tallahassee: Diplomatic Press 1972).

LEDERER, IVO J., ed., *Russian Foreign Policy: Essays in Historical Perspective* (New Haven: Yale University Press 1962).

LENSEN, GEORGE A., *Japanese Recognition of the USSR: Soviet-Japanese Relations, 1921–1930* (Tokyo: Sophia University Press 1970).

LENSEN, GEORGE A., *The Russian Push toward Japan: Russo-Japanese Relations, 1697–1875* (Princeton: Princeton University Press 1957).

MALAZEMOFF, A., *Russian Far Eastern Policy, 1881–1904* (Berkeley and Los Angeles: University of California Press 1958).

MEDLIN, WILLIAM K., *Moscow and East Rome: A Political Study of Church and State in Muscovite Russia* (Geneva: Droz 1952).

MENDEL, DOUGLAS H., *The Japanese People and Foreign Policy: A Study of Public Opinion in Post-Treaty Japan* (Berkeley and Los Angeles: University of California Press 1957).

MORLEY, JAMES W., ed., *Japan's Foreign Policy, 1868–1941: A Research Guide* (New York: Columbia University Press 1974).

OBOLENSKY, D., "Byzantium, Kiev, and Moscow: A Study in Ecclesiastical Relations," *Dumbarton Oaks Papers* 11 (1957), 23–78. Reprinted in *Byzantium and the Slavs: Collected Studies* (London: Variorum Reprints 1971).

OKAMOTO, SHUMPEI, *The Japanese Oligarchy and the Russo-Japanese War* (New York: Columbia University Press 1970).

OKITA, SABURO, "Natural Resource Dependency and Japanese Foreign Policy," *Foreign Affairs* 52 (July 1974), 714–724.

OZAKI, ROBERT S., *The Control of Imports and Foreign Capital in Japan* (New York: Praeger 1972).

PLATONOV, SERGEI F., *Moscow and the West,* trans. J. L. Wieczymski (Hattiesburg, Miss.: Academic International 1972).

SANSOM, GEORGE B., *The Western World and Japan: A Study in the Interaction of European and Asiatic Cultures* (New York: Knopf 1950).

ŠEVČENKO, IHOR, "Byzantine Cultural Influences," in *Rewriting Russian History: Soviet Interpretations of Russia's Past,* ed. C. E. Black, 2nd ed. (New York: Random House 1962), 141–191.

ULAM, ADAM B., *Expansion and Coexistence: Soviet Foreign Policy, 1917–1973*, 2nd ed. (New York: Praeger 1974).

UMETANI, NOBORU, *The Role of Foreign Employees in the Meiji Era in Japan* (Tokyo: Institute of Developing Economics 1971).

WALDER, DAVID, *The Short Victorious War: The Russo-Japanese Conflict 1904–05* (London: Hutchinson 1973).

WHITE, J. A., *The Diplomacy of the Russo-Japanese War* (Princeton: Princeton University Press 1964).

WILBUR, CHARLES K., *The Soviet Model and Underdeveloped Countries* (Chapel Hill: University of North Carolina Press 1969).

Political Structure

AKITA, GEORGE, *Foundations of Constitutional Government in Modern Japan, 1868–1900* (Cambridge: Harvard University Press 1967).

ANWEILER, OSKAR, *The Soviets: The Russian Workers, Peasants, and Soldiers Councils, 1905–1921* (New York: Pantheon 1975).

ARMSTRONG, JOHN A., *Ideology, Politics and Government in the Soviet Union* (New York: Praeger 1971).

AZRAEL, JEREMY R., *Managerial Power and Soviet Politics* (Cambridge: Harvard University Press 1966).

BEASLEY, W. G., *The Meiji Restoration* (Stanford: Stanford University Press 1972).

BYRNES, ROBERT F., *Pobedonostsev: His Life and Thought* (Bloomington: Indiana University Press 1968).

CARR, E. H., *A History of Soviet Russia*, 9 vols. (New York: Macmillan 1951–1971): *The Bolshevik Revolution, 1917–1923*, 3 vols. (1951–1953); *The Interregnum, 1923–1924* (1954); *Socialism in One Country, 1924–1926*, 3 vols. (1958–1964); and with R. W. Davies, *Foundations of a Planned Economy, 1926–1929*, 2 vols. (1971).

CHERNIAVSKY, MICHAEL, *Tsar and People: Studies in Russian Myths* (New York: Random House 1969).

COLE, ALLAN B., GEORGE O. TOTTEN; AND CECIL H. UYEHARA, *Socialist Parties in Postwar Japan* (New Haven: Yale University Press 1966).

CRAIG, ALBERT M., *Choshu in the Meiji Restoration* (Cambridge: Harvard University Press 1961).

CURTIS, GERALD, *Election Campaigning Japanese Style* (New York: Columbia University Press 1971).

DUUS, PETER, *Party Rivalry and Political Change in Taisho Japan* (Cambridge: Harvard University Press 1968).

EMMONS, TERENCE L., *The Russian Landed Gentry and the Peasant Emancipation of 1861* (London: Cambridge University Press 1968).

FAINSOD, MERLE, *How Russia Is Ruled,* rev. ed. (Cambridge: Harvard University Press 1970).

FAINSOD, MERLE, "Bureaucracy and Modernization: The Russian and Soviet Case," in *Bureaucracy and Political Development,* ed. Joseph LaPalombara (Princeton: Princeton University Press 1963), 233–267.

FERRO, MARC, *The Russian Revolution of February, 1917* (Englewood Cliffs, N.J.: Prentice-Hall 1972).

HACKETT, ROGER F., *Yamagata Aritomo in the Rise of Modern Japan, 1838–1922* (Cambridge: Harvard University Press 1971).

HAIMSON, LEOPOLD H., *The Russian Marxists and the Origins of Bolshevism* (Boston: Beacon Press 1968).

HALL, JOHN W., *Government and Local Power in Japan, 500–1700* (Princeton: Princeton University Press 1966).

HAROUTOONIAN, H. D., *Toward Restoration: The Growth of Political Consciousness in Tokugawa Japan* (Berkeley and Los Angeles: University of California Press 1970).

HAUPT, GEORGES, AND JEAN-JACQUES MARIE, eds., *Makers of the Russian Revolution* (London: Allen and Unwin 1975).

HAZARD, JOHN N., *Settling Disputes in Soviet Society: The Formative Years of Legal Institutions* (New York: Columbia University Press 1960).

HELLIE, RICHARD, *Enserfment and Military Change in Muscovy* (Chicago: University of Chicago Press 1971).

HENDERSON, DAN FENNO, *Conciliation in Japanese Law* (Seattle: University of Washington Press 1965).

HOSKINGS, GEOFFREY A., *The Russian Constitutional Experiment: Government and Duma, 1907–1914* (London: Cambridge University Press 1973).

HOUGH, J. F., *The Soviet Prefects* (Cambridge: Harvard University Press 1969).

IKE, NOBUTAKA, *The Beginnings of Political Democracy in Japan* (Baltimore: Johns Hopkins University Press 1950).

ISHIDA, TAKESHI, "Interest Groups under a Semipermanent Government Party: The Case of Japan," *Annals of the American Academy of Political and Social Science* 413 (May 1974), 1–10.

ISHII, RYOSUKE, ed., *Japanese Legislation in the Meiji Era* (Tokyo: Pan-Pacific Press 1958).

JANSEN, MARIUS B., *Sakamoto Ryoma and the Meiji Restoration* (Princeton: Princeton University Press 1961).

JONES, R. E., *The Emancipation of the Russian Nobility, 1762–1785* (Princeton: Princeton University Press 1973).

KUBOTA, AKIRA, *Higher Civil Servants in Postwar Japan* (Princeton: Princeton University Press 1969).

MARUYAMA, MASAO, *Thought and Behavior in Modern Japanese Politics* (London: Oxford University Press 1963).

MASON, R. H. P., *Japan's First General Election, 1890* (New York: Cambridge University Press 1969).

MASSELL, GREGORY J., *The Surrogate Proletariat: Moslem Women and Revolutionary Strategies in Soviet Central Asia, 1919–1929* (Princeton: Princeton University Press 1974).

MEHLINGER, H. D., AND J. M. THOMPSON, *Count Witte and the Tsarist Government in the 1905 Revolution* (Bloomington: Indiana University Press 1972).

MEYER, ALFRED, *The Soviet Political System: An Interpretation* (New York: Random House 1965).

MOORE, BARRINGTON, JR., *Soviet Politics—The Dilemma of Power: The Role of Ideas in Social Change* (Cambridge: Harvard University Press 1950) .

MORLEY, JAMES W., ed., *Dilemmas of Growth in Prewar Japan* (Princeton: Princeton University Press 1969).

NAJITA, TETSUO, *Hara Kei and the Politics of Compromise, 1905–1915* (Cambridge: Harvard University Press 1967).

NORMAN, E. HERBERT, *Japan's Emergence as a Modern State* (New York: Institute of Pacific Relations 1940).

PEATTIE, MARK, *Ishiwara Kanji and Japan's Confrontation with the West* (Princeton: Princeton University Press 1975).

PIPES, RICHARD, *The Formation of the Soviet Union, Communism and Nationalism, 1917–1923*, rev. ed. (Cambridge: Harvard University Press 1964).

RAEFF, MARC, ed., *Plans for Political Reform in Imperial Russia, 1772–1839* (Englewood Cliffs, N.J.: Prentice-Hall, 1960).

RICHARDSON, BRADLEY M., *The Political Culture of Japan* (Berkeley and Los Angeles: University of California Press 1974).

RIASANOVSKY, NICHOLAS V., *Nicholas I and Official Nationality in Russia, 1825–1855* (Berkeley and Los Angeles: University of California Press 1967).

RIGBY, T. H., *Communist Party Membership in the USSR, 1917–1967* (Princeton: Princeton University Press 1968).

SCALAPINO, ROBERT, *Democracy and the Party Movement in Prewar Japan* (Berkeley and Los Angeles: University of California Press 1962).

SCALAPINO, ROBERT, AND JUNNOSUKE MASUMI, *Parties and Politics in Contemporary Japan* (Berkeley and Los Angeles: University of California Press 1962).

SCHAPIRO, LEONARD B., *The Communist Party of the Soviet Union*, rev. ed. (London: Eyre & Spottiswoode 1970).

SCHWARTZ, DONALD V., "Decisionmaking, Administrative Decentralization, and Feedback Mechanisms: Comparisons of Soviet and Western Models," *Studies in Comparative Communism* 7 (Spring/Summer 1974), 146–183.

SHILLONY, BEN-AMI, *Revolt in Japan: The Young Officers and the February 26, 1936 Incident* (Princeton: Princeton University Press 1973).

SILBERMAN, BERNARD S., *Ministers of Modernization: Elite Mobility in the Meiji Restoration, 1868–1873* (Tucson: University of Arizona Press 1964).

SKILLING, H. GORDON, AND F. GRIFFITHS, eds., *Interest Groups in Soviet Politics* (Princeton: Princeton University Press 1971).

SOBOLEV, P. N., ed., *History of the October Revolution* (Moscow: Progress Publishers 1966).

SPAULDING, ROBERT M., JR., *Imperial Japan's Higher Civil Service Examinations* (Princeton: Princeton University Press 1967).

SQUIRE, PETER S., *The Third Department: The Establishment and Practices of the Political Police in the Russia of Nicholas I* (London: Cambridge University Press 1968).

STARR, S. FREDERICK, *Decentralization and Self-Government in Russia, 1830–1870* (Princeton: Princeton University Press 1972) .

STEINER, KURT, *Local Government in Japan* (Stanford: Stanford University Press 1965) .

THAYER, NATHANIEL B., *How the Conservatives Rule Japan* (Princeton: Princeton University Press 1969).

TOTMAN, CONRAD, *Politics in the Tokugawa Bakufu, 1600–1843* (Cambridge: Harvard University Press 1967).

TOTTEN, GEORGE, *The Social Democratic Movement in Prewar Japan* (Princeton: Princeton University Press 1968) .

ULAM, ADAM, *The Bolsheviks: The Intellectual and Political History of the Triumph of Communism in Russia* (New York: Macmillan 1965).

VENTURI, FRANCO, *Roots of Revolution: A History of the Populist and Socialist Movements in Nineteenth Century Russia* (London: Weidenfeld 1960).

VON MEHREN, ARTHUR T., ed., *Law in Japan* (Cambridge: Harvard University Press 1963) .

WARD, ROBERT, ed., *Political Development in Modern Japan* (Princeton: Princeton University Press 1968).

WARD, ROBERT, AND DANKWART RUSTOW, eds., *Political Modernization in Japan and Turkey* (Princeton: Princeton University Press 1964).

WEBB, HERSCHELL, *The Japanese Imperial Institution in Tokugawa Japan* (New York: Columbia University Press 1968) .

WIGMORE, JOHN H., ed., *Law and Justice in Tokugawa Japan*, 5 vols. (Tokyo: Tokyo University Press 1969–72) .

Yanaga, Chitoshi, *Big Business in Japanese Politics* (New Haven: Yale University Press 1968).

Yaney, George L., *The Systematization of Russian Government* (Urbana: University of Illinois Press 1973).

Economic Structure and Growth

Abegglen, James G., *The Japanese Factory: Aspects of Its Social Organization* (New York: Free Press 1958).

Barel, Yves, *Le développement économique de la Russie tsariste* (Paris: Mouton 1968).

Bergson, Abram, "Development under Two Systems: Comparative Productivity Growth Since 1950," *World Politics* 23 (Juy 1971), 579–617.

Bergson, Abram, and Simon Kuznets, *Economic Trends in the Soviet Union* (Cambridge: Harvard University Press 1963).

Bergson, Abram, *The Real National Income of Russia Since 1928* (Cambridge: Harvard University Press 1961).

Berliner, Joseph, *Factory and Manager in the USSR* (Cambridge: Harvard University Press 1957).

Bieda, K., *The Structure and Operation of the Japanese Economy* (New York: John Wiley Publications 1970).

Blackwell, W. L., *The Beginnings of Russian Industrialization, 1800–1860* (Princeton: Princeton University Press 1968).

Blum, Jerome, *Lord and Peasant in Russia* (Princeton: Princeton University Press 1961).

Brown, Emily C., *Soviet Trade Unions and Labor Relations* (Cambridge: Harvard University Press 1966).

Conyngham, William J., *Industrial Management in the Soviet Union* (Stanford: Hoover Institution 1973).

Crisp, Olga, "Russia, 1860–1914," in *Banking in the Early Stages of Industrialization,* ed. Rondo E. Cameron (New York: Oxford University Press 1967), 183–238.

Datta, Amlankusum, *A Century of Economic Development of Russia and Japan* (Calcutta: World Press 1967).

Dobb, Maurice, *Soviet Economic Development Since 1917* (New York: International Publishers 1966).

Ellison, Herbert J., "Economic Modernization in Imperial Russia: Purposes and Achievements," *Journal of Economic History* 25 (December 1965), 523–540.

Ellman, Michael, *Planning Problems in the USSR: The Contribution of Mathematical Economics to their Solution, 1960–1971* (Cambridge, Eng.: Cambridge University Press 1973).

GERSCHENKRON, ALEXANDER, *Continuity in History and Other Essays* (Cambridge: Harvard University Press 1968).

GERSCHENKRON, ALEXANDER, *Economic Backwardness in Historical Perspective* (Cambridge: Harvard University Press 1962) .

GIRAULT, R., *Emprunts russes et investissements français en Russie, 1887–1914* (Paris: Colin 1973) .

GOLDSMITH, RAYMOND W., "The Economic Growth of Tsarist Russia, 1860–1913," *Economic Development and Cultural Change* 9 (April 1961), 441–475.

GRANICK, DAVID, *Managerial Comparisons of Four Developed Countries: France, Britain, United States and Russia* (Cambridge: MIT Press 1972) .

GREGORY, PAUL R. AND ROBERT C. STUART, *Soviet Economic Structure and Performance* (New York: Harper & Row 1974).

The Growth of the National Economies of Japan and the Soviet Union: A Comparison of Economic Growth Rate (Tokyo: Ministry of Foreign Affairs 1963).

HARDT, JOHN P., MARVIN HOFFENBERG, NORMAN KAPLAN, AND HERBERT S. LEVINE, *Mathematics and Computers in Soviet Economic Planning* (New York: Yale University Press 1967) .

HOLLERMAN, LEON, *Japan's Dependence on the World Economy* (Princeton: Princeton University Press 1967).

INUKAI, ICHIRO, AND ARLON R. TAUSSIG, "Kogyo Iken: Japan's Ten Year Plan, 1884," *Economic Development and Cultural Change* 16 (October 1967), 51–71.

JOINT ECONOMIC COMMITTEE, U.S. CONGRESS, *Economic Performance and the Military Burden in the Soviet Union* (Washington, D.C.: GPO 1970).

JOINT ECONOMIC COMMITTEE, U.S. CONGRESS, *Soviet Economic Prospects for the Seventies* (Washington, D.C.: GPO 1973).

KAHN, ARCADIUS, "Continuity in Economic Activity and Policy during the Post-Petrine Period in Russia," *Journal of Economic History* 25 (March 1965) , 61–85.

KAPLAN, NORMAN, AND RICHARD MOORSTEEN, "An Index of Soviet Industrial Output," *American Economic Review* 50:3 (June 1960).

KELLEY, ALLEN C., AND JEFFREY G. WILLIAMSON, *Lessons from Japanese Development: An Analytical Economic History* (Chicago: University of Chicago Press 1974).

KIRSCH, LEONARD, *Soviet Wages* (Cambridge: MIT Press 1972).

KLEIN, LAWRENCE, AND KAZUSHI OHKAWA, *Economic Growth: The Japa-*

nese *Experience Since the Meiji Era* (Hammond, Ill.: Irwin Press 1968).

Komiya, Ryutaro, ed., *Postwar Economic Growth in Japan* (Berkeley and Los Angeles: University of California Press 1966).

Kosobud, Richard, "The Role of International Transfers of Technology in Japan's Economic Growth," *Technological Forecasting and Social Change* 5:4 (1973), 395–406.

Levine, Herbert S., "An American View of Economic Relations with the USSR," *The Annals* 414 (July 1974), 1–17.

Levine, Herbert S., "Input-Output Analysis and Soviet Planning," *American Economic Review* 52 (May 1962), 127–137.

Levine, Herbert S., "The Centralized Planning of Supply in Soviet Industry," in Joint Economic Committee, U.S. Congress, *Comparisons of the United States and Soviet Economies* (Washington, D.C.: GPO 1959).

Lewin, Moshe, *Political Undercurrents in Soviet Economic Debates: From Bukharin to Modern Reformers* (Princeton: Princeton University Press 1974).

Lockwood, William W., *Economic Development of Japan,* rev. ed. (Princeton: Princeton University Press 1968).

Lockwood, William W., ed., *The State and Economic Enterprise in Japan* (Princeton: Princeton University Press 1965).

Lyashchenko, P. I., *History of the National Economy of Russia to the 1917 Revolution* (New York: Macmillan 1949).

Maddison, Angus, *Economic Growth in Japan and the USSR* (New York: Norton 1969).

McKay, John P., *Pioneers for Profit: Foreign Entrepreneurship and Russian Industrialization, 1885–1913* (Chicago: University of Chicago Press 1970).

Miyamoto, Mataji, Yotaro Sakudo, and Yasukichi Yasuba, "Economic Development in Preindustrial Japan, 1859–1894," *Journal of Economic History,* 25 (December 1965), 514–568.

Modernization and Industrialization: Essays Presented to Yoshitaka Komatsu (Tokyo: Ichijo Shoten 1968).

Moorsteen, Richard, and Raymond Powell, *The Soviet Capital Stock 1928–1962* (Homewood, Ill.: Richard D. Irwin 1966).

Nonomura, Kazuo, *Essays on the Soviet Economy* (Tokyo: Institute of Economic Research, Hitotsubashi University 1969).

Nove, Alec, *An Economic History of the U.S.S.R.* (London: Allen Lane 1969).

Ofer, Gur, *The Service Sector in Soviet Economic Growth: A Comparative Study* (Cambridge: Harvard University Press 1973).

OHKAWA, KAZUSHI, AND HENRY ROSOVSKY, *Japanese Economic Growth: Trend Acceleration in the Twentieth Century* (Stanford: Stanford University Press 1973).

PATRICK, HUGH T., AND HENRY ROSOVSKY, eds., *Asia's New Giant: How the Japanese Economy Works* (Washington, D.C.: Brookings Institution Press, forthcoming).

PATRICK, HUGH T., "Japan, 1868–1914," in *Banking in the Early Stages of Industrialization,* ed. Rondo E. Cameron (New York: Oxford University Press 1967), 239–289.

PATRICK, HUGH T., *Monetary Policy and Central Banking in Contemporary Japan* (Bombay: University of Bombay Press 1962).

PORTAL, ROGER, "The Industrialization of Russia," in *Cambridge Economic History of Russia* 6:1 (Cambridge, Eng.: Cambridge University Press 1965), 801–874.

POWELL, DAVID E., "The Social Costs of Modernization: Ecological Problems in the USSR," *World Politics* 23 (July 1971), 618–634.

REICH, MICHAEL R., AND NORIE HUDDLE, *Island of Dreams: Environmental Crisis in Japan* (Kanagawa: Autumn Press 1975).

ROSOVSKY, HENRY, "Japan's Economic Future," *Challenge: The Magazine of Economic Affairs* 16 (July–August 1973), 6–17.

ROSOVSKY, HENRY (ed.), *Industrialization in Two Systems: Essays in Honor of Alexander Gerschenkron* (New York: Wiley 1966).

ROSOVSKY, HENRY, *Capital Formation in Japan, 1868–1940* (New York: Free Press 1961).

SMITH, THOMAS C., "Pre-Modern Economic Growth: Japan and the West," *Past and Present* 60 (August 1973), 127–160.

TAIRA, KOJI, *Economic Development and the Labor Market in Japan* (New York: Columbia University Press 1970).

TANAKA, KAKUEI, *Building a New Japan: A Plan for Remodeling the Japanese Archipelago* (Tokyo: Simul Press 1972).

TREML, VLADIMIR G., ed., *The Structure of the Soviet Economy: Analysis and Reconstruction of the 1966 Input-Output Tables* (New York: Praeger 1972).

TUGAN-BARANOVSKY, M. I., *The Russian Factory in the Nineteenth Century* (Homewood, Ill.: Irwin 1970).

U.S. DEPARTMENT OF STATE, *The Planetary Product, 1973,* Bureau of Public Affairs, Special Report 11 (Washington, D.C.: GPO 1974).

VOLIN, LAZAR, *A Century of Russian Agriculture: From Alexander II to Khrushchev* (Cambridge: Harvard University Press 1970).

VON LAUE, THEODORE, H., *Sergei Witte and the Industrialization of Russia* (New York: Columbia University Press 1963).

YAMAMURA, KOZO, *Economic Policy in Postwar Japan: Growth Versus Economic Democracy* (Berkeley and Los Angeles: University of California Press 1967).

ZALESKI, EUGENE, *The Planning Reforms in the Soviet Union, 1962–1966* (Chapel Hill: University of North Carolina Press 1967).

Social Interdependence

ANDERSON, BARBARA, "Internal Migration in a Modernizing Society: The Case of Late Nineteenth Century European Russia" (Ph.D. diss., Princeton University, 1973).

BEARDSLEY, RICHARD K., JOHN W. HALL, AND ROBERT E. WARD, *Village Japan* (Chicago: University of Chicago Press 1959).

COLE, ROBERT E., *Japanese Blue Collar* (Berkeley and Los Angeles: University of California Press 1971).

CONNOR, WALTER D., *Deviance in Soviet Society* (New York: Columbia University Press 1972).

DE VOS, GEORGE, *Socialization for Achievement: Essays on the Cultural Psychology of the Japanese* (Berkeley and Los Angeles: University of California Press 1973).

DE VOS, GEORGE, "Post-War Social Change in Japan," *Asian Pacific Quarterly of Cultural and Social Affairs* 4 (Autumn 1972), 1–38.

DODGE, NORTON D., *Women in the Soviet Economy: Their Role in Economic, Scientific, and Technical Development* (Baltimore: Johns Hopkins Press 1968).

DORE, RONALD, *British Factory–Japanese Factory* (Berkeley and Los Angeles: University of California Press 1973).

DORE, RONALD, *City Life in Japan* (Berkeley and Los Angeles: University of California Press 1967).

DORE, RONALD, ed., *Aspects of Social Change in Modern Japan* (Princeton: Princeton University Press 1967).

DORE, RONALD, *Land Reform in Japan* (London: Oxford University Press 1959).

EMBREE, J. F., *Suye Mura: A Japanese Village* (Chicago: University of Chicago Press 1939).

FUKUTAKE, TADASHI, *Japanese Rural Society* (Ithaca: Cornell University Press 1972).

FUKUTAKE, TADASHI, *Man and Society in Japan* (Tokyo: University of Tokyo Press 1962).

GEIGER, KENT, *The Family in Soviet Russia* (Cambridge: Harvard University Press 1968).

HALMOS, PAUL, ed., *Japanese Sociological Studies* (Keele, England: University of Keele 1966).

HANLEY, SUSAN B., "Fertility, Mortality and Life Expectancy in Pre-Modern Japan," *Population Studies* 28:1 (1974), 127–42.

HANLEY, SUSAN B., AND KOZO YAMAMURA, "Population Trends and Economic Growth in Pre-industrial Japan," in *Population and Social Change,* ed. D. V. Glass and Roger Revelle (London: Arnold Press 1972).

HARRIS, CHAUNCY D., *Cities of the Soviet Union* (Chicago: Rand McNally 1970).

HEER, DAVID M., "The Demographic Transition in the Russian Empire and the Soviet Union," *Journal of Social History* 1 (Spring 1968), 193–240.

IKE, NOBUTAKE, "Economic Growth and Intergenerational Change in Japan," *American Political Science Review* 67 (December 1973), 1194–1203.

INKELES, ALEX, *Social Change in Soviet Russia* (Cambridge: Harvard University Press 1968).

INKELES, ALEX, AND RAYMOND BAUER, *The Soviet Citizen: Daily Life in a Totalitarian Society* (Cambridge: Harvard University Press 1959).

ISHIDA, TAKESHI, *Japanese Society* (New York: Random House 1971).

KASSOF, ALLEN H., *The Soviet Youth Program* (Cambridge: Harvard University Press 1965).

KATO, HIDETOSHI, *Japanese Popular Culture: Studies of Mass Communication and Cultural Change* (Tokyo: Tuttle 1959).

KERBLAY, BASILE H., *L'Isba d'hier et d'aujourd'hui: L'évolution de l'habitation rurale en U.R.S.S.* (Lausanne: Editions l'Age d'Homme 1973).

KERBLAY, BASILE H., *Les marchés paysans en U.R.S.S.* (The Hague: Mouton 1968).

LEWIN, MOSHE, *Russian Peasants and Soviet Power: A Study of Collectivization* (London: Allen & Unwin 1968).

MATTHEWS, MERVYN, *Class and Society in Soviet Russia* (New York: Walker 1972).

MEISSNER, BORIS, ed., *Social Change in the Soviet Union* (Notre Dame: University of Notre Dame Press 1972).

NAKANE, CHIE, *Japanese Society* (Berkeley and Los Angeles: University of California Press 1970).

OKOCHI, K., B. KARSH, AND S. B. LEVINE, *Workers and Employers in Japan* (Princeton: Princeton University Press 1974).

OSBORN, ROBERT J., *Soviet Social Policies: Welfare, Equality and Community* (Homewood, Ill.: Dorsey 1970).

OSIPOV, G. V., ed., *Town, Country and People* (London: Tavistock 1972).

OSIPOV, G. V., ed., *Industry and Labour in the U.S.S.R.* (London: Travistock 1971).

RIMLINGER, GASTON, *Welfare Policy and Industrialization in Europe, America, and Russia* (New York: Wiley 1971).

ROZMAN, GILBERT, *Urban Networks in Russia, 1750–1800, and Premodern Periodization* (Princeton: Princeton University Press, 1976).

ROZMAN, GILBERT, "Comparative Approaches to Urbanization: Russia, 1750–1800," in *The City in Russian History,* ed. Michael Hamm (Lexington: University of Kentucky Press 1975).

ROZMAN, GILBERT, "Edo's Importance in the Changing Tokugawa Society," *Journal of Japanese Studies* 1:1 (Autumn 1974), 91–112.

ROZMAN, GILBERT, *Urban Networks in Ch'ing China and Tokugawa Japan* (Princeton: Princeton University Press 1973).

SHANIN, TEODOR, *The Awkward Class: Political Sociology of Peasantry in a Developing Society—Russia 1910–1925* (Oxford: Oxford University Press 1972).

SMITH, THOMAS C., *The Agrarian Origins of Modern Japan* (Stanford: Stanford University Press 1959).

SMITH, THOMAS C., "Farm Family By-Employments in Preindustrial Japan," *Journal of Economic History* 29 (December 1969), 687–715.

TAEUBER, IRENE B., *The Population of Japan* (Princeton: Princeton University Press 1958).

TSUKAHIRA, T. G., *Feudal Control in Tokugawa Japan* (Cambridge: Harvard East Asian Monographs 1966).

TSURUMI, KAZUKO, *Social Change and the Individual: Japan before and after Defeat in World War II* (Princeton: Princeton University Press 1970).

VOGEL, EZRA, *Japan's New Middle Class* (Berkeley and Los Angeles: University of California Press 1973).

VUCINICH, WAYNE S., ed., *The Peasant in Nineteenth-Century Russia* (Stanford: Stanford University Press 1968).

WEINBERG, ELIZABETH ANN, *The Development of Sociology in the Soviet Union* (London: Routledge and Kegan Paul 1974).

WHITE, JAMES W., *The Sokagakkai and Mass Society* (Stanford: Stanford University Press 1970).

WILKINSON, THOMAS O., *The Urbanization of Japanese Labor, 1868–1955* (Amherst: University of Massachusetts Press 1965).

YAMAMURA, KOZO, *A Study of Samurai Income and Entrepreneurship* (Cambridge: Harvard University Press 1974).

YANOWITCH, MURRAY, AND WESLEY A. FISHER, eds., *Social Stratification and Mobility in the USSR* (White Plains, N.Y.: International Arts & Sciences Press 1973).

YAZAKI, TAKEO, *Social Change and the City in Japan* (Tokyo: Japan Publications 1968).

ZELNIK, REGINALD E., *Labor and Society in Tsarist Russia: The Factory Workers of St. Petersburg, 1855–1870* (Stanford: Stanford University Press 1971).

Knowledge and Education

ALSTON, PATRICK L., *Education and the State in Tsarist Russia* (Stanford: Stanford University Press 1969).

AZRAEL, JEREMY R., "Soviet Union," in *Education and Political Development,* ed. James S. Coleman (Princeton: Princeton University Press 1965), 233–271.

AZUMI, KOYA, *Higher Education and Business Recruitment in Japan* (New York: Teachers College 1969).

BELLAH, ROBERT N., *Tokugawa Religion: The Values of Pre-Industrial Japan* (Glencoe, Ill.: Free Press 1957).

BENEDICT, RUTH, *The Chrysanthemum and the Sword* (Boston: Houghton Press 1946).

BENZ, E., *The Eastern Orthodox Church* (New York: Doubleday 1963).

BERDIAEV, NIKOLAI, *The Russian Idea* (New York: Macmillan .1948).

BEREDAY, GEORGE Z. F., ed., *The Politics of Soviet Education* (New York: Praeger Publications 1960).

BILLINGTON, JAMES H., *The Icon and the Axe: An Interpretive History of Russian Culture* (New York: Knopf 1966).

BLEWETT, JOHN E., ed. and trans., *Higher Education in Postwar Japan: The Ministry of Education's 1964 White Paper* (Tokyo: Sophia University Press 1965).

BOWEN, JAMES, *Soviet Education: Anton Makarenko and the Years of Experiment* (Madison: University of Wisconsin Press 1962).

DOI, TAKEO, *The Anatomy of Dependence* (Tokyo: Kodansha International Press 1973).

DORE, RONALD, *Education in Tokugawa Japan* (Berkeley and Los Angeles: University of California Press 1965).

FITZPATRICK, SHEILA, *The Commissariat of Enlightenment: Soviet Organization of Education and the Arts under Lunacharsky, October 1917–1921* (Cambridge, Eng.: Cambridge University Press 1970).

GRAHAM, LOREN, *Science and Philosophy in the Soviet Union* (New York: Knopf 1972).

GRANT, NIGEL, *Soviet Education* (Baltimore: Penguin 1964).

HALL, IVAN P., *Mori Arinori* (Cambridge: Harvard University Press 1973).

HANS, NICHOLAS, *The History of Russian Educational Policy, 1701–1917* (New York: Russell & Russell 1964).

HANS, NICHOLAS, *The Russian Tradition in Education* (London: Routledge & Kegan Paul 1963).

HEER, NANCY WHITTIER, *Politics and History in the Soviet Union* (Cambridge: MIT Press 1971).

INKELES, ALEX, *Public Opinion in Soviet Russia* (Cambridge: Harvard University Press 1960).

JANSEN, MARIUS B., AND LAWRENCE STONE, "Education and Modernization in Japan and England," *Comparative Studies in Society and History* 9 (January 1967), 208–232.

JOHNSON, W. H. E., *Russia's Educational Heritage* (Pittsburgh: Carnegie Press 1950).

KRAUSS, ELLIS S., *Japanese Radicals Revisited: Student Protest in Postwar Japan* (Berkeley and Los Angeles: University of California Press 1974).

MEDLIN, WILLIAM, WILLIAM CAVE, AND FINLAY CARPENTER, *Education and Development in Central Asia: A Case Study of Social Change in Uzbekistan* (Leiden: Brill 1971).

MEDVEDEV, ZHORES A., *The Rise and Fall of T. D. Lysenko* (Garden City, N.Y.: Anchor Press 1971).

NOAH, HAROLD, J., ed., *The Economics of Education in the USSR* (New York: Praeger Publishers 1969).

NOZHKO, K. et al., *Education Planning in the USSR* (Paris: UNESCO 1968).

NUNN, G. RAYMOND, "On the Number of Books Published in Japan from 1600 to 1868," *Asian Studies at Hawaii* 3 (May 1969), 110–119.

PASSIN, HERBERT, *Japanese Education: A Bibliography of Materials in the English Language* (New York: Teachers College 1970).

PASSIN, HERBERT, *Society and Education in Japan* (New York: Teachers College 1965).

PASSIN, HERBERT, "Japan," in *Education and Political Development*, ed. James S. Coleman (Princeton: Princeton University Press 1965), 272–312.

PENNAR, JAAN, GEORGE Z. F. BEREDAY, AND IVAN I. BAKULO, *Modernization and Diversity in Soviet Education* (New York: Praeger Publications 1971).

PYLE, KENNETH B., *The New Generation in Meiji Japan; Problems of Cultural Identity* (Stanford: Stanford University Press 1969).

RAEFF, MARC, *Origins of the Russian Intelligentsia: The Eighteenth Century Nobility* (New York: Harcourt, Brace 1962).

ROGGER, HANS, *National Consciousness in Eighteenth-Century Russia* (Cambridge: Harvard University Press 1960).

ROSEN, SEYMOUR M., *Education and Modernization in the USSR* (Reading, Mass.: Addison-Wesley 1971).

SCHAPIRO, LEONARD B., *Rationalism and Nationalism in Russian Nineteenth Century Political Thought* (New Haven: Yale University Press 1967).

Science Policy and Organization of Research in Japan (Paris: UNESCO 1967).

Science Policy in the USSR (Paris: OECD 1968).

SHIVELY, DONALD H., ed., *Tradition and Modernization in Japanese Culture* (Princeton: Princeton University Press 1971).

SIMMONS, ERNEST J., ed., *Continuity and Change in Russian and Soviet Thought* (Cambridge: Harvard University Press 1935).

SINEL, ALLEN, *The Classroom and the Chancellery: State Educational Reform in Russia under Count Dmitri Tolstoi* (Cambridge: Harvard University Press 1973).

SMITH, HENRY D., II, *Japan's First Student Radicals* (Cambridge: Harvard University Press 1972).

Technological Development in Japan (Paris: UNESCO 1971).

VUCINICH, ALEXANDER, *Science in Russian Culture,* 2 vols. (Stanford: Stanford University Press 1963–1970).

ZENKOVSKY, V. V. *A History of Russian Philosophy,* 2 vols. Authorized translation from the Russian by George L. Kline. (London: Routledge & Kegan Paul; New York: Columbia University Press 1953).

BIBLIOGRAPHY OF C.I.S. BOOKS

Books Written Under the Auspices of the Center of
International Studies, Princeton University

Gabriel A. Almond, *The Appeals of Communism* (Princeton University
Press 1954)

William W. Kaufmann, ed., *Military Policy and National Security*
(Princeton University Press 1956)

Klaus Knorr, *The War Potential of Nations* (Princeton University Press
1956)

Lucian W. Pye, *Guerrilla Communism in Malaya* (Princeton University
Press 1956)

Charles De Visscher, *Theory and Reality in Public International Law*,
trans. by P. E. Corbett (Princeton University Press 1957; rev. ed. 1968)

Bernard C. Cohen, *The Political Process and Foreign Policy: The Making of the Japanese Peace Settlement* (Princeton University Press 1957)

Myron Weiner, *Party Politics in India: The Development of a Multi-
Party System* (Princeton University Press 1957)

Percy E. Corbett, *Law in Diplomacy* (Princeton University Press 1959)

Rolf Sannwald and Jacques Stohler, *Economic Integrations: Theoretical
Assumptions and Consequences of European Unification*, trans. by
Herman Karreman (Princeton University Press 1959)

Gabriel A. Almond and James S. Coleman, eds., *The Politics of the
Developing Areas* (Princeton University Press 1960)

Herman Kahn, *On Thermonuclear War* (Princeton University Press
1960)

Sidney Verba, *Small Groups and Political Behavior: A Study of Leadership* (Princeton University Press 1961)

Robert J. C. Butow, *Tojo and the Coming of the War* (Princeton University Press 1961)

Glenn H. Snyder, *Deterrence and Defense: Toward a Theory of National
Security* (Princeton University Press 1961)

Klaus Knorr and Sidney Verba, eds., *The International Systems: Theoretical Essays* (Princeton University Press 1961)

Peter Paret and John W. Shy, *Guerrillas in the 1960's* (Praeger 1962)

George Modelski, *A Theory of Foreign Policy* (Praeger 1962)

Klaus Knorr and Thornton Read, eds., *Limited Strategic War* (Praeger
1963)

Frederick S. Dunn, *Peace-Making and the Settlement with Japan* (Princeton University Press 1963)

Arthur L. Burns and Nina Heathcote, *Peace-Keeping by United Nations Forces* (Praeger 1963)

Richard A. Falk, *Law, Morality, and War in the Contemporary World* (Praeger 1963)

James N. Rosenau, *National Leadership and Foreign Policy: A Case Study in the Mobilization of Public Support* (Princeton University Press 1963)

Gabriel A. Almond and Sidney Verba, *The Civic Culture: Political Attitudes and Democracy in Five Nations* (Princeton University Press 1963)

Bernard C. Cohen, *The Press and Foreign Policy* (Princeton University Press 1963)

Richard L. Sklar, *Nigerian Political Parties: Power in an Emergent African Nation* (Princeton University Press 1963)

Peter Paret, *French Revolutionary Warfare from Indochina to Algeria: The Analysis of a Political and Military Doctrine* (Praeger 1964)

Harry Eckstein, ed., *Internal War: Problems and Approaches* (Free Press 1964)

Cyril E. Black and Thomas P. Thornton, eds., *Communism and Revolution: The Strategic Uses of Political Violence* (Princeton University Press 1964)

Miriam Camps, *Britain and the European Community 1955-1963* (Princeton University Press 1964)

Thomas P. Thornton, ed., *The Third World in Soviet Perspective: Studies by Soviet Writers on the Developing Areas* (Princeton University Press 1964)

James N. Rosenau, ed., *International Aspects of Civil Strife* (Princeton University Press 1964)

Sidney I. Ploss, *Conflict and Decision-Making in Soviet Russia: A Case Study of Agricultural Policy, 1953-1963* (Princeton University Press 1965)

Richard A. Falk and Richard J. Barnet, eds., *Security in Disarmament* (Princeton University Press 1965)

Karl von Vorys, *Political Development in Pakistan* (Princeton University Press 1965)

Harold and Margaret Sprout, *The Ecological Perspective on Human Affairs, With Special Reference to International Politics* (Princeton University Press 1965)

Klaus Knorr, *On the Uses of Military Power in the Nuclear Age* (Princeton University Press 1966)

Harry Eckstein, *Division and Cohesion in Democracy: A Study of Norway* (Princeton University Press 1966)

Cyril E. Black, *The Dynamics of Modernization: A Study in Comparative History* (Harper and Row 1966)

Peter Kunstadter, ed., *Southeast Asian Tribes, Minorities, and Nations* (Princeton University Press 1967)

E. Victor Wolfenstein, *The Revolutionary Personality: Lenin, Trotsky, Gandhi* (Princeton University Press 1967)

Leon Gordenker, *The UN Secretary-General and the Maintenance of Peace* (Columbia University Press 1967)

Oran R. Young, *The Intermediaries: Third Parties in International Crises* (Princeton University Press 1967)

James N. Rosenau, ed., *Domestic Sources of Foreign Policy* (Free Press 1967)

Richard F. Hamilton, *Affluence and the French Worker in the Fourth Republic* (Princeton University Press 1967)

Linda B. Miller, *World Order and Local Disorder: The United Nations and Internal Conflicts* (Princeton University Press 1967)

Henry Bienen, *Tanzania: Party Transformation and Economic Development* (Princeton University Press 1967)

Wolfram F. Hanrieder, *West German Foreign Policy, 1949-1963: International Pressures and Domestic Response* (Stanford University Press 1967)

Richard H. Ullman, *Britain and the Russian Civil War: November 1918-February 1920* (Princeton University Press 1968)

Robert Gilpin, *France in the Age of the Scientific State* (Princeton University Press 1968)

William B. Bader, *The United States and the Spread of Nuclear Weapons* (Pegasus 1968)

Richard A. Falk, *Legal Order in a Violent World* (Princeton University Press 1968)

Cyril E. Black, Richard A. Falk, Klaus Knorr and Oran R. Young, *Neutralization and World Politics* (Princeton University Press 1968)

Oran R. Young, *The Politics of Force: Bargaining During International Crises* (Princeton University Press 1969)

Klaus Knorr and James N. Rosenau, eds., *Contending Approaches to International Politics* (Princeton University Press 1969)

James N. Rosenau, ed., *Linkage Politics: Essays on the Convergence of National and International Systems* (Free Press 1969)

John T. McAlister, Jr., *Viet Nam: The Origins of Revolution* (Knopf 1969)

Jean Edward Smith, *Germany Beyond the Wall: People, Politics and Prosperity* (Little, Brown 1969)

James Barros, *Betrayal from Within: Joseph Avenol, Secretary-General of the League of Nations, 1933-1940* (Yale University Press 1969)

Charles Hermann, *Crises in Foreign Policy: A Simulation Analysis* (Bobbs-Merrill 1969)

Robert C. Tucker, *The Marxian Revolutionary Idea: Essays on Marxist Thought and Its Impact on Radical Movements* (W. W. Norton 1969)

Harvey Waterman, *Political Change in Contemporary France: The Politics of an Industrial Democracy* (Charles E. Merrill 1969)

Cyril E. Black and Richard A. Falk, eds., *The Future of the International Legal Order*. Vol. I: *Trends and Patterns* (Princeton University Press 1969)

Ted Robert Gurr, *Why Men Rebel* (Princeton University Press 1969)

C. Sylvester Whitaker, *The Politics of Tradition: Continuity and Change in Northern Nigeria 1946-1966* (Princeton University Press 1970)

Richard A. Falk, *The Status of Law in International Society* (Princeton University Press 1970)

John T. McAlister, Jr. and Paul Mus, *The Vietnamese and Their Revolution* (Harper & Row 1970)

Klaus Knorr, *Military Power and Potential* (D. C. Heath 1970)

Cyril E. Black and Richard A. Falk, eds., *The Future of the International Legal Order*. Vol. II: *Wealth and Resources* (Princeton University Press 1970)

Leon Gordenker, ed., *The United Nations in International Politics* (Princeton University Press 1971)

Cyril E. Black and Richard A. Falk, eds., *The Future of the International Legal Order*. Vol. III: *Conflict Management* (Princeton University Press 1971)

Francine R. Frankel, *India's Green Revolution: Economic Gains and Political Costs* (Princeton University Press 1971)

Harold and Margaret Sprout, *Toward a Politics of the Planet Earth* (Van Nostrand Reinhold Co. 1971)

Cyril E. Black and Richard A. Falk, eds., *The Future of the International Legal Order*. Vol. IV: *The Structure of the International Environment* (Princeton University Press 1972)

Gerald Garvey, *Energy, Ecology, Economy* (W. W. Norton 1972)

Richard H. Ullman, *The Anglo-Soviet Accord* (Princeton University Press 1973)

Klaus Knorr, *Power and Wealth: The Political Economy of International Power* (Basic Books 1973)

Anton Bebler, *Military Rule in Africa: Dahomey, Ghana, Sierra Leone, and Mali* (Praeger Publishers 1973)

Robert C. Tucker, *Stalin as Revolutionary 1879-1929: A Study in History and Personality* (W. W. Norton 1973)

Edward L. Morse, *Foreign Policy and Interdependence in Gaullist France* (Princeton University Press 1973)

Henry Bienen, *Kenya: The Politics of Participation and Control* (Princeton University Press 1974)

Gregory J. Massell, *The Surrogate Proletariat: Moslem Women and Revolutionary Strategies in Soviet Central Asia, 1919-1929* (Princeton University Press 1974)

James N. Rosenau, *Citizenship Between Elections: An Inquiry Into The Mobilizable American* (Free Press 1974)

Ervin Laszlo, *A Strategy For The Future: The Systems Approach To World Order* (Braziller 1974)

John R. Vincent, *Nonintervention and International Order* (Princeton University Press 1974)

Jan H. Kalicki, *The Pattern of Sino-American Crises: Political-Military Interactions in the 1950s* (Cambridge University Press 1975)

INDEX

Date Due